AMERICA
THE VINCIBLE

AMERICA THE VINCIBLE

U.S. FOREIGN POLICY FOR THE TWENTY-FIRST CENTURY

Earl H. Fry
Brigham Young University

Stan A. Taylor
Brigham Young University

Robert S. Wood
U.S. Naval War College

248943

Prentice Hall, Englewood Cliffs, New Jersey 07632

Library of Congress Cataloging-in-Publication Data

FRY, EARL H.
America the Vincible : U.S. foreign policy for the twenty-first
century / EARL H. FRY, STAN A. TAYLOR, ROBERT S. WOOD.
 p. cm.
 Includes bibliographical references and index.
 ISBN 0-13-028457-2
  1. United States—Foreign relations—1989- 2. Twenty-first
century. I. Taylor, Stan A., [date]. II. Wood, Robert S., [date].
III. Title.
E840.F78 1994 93-24566
327.73'009'049—dc20

Editorial/production supervision and interior design: *Edie Riker*
Cover design: *Design Source*
Production coordinator: *Mary Ann Gloriande*
Editorial assistant: *Nicole Signoretti*

©1994 by Prentice-Hall, Inc.
A Paramount Communications Company
Englewood Cliffs, New Jersey 07632

Printed in the United States of America

10 9 8 7 6 5 4 3 2 1

ISBN   0-13-028457-2

Prentice-Hall International (UK) Limited, *London*
Prentice-Hall of Australia Pty. Limited, *Sydney*
Prentice-Hall Canada Inc., *Toronto*
Prentice-Hall Hispanoamericana, S.A., *Mexico*
Prentice-Hall of India Private Limited, *New Delhi*
Prentice-Hall of Japan, Inc., *Tokyo*
Simon & Schuster Asia Pte. Ltd., *Singapore*
Editora Prentice-Hall do Brasil, Ltda., *Rio de Janeiro*

CONTENTS

PREFACE

As the title of this book emphasizes, America is a "vincible" nation as it prepares to enter the highly complex and interdependent world of the twenty-first century.

Vincibility does not mean that the United States, home to more than a quarter billion people, will soon relinquish its position as the planet's most powerful nation-state, possessing an awesome strategic and conventional military capability bolstered by a huge and resilient national economy. Indeed, one might argue with some justification that the end of the Cold War and the dismantlement of the Soviet Union have resulted in the United States being the world's only superpower.

Even a superpower, however, cannot guarantee stability, peace, and democracy in a global community fragmented into more than 180 nation-states. Perhaps the threat of an imminent nuclear confrontation with another military superpower is now behind us, but many more nations are expected to possess nuclear weapons and delivery systems over the next few decades. With the proliferation of such deadly weapons, the chances that they will be used in combat somewhere around the globe have increased dramatically.

Moreover, decision-makers in Washington, D.C., are just beginning to grapple with the intricacies of peacekeeping and peacemaking operations in areas as diverse as Africa, Eastern Europe, and Central America. Just during the early period of the 1990s, American troops have been deployed in an effort to combat aggression in the Persian Gulf, end starvation and anarchy in East

Africa, quell civil strife in the Adriatic, and restore democratic government in the Caribbean. As tensions flare around the world, will the United States be expected to assume the role of global cop and take responsibility for maintaining international and regional law and order?

At home, the average American citizen is beginning to comprehend both the opportunities and vulnerabilities present in an increasingly interdependent community of nations. It is now easier than ever before to travel around the world or to procure goods and services produced in distant lands. More U.S.-based companies than ever before are now exporting their products, and foreign-owned enterprises in the United States provide 5 million jobs for American workers.

On the other hand, the United States has the world's largest government debt and is very dependent on foreign investors to buy U.S. Treasury bills and bonds which help finance this debt. Washington, D.C. can no longer determine the value of the dollar or the level of domestic interest rates without first taking into account how these decisions would impact upon America's global competitiveness. Moreover, the U.S. government could outlaw the use of CFCs, a substance which damages the earth's ozone layer, but this would do little to solve the problem unless other nations were also willing to curtail the production of this chemical compound.

In other words, many vital issues linked to the military, the economy, the environment, and natural resources and energy are beyond the capacity of the U.S. government to solve unilaterally. As a consequence, the well-being of the American people may be more vulnerable than ever before to decisions rendered and actions taken outside the borders of the United States. This, when combined with the overlapping of "domestic" and "international" issues in an era of interdependency and interconnectedness, renders the making of U.S. foreign policy in the twenty-first century a very difficult task indeed.

The end of World War II and the rise of the Soviet Union were watershed events which indelibly differentiated the world of the first half of the twentieth century from the world of the second half. The end of the Cold War, the demise of the Soviet Union as a nation and communism as an ideology, and the growing thrust of global interdependence, may prove to be equally monumental events which differentiate the latter half of the twentieth century from the first few decades of the twenty-first century. *America the Vincible* highlights the major challenges facing U.S. policy-makers in a vastly transformed international system and illustrates why bold new thinking will be needed in both America's domestic and foreign policy arenas.

AMERICA
THE VINCIBLE

AMERICA THE VINCIBLE

THE SHIP OF STATE IN HAZARDOUS WATERS

MILLENARIAN REFLECTIONS

Time is a human invention. It is true that day flows into night and that the seasons pass from warm to cold and from dry to wet, but the punctuations of life are inserted by man. The continuum is broken by human decision, and in those mental ruptures human beings find meaning. The notions of ages and of eras, of schedules and of history, of daily work and of sabbaths—all of these constitute the grammar that gives coherence to the statements of life.

In Western civilization, we are now approaching two of these punctuation marks: the end of a century and, in more visionary perspective, the onset of a new millennium. One can reasonably expect that learned commentary will be published, sermons will be preached, popular imagination will be titillated, and proverbial mountains will be climbed—all signaling the end of the twentieth century as well as the end of the second common millennium.[1]

If the end of a human-defined fragment of time inspires reflections on who we individually and collectively are and where we are going, we can be excused for beginning a study on U.S. foreign policy by examining the nature of the era in which we now find ourselves and into which we are moving. Moreover, as the title of this book indicates, we are concerned not only with the movement into another century and millennium, but the unprecedented vincibility and vulnerability of the United States of America as it prepares for the challenges which lie ahead.

There are moments in human history when people from many walks of life, and subject to widely diverse conditions, sense that the answers which they had learned to the problems of life no longer quite fit. Not that they were irrelevant but that they were incomplete. New circumstances shaped the old problems and new problems for which the wisdom of the ages had not yet devised answers pressed upon the consciousness. Such periods are later seen to have been great transitions in civilization itself. The end of the Roman empire and the beginning of the Middle Ages was such an era. The conditions of security and public order, the requirements of economic life, the definition of ethics, the relationship with the "gods"—these were all at best ambiguous and at worst collapsing. So it was with the end of the Middle Ages and the onset of the modern state system. The feudal structure of obedience and order, the rigid connection between the land and one's economic role, the highly stratified social structure, the limits on commerce and lending, the dominant role of the Church and the restrictions on private conscience—all of the pillars of meaning were at first eroded and then crumbled. Some now suggest that the latter part of the twentieth century may also be such a period of transition. If so, the turn of the century and a new millennium now almost upon us may yet be seen as marking a decisive turning point in history.

DECIPHERING THE NEW ERA
OF INTERNATIONAL POLITICS

Thomas Kuhn, noted commentator on the history of science, argued that science is characterized by a shared understanding of what constitutes the correct questions to ask, the ways to go about answering them, and the parameters of acceptable responses. Many social scientists have observed that this characterization goes quite beyond science. Political and social culture itself is bound together in much the same way. Kuhn argued that when observed phenomena could no longer quite fit within the accepted questions and answers and could not be studied using the standard techniques, complicated theoretical elaborations were often constructed both to accommodate these "anomalies" and to secure the accepted approaches.[2] And so it is in the broader society. We go to extraordinary lengths to preserve the traditional understanding and develop marvelous rationalizations. Demographic patterns change, the conditions of work and of wealth are transformed, the means of communication vary, new ideas (or old ideas rediscovered) emerge, social patterns and individual expectations are remolded—but we try desperately to maintain older patterns of behavior and of rule. Indeed, as Kuhn demonstrated in the history of science, it is not that the older approaches were utterly wrong but that they were substantially inadequate. Revolutions seldom annihilate completely the ancient ways of thought and behavior, but rather they develop coexistent ways or rework the old.

Many students of international relations and foreign policy contend that we do indeed live in a period where ancient understandings and new conditions uneasily coexist. The understanding of international politics that emerged from the transition from the Middle Ages to the modern state system is seen as at best incomplete and at worst utterly irrelevant. The "classical" conception stemmed from a period in which new and relatively self-contained units of political authority arose which were territorially defined and effectively sovereign. The resultant "system" was a collection of states claiming total secular independence and actively seeking the military, economic, and ideological conditions necessary to make good on that claim. Integration within each state, and anarchy among the states, represented the basic presumptions upon which policy was to be grounded. Even if concepts of political liberty and economic wealth would prompt states to permit a free flow of peoples, goods, and money, they always insisted on the right to define the terms of the flow and to limit or end such interdependence should security requirements, economic advantage, or political control dictate such restrictions.

It is true that this model of international relations was never the whole of social reality nor was it particularly applicable to many smaller or weaker states. Indeed, on the latter point, Raymond Aron noted that the system was always tilted toward the great states; in other words, the system was oligopolistic and hegemonic in its basic power relations.[3]

Nonetheless, the paradigm, if simplified, sufficiently explicated for the statesman the world that he saw and, more importantly, provided a guide to action that seemed to promise reasonable control of his domestic and international environment.

Even today this abstract model of reality serves statesmen in the formulation and execution of their policies, and quite frequently with acceptable results. Particularly when we examine the politics of national defense, it is clear how dominant this approach is. Balance of power, alliance management, containment, deterrence, power projection—all of these words and phrases are the very staples of strategic discussion and analysis. Moreover, they are ideas with which a Frederick the Great or a Bismarck would feel comfortable. Even in economic areas, commentaries on foreign investment in the United States or on measures of protection for domestic industry are well within the parameters of the classical model. And yet, if the interdependence of societies is not a new phenomenon, the nature, range, depth, and impact of such interdependence may create a qualitatively different condition. The intertwining of capital markets, the truly multinational corporation, the global environmental linkages, the intrusiveness of modern communications, the range and speed of movement of peoples and goods, the apocalyptic destructiveness of modern weapons, the potential empowerment of countless millions through the information revolution—all signal a transformation of the human condition that is at times utterly bewildering. In a real sense statesmen find themselves "between two worlds," struggling to apply tested concepts in untested terrain and to develop new approaches to a world whose dimensions are still uncertain.

AMERICA THE VINCIBLE

It is the world thus portrayed that the United States confronts as it moves through the last decade of the twentieth century and into the twenty-first. It is a decade, some prominent commentators argue, for which the United States is terribly unprepared and in which it finds itself vulnerable to forces that are perhaps beyond its control. For example, Paul Kennedy insists that the United States has already seen its best days as a global economic and military power.[4] He offers the following admonition concerning the linkage between economic and strategic prowess:

> For it has been a common dilemma facing previous "number-one" countries that even as their relative economic strength is ebbing, the growing foreign challenges to their position have compelled them to allocate more and more of their resources into the military sector, which in turn squeezes out productive investment and over time, leads to the downward spiral of slower growth, heavier taxes, deepening domestic splits over spending priorities, and a weakening capacity to bear the burdens of defense.[5]

The popular British magazine, *The Economist,* observes that the major task facing America's political leadership "is to help the country come to terms with its diminishing preeminence in the world, both as a military and, above all, as an economic power."[6] David Calleo dishearteningly adds that the "United States has become a hegemon in decay, set on a course that points to an ignominious end."[7] Tokyo's leading business newspaper writes of the Japanese belief in the "American decay," referring to the United States as "a sick and ill-humored uncle who is suffering from financial and family problems, paying no attention to chastity or discipline."[8] Tokyo-based Nikko Research stresses that "there are many unfavorable factors rooted deeply in American society, such as the declining work ethic, increases in crime, deterioration of education, as well as social discipline and order."[9]

The American people also harbor some ambivalent feelings about their nation's future. In 1989, about half optimistically believed that the Cold War was about to end and that the Kremlin was sincere in seeking much better relations with the West, and two-thirds no longer viewed the USSR as an immediate military threat.[10] On the other hand, almost 60 percent perceived that Japan had now become the world's leading economic power, giving some credence to Richard Rosecrance's parallel observation that if "things continue as they are now, it won't be much beyond 2010 before Japan becomes the leading power in world politics."[11]

There is little doubt that some of this criticism directed at the United States is justified, especially in the economic arena. For example, the U.S. share of the world export market has declined 30 percent since 1950. Between 1970 and 1987, the U.S. manufacturers' share of America's own domestic telephone market decreased from 99 percent to 25 percent, the machine tool market from 100 percent to 35 percent, and the color television market from 90 percent to 10 percent.[12] At the end of 1987, of the 100 largest industrial companies in the world (based on stock market value), 53 were Japanese, 34 were American, and 5 were British. Of the 100 largest banks (based on assets), 28 were Japanese, 11 French, 11 West German, and 11 American. Citizens of the United States have long taken pride in their high-technology sector, but U.S. trade in these products moved into the red in 1986 for the first time in the post-World War II era. Moreover, foreign corporations and individuals now receive almost 50 percent of all the patents issued by the U.S. Patent and Trademark Office, nearly twice as many as in 1980.

Do these statistics indicate that America is destined to be a much weaker economic power in the twenty-first century, and how will America's strategic and diplomatic choices be impacted by the nation's overall performance in an increasingly interdependent global economy? Has Henry Luce's 1941 vision of the "American Century" actually ended after only three or four decades?[13] Does an "America the Vincible" stand at the portal of an age of great uncertainty?

We do not share the perspective of these prophets of decline. As one does a comparative trend analysis of the world's powers, one cannot help but be impressed at the resilience of the American people and their institutions. Indeed, by 1993 many of the economic ills which some seemed to attribute to the United States were visible elsewhere, including Japan, and American social stability and political adaptability were even more impressive. We use the concept of vincibility in its precise meaning in this book. We do not mean that America will play a less significant role in world affairs nor that America is destined to be characterized by weakness. To be vincible is to be vulnerable, to be capable of being overcome. Such a condition is the normal fate of men, individually or collectively. The founders of the American republic were keenly aware how fragile social arrangements and political institutions are and how much attention, therefore, needs to be given to the foundations of our polity and to the direction of our policies.

To acknowledge vulnerability is to understand that security is not automatic, that national preservation comes only through prudent, thoughtful, and wise policies. A sense of vincibility implies not an end of Great Power status, but a sober assessment of the conditions and responsibilities of great power. A sense of invincibility is often associated with arrogance and is marked by bravado and a reckless disregard of one's permanent interests. The history of this century is littered with the political wreckage of regimes so animated. A truly strong and powerful country is one which recognizes national limitations and comfortably accepts social interdependence. America is the largest, continuous constitutional democracy in the world, but, as Abraham Lincoln observed, our form of government is always an experiment to which even today the cause of mankind is linked.

How will the United States validate its founding principles and aspirations in a changing and increasingly interdependent international environment? In a simplified sense, there is a continuum of possible responses. At one extreme of the continuum is the option to withdraw into a state of isolation so that the United States has very limited international dealings. Various states have tried permutations of this policy at different times with little success. The United States moved towards this kind of policy after World War I in response to public desires to avoid the kind of policies that had drawn America into that war. In today's interdependent world, however, few see isolationism as a viable option although its proponents occasionally appear on the domestic political stage, most frequently during national presidential campaigns. It is not a viable option today because of the extensive intertwining of peoples and economies which exists in the contemporary world and about which more will be said later in this book.

At the other extreme of the continuum is the option of acquiring such overwhelming power, and the reputation for using it, that, rather than dealing with the complexities of the world, America merely has to let its wishes be known and be prepared to enforce policies to achieve those interests regardless of the implications for other actors. This archetype has never existed to the degree that some would suggest, but the phrases *pax romana* and *pax britannica* have been used to describe earlier international systems which were dominated so thoroughly, either by the Romans in ancient times or by the British in more recent times, that most other states complied with the wishes of the empire.

Some have suggested that the period of time from World War II down to the end of the Vietnamese War was a period of *pax americana,* a global system heavily dominated by the preponderance of American power. Some have even talked of an "American Century." While these generalizations are much too broad, it is fair to say that the United States has been the predominant actor at least through much of the twentieth century. A commitment of American military could turn the balance of power in a conflict (or potential conflict) situation, the American dollar was (and continues to be) the international currency, and the sheer size of the American economy made all other economies, especially those of war-torn Europe, pale into insignificance. American assistance was needed not only to win World War II but it was also needed to reweave the political and economic fabric of Western Europe.

One of the most fundamental changes in the post-World War II international political system, however, has been not only the end of the age of empire, but the disappearance of the type of international system in which empires can develop and exist. People who talk of a *pax japonica* or *pax americana* or any other kind of single power dominant system fail to recognize these changes. The great powers of today have difficulty governing their domestic affairs and they are unable to manage their own allies, let alone other hostile states within the international system. The United States cannot control events in Nicaragua, Panama, the Philippines, or other states where U.S. intervention traditionally has altered political developments. Even more dramatically, Russia, having lost both its internal and external empire, may only with great difficulty, if at all, establish its imperium over its erstwhile provinces and dependent allies.

Surely, some nations will continue to be more influential than others and today's influential nations may be less influential tomorrow, but today's decision-makers must pursue national security in a vastly different international environment—one that has never existed quite this way in history.

This era is unique in a number of ways. In the contemporary international political system neither isolationism nor single power hegemony is possible. The U.S. must deal with other nations, large or small, as if those relations mattered. It must recognize the many facets of interdependence and understand that other peoples and nations cannot be ignored or bullied. Never before in the history of mankind have the interests of all nations been so intertwined. Scores of books have been written describing in various details the complex web of interdependence that exists. Some of the most fundamental notions of traditional international politics have been challenged. To some degree, this also is what we mean in this book by the phrase "vincibility." Today's world is no longer controlled by the actions of powerful states; nonstate actors play significant roles, in some cases more significant than those played by some state actors, and some relatively weak states also have considerable influence. The very idea of political sovereignty has been challenged by historical forces. The notion that a state has supreme authority within its own borders has been challenged by many developments, at least two of which have little to do with economics and trade.

First, many states have treaty obligations which make it extremely difficult for them to exercise unilateral control over matters traditionally considered solely within their domestic jurisdiction. To be sure, states may still take unilateral actions; but, in an increasing number of situations, political and economic costs make it unwise to do so. Members of the European Community (EC), for example, effectively share powers over some political and economic matters for which states in the past have fought for the right to control unilaterally. It is true that members can always withdraw from the EC if they are dissatisfied, but after forty years of integration, it is increasingly difficult to do so.

Second, a panoply of cross-national social, commercial, financial, and personal contacts have intertwined societies so completely that even legal, unilateral action by a state within its own borders can be undertaken only with considerable concern for the international implications. For every segment of American society which wants higher duties on imported goods, there will be another segment who will worry that such action will spark retaliation by foreign nations and subsequently hurt American exports. The legal concept of sovereignty has thus lost much of the factual political and economic base that historically undergirds it.

The era is unique in another way. At a time when the global system is becoming *more* homogeneous, nations themselves are becoming *less* homogeneous. This reverses an historic process that has been going on at least since the modern nation-state system came into existence in the mid-seventeenth century. Generally speaking, from the 1648 Peace of Westphalia which ended the Thirty Years War up to World War II, nations grew more *homogeneous* while the international system grew more *heterogeneous*. That is, domestic societies were being created through linguistic, economic, social, cultural, and political unification while, at the same time differences between nations were becoming greater as peoples began to define themselves ever more distinctly as Germans, Italians, Englishmen, etc. This is often referred to as the classical period for the development of nationalism. Nationalism was an integrative force within nations while at the same time it was a disintegrative force between nations.

But today the opposite is occurring. There is an increasing fragmentation within nations (more and larger communities of immigrants and refugees, greater language diversity, an explosion of separatist sentiment, demographic cleavages, etc.) while, at the same time, the states which make up the international system, particularly the western industrial nations and other states whose development has been influenced by the Enlightenment, are becoming more like one another.

Today, the forces of interdependence create common dilemmas as well as common enemies for all nations.[14] Small states have as much at stake in a nuclear war between major powers as the major powers themselves have. All nations are equally vulnerable to economic disruption, to environmental and ecological degradation, and to terrorism. The major powers have as much interest in developments in smaller states as those states themselves have. Diplomats from all states are potential hostages and the resource policies of even the smallest states can create serious consequences for larger states. Again, it is developments like these that contribute to the vincibility of all nations.

Another manifestation of this phenomenon is that certain segments of national populations are becoming more like related segments in other nations and less like disparate segments in their own nations. An almost guild-like relationship has developed between people in similar occupations across national boundaries. For example, computer programmers in Japan, Russia, Italy, and the United States share common languages, communicate frequently through scholarly publications and personal correspondence, meet together often in international and regional conferences, have loyalty to certain common principles (a commitment to certain kinds of technological developments, etc.), have been trained at the same universities, and have been socialized by many similar ideas and values. In fact, they have more in common with similar groups in other nations than they have with their own countrymen in different professions. This principle may be more noticeable within high technology professions than others, but it is also present in other professions (for example, musicians, artists, academics, homemakers). This decreasing homogeneity within nation-states makes it more difficult for governments to define their national interests with pristine clarity. Increasingly, the critical question for foreign policy analysts is which particular group's interests are being furthered by the external policies of the government.

Beyond that, once national interests are defined, pursuing them in a fragile and interdependent world is equally more difficult. All nations have lost some of their abilities to control global economic and political forces. Fluctuating exchange rates, the tenuousness of energy sources, the vulnerability of the global environment to adverse ecological developments, the uneven distribution of commodities, small wars that can turn into large ones, subnational groups who can carry out severely damaging acts of terrorism, capital flows—all of these forces and many more are beyond the control of any single nation-state. In fact, in the contemporary world there are a decreasing number of national problems which can be solved solely by national policies.

The contemporary period thus fascinates and challenges by the way that the traditional concept of state sovereignty is being challenged from both above and below at the same time. In many regions of the world, traditional state sovereignty is qualified by supranational authority, such as the European Community or the North American Free Trade Area or even the United Nations, while being challenged at the same time by ethnic, tribal, religious, and political groups within.

In the face of this diversity and interdependence, America will continue to play an extremely significant, perhaps the dominant, role in the drama of international politics. But it can ill afford to do so except from a sense of the limits as well as reach of its power. Above all, American power in the twenty-first century, as in the past, will depend on the totality of America itself—on its economic, political, military, and moral qualities.

Interdependence and vincibility, like political independence and invul-nerability, are always relative. But, as indicated above and as shall be further illustrated in the following chapters, the United States has occupied a virtually unique position among great world powers in its self-containment—geo-graphically, politically, materially, intellectually. Not only the fact of growing interdependence, but the vast dimensions of it, are thus particularly disorient-ing to the American public and its leaders. The vincibility associated with this interdependence covers the whole spectrum from the cosmic to the pedestrian. Although it will be argued in Chapter 6 that the United States is still largely immune to invasion and occupation, it is clear that it is not immune to genocidal destruction. Not only the United States but the planet now lives under multiple swords of Damocles—nuclear, chemical, and biological in character—not to mention the potential for environmental destruction arising from our daily work and play.

On a personal note, if you look around the room in which you are sitting, you will see more mundane evidences of vulnerability. The chair upon which you sit, the clothes you wear, the hand-held calculator in your briefcase, the car outside for which the keys are in your pocket—all in some degree probably come from a foreign market or from a U.S.-based company under foreign ownership. The very notion of "foreign" may be undergoing substantial alterations. The social web that ties us to others also defines who we are. Even the music to which you listen and the ideas which move you may originate in places far removed from your home and your country. Your vacation to a faraway nation may be threatened by quarrels to which you are seemingly not a party and which you may not even comprehend. Vulnerability is not simply a condition of the abstraction called the "United States of America," but of your daily life.

Returning to the earlier theme of this introduction, the transition through which we are now going, whether it be civilizational or more modest in proportion, is not simply an intellectual curiosity but rather the very warp and woof of our lives. *America the Vincible* is not a counsel of despair but a call for a new enlightenment from which new heights can be climbed. All Ameri-cans must understand that the quality and substance of their lives are poten-tially at risk, but that an informed citizenry and prudent policies are the preconditions to forestall dire consequences and to grasp the splendid oppor-tunities which will also be found in the era of 2001 and beyond.

ENDNOTES

1. At the end of the first common millenium, legend suggests that millenarian fervor was so great that on January 1, 1000, the entire population of Iceland was converted en masse to Christianity. One does not anticipate that the fervor will be as strong at the completion of the second millennium. Even here, of course, not everyone subscribes to the calcula-

tions of the Gregorian calendar. In the year 2000 by Gregorian estimates, the Chinese will be celebrating Kang-shin in the 17th cycle, the Islamic world the year of Hegira 1421, and the Hebrews year 5761.

2. Thomas S. Kuhn, *The Essential Tension: Selected Studies in Scientific Tradition and Change* (Chicago: University of Chicago Press, 1977).

3. Raymond Aron, *Politics and History,* ed. and trans. by Miriam Bernheim Conant (London: Collier Macmillan, 1978), especially Chapter 9.

4. Paul Kennedy, *The Rise and Fall of the Great Powers* (New York: Random House, 1987), 529.

5. Kennedy, *The Rise and Fall of the Great Powers,* 533.

6. "The Perfect President," *Economist,* 17 October 1987, 13.

7. David P. Calleo, *Beyond American Hegemony* (New York: Basic Books, 1987), 220.

8. Margaret Shapiro and Fred Hiatt, "Confident Japanese See United States in Serious Decline," *Washington Post,* 3 July 1988, 1. The Japanese newspaper is the *Nihon Keizai Shimbun.* As discussed in this article, the "American decay" is linked to the Challenger disaster, trade and budget deficits, external debt, the fall in the value of the dollar, drug abuse, AIDS, teenage pregnancy and illiteracy, and the shoddy quality of U.S. goods.

9. Clyde V. Prostowitz, Jr., *Trading Places: How We Allowed Japan to Take the Lead* (New York: Basic Books, 1988), 332.

10. ABC poll, May 1989, *The New York Times*-CBS poll, May 1989. See the *Washington Post,* 23 May 1989, A13.

11. Bill Powell, "The Pacific Century," *Newsweek,* 22 February 1988, 42-51. The recent Times Mirror/Gallup poll indicated that 58 percent of Americans described Japan as the world's leading economic power versus 29 percent who placed the United States first.

12. A report of the Council on Competitiveness, September 1988.

13. Henry R. Luce, "The American Century," *Life,* 17 February 1941, 61-65.

14. Some of this same logic prompted Daniel Bell to write that "The nation-state is becoming too small for the big problems of life, and too big for the small problems of life." See his "The World in 2013," *New Society,* 8 December 1987, 35.

PART I

THE CONTEXT OF U.S. FOREIGN POLICY-MAKING

There was a time when the preponderance of American military power and the relative independence and global influence of the American economic system created a foreign policy environment that was quite unique. It was unique not because it was easier for America to deal with other nations during this period. There were then, and will be always, friends and foes of varying intensities, both of whom make the conduct of foreign policy a very difficult and complicated process.

It was unique because of the domestic context of foreign policy-making. There were fewer legal and political challenges to foreign policy authorities, the foreign policy institutions were more moderate and accommodating and less ideological in their dealings with one another, and there was a fairly strong foreign policy consensus among the American people.

Moreover, there was a fairly widespread self-confidence among both American elite groups as well as the general public which tended to moderate the partisan foreign policy squabbles that did exist between political parties. That self-confidence led to a fairly widespread consensus based on, among other things, the perception that America's mission was to defeat threats to democracy and that created a willingness to spend, invest, or loan U.S. dollars to accomplish this mission.

Those conditions exist no more.[1] We have become, to use the title of one book, "our own worst enemy."[2] Foreign policy issues have become the stuff of political and ideological battles between parties, institutions, and bureaucracies as well as between different segments of the American people. The national security consensus evaporated.

The exact dates of this period are difficult to set precisely, but it probably began with the American entry into World War I, peaked during the 1950s and 1960s, and ended in the 1970s. The oil shocks of the early 1970s forced many Americans to believe that the actions of other, even relatively obscure, nations could have a profound effect on American life and that there was not a lot that America could do about it. Additionally, the Vietnamese conflict convinced many Americans that American military might was not unlimited and that the vision of global intervention to prevent the spread of communism was more clouded than many believed.

Precisely how these changes came about is not the subject of this book, but it has to do with personal ambition, with the loss of political comity, and with the increasing significance of international affairs on American life. Office seekers, particularly those seeking the presidential office, launch full-scale attacks on existing or previous foreign policies and then, if they win, become hoisted on their own rhetorical petards. Once in office they find that many of the developments about which they were so critical have a life of their own somewhat independent of American policies. They find that campaign rhetoric is not a sound basis for foreign policy.

Moreover, they find that their own ability, as head of arguably the last remaining superpower, to strike a policy that will alter the situations which they once criticized is much more limited than they thought. They find that their earlier political pronouncements were founded on faulty assumptions, that their ability to steer the ship of state through international waters requires more than rhetoric—it requires vision, leadership, and the ability to create and sustain coalitions. They also find that preelection promises to diverse segments of American society are difficult to fulfill and that the very act of trying to fulfill promises to one segment of the population can alienate other segments.

It is not the argument of this book that the United States is no longer the strongest nation in the world. Rather, it is our contention that changing global and domestic conditions now require greater skill, greater unity and continuity, more comity between the institutions of foreign policy, and more effective fforts to both shape and build on American values in the foreign policy process.

In Part I we try to describe the constitutional, legal, political, institutional, and social contexts that define the contemporary foreign policy process. Chapter 2 focuses on problems between the president and Congress over the control and formulation of American foreign policy. Some of these problems

It is not the argument of this essay

have become so pervasive that foreign powers have wondered who indeed is in charge of American foreign policy. At the conclusion of Chapter 2, as at the conclusion of each chapter, we make modest proposals, the discussion of which might lead to ways to get beyond deadlock and inaction and lead to more effective foreign policies in the twenty-first century.

Chapters 3 and 4 focus on institutional and bureaucratic issues. In these two chapters we discuss some of the primary executive branch institutions involved in the foreign policy process and call attention to various problems they face. Again, we suggest why certain problems exist within and between these institutions and hope to contribute to discussions that might make a vincible nation more secure.

Chapter 5 turns to the ultimate source of U.S. foreign policy, American society itself. In this chapter we describe a more fragmented American society in which ideals and values are becoming increasing diverse. We also try to describe what we believe are some problems and challenges in both formulating and interpreting a foreign policy consensus. Many of the problems we point out would not be very serious were America an invincible nation. Increasing vincibility requires greater foreign policy skills, it requires improved relations between the foreign policy institutions, and it requires a better understanding of the changing social and cultural contexts of foreign policy-making.

ENDNOTES

1. There is a vast literature which explores this consensus and its demise. Ronald H. Hinckley, in *People, Polls, and Policymakers* (New York: Lexington Books, 1992), discusses "The Consensus Myth" in Chapter 2 and cites much of the relevant literature. Of considerable importance are the many publications of James N. Rosenau and Ole R. Holsti on this topic. See, for example, their "U.S. Leadership in a Shrinking World: The Breakdown of Consensus and the Emergence of Conflicting Belief Systems," in *World Politics* 25 (April, 1983): 368-92. Eugene R. Wittkopf, another leading scholar on this subject, has reproduced much of his vast work in his *Faces of Internationalism: Public Opinion and American Foreign Policy* (Durham, North Carolina: Duke University Press, 1990).
2. I. M. Destler, Leslie H. Gelb, and Anthony Lake, *Our Own Worst Enemy: The Unmaking of American Foreign Policy* (New York: Simon & Schuster, 1984).

2

WHO STEERS
THE SHIP OF STATE?

THE CONSTITUTIONAL BASIS
OF FOREIGN POLICY

A constitution is a basic law which proscribes the power of a government and prescribes the procedures by which a government exercises those powers.[1] As everyone knows, the American Constitution created a unique separation of powers system in which legislative, executive, and judicial functions were assigned to separate branches of government. At the same time, the framers created what is called a system of checks and balances in which each separate branch was given authority, under certain circumstances, to exercise some limited authority in the functions performed by the other branches. It is no wonder that almost since the Constitution was written people have asked "[w]here does the Constitution lodge the power to determine the foreign relations of the United States?"[2] Since the Constitution does not make a distinction between domestic and foreign affairs, the responsibility for both is spread across all three branches of government. That is the very nature of a separation of powers system. The question then becomes, what are the various responsibilities of the separate branches of government? On this question the Constitution does have something to say.

Before turning to the Constitution, however, it is useful to ask how differing interpretations of constitutional authority are settled. One school of thought is that the Constitution itself should be consulted. Unfortunately, the original document, while it is very clear on some aspects of this question, leaves other aspects of the question unanswered. The Constitution spells out specific duties of the various branches, but it says nothing about how constitutional words and phrases should be interpreted through changing times.

Who has the authority to settle unanswered questions about the constitutional framework for foreign policy governance? This question itself is not easily answered. Some argue that on all questions requiring constitutional interpretation, it is the intentions of the framers which must be determined and followed. Unfortunately, however important these intentions, the Constitution itself was the result of many compromises between various political factions. Those compromises have left a legacy of different and varying "intentions" rather than a single common one. As one leading constitutional authority has said, "In large measure what the framers intended can be inferred only from what they did . . . ."[3]

Some have argued that neither the framers themselves nor the Constitution which they produced can be of much help in settling this issue since "foreign policy," at least as we now conceive it, was not of great concern in the mid-1780s.[4] While it is true that the main goal of the framers was to curb the excesses of both centralization (such as that of King George III) and decentralization (such as that of the Articles of Confederation), a careful reading of the events of the 1780s reveals several significant foreign policy concerns, some of which presage the very separation of powers controversies with which the nation grapples to this day.[5]

Another way to settle these ambiguities is to turn to the judicial process. The Supreme Court, in response to cases brought before it, has the authority to interpret the Constitution and to settle disputes according to those interpretations. However, changing historical and political realities have resulted in widely varying interpretations over time stemming from, among other things, Supreme Courts with different shades of political beliefs. Moreover, the Supreme Court has been shy about trying to settle arguments between Congress and the president, particularly arguments over foreign policy powers. The Court has viewed such arguments as nonjusticiable because of their political, rather than legal, origins.[6]

Who is the final arbiter of such questions? The intentions of the framers and Supreme Court interpretations of those intentions are of great importance; however, in the final analysis, questions about the relative powers of the different branches of government must be settled by the same authority that created the Constitution. It was by this authority that the document was written, it was by this authority that it became the fundamental law of the land, and it is only by this same authority that it can be interpreted with finality. This authority is the democratic political process.

Ultimately, it is the American people—through the ebb and flow of the political process—who interpret the meaning of the Constitution.[7] Thus, while the Supreme Court plays a significant role in settling questions involving foreign policy powers, ultimately these disputes between Congress and the executive branch are resolved according to what the American people, through the political process, will allow. And, given the separation of powers and checks and balances, it is important to understand that all such questions will never be settled with finality.

This chapter examines the constitutional allocation of foreign policy powers as well as the extraconstitutional forces of the political process that have shaped the exercise of those powers. It also relates this discussion to the theme of this book—American vincibility in the contemporary world.

AN "INVITATION TO STRUGGLE"?

The widespread view that the Constitution created an "invitation to struggle" between the executive and legislative branches in the foreign policy arena may be a bit overstated.[8] It is clear that there *has been* a struggle over the exercise of those powers, but that struggle does not stem from constitutional ambiguity. In fact, the Constitution is quite explicit on this issue—Congress is given primacy in setting policies which govern foreign relations, just as it has primacy in setting policies which govern domestic matters. The widespread misunderstanding of this primacy stems partially from a failure to make an adequate distinction between setting and implementing policy. Clearly the president has supremacy in the execution of foreign policy and that supremacy creates ample opportunities to shape, mold, define, and redefine foreign policy goals and objectives. However, the basic function of setting the policies which should guide the United States in its foreign relations is allocated to Congress by the Constitution.

Some commentators perpetuate the misunderstanding that the chief executive is ultimately responsible for making foreign policy.[9] According to the Constitution, as we will see later, the president is ultimately responsible for executing foreign policy while Congress is ultimately responsible for making it. As long as the word "making" is understood as setting U.S. foreign policy goals and objectives, there should be no objection to this conclusion. To return to the metaphor used at the head of this chapter, Congress, according to the Constitution, is responsible for setting the sails of the foreign policy ship, and the president is responsible for navigating the ship of state through the murky waters of world politics.

It is not difficult to explain how this misunderstanding came about. Though Congress is endowed by the Constitution with foreign policy primacy, it has seldom exercised that role and, indeed, may be institutionally incapable of doing so. But one should not confuse practice with theory. The framers of the Constitution clearly believed that Congress should be the primary source of policies to guide the American nation in its global role. They also believed that the president should execute those policies "faithfully." An explanation of the ensuing "struggle" lies not in the Constitution but rather in extra-constitutional developments and in changing political realities.

The Constitutional Sources of Congressional Power

It was not by accident that the first article of the Constitution bestows powers on Congress. "For the framers, Congress came first."[10] In fact, after the brief preamble, the first words of the Constitution give "all legislative Powers" to the Congress of the United States. If legislative power is defined as the right to make laws and establish principles which direct the affairs of this nation— both at home and abroad—then the primacy of Congress, even in the field of foreign policy, is established very early in the Constitution. It is often believed that the strongest weapon Congress has in its competition with the president for foreign policy supremacy is its power to declare war. In fact, that is not the case. Congressional supremacy in foreign policy rests on the "all legislative power" clause of the Constitution.

Additional support for this idea is found in the remainder of Article I which goes on to enumerate specific foreign policy powers vested in Congress: the power to establish conditions of trade;[11] the authority to borrow money; the obligation to regulate international trade and commerce; the sovereign right to determine both the existence of, and the appropriate punishment for, acts committed against U.S. national interests in international territory; the right to declare a state of war; the authority to raise, maintain, and set policies for the various branches of the armed services; the obligation to repel invasions; and the final, all inclusive, right to "make all Laws which shall be necessary and proper for carrying into Execution the foregoing Powers...."[12] By any interpretation, that is a very broad grant of foreign policy powers. Each phrase is pregnant with implications for contemporary foreign policy. The fact that Congress has virtually never lived up to these expectations is another issue and will be discussed later in this chapter.

The Constitutional Sources of Executive Powers

Article II of the Constitution defines the scope of presidential power. Section 2 of Article II mentions four specific presidential foreign policy powers: The president is the Commander-in-Chief of the armed services and he or she has the authority to make treaties with other sovereign states, to appoint foreign policy officials, and to "receive" ambassadors from foreign nations. Beyond these specific powers, the president is enjoined to see that "the Laws [passed by Congress] be faithfully executed." With the exception of the Commander-in-Chief power, this is a rather narrow grant of foreign policy power and each specific authority needs some explanation.

The Commander-in-Chief Power. It must be recalled that the president is Commander-in-Chief of the armed services *only* once those services are created, funded, and called into existence by Congress. Moreover, as Hamilton argued, the powers of the Commander-in-Chief are less than the military authority enjoyed by the King of England.[13] Even with this caveat, however, the Commander-in-Chief role of the president is the least challenged presidential foreign policy power. Once authorized by Congress, few deny the need for a single source of command authority. Controversies have arisen, however, when presidents have used their Commander-in-Chief powers as a way of getting around the specifically mentioned congressional powers, particularly the treaty powers of the Senate and the war-making powers of Congress.

From the mid-nineteenth century on, the Commander-in-Chief authority of the president has been interpreted, on the whole, very broadly and in a way which has impinged more or less directly on the war-making authority of Congress. President Polk provoked the Mexicans into war in 1846 using this authority; President Franklin D. Roosevelt authorized the U.S. Navy to fire upon German submarines months prior to the Japanese attack on Pearl Harbor; the conflicts in both Korea and Vietnam were entered into under the authority of the president acting as Commander-in-Chief; President Kennedy authorized a clandestine incursion into Cuba, President Carter authorized an ill-fated rescue of U.S. hostages in Iran, President Reagan ordered the invasion of Grenada and the attack on Libya, and President Bush ordered the attack on Panama and the buildup of offensive forces in the 1990 Gulf crisis, all acting under the same constitutional authority as Commander-in-Chief. In virtually every case, critics have responded with cries of presidential excess and with demands for more legislative restraints on the president.

In fact, there has not been a congressional declaration of war since 1941, yet the nation has been involved in both minor and major conflicts up to the present day. The controversial War Powers Resolution of 1973 (Public Law 93-148), which requires the president to consult with Congress before sending U.S. troops into a foreign conflict, fundamentally was a congressional attempt to reclaim its constitutional power to declare war. The Resolution allows the president to send troops abroad without consulting Congress only in an emergency. Congress must then be informed within forty-eight hours and the troops must return after sixty days (or, in ninety days under special circumstances) unless Congress fails to meet, approves an extension, or declares war.[14]

In spite of a host of Supreme Court cases reaffirming the monopoly of Congress on the right to declare war and the right to engage in all other legislative activities pertaining to war-making, "the power of Congress *vis-á-vis* the president has . . . inexorably receded."[15] The attempt by Congress to reassert its authority through the War Powers Resolution, since it also impinged on the president's Commander-in-Chief role, was of dubious constitutionality at its inception and became moribund when the legislative veto (discussed below) was successfully challenged in the *INS* v. *Chadha* case in 1983.

The role of Congress in "Operation Desert Storm," the U.S.-led international coalition that invaded Iraq on 16 January 1991, was, in a sense, neither fish nor fowl. A long series of UN resolutions culminated in Resolution 678 of 29 November 1991 which authorized the use of force in the face of Iraqi non-compliance with UN demands. The UN resolutions had required an Iraqi withdrawal from Kuwait by 15 January 1991. All of this was done by the Bush administration without specific authorization from Congress. As the political and military conflict developed in the Gulf, a constitutional conflict between Congress and the White House developed in Washington. The issue was whether or not the president could authorize the buildup of forces, and commit the U.S. to the use of force, without meeting the specific requirements of the 1973 War Powers Resolution. On 12 January 1991, both houses of Congress authorized the use of force against Iraq in the event of Iraqi noncompliance. The last minute nature of the congressional authorization, without addressing the issue of the constitutionality of the War Powers Resolution, did lend some support to the idea that the Act was moribund, if not dead. Nevertheless, the Commander-in-Chief authority of the president is the least challenged, the most broadly stated, and the least shared of all presidential powers when it is used in conformity with "rules" set by Congress and for purposes congressionally mandated (Art. 1, Sec. 8). When presidents go beyond this, cries of presidential abuse, calls for reform, and a resurgence of congressional power inevitably follow.

Treaty-Making Power.   The treaty-making power is another matter— it is not assigned to the president alone. The Constitution specifies that the president shall "make treaties" only "by and with the Advice and Consent of the Senate."

Consent.   In a literal sense, the "Consent" portion of this clause does not present any difficulties. All treaties are submitted to the Senate for its consent and no treaty is ratified without its consent.[16] In a practical sense, however, the consent requirement has sparked frequent political battles. From the beginning of the Republic down to the present day, presidents have attempted to enjoy the fruits of international agreements without paying the price of senatorial consent. They have done this through the means of executive agreements which, for all intents and purposes, have the same legal standing, both domestically and internationally, as treaties but which can be entered into solely on the initiative of the executive.[17]

In practice, three forms of agreements with other nations have developed. The traditional treaty requires the consent of two-thirds of the Senate. A congressional-executive agreement, though not specified in the Constitution, is permitted by various interpretations of existing congressional and presidential powers and requires the consent of a simple majority of both houses of Congress. The pure executive agreement, also not mentioned in the Constitution but based on inherent executive powers of the president, requires no congressional involvement. It is the latter type of agreement which has caused the greatest problems with Congress.[18]

Some of the more famous executive agreements include: the Rush-Bagot Notes of 1817 (which a year later were sent to the Senate and became the Rush-Bagot Treaty limiting the presence of naval vessels on the Great Lakes); President McKinley's 1900 arrangements regarding China which promised 5,000 troops with naval support to rescue besieged legations in Beijing; President Theodore Roosevelt's agreements with the Dominican Republic in 1905; the Lansing-Ishii Agreements in 1917; and President Franklin Roosevelt's destroyer deal with Great Britain, a major event in convincing the Germans that the United States would not remain neutral in World War II. The various agreements which came out of the Cairo, Yalta, and Potsdam conferences at the end of World War II were all executive agreements. The early American obligations in Southeast Asia were created by executive agreements under both Presidents Eisenhower and Kennedy. Neither President Nixon's agreements with Hanoi nor President Carter's agreements with the People's Republic of China were treaties. President Reagan's accord with the People's Republic of China regarding the peaceful use of nuclear energy was also an executive agreement.[19]

Table 2-1 shows the dramatic increase in international agreements other than treaties (although it does not distinguish between pure executive agreements and congressional-presidential agreements). In most cases, Congress does not object to this trend. In fact, Congress frequently authorizes the executive branch to enter into such agreements, following basic congressional guidelines, without congressional consent. Were this not the case, Congress would become clogged with largely noncontroversial agreements with foreign powers.

TABLE 2-1 Treaties versus Executive Agreements

Period	Treaties	International Agreements Other than Treaties
1789-1839	60	27
1840-1889	215	238
1890-1939	524	917
1940-1984	554	9,987

Source: Thomas G. Ingersoll and Robert E. O'Connor, *Politics and Structure* (Monterey, California: Brooks/Cole Publishing Co., 1986), p. 8.

Congress has occasionally attempted to limit the president's use of executive agreements viewing it as a circumvention of the normal treaty-making process. Though not the only attempt, the effort led by Senator John Bricker (R-Ohio) came the nearest to succeeding. In 1952, congressional opposition to executive agreements was so widespread that Senator Bricker's constitutional amendment to require, among other things, that executive agreements be regulated by Congress failed by only one vote in the Senate.[20]

However, one type of executive agreement is very troublesome to Congress—the secret executive agreement. Since they are secret, few know how many such agreements are made. A 1970 Senate subcommittee led by Senator Symington reported hundreds of such agreements.[21] In an attempt to gain some control over secret executive agreements, Congress passed a law in 1972 (Public Law 92-403) which required that the secretary of state report to Congress the texts of any international agreements entered into by the government within sixty days of the agreement. Yet, a Government Accounting Office study found that in the case of one bilateral relationship—United States-South Korea—there were thirty exceptions to this requirement in 1976 alone.

Nevertheless, when dealing with formal treaties, as opposed to executive agreements, the consent of the Senate is always sought and on some significant occasions has been withheld. The Treaty of Versailles, which ended World War I and which included the Covenant of the League of Nations, was rejected by the Senate in 1919, and, for fear of being rejected by the Senate, the SALT II Treaty was withdrawn from the Senate in 1979 before a vote was taken.[22]

Advice. The "Advice" portion of the "Advice and Consent" clause is quite a different thing. To begin with, no one knows precisely what the framers meant in requiring the advice of the Senate in the treaty process. At face value, it seems to suggest that the president (and, one supposes, the State Department) should consult with the Senate at some point during the treaty-making process.

In practice, this is virtually never done. George Washington was both the first and perhaps the last president to do so. He is reported to have met with members of the Senate to consult with them on a treaty with a southern Indian tribe. After two days of what he considered rude treatment, President Washington left the Senate and said "he would be damned if he ever went there again." He never did, nor have any of his successors ever sought Senate advice in that way.[23]

Scholars and politicians quibble over distinctions between treaties and executive agreements, but all agree that the Senate has seldom been called upon for its institutional advice in such matters. It is easy to question the wisdom of seeking Senate advice on a treaty, but it is difficult to question the constitutional requirement to seek such advice. One of the more successful ways of meeting this requirement, while at the same time working with less than the entire membership of the Senate, has been for the president to seek the advice of a few key Senators or with the leadership on relevant committees.

If nothing else, prudence should compel presidents to do this. If one compares the success of Presidents Roosevelt and Truman in securing the near unanimous support of the Senate on the United Nations treaty with the failure of President Wilson on the League of Nations, it is clear that ignoring the Senate is done at considerable peril. President Wilson virtually ignored the Senate during the period leading up to the Paris Peace Conference in 1921. The Senate was not informed about the negotiating process nor about Wilson's goals. And to make matters worse, Wilson's chief negotiator, Colonel House, was not liked by the Senate. For these, and other reasons, there was widespread Senate opposition to the Covenant of the League of Nations.

In contrast, President Roosevelt's secretary of state, Cordell Hull, vowed that the birth of the United Nations would not have these kinds of complications and involved members of both houses of Congress over a period of several years in a process which led to the near unanimous (there was one negative vote) support in the Senate for the treaty allowing U.S. participation in the United Nations.

Power of Appointment.   The third specified foreign policy power of the president is the power to appoint ambassadors, which by interpretation includes the power to appoint nearly all senior foreign policy officials. This power, however, is also shared with the Senate which must give its "Advice and Consent" (now generally called "confirmation" and limited to consent with no advice) on all such appointments. On a few occasions, the Senate has objected to some presidential appointments to foreign policy positions, but for the most part presidents have had their way in ambassadorial and other State Department appointments even when the only qualification for such an appointment has been the amount of money contributed to a presidential campaign.[24]

Occasional opposition by a single senator on ideological grounds is probably a clear abuse of the congressional share of this authority. Senator Jesse Helms (R-SC), strongly committed to a conservative agenda in foreign policy, single-handedly delayed several of President Reagan's early foreign policy appointments for so long that the president was forced to withdraw the names.

Another question regarding the power to appoint senior foreign policy officials has arisen in recent years concerning the president's national security affairs adviser.[25] The National Security Act of 1947 has been interpreted to allow the president to appoint such an adviser. For many years this official has staffed the National Security Council, created by the same act, and acted as the president's chief adviser on national security matters.

The role performed by the national security affairs adviser, however, has changed quite dramatically over the years. Some argue that it was President John F. Kennedy's adviser, McGeorge Bundy, and President Lyndon Johnson's adviser, Walt Rostow, who initiated these changes. Others argue that it was President Richard Nixon's national security affairs adviser, Henry Kissinger, who most significantly altered this role. Clearly, Kissinger went beyond being an adviser and became both the architect and the administrator of foreign policy and national security affairs. His secret trip to China, aimed at reopening U.S.-Chinese relations, was clear evidence of this gradual change. President Carter's national security affairs adviser, Zbigniew Brzezinski, continued this same trend with his operations in Iran. President Reagan's string of national security affairs advisers became so involved in actual operations, including the management of covert activities, that Congress again raised the recurring question of whether or not the position of national security affairs adviser ought to be subject to Senate confirmation.

If the national security affairs adviser is a major architect of foreign policy, there is a powerful argument that the constitutional requirement of Senate confirmation should be followed. If he or she merely acts as the coordinator for National Security Council meetings, then the question becomes less urgent. On the other hand, Senate confirmation of this position might alter the traditional executive privilege protection the position enjoys and tempt any president to create a new adviser for national security affairs who was beyond the reach of the Senate. However, with the exception of the occasional encroachment by individual, ideologically motivated senators or the overly broad role played by the national security affairs adviser, the appointment authority has been relatively free of controversy.

Power of Recognition. The constitutional authority to "receive Ambassadors" has been interpreted as the power to bestow U.S. recognition upon other governments. This is no small power. Traditional international law treated recognition as somewhat automatic once certain minimal objective conditions had been met. However, it was President Wilson who first used the power of recognition as a foreign policy weapon. He viewed the 1913-14 Mexican regime led by Victoriano Heurta as a "government of butchers" and withheld American recognition for fear that recognition would signal U.S. approval of the regime and would also assist the regime in gaining further international recognition and legitimacy.

The revolutionary Soviet regime came to power in 1917 but was not recognized by the United States until 1933 and even though Mao Tse-tung and the Chinese Communists defeated the Nationalist government of Chiang Kai-shek in 1949, the communist People's Republic of China was not officially recognized by the United States until 1979. In neither of these cases was the "Advice and Consent" of the Senate sought nor was it constitutionally required. In both cases, however, cries of presidential abuse were heard from critics of these policies.[26] Tensions arose between Congress and the president as former Soviet republics sought American recognition during the early 1990s.

Thus, these four specified foreign policy powers of the president—the appointment and treaty-making powers and the Commander-in-Chief and recognition powers, the first two of which are shared with the Senate and the latter two are held alone—have been the basis for the expansion of presidential powers in the foreign policy field. These four specifically stated grants of presidential foreign policy authority have been the pegs on which all expansions of these powers have been hung.

It has been argued that the president has a foreign policy preeminence inherent in his role as chief executive.[27] Of all justifications of presidential power, this is probably the weakest. What follows the Article II statement that the "executive Power shall be vested in a President of the United States of America," is a specific enumeration of those executive powers. Any claim to inherent powers must be based on one of those specified powers, such as the Commander-in-Chief power. "The framers would be incredulous at what has become of their original creation, the presidency, an office conceived in doubt and controversy, its powers seemingly strictly limited, yet commonly described today as the most powerful in the world. It would, as President Truman once said, make Genghis Khan green with envy."[28]

THE SWING OF THE PENDULUM
BETWEEN CONGRESS AND THE PRESIDENT

What has been described above is clearly the Madisonian view of the locus of foreign policy power in the Constitution. Hamilton, among others, had a different view. He believed that when dealing with foreign nations the newly created government had to act quickly and responsibly, goals which could be met only by a strong president with foreign policy preeminence. While the actual Constitution favored Madison's more limited views, circumstances, tradition, and practice have created an executive office marked by Hamilton's conception of presidential preeminence in the field of foreign policy.[29]

It was, however, this same Hamilton who wrote in the *Federalist*, paper no. 75:

> The history of human conduct does not warrant that exalted opinion of human nature which would make it wise in a nation to commit interests of so delicate and momentous a kind, as those which concern its intercourse with the rest of the world, to the sole disposal of . . . a President of the United States.

This increase in presidential power has been uneven, but inexorable. Occasionally the pendulum has shifted and Congress has expanded its powers at the expense of the president. But it is important to note that even though the pendulum has swung back and forth between the president and Congress, the very axis of the swing has drifted inexorably towards the president.[30] In fact, other than the early presidencies of Madison, Monroe, and John Quincy Adams, where "the plan rejected by the Framers, of having the president chosen by Congress, was substantially in operation," the power of the president relative to Congress has grown steadily.[31] In summarizing the last half century, one scholar has written that "the Oval Office is where foreign policy for better or for worse has been made."[32] Both the swing of the pendulum and the changing axis of the swing can be explained, at least partially.

The Pendulum Swing

There are several principles which explain the shifting balance of foreign policy preeminence between the executive branch and Congress.

1. International crises usually favor a strong executive. There is a natural tendency to "look to the president" during periods of international tension and conflict. Clearly, Congress cannot "run a war" and the president's role as Commander-in-Chief gives him a considerable advantage in these settings. "Congress" cannot meet with allied heads of state nor can theater commanders report to and receive instructions from 535 elected representatives.

President Polk often is credited as being the first president to expand vastly the foreign policy powers of the presidency during the war with Mexico. Polk's unprecedented use of presidential power was severely criticized by a young representative from Illinois, Abraham Lincoln, who said that if the nation were to "allow the President to invade a neighboring nation, whenever he shall deem it necessary to repel an invasion, and you allow him to do so, whenever he may choose to say he deems it necessary for such purpose. . .[then] you allow him to make war at pleasure."[33] But wars, police actions, humanitarian operations, or any other kind of international tension have inevitably created both public and congressional attitudes that have favored strong presidential leadership.

2. At the conclusion of wars and other acts of international conflict, however, there is usually a resurgence of congressional power in foreign policy. Some of this is explained merely by the desire to "get on" with domestic problems which are usually neglected during wars. "Getting on" with domestic problems usually requires an extensive legislative agenda devoted primarily to domestic matters and more clearly within the bailiwick of Congress.

But other parts of this reaction are explained by a feeling that now is the time to change direction. The president has been resurgent during the international conflict, but perhaps that was part of the problem. After military action in both Korea and Vietnam the public mood supported a resurgence of congressional power, occasionally at the expense of sound legislation. There is always a tendency to seek legislation to prevent the kind of war which has just ended rather than the kind that is just ahead, the causes of which, unfortunately, are unknown.

Causes of More Systemic Shifts of Power

As noted above, even as the pendulum swings back and forth between Congress and the president, the very axis of the pendulum has shifted towards the president. A variety of informal and extra-constitutional circumstances and conditions have favored the president in the competition for foreign policy primacy.

1. The president has unrivaled access to foreign policy information. All of the nation's foreign policy institutions—the State Department, the intelligence agencies, the defense establishment, and others—are part of the executive branch of government. Their heads are all appointed by, and report to, the president.

It is true that representatives of these institutions can be called before congressional committees and asked for information, but that information is usually selective and only given in response to specific congressional requests. Congress is never certain that it is receiving complete information. If things go wrong and Congress conducts subsequent investigations to determine responsibility, members of Congress frequently ask executive branch witnesses why they did not tell Congress certain pertinent information at earlier hearings. The most common executive branch response is: "You didn't ask us that specific question."

Moreover, Congress lacks the means of information gathering. Even with bloated staffs, congressional committees cannot (and should not) maintain observers at all significant international events and monitor all international developments. Attempts to do so violate the separation of powers principle as surely as do executive abuses.[34]

2. The president has a virtual monopoly on the ability to influence public opinion. Some members of Congress attain sufficient celebrity status to make public opinion ripples, but only the president (and some more than others) can make waves. The president commands global media attention at the drop of a word. One pollster has estimated that, at least prior to Watergate, any president automatically could expect fifty percent of the public to support any decision he or she made.[35] Whether it was President Franklin D. Roosevelt with his innovative use of radio or President Reagan with his commanding television presence, the president of the United States has unprecedented preeminence in shaping public opinion. It appeared that President Clinton even found ways to get to public opinion while circumventing traditional print and electronic journalists through his use of electronic town hall types of meetings.

3. The president has become the "principal author of the national legislative program."[36] Even though the Constitution requires only an annual report
from the president and commits Congress to consider "such measures as he
shall judge necessary and expedient," in practice the president is the chief
initiator of legislation. Determining the ultimate source of legislation is a very
difficult task. Clearly, there is complicated interaction in which Congress,
representatives of hundreds of executive branch agencies, and interest groups
all participate in drafting legislation. It is also clear that Congress has the last
word and may alter any legislative proposals or even fail to enact them—thus
the old saying that the president proposes and Congress disposes. But the
degree of executive branch participation in the initiation and development of
legislation is generally surprising to new members of Congress.[37] Thus, even
in an area where one would expect a congressional advantage, the president
enjoys a legal and overwhelming advantage stemming from his role as head
of the entire executive branch of government.

4. The president controls the political machinery of the United States.
Employees of the vast federal bureaucracy take their orders from the president
who appoints the heads of all executive agencies. This also supports presidential primacy in the field of foreign affairs.

5. Finally, there is some logic to the Hamiltonian argument; other peoples
and nations look to the president of the United States for leadership. This is a
role that no aggregation of domestic political leaders can play. There is only
one chief executive of the most powerful nation in the world. All heads of
sovereign states are legally and juridically equal, but politically, the president
of the United States is first among equals. No individual member of Congress
nor congressional committee can play this role.

Two Developments Which Have Favored Congress

Thus far we have seen that while the Constitution favors Congress in the bid
for foreign policy primacy, extra-constitutional privileges, practice, and tradition have favored the executive. Nevertheless, there have been two fundamental developments over the history of the Republic which have kept Congress
at least partially in the competition for foreign policy leadership.

1. The first development was the democratization of foreign policy.
Exact dates are elusive in these kinds of broad developments, but roughly it
has been only in the twentieth century—the Age of Ideologies—that heads of
state have consciously tried to enlist public support for foreign policy. As the
United States found itself involved in foreign, and not always popular, wars
in 1917 and 1941, presidents felt compelled to convince the American public
that these wars had consequences beyond those of traditional European
dynastic conflicts. These wars, the people were told, were being waged over
the very foundations of civilization.

With so much at stake and with so much required from the American people—military personnel, new factory workers, personal sacrifices, and tax dollars—the government sought to build a popular consensus to support the war effort. And Congress had to be involved in this effort. Senators and representatives have much smaller constituencies than the president. In that sense, they are closer to the people and better able to generate local support for a war effort.

As it later turned out, there was another side of this coin. When unpopular foreign conflicts came along, the American people, now enlisted in the foreign policy cause, became less a source of support and more a restraint on the foreign policy of the government. In Korea and, even more dramatically, in Vietnam, the American people, who for the previous fifty years had been told that their support was vital for national security, were now told that they did not fully understand the complexities of foreign policy.

Perhaps much of the change came about because of the neglect of Congress. In both Korea and Vietnam, American presidents acted virtually unilaterally in involving the American nation in foreign conflicts. In regard to the one legitimizing legislative act during the Vietnamese conflict, the Gulf of Tonkin Resolution (1964), Congress later came to feel that its acquiescence may have been secured fraudulently. Congress, angry over being deceived and with the support of much of the public, began to search for ways to limit or end U.S. military activities in Southeast Asia.

As the American public, particularly the young, became increasingly restless about U.S. involvement in Southeast Asia, members of Congress became the first to reap the political ill wind from the changing climate. With their smaller constituencies and closeness to the people, the democratization of foreign policy had now come full circle as the American people, through their closest national officials, gradually made it impossible for the president to continue the undeclared war. Historians continue to debate the wisdom of this, but few doubt its occurrence.

Even in areas not involving foreign conflict, the democratization of foreign policy has briefly (and some would say unfortunately) resuscitated Congress. When President Eisenhower needed widespread public support for his rejection of Mao Tse-tung and the newly victorious Chinese Communists, it was to the American people he turned. What Secretary of State John Foster Dulles continually referred to as the Red Chinese "Bandit Regime," became anathema to the American public and its elected members of Congress.

But when subsequent presidents wanted to initiate some kind of accommodation with Red China, the now-conditioned American public could not be changed quite so easily. As the realities of international politics came to demand a shift in American alliance patterns, Presidents Kennedy, Johnson, and Nixon found that talk about easing relations with Red China was not popular with the American public. Ultimately, it took twenty-three years and a president (Richard Nixon) whose anticommunist reputation was so secure that he could survive any criticism before rapprochement could be reached with the People's Republic of China in 1972. It is interesting to note that even in the Gulf War of 1990, President Bush asked Congress to "authorize" American participation, not to declare war.[38]

The democratization of foreign policy has meant an increased role for wider public voices. Because of this, "public opinion influence in executive and legislative governance and foreign policy-making is growing. It does not appear possible to reverse this tide. The intellectual and political challenges for foreign policymakers are to come to grips with the actuality and direct it in a positive and beneficial course."[39]

2. The second "thread" which has kept Congress alive in the competition for preeminence in the foreign policy process has been the changing role of American dollars as a foreign policy tool. Prior to World War II, the important commodities of international politics were treaties, trade arrangements, and military might.

But after World War II, American dollars became increasingly important as an instrument of foreign policy. The Marshall Plan, for example, rebuilt the war-torn economies of Europe and cost the United States over 13 billion dollars. Various other "plans" and "doctrines" also came along which supplied economic, political, and military aid to other nations in America's relentless search for Cold War allies. But this required vast sums of money which could be raised only with congressional assent.

The military doctrines of massive retaliation and deterrence also created a somewhat different situation. Vast and expensive weapons systems, never meant to be used, had to be brought into existence. These new weapons systems and large numbers of peacetime military personnel required an unprecedented share of the peacetime federal budget. And this required the cooperation of the one political institution which controlled the purse strings of the American people—Congress, particularly the House of Representatives.

There are some parallels between the end of World War II and the end of the Cold War. Just as the war-torn economies of defeated European states required large injections of American money, so also did the states of the former Soviet Union and the Warsaw Pact require vast sums of money in order to rebuild their debilitated economies. This again required congressional assent.

While most of the constitutionally granted foreign policy powers enjoyed by Congress were given solely to the Senate (with the exception of the power to declare war), the increasing importance of money as an instrument of foreign policy favored the House of Representatives where, by tradition, all revenue bills must originate. This explains why in the Senate it is the Foreign Relations Committee which plays the most significant role in foreign policy matters (this committee has jurisdiction over treaties and appointments), but in the House of Representatives it is the Appropriations Committee and the Ways and Means Committee which have foreign policy cards to play.[40] It is through these committees that money is appropriated and tax policies adjusted to raise the necessary revenue to carry out these policies.

In the historical tug of war for foreign policy primacy, it has been the democratization of foreign policy and the increasing role of money in foreign affairs which have kept Congress from being rolled over completely by the executive branch steamroller.

OBSTACLES WHICH PREVENT CONGRESS FROM PLAYING ITS FOREIGN POLICY ROLE

It has taken more than the extra-constitutional powers of the president, however, to affect the changing axis of the pendulum swing. There are some fundamental obstacles inherent in Congress itself which have facilitated its loss of foreign policy powers. These obstacles have to do with the organization and makeup of Congress. In many ways, Congress is its own worst enemy.

1. First, there are a number of impediments which stem from the size, diversity, and varying personalities and styles of Congress and its members. There are 100 Senators and 435 members of the House of Representatives. To an extraordinary degree, they are a microcosm of the American population. Some are brilliant, some are not; some are very ideological while others are very pragmatic; some are arrogant, a few humble; and some are very interested in foreign affairs while others could not locate Korea on an unmarked map and could not care less about foreign affairs unless they have rather immediate domestic political significance.

Often, those who have an interest in foreign affairs are assigned to committees with solely domestic jurisdiction and those with no international interests are assigned to significant foreign policy committees. Members of Congress with no international interests, but in whose districts industries are threatened by foreign competition, can very quickly become strident trade protectionists. A congressman with a large steel plant in his district once worked vigorously to restrict foreign steel imports until he learned that the same Japanese steel industries whose exported steel products were hurting "his" plant were purchasing coal used in the manufacture of their steel from previously idle mines also located in his district. His attitudes towards tariffs on imported steel changed.

Given such diversity, it may be too much to expect either institutional or individual consistency. The interests of Congress change from time to time and the interests of individual congressmen can change more quickly and rather quixotically. Senator Barry Goldwater (R-AZ) argued against the War Powers Resolution all through 1972 on the basis that committing U.S. troops abroad was a presidential prerogative of no concern to Congress whose judgment could not be trusted on such matters anyway. However, when President Carter unilaterally proposed the gradual withdrawal of U.S. troops from South Korea in 1977, Senator Goldwater opposed this on the basis that such unilateral action, without the approval of Congress, violated the president's more limited foreign policy prerogatives. He suggested that President Carter should send his request to Congress where it would receive the attention it deserved. Senator Goldwater also voted against the War Powers Resolution as an intrusion on inherent and necessary presidential powers and then, in 1978, went before the Supreme Court to argue that it was unconstitutional for President Carter to rescind the security treaty the United States had with Taiwan without congressional assent.

Clearly, it is difficult, if not impossible, to expect the kind of single-mindedness of purpose, the sense of long-range planning, and the consistency needed in the direction of foreign policy from a national body of this size and diversity. Congress can, however, when its attention is seized, respond quickly and purposefully.

The War Powers Resolution of 1973 is an example of how and why Congress changes its mind. An inability to alter the course of the war in Vietnam created considerable congressional frustration in the early 1970s. This frustration led to a series of legislative attempts to end U.S. involvement in Southeast Asia. The McGovern-Hatfield Amendment (1970-71) required U.S. withdrawal from Indochina in stages (it did not pass); the Cooper-Church Amendment (1971) cut off funds needed for U.S. involvement in Cambodia (it passed); and the Eagleton Amendment (1973) called for a withdrawal from Cambodia and Laos (it did not pass).

But the handwriting was on the wall. The War Powers Resolution came next and was far more sweeping in its effects. It required the president to consult with Congress prior to inserting U.S. troops into any foreign conflict. In emergency circumstances, the president could send troops abroad on his or her own authority but had to report such developments to Congress within forty-eight hours and, in the absence of congressional authorization or a declaration of war, withdraw those troops within sixty (or ninety) days.

The resolution was attacked from both left and right. The left did not like the notion that the president had the authority to send troops abroad without congressional approval even for sixty days. They saw the resolution as weakening the already clearly stated constitutional principle that only Congress could declare war. The right saw the resolution as an infringement on the president's Commander-in-Chief powers.

In any event, the Resolution was passed three times by Congress and vetoed by President Nixon each time. Congress could not muster enough votes to override the veto. However, as the political fallout from the Watergate scandal began to settle and a favored Republican congressional candidate in

New Jersey was defeated in an off-year election, congressional interest was captured and Congress came up with enough votes to override the veto and passed the War Powers Resolution.

2. A second set of obstacles stem from organizational problems within Congress. The absence of any meaningful leadership structure in Congress creates what can only be described as anarchy. Each member of Congress feels responsible only to his or her constituency. It has been years since a Speaker of the House of Representative actually "spoke" for the House and the president of the Senate (the vice president of the United States) is virtually never in attendance. Party leaders in both houses lack effective means of enforcing party discipline.

Foreign policy cacophony results from the fact that Congress is an orchestra without a conductor. Party discipline has become so weak that one strains to find examples of it. Each member of Congress has unfettered access to local media without working through congressional leadership. Campaign funds are raised primarily by the members of Congress and by the aspirants for those seats—little of the money necessary to run political campaigns comes from party headquarters. This does not help build party loyalty.

Whether apocryphal or not, the story told by Representative Synar (D-OK) strikes an all-too-truthful chord to anyone who has dealt with Congress. He claims that when he asked a Cub Scout pack to which he was speaking if they knew the difference between the United States Congress and the Cub Scouts, one young boy raised his hand and said, "We have adult supervision."[41]

The lack of effective leadership and the absence of party discipline lessen the ability of Congress to play its constitutionally permitted foreign policy role. When the Soviet Union shot down a Korean civilian airliner in 1983, the Senate took eight different votes on as many separate resolutions, each condemning the action in slightly different language. It was not that the Soviet act required that many resolutions in order to express the required degree of repugnance. Rather, different Senators, in playing to their constituencies, felt that slight variations on language were needed and, of course, no one wanted to be left off the list of those who condemned the Soviet act. During President Reagan's first term, there were thirty-six "test votes" on the MX missile. A House vote in December of 1982 to cut 1 billion dollars from the MX was reported by many newspapers as the end of the MX. But the very next day, the House voted to retain 25 billion dollars for MX research and development.[42] In the early days of the Nicaraguan conflict, Congress took ten months to deal with an important piece of legislation which related to the conflict. This delay vitiated any possible beneficial effects of the policy.[43] Clearly, a more effective leadership system in Congress could run a more efficient legislative body.

3. The committee structure of Congress also dulls its effectiveness in foreign affairs. There is no single committee in either house which can claim

sole jurisdiction over foreign policy matters. In spite of the significant role of the Senate Foreign Relations Committee, nine of the other thirteen standing committees of the Senate exercise some jurisdiction over foreign policy issues. It is this problem, among others, which led to one of the more odious requirements of the Hughes-Ryan Amendment to the 1974 Foreign Assistance Act. While there was widespread congressional agreement with the purpose of the Amendment (to limit the ability of the CIA to engage in covert operations abroad without informing Congress), the original language required the reporting of the most sensitive of all national security secrets to eight congressional committees theoretically involving up to 200 members of Congress plus additional staff. In 1980, this process was amended to require reporting only to the two intelligence committees of Congress or, in special cases, only to the leaders of the intelligence committees and to senior party leaders.

Multiple claims of jurisdiction often result in important legislation being subjected to so many committee hearings that it is "heard to death." The Anti-Terrorism Act of 1978, for example, was subjected to hearings before five separate committees of the Senate. This allowed opponents of the legislation to search for the most vulnerable committee in the process and focus all of their efforts to defeat the legislation at that spot.

4. The effectiveness of Congress is also limited by the multiple committee assignments which each member has. Senators currently sit on an average of 3.56 full committees and 7.89 subcommittees while members of the House of Representatives sit on an average of 2.15 full committees and 4.91 subcommittees. This situation results in unreasonable time demands on senators and representatives. This is especially true now that each committee or subcommittee has a full professional staff with nothing to do but to look out for the interests of that committee or subcommittee (which means that they have nothing to do but generate work that eventually requires the attention of their principals). Yet the senators and representatives must divide their time between all of their committee assignments as well as meet the many other time obligations they face.

Staff members are often frustrated as they schedule hearings for important executive branch officials only to find that no committee members are free to attend the hearing, even though it was scheduled at the request of the members. Other committee business, roll call votes, meetings with special interest groups or journalists, or local constituency matters can come up at any time and take committee members away from hearings.[44] These events compete not only for the time of the members but also for their interest and energy.

5. Congress also suffers from a lack of information about foreign policy. Congress has few independent sources of information and even those they have (the Congressional Reference Service, the Congressional Budget Office, etc.) often rely on executive branch sources of information. It is very frustrating for

members of Congress to consider legislation sponsored by the executive branch while relying almost solely on that same branch for information to evaluate that legislation. There is a natural and understandable tendency for executive agencies to be selective in the information transferred, to phrase the information in the most favorable manner, and to suppress information which would be unfavorable to the policies or legislation being proposed.

The same is true when congressional committees hold oversight hearings. It falls to Congress to see that the executive departments and agencies are administering the laws according to the intent of the authorizing legislation. These oversight hearings are vital to the legislative duties of Congress. Yet, here too there is a tendency for the executive agencies to reveal only the bare minimum of what is requested and to present all information in a manner which will protect existing practices and policies.

Shortly after the Soviet invasion of Afghanistan, the Senate Intelligence Committee was being briefed on developments in Afghanistan by senior officials and analysts from the intelligence community. After several minutes of very general statements, one senator interrupted the briefing and said in frustration that his wife had just returned from an extended trip to that country and seemed to know more about what was going on there than did the CIA. The lack of current and complete information about global developments is a serious impediment to the effective functioning of Congress in the field of foreign affairs. The creation of congressional committees equipped to receive and handle sensitive classified information has relieved this problem a bit.

The greatly increased size of congressional staffs, both personal and committee, has not solved this problem as effectively as advocates of increased staffing had hoped. The fact that each staff person, whether attached to the member's personal office or to a committee staff, reports to the member who appointed them inevitably creates a bottleneck. Thus, much of the increased level of staff work merely reinforces the independent and anarchical tendencies of Congress previously mentioned. The problem is exacerbated by competition for the member's time by his or her staff. Staff members literally fight for access to the senator or representative which further reduces the time available to them. In order to capture the time and attention of their bosses, there is a tendency for staff members to do ever more outlandish and immoderate things, a practice that does not promote moderation.

6. A further obstacle to Congress in the exercise of its foreign policy powers is that Congress lacks the institutional means to see that its policies are followed. It has no operational handles to pull when executive agencies ignore the wishes of Congress. One of its operational handles, the legislative veto, was declared unconstitutional by the Supreme Court.[45] The legislative veto (first used in 1932) allowed the president to submit a proposal which a legislative committee, either of the two houses, or both chambers could either approve or disapprove within a specified time limit. The Supreme Court said

in 1983 that the single house congressional veto strained the separation of powers doctrine.

And Congress's ultimate weapon—the power of the purse—has turned out to be both too broad and too blunt to be used for effective oversight. Congress may enact various pieces of legislation either mandating or prohibiting certain foreign policy actions, but shifting political winds, changing circumstances, and especially the absence of strings to pull cause Congress to lose interest in constantly monitoring foreign policy behavior which it can change only with great effort.

The role of President Reagan's National Security Council in the Iran-Contra-Israel arms arrangement illustrates this point. Even with over ten committees or individuals investigating this affair, it was difficult for Congress to find out the extent to which its laws had been circumvented or contravened. Moreover, within a short time after the last report had been published, most members of Congress had lost interest in the matter.

7. However, the major obstacle to more effective congressional participation in the foreign policy process is the attitude of the executive branch. The problem goes beyond information, organization, and interest. Every president expects Congress to rise above partisanship and support major foreign policy initiatives. And every president knows that congressional support for such initiatives is essential, if for no other reason than to finance them. After all, it is Congress that must face the wrath of the American people for raising taxes to pay for foreign policy and national security initiatives. Yet, Congress is seldom, if ever, involved in any meaningful way in the development of a rationale for U.S. foreign policy. In the absence of any meaningful collaboration with Congress on these matters, administration after administration finds itself isolated from its most important base of support.

> But the only way it [an administration] will ever gain any leeway for its tactics is by elaborating an overall strategy—not merely in consultation with Congress, but in partnership with it. If Congress does not know and approve of the general purpose of a treaty, and of its place in U.S. global diplomacy, how can it be expected to show tolerance for the inevitable verbal ambiguities and obscurities without which few deals can be had? If Congress is not brought in at the stage of definition, it will not allow the executive any latitude at the stage of execution.[46]

A prudent president will initiate substantive discussions with Congress well in advance of the need for congressional support; he or she will focus on substantive issues with Congress and will seek broad centrist policies around which congressional support can coalesce; such a president will be willing to share both information and credit with members of Congress and to involve

Congress in a meaningful way in discussions about both specific policies and about the fundamental politico-strategic foundations on which those policies must rest. "More, better, earlier consultation with the Senate will surely improve the treaty-making process."[47]

In a sense, constitutional arguments are less important in this regard than are pragmatic ones. The executive branch cannot afford to be smug about its foreign policy experience. Congressional foreign policy leaders have more experience dealing with regional and global questions than their executive branch counterparts. From 1972 to 1985, the staff directors of congressional foreign policy committees and subcommittees had an average of forty months experience compared with twenty-three months experience for their counterparts in the State Department. Even at the principal level, the congressional advantage holds. Secretaries of state, defense, and treasury averaged twenty-nine months experience between 1972 and 1985 while the chairmen of the foreign policy committees of Congress averaged sixty-eight months.[48]

In spite of these formidable obstacles, Congress has several things in its favor. As mentioned above, in many cases Congress has expertise, knowledge, and experience—ingredients often in short supply when new administrations come into power. Congress also is the most representative branch of the government. Its members must face constant reelection battles which force them, particularly members of the House, to listen to public opinion more closely than often is realized. There is one significant advantage in strengthening the congressional role in foreign policy—it increases the influence of public opinion in the foreign policy process. "History suggests that the most effective and durable foreign policy is generally that which has the broadest public support."[49] Democratic theory is relevant to more than domestic politics.[50]

Contrary to popular myth, Congress also does a better job than the executive branch in keeping secrets. A deputy director of the Central Intelligence Agency reported that out of 500 attributed "leaks" or unauthorized disclosures of classified material between 1975 and 1987, only 25 could be attributed to Congress and the remaining 475 were from various executive branch agencies.[51]

TOWARDS THE TWENTY-FIRST CENTURY

While the provisions of the Constitution seem to point to Congress as the primary source of foreign policy and national security direction and policies, extra-constitutional powers of the president, general historical developments, and the structure and operations of Congress have supported a steady expansion of presidential powers. There has been a struggle for primacy in the foreign policy process, not a struggle invited by the Constitution, but a struggle made inevitable by changing historical forces, by institutional realities, and by the continuing adaptation of American political institutions to new domestic and global circumstances.

The twenty-first century will see an increasing interdependence of nations marked by a growing intertwining of foreign and domestic affairs. America may well continue to be the major actor, if not hegemonic, actor, in this world. It must continue to play a lead role, but it cannot do that alone. That is what we mean by increasing vincibility. Much greater reliance must be placed on diplomacy, as, in fact, was done during the Gulf War. If chess has been the accepted metaphor of international politics, for the twenty-first century the metaphor will be multilevel chess. That means, among other things, that the foreign policy process must be more unified, consistent, and coordinated.

Given existing powers and prerogatives, what is needed to accomplish this? Constitutionally, probably nothing is needed nor is it likely that any significant constitutional reforms could be achieved. Through legislative action and executive orders, much could be accomplished. Many years ago, one scholar argued that legal structures which would promote interbranch dialogue were essential to sound foreign policy and, more recently, another scholar has reminded us that legal changes in the foreign policy process should not attempt to "establish congressional control over the president, but rather to institutionalize the dialectic between presidential policy purpose and democratic process."[52]

Perhaps more than anything else, the American people need to understand two things about the foreign policy process as it has developed over the last 200 years.

First, it may not be as bad as people, even the authors of this book, make it out to be. Mark Twain's comment about Wagner's music might be apt: "It is not as bad as it sounds." Clearly the constitutional foreign policy process has some weaknesses, but it has permitted the United States to play a significant and, with a few glaring exceptions, constructive role in world politics. As the commission appointed to investigate the Iran-Contra Arms scandal (the Tower Commission) pointed out, our problems usually stem from individuals, not from institutions.

The genius of the American Constitution may well be that its broad foundation of fundamental principles (its proscription of power) and its firm yet flexible commitment to fairness and equity (its prescription of procedures) have permitted the global pursuit of prudential power restrained by the ever present possibility of change and correction that has, at times, bordered on self-abuse. Those who view a constitution as a static parking lot on which principles are parked never to be moved miss the point. A constitution must be seen as a dynamic system of streets and roads which permits movement and change, even the occasional dead end or one way street. The American Constitution has performed that function quite well.

Second, the American people need to understand that the goal of the framers of the Constitution was not efficiency; it was to protect individual rights against the encroachment of central government.[53] Sir Denis Brogan, a British scholar, may have had this in mind when he said that "an authoritarian government is like a great ship moving smoothly through the ocean until it strikes an iceberg and sinks abruptly. A democracy, on the other hand, is like a raft, the damned thing won't sink but your feet are always wet." That is not an easy concept to understand when, in the wake of every crisis (Vietnam, Watergate, Iran-Contra, etc.) few politicians can resist calling for legal, constitutional, or institutional reforms all of which are promised to make the foreign policy process more efficient.

Calls for bipartisan cooperation in the field of foreign policy are easily and frequently made. Such appeals are usually appropriate. Clearly, a broadly based bipartisan approach to U.S. foreign policy is needed. Unfortunately, bipartisanship cannot be invoked by rhetoric. It must grow from presidential prudence and congressional constraint. A president, willing to share credit and seeking moderate, centrist policies, coupled with a Congress sticking to general principles, would do more to enhance bipartisanship than anything else.

Strident calls for bipartisanship are usually nothing but thinly disguised calls for capitulation—a plea by those on one side of an issue asking others to abandon their policies. And the end result of successful bipartisanship may not always be beneficial. The end result of greater collaboration between Congress and the president "may not be better policies, but simply greater legitimacy for bad ones."[54]

Are there any procedural changes, short of constitutional amendments, which would help? On the congressional side much needs to be done to take the anarchic edges off Congress. Most of these changes could be brought about by strong bipartisan leadership in both houses. But that is not easy to obtain. Any proposed congressional reform is evaluated immediately according to who it helps and who it hurts in terms of current power struggles and not according to the goal of long range improvement in the congressional process. For example, the early 1970s reforms in the House of Representatives were supported by many because it seemed a good thing at the time to prevent the chair of a full committee from also chairing several subcommittees. The reforms were touted as a way to open up clogged congressional leadership to new blood with new ideas. In fact, they were a means of bringing congressmen opposed to the Vietnamese war into positions of leadership. Now, nearly twenty years later and long after Vietnam, it is evident that these reforms also weakened the effectiveness of the House leadership, thus contributing to congressional anarchy.

It would certainly help to eliminate overlapping jurisdiction of congressional committees. A committee charged with foreign affairs, for example, ought to have a fairly tight monopoly on legislation, oversight, and authorizations in that field. Again, strong leadership could bring that about but there may be little incentive to do so since, to some degree, jurisdictional ambiguity gives congressional leadership increased maneuverability.

Along with restructuring congressional committees and increasing the authority of its leadership, Congress needs to consider ways to approve multiyear budgets and to avoid rollercoaster financing of defense and national security areas.

Unitary staffs (staff members who work under the direction of the committee chief of staff rather than at the whim of committee members) would also improve consistency and strengthen the forces of moderation. They would lessen the divisive impact of extreme partisanship at the staff level which contributes significantly to partisanship among the principals. One of the most experienced congressmen in Washington, Congressman Morris Udall (D-AZ), once said that he spent most of his time getting out of fights into which his staff had placed him. But few members of Congress want to lose control over their staff appointees, even those that work on committee staffs.

Many people have suggested the creation of a "Foreign Affairs Supercommittee"—a single committee made up of representatives of all of the committees which have some jurisdiction in foreign policy matters which would have higher and more final authority on foreign policy matters. The track record of such supercommittees, however, is not very good. When the budget process was "streamlined" by the creation of an overall Budget Committee, rather than realizing the desired efficiency, it merely added another layer to the already too high layer cake of committees involved in the budget process. More exclusive jurisdiction would accomplish the desired goal more effectively.

A joint committee has also been suggested. A joint committee is one made up of members of both the House and the Senate. The Joint Economic Committee has often been cited as a model for this kind of reform. However, the Joint Economic Committee has no legislative or budgetary authority. It does only one thing—it publishes interesting documents on economic matters. It is certainly not a model for working foreign policy committees. In the late 1940s there was also a Joint Atomic Energy Committee. That is a more apt model, but its success rested primarily on the unique and secretive nature of atomic energy matters at that time. When that condition changed, the committee became less effective and was eventually disbanded.

Congress also must draw a more circumspect line around the extent of its authority. It is a deliberative body and must limit its role to providing general principles which guide U.S. foreign policy but not try to administer that policy. Related to this, Congress needs to develop ways to vent its anger short of criminal litigation which ought to be reserved only for the most serious cases of actual criminal wrongdoing, not merely for the pursuit of unwise policies. There is a vicious cycle which seems to operate in presidential-congressional relations. If Congress often seems to drive the president to bypass congressional collaboration, presidential circumvention forces Congress toward more extensive legislated restrictions. If this cycle is not broken, both the integrity and effectiveness of U.S. foreign policy will suffer.

But it is not only Congress that must change. Presidents bear considerable responsibility for the foreign policy mess.

> If Presidential conduct of foreign policy up to 1964 can be described as "imperial," it is not stretching reality too far to see it thereafter as irresponsible. Before the breakdown, Presidents derived much of their power and authority over national-security matters from the belief that they stood above politics, that they would sacrifice short-term political gains for long-term goals, and that they somehow embodied the enduring national interest. Too many times since 1964 they have used foreign policy to enhance their personal positions, thus personalizing, politicizing and sometimes even trivializing the content and conduct of foreign affairs.[55]

Presidential pleas for more substantive congressional collaboration are always timely but not often effective, at least for long periods of time. Nor are calls to turn back the clock to recreate the congressional-executive relations that existed in the 1950s and early 1960s very realistic.[56] Without moving all the way towards a cabinet government of the British type (which would require a constitutional amendment), perhaps a useful small nod in that direction would be a modified Question Time borrowed from British practice.[57]

In Britain, cabinet ministers (who themselves are members of Parliament) must meet with Parliament on a weekly basis to be questioned about their ministerial duties. In the United States, cabinet members are frequently called to testify before committees of Congress, but such calls are sporadic and usually focused on some current crisis. Perhaps periodic and formalized appearances before single or combined committees might force more regular and routine cooperation. Former Secretary of State Vance has made such a suggestion.[58] Another former secretary of state, George Shultz, estimated that he spent 25 percent of his time dealing with Congress anyway, so perhaps a routinized question time would be welcomed by both Congress and the executive branch.

Presidents must understand that they need to pay as much attention to lobbying for foreign policy goals as they do for domestic goals. The forging and reforging of coalitions, the trade-offs, and the bargaining are as applicable to the making of foreign policy as they are to the making of domestic policy. In fact, most recent presidents have acted in this way, but this activity seems never as clearly understood, perhaps because of the constant, and inaccurate, refrain that politics stops at the water's edge. There *should* be some solidarity in our foreign policy orientation, but given the shattering of the national security consensus during the Vietnam period, this solidarity will emerge and be sustained only within a vigorous political process. Moreover, executive branch practices of misleading, deceiving, or overlooking Congress will not only damage Executive initiatives, but also will delay indefinitely the reestablishment of "plain and general truths" (to use Madison's phrase) about the Republic's role in world affairs.

Any serious reforms will work only if Congress and the president hold each other hostage on all such proposals. That is, helpful reforms in one branch must be tied to concomitant reforms in the other. Each side might be thus willing to "give up" something as long as it thought it was getting concessions from the other side. The nature of those mutual reforms ought to involve, as Warren Christopher has said, at a minimum, a "compact" (mutual commitments to reform) which (1) reaffirms the president's basic authority to articulate foreign policy, (2) requires full cooperation and consultation between the president and Congress, (3) holds the president to broad basic policy guidelines imposed by Congress, (4) renews a bipartisan spirit, (5) increases resources to support foreign policy, and (6) acknowledges that the United States will never be as efficient in making and executing foreign policy as authoritarian regimes.[59]

Any consideration of ways to improve relations between Congress and the White House in the field of foreign policy must examine the role of the NSC. There is an inverse relationship between the influence of the NSC and healthy congressional participation in foreign policy. A too powerful NSC detracts from the role of the State Department and the secretary of state, a development which invariably lessens the information Congress receives and its sense of importance. "To the extent the secretary of state feels excluded from foreign affairs decision, Congress feels excluded; and that is ultimately unhealthy for the president."[60]

Successful reform also requires widespread commitment to moderation and integrity. A consensus adequate for the twenty-first century cannot be built on zealotism and acrimonious censure. After virtually any foreign policy embarrassment, the president and Congress blame each other. Former Secretary of State Kissinger, for example, whose contempt for Congress was worn on his sleeve, blamed congressional reaction to Watergate for President Nixon's inability to live up to agreements made with South Vietnam during the peace talks. But a Southeast Asian policy that had been built on a solid consensual base of congressional support surely could have survived even Watergate. On the other hand, even sound foreign policies become weak when they are not built on that consensus.

Enhancing presidential-congressional cooperation is difficult in the absence of a consensus between our political leaders on the meaning and role of American power in the world. The consequence of such a divergence will be either persistent attempts by Congress or the White House to pursue unilateral policies or the inability to pursue any consistent line of policy—that is, government by cabal or government in deadlock, or both. One scholar, after reviewing the successes and failures of U.S. foreign policy from 1941 to 1991, concluded that "successes . . . tend to come in those areas in which there is a consensus . . . [while f]ailures tend to come in those areas where there is not a consensus."[61]

The foreign policy process, as established in the Constitution and as developed over the years, has served America fairly well over its past two centuries. The new century will require an America willing to invest in international affairs, an America whose leadership is not based solely on military might or on the relative weakness and disunity of other states, and an America whose foreign policy consensus is not based on the existence of a real or imagined foe.

ENDNOTES

1. William G. Andrews, ed., *Constitutions and Constitutionalism* (Princeton, New Jersey: D. Van Nostrand, 1961), 16.
2. The question has been asked frequently, however this version of it comes from Robert A. Goldwin and Robert A. Licht, eds., *Foreign Policy and the Constitution* (Washington, D.C.: The AEI Press, 1990), ix.
3. Louis Henkin, "Foreign Affairs and the Constitution," *Foreign Affairs* 66 (Winter 1987/88): 288.
4. See, for example, the letter from Michael H. Shuman in *Foreign Policy,* No. 88 (Fall 1992): 190.
5. See Jack N. Rakove, "Making Foreign Policy—The View from 1787," in *Foreign Policy and the Constitution,* eds. Goldwin and Licht (Washington, D.C.: The AEI Press, 1990) for a discussion of some of these issues.
6. Harold Hongju Koh, in his *The National Security Constitution: Sharing Power after the Iran-Contra Affair* (New Haven, Connecticut: Yale University Press, 1990), Chapter 6, makes a compelling argument that the Supreme Court has been *too* tolerant of executive initiatives.
7. An excellent discussion of this principle can be found in Inis L. Claude, Jr., *The Changing UN* (New York: Random House, 1967).
8. The phrase, "an invitation to struggle" is frequently used in describing the constitutional division of foreign policy powers. It is the title of a well-known book—Cecil V. Crabb, *An Invitation to Struggle: Congress, the President, and Foreign Policy,* 2d ed. (Washington D.C.: Congressional Quarterly Inc., 1984)—and an oft quoted description of the bifurcated basis for foreign policy making. The phrase itself was first used by Edwin S. Corwin in his *The President: Office and Powers* (New York: New York University Press, 1957), 171. The same theme is frequently used by political cartoonists who love to describe foreign policy-making as the only car with two steering wheels, etc. The idea that the Constitution is "an invitation to struggle" ignores the fundamental fact stated clearly by Dick Cheney just before he became Secretary of Defense in the Bush administration. "The Constitution does not really distribute powers at random; it is not simply 'an invitation to struggle.'" "Congressional Overreaching," in *Foreign Policy and the Constitution,* eds. Goldwin and Licht, 102.
9. See, for example, the review by Margaret Jane Wyszomirski in *Presidential Studies Quarterly* 18 (Winter 1988): 178 of Cecil V. Crabb and Kevin V. Mulcahy, *Presidents*

and Foreign Policy Making; From FDR to Reagan (Baton Rouge, Louisiana: Louisiana State University Press, 1986).

10. Henkin, "Foreign Affairs and the Constitution," 286.
11. These powers are phrased in more contemporary language than that found in the Constitution; however, the meaning is not changed in any significant way.
12. All of these powers are enumerated in Section 8 of Article I.
13. Federalist 69: "The President will have only the occasional command of such part of the militia of the nation as by legislative provision may be called into the actual service of the Union. The King of Great Britain and the governor of New York have at all times the entire command of all the militia within their several jurisdictions. In this article, therefore, the power of the President would be inferior to that of either the monarch or the governor." This quote is on p. 430 of *The Federalist,* edited by Henry Cabot Lodge and published in 1888 by G.P. Putnam's Sons of Boston.
14. An excellent, brief discussion of the Resolution is contained in Pat M. Holt, *The War Powers Resolution: The Role of Congress in U.S. Armed Intervention* (Washington, D.C.: American Enterprise Institute for Public Policy Research, 1978).
15. Jean E. Smith, *The Constitution and American Foreign Policy,* (St. Paul, Minn: West Publishing Company, 1989), 228. Smith also gives a brief summary of significant Supreme Court cases pertaining to war powers on pages 227-30.
16. It is widely, but erroneously, believed that the Senate ratifies treaties. Under common practices of international diplomacy, however, only the treaty-making authority has the power to ratify a treaty. The best explanation of this is in Herbert W. Briggs, ed., *The Laws of Nations,* 2d ed. (New York: Appleton-Century-Crofts, 1952), 853 ff. Under the U.S. constitutional system, the making of treaties requires three separate steps: first, the treaty is negotiated; second the consent of the Senate is sought; and third, the treaty is ratified by the president. This is an easily misunderstood point since it is an act of the Senate which allows or prevents a treaty from being ratified.
17. In *United States* v. *Belmont* (1937) the Supreme Court ruled that when President Roosevelt recognized the Soviet government and entered into various agreements with that government, he was acting "as the sole organ" of international relations for the government of the United States and that his agreements had the same effect on state laws as did treaties. Some argue that Art. II, Sec. 1 gives this authority to the president when it states that "The executive Power shall be vested in a President of the United States of America." Others believe that this phrase should be seen as flowing from the later phrase which states that the president "shall take care that the Laws be faithfully executed. . . ." (art. II, sec. 2).
18. See Thomas G. Ingersoll and Robert E. O'Connor, *Politics and Structure* (Monterey, California: Brooks/Cole Publishing Co., 1986) and Loch K. Johnson, *The Making of International Agreements: Congress Confronts the Executive* (New York: New York University Press, 1984) for discussions of these distinctions.
19. A good discussion of the use of executive agreements in American history is found in Wallace McClure, *International Executive Agreements: Democratic Procedure under the Constitution of the United States* (New York: AMS Press, 1967).
20. President Eisenhower commented privately that appointing a Bricker Commission to look into the problem would satisfy Senator Bricker's need for publicity, which was all the senator really wanted from the amendment. This assessment of Senator Bricker was probably partially true, but does not explain the widespread support the proposal had in Congress.
21. Congress, Senate, Committee on Foreign Relations, *Hearings before the Subcommittee on U.S. Security Agreements and Commitments Abroad,* 91st Cong., 1971.
22. A number of factors caused Senate support of SALT II to diminish. Of great significance was the ongoing presidential primary race in which, partially in response to Senator Frank

Church's "discovery" of a Soviet combat battalion in Cuba, there was a recurring resurgence of anti-Soviet rhetoric. The Soviet invasion of Afghanistan gave President Carter his justification to withdraw SALT II from the Senate. However, even without Soviet adventurism, it is doubtful that the Carter administration had sufficient votes to secure passage of the treaty. See *The New York Times,* 15 March and 9 June 1980. The impact of domestic political considerations is demonstrated quite clearly in the subsequent Senate Foreign Relations Committee appeal to President Ronald Reagan that the U.S. continue to comply with the terms of SALT II. (See *The New York Times,* 10 June 1982.)

23. The actual words of Washington are second- or third-hand and originated in the writings of John Quincy Adams. The story is told, in part, in Edwin S. Corwin, *The President: Office and Powers* (New York: New York University Press, 1957), 209-10, and 442. Corwin gives the genealogy of the story. The most accurate recounting of the event is, Douglas S. Freeman, *George Washington: A Biography,* Vol. 6 (New York: Scribners, 1954), 223-25.

24. President Nixon's personal lawyer, Herbert Kalmback, admitted to the House Judiciary Committee's impeachment hearings that he had the responsibility of, in effect, selling ambassadorial posts to the highest bidders, a crime for which he later went to prison. See Walter Pincus, "The Case of Peter Flanigan," *The New Republic,* 19 October 1974, 12.

25. Throughout this book, we use the term national security affairs adviser even though the actual title has changed under various presidents from Executive Assistant, to Special Assistant for National Security Affairs, to Assistant for National Security Affairs. When in lower case, we always refer to the role, regardless of the changing official title.

26. It is ironic that those who choose to ignore the Constitution when they are expanding their own powers derived from it are the first to invoke the Constitution to condemn the increase of power by others.

27. See, for example, William D. Rogers, "Who's In Charge of Foreign Policy?" *The New York Times Magazine,* 9 September 1979.

28. Henkin, "Foreign Affairs and the Constitution," 286.

29. It is difficult to generalize in this short space the complicated views of the framers of the Constitution. There were widely varying opinions about the relative power of the president and Congress and opinions often changed when the authority to deal with other nations was the point in question. It is safe, however, to say that people such as Morris and Hamilton pushed for a strong executive, while those such as Madison and Jefferson (who was not a member of the convention) favored a stronger legislature. Hamilton, however, "did not claim any authority for the president to exclude Congress, or to act contrary to direction by Congress," according to Louis Henkin in "Foreign Affairs and the Constitution," 295.

30. This point is made well in Koh, *The National Security Constitution,* Chapter 2.

31. Corwin, *The President: Office and Powers,* 19.

32. Stephen E. Ambrose, "The Presidency and Foreign Policy," *Foreign Affairs* 70 (Winter 1991/92): 137.

33. Lincoln went on to say: "The provision of the Constitution giving the war making power to Congress, was dictated, as I understand it, by the following reasons: kings had always been involving and impoverishing their people in wars, pretending generally, if not always, that the good of the people was the object. This our Constitution undertook to be the most oppressive of all kingly oppression and they resolved to so frame the Constitution that no one man would hold the power of bringing that oppression upon us. But your [Polk's] view destroys the whole matter and places our President where kings have always stood." Roy P. Basher, ed., *The Collected Works of Abraham Lincoln,* vol. 1 (New Brunswick, N.J.: Rutgers University Press, 1958), 451.

34. It is difficult to find a more dramatic demonstration of this principle than the appearance at the British sponsored Zimbabwe-Rhodesia talks in 1979 of two personal staff members from the office of Senator Jesse Helms (R-NC). At a very delicate stage of the British attempt to bring about a peaceful solution to the long standing problem in Rhodesia, Helms' aides appeared to "stiffen the spine" of former Rhodesian Prime Minister, Ian Smith. Helms said, in response to the flap created by the episode, "I don't trust the State Department on this issue." Don Oberdorfer, "British Say Helms Aids Hurt Talks," *Washington Post,* 20 September 1979, 1.

35. Daniel Yankelovich, "Farewell to 'President Knows Best,'" *Foreign Affairs* 57 (1978): 670-93.

36. Henkin, "Foreign Affairs and the Constitution," 286.

37. One study in 1946 credited Congress with the initiative in 40 percent of the 90 laws studied, the President with initiative in 20 percent, shared initiative in 30 percent, and interest group initiative in 10 percent. See Lawrence H. Chamberlain, *The President, Congress and Legislation* (New York: Columbia University Press, 1946). A 1970 study obtained basically the same results. See Ronald C. Moe and Steven C. Teel, "Congress as Policy-Maker: A Necessary Reappraisal," *Political Science Quarterly* 85 (1970): 443-70. Both studies are cited in Randall B. Ripley, *Congress: Process and Policy* (New York: Norton, 1975), 259. People who have worked on Capitol Hill suspect that the influence of the executive branch is greater but more difficult to isolate in the process.

38. We are indebted to an anonymous reviewer for this point.

39. Ronald H. Hinckley, *People, Polls, and Policymakers: American Public Opinion and National Security* (New York: Lexington Books, 1992), 140.

40. There is an oft-repeated story, perhaps apocryphal but very plausible, that when a newly elected young congressman sought President Eisenhower's advice as to whether he should seek a position on the Foreign Affairs Committee or the Ways and Means, Ike directed him to Ways and Means saying that on tax matters Ways and Means was king, but that on Foreign Affairs the President was king.

41. Quoted in Gregg Easterbrook, "What's Wrong With Congress," *Atlantic Monthly* (December 1984): 57.

42. Easterbrook, "What's Wrong with Congress?" 61.

43. I. M. Destler, "Congress as Boss?" *Foreign Policy,* No. 42 (Spring 1981).

44. There are approximately 4,000 accredited journalists in Washington, D.C., over seven for each member of Congress. There are also approximately 20,000 registered and unregistered lobbyists who can make demands on the time of members of Congress and each member receives an average of 1,200 pieces of mail each day. (See Easterbrook, "What's Wrong With Congress.")

45. If Congress authorizes a general category of executive branch activity but inserts within that authorization a provision which gives Congress a period of time in which it can prevent a specific case of that activity, that is called a legislative veto. In 1976, for example, Congress lowered the threshold amount for military equipment sales down to $7 million . The executive branch was free to enter into arms sales at any level, but any sale over $7 million could be stopped by Congress within thirty days of the announcement of the sale. The case which threatened the legislative veto was *Immigration and Naturalization Service v. Chada,* 462 U.S. (1983). The best discussion of this case appears in I. M. Destler "Life After the Veto," *Foreign Policy,* No. 52 (Spring 1983): 181.

46. Stanley Hoffmann, "The Hell of Good Intentions," *Foreign Policy,* No. 29 (Winter 1977-78): 22.

47. Henkin, "Foreign Affairs and the Constitution," 305.

48. These data were calculated by measuring tenure in office from a variety of annual personnel and organization manuals.

49. "President, Congress, and Public: A Shared Foreign Policy Role," *The Christian Science Monitor,* 4 March 1987, 15.

50. Benjamin L. Page makes this argument quite effectively in his "Representation as well as Competence; Congress and President in U.S. Foreign Policy," a paper presented at the Constitutional Bicentennial Conference, Nelson A. Rockefeller Center, Dartmouth College, 17 February 1987. Stephen E. Ambrose also argues that, over the last fifty years, "the policies that have failed have tended to be those adopted by presidents without meaningful debate. . . . The policies that have succeeded have been adopted by Congress and the people after meaningful debate. . . ." in "The President and Foreign Policy," 136.

51. Robert M. Gates, "Unauthorized Disclosures: Risks, Costs, and Responsibilities," *American Intelligence Journal* (Special Issue 1988): 6, 7.

52. The first scholar is Hans Morgenthau and the second is I. M. Destler. Both are cited in Koh, *The National Security Constitution,* 230.

53. As Justice Brandeis stated in *Myers* v. *United States,* 272 U.S. 52 (1926), the system of checks and balances was created "not to promote efficiency but to preclude the exercise of arbitrary power."

54. I. M. Destler and Eric R. Alterman, "Congress and Reagan's Foreign Policy," *The Washington Quarterly* (Winter 1984): 99.

55. I. M. Destler, Leslie Gelb, and Anthony Lake, *Our Own Worst Enemy: The Unmaking of American Foreign Policy* (New York: Simon & Schuster, 1984), 21.

56. Senator John G. Tower made just such a call in his "Congress Versus the President: The Formulation and Implementation of American Foreign Policy," *Foreign Affairs* 60 (Winter 1981-82).

57. Former presidential counselor Lloyd Cutler has proposed a major nod in that direction, one that would require a constitutional amendment in his "To Form a Government," *Foreign Affairs* 59 (Fall 1980): 126-43.

58. Vance participated in a panel discussion with three other former secretaries of state. His remarks are summarized in William O. Chittick, "The Secretarys on Continuity and Bipartisanship in American Foreign Policy," *International Studies Notes* 11 (Fall 1984): 6.

59. This list is adapted from Warren Christopher, "Ceasefire Between the Branches: A Compact in Foreign Affairs," *Foreign Affairs* 60 (Summer 1982): 989-1005.

60. Theodore C. Sorenson, "The President and Secretary of State," *Foreign Affairs* 66 (Winter 1987/88): 239.

61. Ambrose, "The Presidency and Foreign Policy," 123. Ambrose argues that consensus creates consistency and that "consistency in foreign policy is difficult to achieve but immensely powerful when it happens" (136). For a set of well-formulated but somewhat more legalistic suggested reforms in the foreign policy process, see Koh, *The National Security Constitution,* Chapter 7.

3

THE WHITE HOUSE OFFICE AND THE NATIONAL SECURITY COUNCIL IN THE FOREIGN POLICY PROCESS

In this chapter we talk briefly about the foreign policy-making process and then turn our attention to those institutions attached to the White House Office from which presidents receive assistance as they execute the nation's foreign policy. We pay particular attention to what has become a very significant locus of foreign policy power, the National Security Council (NSC). We will talk about both the origins as well as the strengths and weaknesses of the National Security Council system and make suggestions on how to improve this system in order to deal with increasing American vincibility as well as to prepare the nation for the twenty-first century.

TWO VIEWS OF THE FOREIGN POLICY PROCESS

There is a fairly widespread, yet considerably overly simplified view of the foreign policy process, the perception of which misrepresents and distorts the actual process. This model suggests that somewhere out of the American political cauldron, certain general ideas and ideals about the role of America in a world of other sovereign states will emerge. These ideas and ideals then shape hundreds of electoral outcomes which ultimately result in the election of national political leaders, particularly members of the House and Senate, who will articulate these ideas and ideals and refine them into a general legislative agenda for the United States in world affairs. There are, obviously, opposing voices throughout this process, but it does lead to the closest thing that we have to a consensual national foreign policy agenda in America.

According to this view, this agenda, still somewhat general and vague, will be focused into logical and coherent priorities by the president with the assistance of the foreign policy bureaucracy. The Department of State will both provide general information about the nature of the international environment as well as carry out the president's policies, and the intelligence agencies will give to the president "denied information" which will guide him or her in this process.

The president, with advice and counsel from the NSC, will then add greater specificity to these policy preferences and, in concert with the Department of State (and with the assistance of other executive agencies which have foreign policy responsibilities), detailed foreign policy positions for the United States will be identified, formulated, and carried out. The NSC staff will coordinate the execution of these policies throughout all of the foreign policy agencies and departments.

The State Department is the primary agency for carrying out these policies, according to this view, and the Department of Defense stands ready to use armed force, if necessary, for the protection of vital U.S. interests. If, on rare occasions, the vital interests of the United States require something more than diplomatic action and less than military action, the covert action capabilities of the Central Intelligence Agency (CIA) may be utilized.

This view then suggests that as all of these actions unfold, the American people are kept informed and the process kept honest by the careful and objective reporting of the news media. As this process unfolds and as foreign policy information returns to the American people, changes and shifts in foreign policy goals are kindled and the process is either corrected or confirmed. In recent years a version of this view has developed which argues that the system is gridlocked, primarily because of the inability of the president and Capitol Hill to work cooperatively.[1]

A MORE COMPLEX REALITY

This overly simplified view is obviously both wrongfully simple and simply wrong. It has never existed in the past and probably will never exist in the future. The input side of the model is capriciously complex consisting of innumerable and interchanging groups of citizens who neither understand the interlocking intricacies of contemporary world politics nor the long-run effects of their own preferences or actions. The decision matrix itself is both complex and chaotic with scores of government agencies vying for influence in a

labyrinthian political process which few understand fully—a process characterized at times by issues unable to find a decision center in which to be settled
and, at other times, by the same issues being settled in different ways in a
variety of competing decision centers. And the output side of the foreign policy
process is also in disarray as individuals and agencies compete for supremacy
and "lead agency" status in a bureaucratic sea where, at times, it is difficult to
tell just who is carrying out a particular policy and who is trying to subvert it
since both efforts are always done "in the name of the president."

Reality can be most easily summarized by resorting to a widely used, but
apt, metaphor. For the United States, the drama of international affairs is
played on two adjoining stages—one domestic (where goals and policies are
established) and the other global (where those policies are carried out). At one
time these two stages were more clearly delineated, but as we move towards
the twenty-first century they overlap and their borders are blurred.

On the domestic side of the stage, individuals and institutions vie for the
opportunity to influence the role played by the American nation on the global
stage. This competition for influence is played by actors (local, state, and national
government officials, myriads of interest groups represented by lobbyists, representatives of other nations and of multinational organizations, and private citizens)
who disagree both on the script and on the purpose of the drama being performed.
They disagree on the very importance of the drama and they even have disparate
visions of the most desirable outcome. Moreover, these actors engage in frequent
and debilitating arguments about star versus supporting roles and billings as well
as about the script to be followed on the global side of the stage. They play to
different audiences, are promoted by different and competing agents, and all view
the nominal director of the play—the president of the United States—with varying
degrees of suspicion or trust.

Fortunately, there is one basic consensus on the domestic side of the
stage—a broad agreement on the rules governing the competition (this is the
constitutional consensus discussed in the previous chapter). To switch metaphors and use Stanley Hoffmann's useful distinction, this "fight" to shape U.S.
foreign policy resembles a prize fight under agreed rules whereas the competition on the global stage is much more like a street fight in a dark alley.[2] It is
easy to see why, without anyone wanting it to be so, this domestic drama can
easily turn into comedy or even farce.

On the global side of the stage, actors representing other nations, as well as
a growing number of players representing both multinational and nonnational
organizations, compete to shape the outcomes of world politics.[3] On this stage
there is an even greater number of actors representing an even greater variety of
political cultures; but here there is no director, virtually no consensual script of
any kind, and, often, violently opposite desired outcomes. This stage was once
characterized by single actors each representing his nation's interests. Today, with
the line between the two stages blurred, actors from several domestic stages spill

over onto the global stage and each nation's domestic stage is full of bit players wandering about in an attempt to influence the foreign policy process. Other actors in the drama are often unsure just who is representing other nations or groups on this stage and subplots and peripheral intrigue are rampant. And, as stated earlier, this competition is played virtually without rules. Even more confusion is created by the presence of an increasingly large number of nonstate actors whose roles are often more important than those of some traditional state actors. It is easy to see why this side of the drama can easily turn into tragedy.

In this and the following chapter, we will deal primarily with the domestic side of the drama by looking at the institutions which compete for foreign policy influence on the domestic stage and describe the ways they engage in this competition.

THE WHITE HOUSE

Any review of the institutions which both shape and carry out U.S. foreign policy must begin with those agencies and offices which, one way or another, operate as part of the Office of the White House—the apex of executive branch power in the United States. In practice, the president is perceived as the most significant actor in the foreign policy process. He enjoys both constitutional privileges as well as the extraconstitutional advantages discussed in the previous chapter.

We also pointed out in the previous chapter that some scholars argue that the Constitution meant this to be the case, some argue that this situation has developed in spite of the constitutional primacy of Congress, while yet others argue that the Constitution was not specific enough to prevent an historically inevitable and irrevocable drift towards individual predominance. But whatever the cause, few doubt there is a widely held perception of presidential supremacy, either occasionally tempered by congressional actions or occasionally thwarted by congressional tampering, depending on one's point of view.

Surrounding the president are scores of individuals and institutions who assist in the foreign policy process. As is the case with all chief executives, the president of the United States must rely on individuals both for ideas and information as well as for the execution of his instructions.

UNOFFICIAL ADVISERS

There is an inner network of personal friends and colleagues who can both shape and conduct foreign policy. These are the personal friends of a president who in some cases may hold no government positions and in other cases may hold government, but nonforeign policy, positions. This inner circle has occasionally been called the "kitchen cabinet" to indicate its unofficial, but influential, status. The very unofficial nature of this network clouds a full understanding of its functioning.[4] Wives, relatives, personal friends, and political party associates are among those on whom presidents historically have relied but who have not held official foreign policy positions. Some may hold government, but nonforeign policy, positions yet may provide essential foreign policy advice and service to a chief executive.[5] In some cases these individuals have done trivial tasks and on other occasions they have made major contributions or blunders, again depending on one's perspective.[6]

Neither the presence nor the absence of formal or legal arrangements can prevent a president from discussing foreign policy with these people nor prevent them from being used to carry out foreign policy tasks at the behest of the president. This is an important point which warrants repeating—presidents want to be able to seek advice and assistance from whomever they wish and in manners most suitable to their needs. They do not want either bureaucratic or legislative restraints to prevent this.

During the second term of President Reagan the complex interweaving of this kitchen cabinet was revealed dramatically in the Iran-Contra affair where a coterie made up of White House officials, current and former CIA personnel, private citizens (some retired government officials), official representatives from other nations, and international arms dealers made and carried out U.S. foreign policy in the absence of congressional or State Department awareness and perhaps even without the participation of the president.[7]

OFFICIAL INSTITUTIONS

Although more is understood about the role of official foreign policy institutions and agencies, even here the size and complexity is amazing. A 1975 report from the Commission on the Organization of the Government for the Conduct of Foreign Policy listed five primary foreign affairs agencies (State Department, Agency for International Development, United States Information Agency, Arms Control and Disarmament Agency, and Peace Corps) and twenty-one departments or agencies with significant international activities ranging from the Agriculture Department to the Smithsonian Institution.[8] This report claimed there were over 26,000 American nationals employed by the government in international activities. Even that very comprehensive report failed to consider a large array of intelligence agencies, congressional personnel who work with foreign policy matters, military officers whose responsibilities go beyond defense, and others. Of the executive branch foreign policy institutions, however, the National Security Council has emerged as the most significant.

The National Security Council (NSC)

Created by the National Security Act of 1947, the NSC was to be a cabinet level council which would coordinate military and foreign policy at the highest level of government. In fact, the Act initiated a process that through subsequent legislation and executive practices has resulted, at times, in a NSC staff which has devised and carried out foreign policy, both overt and covert, and which has weakened the authority of other cabinet officers with foreign policy responsibilities, particularly the secretary of state. Moreover, this process has also strengthened the office of the secretary of defense (OSD), the combatant commanders (i.e., unified and specified commanders-in-chief—CINCs), and the chairman of the Joint Chiefs of Staff (JCS) while weakening the roles of the service secretaries.

There is much confusion in discussing the NSC, however, because it has developed at two somewhat different levels. At the first level are the statutory members of the NSC which constitute the actual "council" of the NSC.

This "council" is clearly the most prestigious of all official foreign policy bodies and officially consists of the president, the vice president, the secretary of state, and the secretary of defense. The National Security Act of 1947 authorized this cabinet level body "to advise the president with respect to the integration of domestic, foreign, and military policies relating to the national security so as to enable the military services and other departments and agencies of the government to cooperate more effectively in matters involving national security."[9] Other cabinet level officers (the chairman of the Joint Chiefs of Staff, the director of Central Intelligence, and the Director of the Arms Control and Disarmament Agency) have served at times as statutory advisers to the Council at the invitation of various presidents, some of whom also have invited the attorney general, the secretary of commerce, the secretary of the treasury, and others to be official observers. In recognition of the increasing importance of economic affairs to American national security and foreign policy, President Carter invited the director of the Office of Management and Budget (OMB) and the chairman of the Council of Economic Advisers to attend NSC meetings.

At the second level is the NSC staff. Most press references to the NSC refer not to the "council" itself but to the NSC staff and to the chief of that staff, the president's national security affairs adviser. At this level there have been roller coaster changes in the way foreign policy is coordinated and conducted.[10] Given historical developments, it is ironic that the 1947 Act did not even call for such an official nor provide for such a staff. One of the drafters of that legislation has said that the Act did not intend to create a national security adviser for the president.[11]

Organization of the NSC Staff. Although presidents have organized the NSC system differently, in virtually every case the purposes of the organizational schemes have been the same: to coordinate both the planning and the execution of national security policy, to provide advice to the president on national security matters, to act as a crisis decision-making center for the president, and to review proposals for sensitive intelligence operations and covert actions. Just a few examples will show the range and variety of NSC staff organizations.

The NSC staffs of Truman and Eisenhower consisted of a handful of individuals, most of whom believed they were to perform a strictly coordinating and custodial function. The NSC staffs of Kennedy, Johnson, Nixon, Ford, and Carter assumed much broader roles. They took the appearance of a miniature State Department or, at times, like a combination State Department and Department of Defense. There have been geographical desks (Middle East, Soviet Affairs, etc.) and functional desks (Terrorism, Human Rights, etc.) as well as various committees for special purposes. Under President Carter, for example, there was a Policy Review Committee and a Special Coordinating Committee. The latter committee handled crisis management, covert actions, and broad functional matters such as terrorism while the former dealt with more traditional foreign policy matters.

The Reagan-Bush NSC staff looked less like a miniature State Department. It was characterized by three Senior Interdepartmental Groups (SIGs), one for foreign policy chaired by the secretary of state, one for military and defense affairs chaired by the secretary of defense, and one for intelligence matters chaired by the director of the CIA. Beneath these there were several Interdepartmental Groups (IGs) and even some Restricted Interagency or Interdepartmental Groups (RIGs) whose membership and activities were secret.

Reagan's NSC staff looked a little more like a miniature Defense Department as there were approximately twenty active-duty military officers serving on the NSC staff in addition to several key NSC officials who were recently retired military personnel. That number may not seem disproportionate out of a staff of just under 200, but approximately two-thirds of that total are support staff (either secretarial or information management specialists). President Bush's NSC staff returned to the earlier model and was organized somewhat like a miniature state department.

The President and the NSC. The personal style of the president has been the most significant variable in explaining the organization and functioning of all NSC systems. Any attempt to alter the NSC system by rearranging bureaucratic lines and charts will ultimately fail because of this fact.

> It is not an institutional problem, susceptible to bureaucratic reform.
> . . . It has almost everything to do with [the] personality . . . of the
> president; his character and temperament; his work habits and manage-
> rial skills; his past experience and the knowledge of foreign policy
> that he brings to the job; [and] his relationship with (and confidence
> in) his secretary of state.[12]

Some presidents, President Kennedy for example, have not wanted to be locked into a single statutory source for national security policy advice. He viewed the existence of a single body for the coordination of national security advice and policies as an unacceptable narrowing of his field of choices. He did not want to rely on a single body for policy recommendations for two reasons. Kennedy also wanted to restore the State Department to some pre-eminence in the foreign policy process. Disappointment with the State Department, however, quickly caused him to abandon this goal and to go to a very free-floating national security system. On the one hand, he liked the freedom of informal bureaucratic structures—he liked to pick and choose from among his advisers and from among various federal agencies. On the other hand, he also liked to make his own national security decisions. He liked to receive information from the NSC, as well as other groups, but he resisted the notion of being bound in any way to its recommendations.

In contrast, his predecessor, President Eisenhower, preferred a much more ordered NSC. His NSC staff, consisting of three or four persons, and other White House advisers, would review policy alternatives and present Eisenhower with a very ordered set of policy alternatives. This made Eisenhower's NSC meetings rather routine and formal. In some respects, President Reagan followed the Eisenhower model and President Carter the Kennedy model.

Both the frequency of NSC meetings and the degree of participation by the president in those meetings have varied over time. Eisenhower's NSC, following his tradition of routine meetings with his wartime staffs, met frequently with the president himself in attendance.[13] Kennedy and Johnson used the NSC quite differently and both the frequency of meetings as well as presidential participation declined. Nixon announced that he would meet regularly with his NSC but after the first year changed that pattern as Kissinger emerged as the primary source for both the coordination of foreign policy as well as the source of foreign policy ideas.

Two presidents with vastly different management styles, Carter and Reagan, both entered office with the publicly avowed intention of de-emphasizing the role of the NSC staff. President Carter, however, soon returned to the practices of his predecessors in the White House.[14] He let the NSC staff, headed by Brzezinski, gradually take control of the foreign policy process. On the other hand, President Reagan's neglect of the NSC staff created what two experts have called,

> . . . times of turbulence involving a forced resignation over suspected impropriety by one director (Allen, exonerated a year later from the allegation that he had given special White House access to a Japanese news magazine in exchange for a cash payment); sharp criticisms of

inadequate experience directed against another (Clark); a suicide attempt soon after a troubled resignation by a third (McFarlane); and charges of unlawfulness leveled at a fourth (Poindexter).[15]

Perhaps President Reagan's greatest mistake in this regard was to not constrain the NSC staff as it engaged in controversial, arguably illegal, and (perhaps the ultimate political sin) unsuccessful operations which, though they began as clandestine operations, were soon subject to press, public, and congressional scrutiny.[16] Reagan's final national security advisers (Frank Carlucci and General Colin Powell) as well as Bush's national security adviser (Brent Scowcroft) did much to reestablish the integrity of the early Reagan NSC staff.

The degree of confidence a president has in his secretary of state is another predictor of the NSC staff role. It was, in fact, a secretary of state, Dean Rusk, who knew by personal experience of what he was speaking, who said that "the organization of government at higher echelons" depends on "how confidence flows down from the president."[17] President Reagan, for example, had considerable confidence in Secretary of State Shultz and Secretary of Defense Weinberger and, therefore, began to pay less and less attention to the formal apparatus of the NSC system and to settle significant foreign policy matters outside of formal NSC meetings. President Reagan had much less confidence in his first secretary of state, Alexander Haig, who publicly embarrassed him on inauguration day by presenting the president with a written document acknowledging Haig's preeminence and calling for the president's signature. The president refused to sign, his confidence in Haig dropped, Haig's effectiveness was diminished, and the NSC staff gained in importance.[18]

President Nixon relied less and less on his cabinet officers, particularly his secretary of state, and on the formal NSC and came to rely more and more on the NSC staff under Henry Kissinger. This was virtually inevitable since Nixon's choice for secretary of state, William Rogers, was based partially on the president's belief that Rogers knew nothing about foreign affairs and that policy coordination would therefore remain in the White House. NSC meetings became a forum in which Kissinger would pronounce the foreign policies of the government. This led inexorably to less frequent meetings of the NSC. One scholar has described Nixon's NSC as a device to shield the president from his advisers.[19]

Growth of the NSC Staff. Two of the more significant developments in the foreign policy process since 1947 have been the increasing *size* and *role* of the NSC staff and the increasing preeminence of the chief of that staff, the president's national security affairs adviser, as the central figure in the national security system. It is possible to argue that the NSC was never meant to have a staff, at least beyond that of an executive secretary who would prepare agenda, keep minutes, and brief the president on NSC matters. The comments of Secretary of State Dean Acheson who was (to use the title of his book) "present at the creation," are useful to review in this context.

> This [the National Security Council] was created in the Truman years and reached its highest usefulness during them. It was kept small; aides and brief-carriers were excluded, a practice—unfortunately not continued—that made free and frank debate possible. Those present came prepared to present their views themselves, and had previously filed memoranda. Matters brought before the council were of importance worthy of the personal attention of the highest officers and decisions by the President. In succeeding administrations practice deteriorated in two ways. The first was toward a desire by the President for "agreed recommendations." This was a deathblow. Agreement can always be reached by increasing the generality of the conclusion. When this is done, the form is preserved but only the illusion of policy is created. The President gives his hierarchical blessing to platitudes. To perform his real duty must involve the anguish of decision, and to decide one must know the real issues. These have to be found and flushed like birds from a field. The adversary process is the best bird dog.[20]

As is often the case, significant international events shape policy-making styles and procedures. The policy and coordinating demands of the Korean War brought about an enlargement of both the size and significance of what began as a one or two person staff. Eisenhower abolished the title of executive secretary and created instead a special assistant for national security affairs who, with a larger staff, would serve the needs of the NSC, but more significantly, the needs of the president. A further blurring of roles occurred when Eisenhower named General Andrew Goodpaster as his White House Office staff secretary and also assigned him substantive National Security Council duties. Almost imperceptibly the NSC chief of staff was becoming the president's personal national security affairs adviser.

President Kennedy named the Dean of Faculty at Harvard, McGeorge Bundy, as his special assistant for national security affairs. Kennedy's desire to manage the national security system himself and his early experience with the Bay of Pigs debacle in the spring of 1961, brought about major changes in the NSC system. Kennedy's disappointment over the way the traditional NSC system had served him during the Cuban crisis led to increasing informality in the system and to a greater role for Bundy who now, with a larger staff and flourishing in Kennedy's dislike of formal structures, began to coordinate and to be a spokesman for national security policy throughout the vast bureaucratic sea of foreign policy institutions.

President Johnson came into the White House with a vastly different operating style and with much less interest in foreign affairs. Nevertheless, he continued both Kennedy's personnel and procedures. That is, he kept Bundy as his national security affairs assistant and he maintained the use of the NSC and its staff as the coordinating point for all national security policy. When Walt Rostow succeeded Bundy, and in spite of a public diminution of the role of the national security affairs assistant, Rostow continued to coordinate policy, to manage the flow of national security information to the president, and to carry presidential decisions to the foreign policy bureaucracy. Perhaps this would not have been the case had not the war in Vietnam placed such a high premium on policy coordination.

Both the title and the role of the president's national security affairs adviser was changed during the Nixon administration. President Nixon appointed Harvard professor Henry Kissinger as presidential assistant for national security affairs. And with an ever increasing staff, Kissinger not only coordinated national security policy, but also became the chief architect of that policy.[21] While it is easy to exaggerate the changes in the NSC staff under Kissinger, both in terms of size and importance, few would disagree that Kissinger's tenure as the national security affairs adviser was the high point of that position in terms of size of staff, prominence, and power.

The development of the Nixon-Kissinger NSC system illustrates, however, an interesting bureaucratic principle. Early in his administration, Nixon announced that he wanted to restore the NSC system to its original role. He was very critical of Johnson's neglect of the NSC and felt that key foreign policy and national security decisions had been made haphazardly. Thus, Nixon appointed Kissinger as chief of staff of a new NSC system which was to be the central hub of the foreign policy wheel. All spokes of the foreign policy process led to the NSC, but the only route to the president was through Kissinger whose NSC staff grew both in size and importance.

Now larger and encumbered with greater procedural impediments, however, the NSC system began to play a less significant role in the process. For example, the 1973 decision to bomb Cambodia was made outside of the NSC system. It appears that in spite of organizational efforts, decision-making processes are shaped by the interplay of individual personalities and the confidence and power inherent therein. It also appears that the larger a bureaucratic structure grows, the less useful it is to a president.

President Ford separated Kissinger from one of the two hats he had worn under President Nixon when he designated Brent Scowcroft, Kissinger's former deputy, as the national security affairs adviser. Scowcroft's NSC and staff operated more like the early NSC and its staff in the Truman administration. But, with Kissinger at State, power did shift temporarily away from the NSC system to the State Department.

Carter's assistant for national security affairs, Zbigniew Brzezinski, began his four-year tenure by publicly disavowing the Kissinger model, both for the NSC staff as well as for the national security affairs adviser. To no one's surprise, however, he ended up behaving very much like Kissinger but without Kissinger's wit, charm, or sense of global mission.

Reagan made the same kind of commitment to a diminished role for the NSC staff and for his national security affairs adviser and, to a considerable degree, lived up to that commitment. First, Reagan appointed as his first and second secretaries of state strong individuals who accepted their appointments on the condition that they were to be the primary source of foreign policy advice for the president. Both Alexander Haig and George Shultz were familiar with the way past national security affairs advisers Bundy, Rostow, Kissinger, and Brzezinski had overshadowed Secretaries of State Rusk, Rogers, Vance, and Muskie and they accepted their appointments only with an understanding that this would not happen to them.

In fact, Reagan's first secretary of state, retired General Alexander Haig, went to considerable lengths to let the foreign policy bureaucracy know that he was in charge. He publicly announced that he was to be the foreign policy/national security affairs "vicar" in the Reagan administration and that all foreign policy advice would be correlated through him.

Even though this act caused some embarrassment to President Reagan, it nevertheless sent a very clear message to Reagan's first national security affairs adviser, Richard Allen, that Haig was not going to settle for anything other than first place in the race to be the president's chief agent in foreign policy matters. The message was remembered and repeated (albeit more tastefully) by George Shultz, Reagan's second secretary of state.

Secondly, five of Reagan's six national security affairs advisers were seen as officials who lacked both substantive foreign affairs experience as well as the concomitant respect that such experience would have brought them. Richard Allen, William Clark, Robert McFarlane, John Poindexter, and Lt. General Colin Powell were clearly not in the Bundy, Rostow, Kissinger, or Brzezinski mold.[22] Only Frank Carlucci, who held that office for a short time until he was made secretary of defense, brought to the office extensive experience in foreign and national security affairs.

Perhaps as a result of its less elevated status, Reagan's NSC staff fell back on a time-honored bureaucratic axiom: If your office has not been given a significant role to play, then invent one. President Reagan's second-term NSC staff apparently did just that. The NSC staff under McFarlane and Poindexter became heavily involved in supporting private efforts to fund the Contras (the guerilla movement in Nicaragua fighting against the Sandinista government) with moneys gained from the sale of weapons to the Khomeini government of Iran, as well as from other sources.

The degree of Reagan's awareness of these activities has never been fully established, but it is clear that members of the NSC staff and the president's national security affairs adviser believed they were carrying out the desires of the president.[23] It is also clear that Reagan's aloofness from the details of NSC activities made this possible. This was in marked contrast to his predecessor in the White House, Jimmy Carter, whose involvement in the details of running the nation sometimes stunned his aides and other senior government personnel.[24]

President George Bush named Brent Scowcroft as his national security affairs adviser. Scowcroft was a deputy to Kissinger in the Nixon administration and then served as the head of the NSC staff under President Ford. Scowcroft brought considerable experience to that position and became known for his quiet, less public, and effective work. Bush's strong secretary of state, James Baker, came to that office highly touted as an experienced and effective foreign policy leader.

Operational Activities of the NSC. It has been the intrusion of the NSC staff into operational roles that has attracted the most criticism. From its original creation as a council of cabinet level officers assigned to coordinate foreign and national security policy, the council itself became less significant than the staff which gradually turned into an alternate Department of State, personally attached to the White House, whose duties, at times, even included conducting both foreign policy and clandestine operations.

Some argue that the war in Indochina was the culprit—that Walt Rostow began to use the NSC staff to shape the flow of information headed for President Johnson and thus alter the original purpose of the NSC. Others scoff at this insignificant change and assert that it was Kissinger who fundamentally restructured the role of the NSC and its staff.

Clearly, prior to Kissinger, no national security affairs adviser had ever been seen by other international actors as the chief foreign policy spokesman for the American government. Yet Kissinger was seen as just that. None had been involved in government to government negotiations nor made official representations abroad nearly as much as did Kissinger. His secret trip to China in 1972 illustrates this point. That trip was of enormous significance to U.S. foreign policy, yet it was conceived, staffed, and conducted by the NSC staff without the participation of the State Department or any other traditional foreign policy office. Ironically, then Vice President Spiro Agnew, a statutory member of the National Security Council, did not even know about the trip and was publicly condemning the People's Republic of China at the very time that Kissinger was on his way to forge a rapprochement with the Beijing government.[25]

That was not Kissinger's only experience at secret diplomacy nor was Kissinger the only national security affairs adviser to be so involved. Kissinger, between 1971 and 1973, made thirteen secret trips to Paris during the Vietnam negotiations, six trips to China, and five to Moscow.[26] Brzezinski was also involved in critical negotiations without the knowledge of the State Department, this time in the Middle East, and Poindexter and his staff participated in possibly illegal and secret diplomatic interventions conducted not only without the knowledge of the State Department but perhaps without the full awareness of the president.

The extracurricular activities of the Reagan NSC staff rose to new heights of creativity. From selling weapons to the Khomeini regime in Iran to facilitating aid to the Contras in Nicaragua, the Reagan administration NSC staff skirted legal niceties and violated, at a minimum, the spirit of U.S. laws. The full details of this affair may never be known and scholars will debate its wisdom for many years. Supporters of the NSC staff will argue that it was carrying out the will of the president and trying to compensate for a short-sighted and irresponsible Congress. Critics will argue that no end can justify a means which violates the law. But no one will disagree with the conclusion that the second-term Reagan NSC staff used the NSC system in a novel way unintended by the National Security Act of 1947 and in violation of the will of Congress.

Since the will of Congress had been violated, the objectivity of its report on the matter may be biased. But the report's recitation of National Security Affairs Adviser John Poindexter's conscious decision to protect the president by not informing him of details seemed to justify Senator Inouye's conclusion that the NSC staff was attempting to run a government outside of the legally constituted government.

As one scholar has noted,

> The National Security Act of 1947, which had established both the NSC and the CIA, did not create the NSC as a decision-making, much less a decision-executing body. Congress no more designed the NSC to execute national security policy than it designed the Council of Economic Advisers to print the nation's money.[27]

Why the NSC staff, rather than the CIA, was used for these kinds of covert and shadowy operations is quite clear. Since 1976, the CIA has been subject to congressional oversight. Its director is appointed with the consent of the Senate, its budget is appropriated by Congress, and its actions are fair game for congressional investigations. The NSC staff, on the other hand, is part of the White House and is protected from full congressional inquiry by the doctrine known as "executive privilege," a very controversial doctrine, especially when broadened to include any matter touching on national security.[28] Since the president's national security affairs adviser is appointed solely by the president without Senate consent, Congress cannot subject the NSC or its staff to oversight investigations in the same way that it can other agencies.[29]

The Reagan NSC staff scandal reawakened cries for legislation requiring Senate consent of national security affairs advisers, it rekindled congressional dislike of executive privilege, and it reaffirmed executive perceptions of the evil effects of congressional meddling in national security affairs. The American system of government being what it is, however, it is unlikely (and perhaps unwise) that executive branch officials will ever come completely out from under the protection of executive privilege. A head of state needs some latitude for actions without worrying that every verbal or written word will be scrutinized by a potentially hostile congressional committee. Similarly, it is both unlikely and unwise, given the constitutional division of foreign policy power, that Congress will ever abdicate to the president the sole management of national security affairs.

The NSC System Under President Bush.   President Bush, in his first National Security Decision Directive, tilted towards an interagency coordination approach, although his national security affairs adviser clearly maintained a preeminent position. In a little-noticed but rather unique organizational departure, President Bush established the *Principals Committee* of the NSC with the secretary of state, the secretary of defense, the director of Central Intelligence, and the chairman of the Joint Chiefs of Staff as members, and, by invitation, the secretary of transportation, the attorney general, and other heads of executive departments and agencies as appropriate. What was unique, however, was that the *national security affairs adviser chaired the Principals Committee.* Since this committee reviewed, coordinated, and monitored the development and implementation of national security policy, the adviser's position as chairman held the potential for enormous influence. Moreover, the NSC Deputies Committee, immediately under the Principals Committee and attended by the number two officers in each of the participating agencies mentioned, *was chaired by the deputy to the national security affairs adviser.* The Deputies Committee both made recommendations on policy development and implementation to the NSC Principals Committee and oversaw the interagency committees.

Only at the interagency level, the NSC Policy Coordinating Committees, organized along the regional and functional lines of the Departments of State and of Defense and entrusted as well with crisis management (a separate function chaired by the vice president under Reagan), were the chairmen drawn from the State Department or from Defense, Treasury, and the CIA, depending on the issues involved. There was one exception: The policy coordinating committee on arms control was chaired again by a representative of the national security affairs adviser.

Despite the highly visible role of the national security affairs adviser, the Bush NSC system represented a departure in two ways from the Reagan administration. First, the presidential directive returned the NSC organization to its statutory role of interagency coordination. Second, the directive also seemed to aim at precluding policy development and implementation by the NSC staff as an independent process. However, given the intertwining of a host of domestic and international issues in contemporary American life, and, given the fact that the national security affairs adviser is a principal actor with offices next to the president (propinquity is power), it is probably prudent to assume that competition between the NSC staff and the other cabinet level foreign policy departments will continue. The phrase, an "invitation to struggle," which has been used to describe executive-congressional arrangements for the direction of U.S. foreign policy, applies more aptly to the struggle which has gone on within the executive branch between the NSC and other foreign policy institutions, primarily the State Department. With a strong and personally close secretary of state, this "struggle" was less apparent in the Bush administration than in most post-World War II administrations.

Given past history and legal ambiguities, however, it is likely that a divisive struggle between future NSC systems and other foreign policy agencies will erupt. Much as one scholar described the constitutional formula for presidential-congressional relations, the current structure remains an "invitation to struggle."

TOWARD THE TWENTY-FIRST CENTURY

In an age of increasing vincibility, U.S. foreign and national security policies require greater continuity and consistency than they have ever had before. One scholar has asked, "Can a system with divided authority, with two major foreign policy decision-making institutions, meet the need for united national action on life-or-death matters. . . ?"[30] We wish to expand the scope of "life-or-death matters" and ask whether such a system can meet the need for prompt, consistent, and effective national action on a broad range of foreign policy issues which include economic, energy, trade, and environment, as well as traditional national security matters?

The foreign policy system of President Clinton could well be the system that takes this nation into the twenty-first century. America may still continue to play a significant leadership role in a century in which the distinction between foreign and domestic policies will disappear virtually completely, in which national and international economies will become even more intertwined and complex, in which the importance of national and ethnic boundaries lessens in importance in some areas of the world while they increase in importance in others, and in a century in which the elements of national power are both less and more than military force.

If America is, however, to continue its traditional leadership role, some attention must be paid to the foreign policy system. In the previous chapter we talked about the need to prevent debilitating squabbles between Congress and the president. We suggested that Congress must rationalize its own process and exercise more restraint and discipline. We also suggested that the president must defer to such a reformed Congress in general policy formulation while at the same time be more efficient and effective in his or her execution of such policies. In this chapter we are suggesting that the executive branch must also be willing to explore ways to attack the pluralization of foreign policy formulation, coordination, and execution. It must be kept in mind that the most debilitating competition for foreign policy influence occurs not between the White House and Congress, but within the executive branch (even within the White House) between various executive departments and agencies. Most attempts to fix this problem have merely exacerbated it.

Some have argued that it will be necessary to reorganize the NSC system.[31] Unfortunately, many reorganization schemes merely add an additional bureaucratic layer over the existing one. Calls for a reduced role for the national security affairs adviser have also been plentiful.[32] Indeed, that call was met under the Scowcroft NSC system during the Bush administration. However, voluntary self-restraint or restraint that relies solely on the personality mix between a president, a secretary of state, and a national security adviser are insufficient. Such arrangements are easily overturned by subsequent individuals. As long as the potential exists for a NSC system in which the national security adviser formulates, coordinates, and executes foreign policy with a staff whose role resembles a combined State Department and CIA, the requirements of consensus, coordination, and consistency will be at risk.

While the NSC system since 1947 has not served faithfully the purposes for which it was created, it is fair to say that it has served the purposes of individual presidents quite well. Most NSC staffs and national security affairs advisers have reflected the preferences of the president—they have assisted him in steering the foreign policy ship.

But it is ironic that the American government, which has more information and ideas available to it than any other government in history, has suffered from several bureaucratic blunders in its foreign policy over the last twenty years. It suggests that the government is not being well served by all of the information and ideas available to it.[33] And that suggests a weakness in the NSC system which needs to be examined as the U.S. prepares for the twenty-first century.

One can argue that the critical goals of continuity and coordination might be better served if both the existing NSC staff and the role of the national security affairs adviser were abolished completely. Surely the president ought to continue to meet with cabinet level officials who have major foreign policy responsibilities (the *council* part of the NSC), but coordination might be more easily obtained if a White House-based secretary of state assumed the role of the president's national security affairs adviser with a senior interdepartmental committee under him taking the role of the NSC staff.[34] The secretary could then designate a senior assistant to direct the usual business of the State Department and another to act as the staff director or (to use a title from the first NSC) executive secretary of the reconstituted NSC. That would more closely approach the parliamentary-ministerial model used by some other governments. Above all, it might be the only way to restore the sagging morale of the State Department, end the ofttimes bitter competition between NSC and State, and do away with the expensive and unnecessary "luxury" of two "State Departments."

One variation of this proposal calls for the creation of an "executive committee of the cabinet" to take the place of the NSC. This "ExCab" would "become the chief forum for high-level review and discussion of all major policy issues that combine substantial 'foreign,' 'domestic,' and 'economic' concerns."[35]

In establishing the NSC, Congress never intended to create a body that was constitutionally unaccountable. Yet, to some extent, that is what has happened. To the contrary, Congress was attempting, through the NSC system, to force coordination of those departments of government whose secretaries are confirmed by Congress and who are constitutionally responsible—a requirement which the national security affairs adviser and his staff escape.

On the other hand, it is possible to argue that the secretary of state cannot be the president's national security affairs adviser and run the State Department at the same time. Perhaps one cannot be concurrently an administrator and an adviser. But that really depends on the managerial style of the persons involved and on the organizational framework they set in place. It is not clear why a secretary of state could not be the president's chief foreign policy aide while one assistant secretary of state administered the State Department and another acted as the executive secretary of the National Security Council. Under this arrangement, there would be no NSC staff beyond senior State Department officials and other subsecretary officials working with them on various committees and subcommittees.

All pleas to alter the NSC merely by reducing the role of the national security affairs adviser or the size of NSC staff ought to be viewed with suspicion. According to one observer, it is not difficult to prune branches, but they will always grow back. "The question is not whether to cut the staff; it's whether to scale down the job description of the president's adviser for national security. What needs pruning is not the branches but the roots; do that, and the staff's influence and activity will inevitably die back."[36] This advice may be on the right track but may not go far enough. It may be necessary to abolish completely the separate position of national security affairs adviser and have the secretary of state assume that role.

There are, of course, arguments against this proposal.[37] The very establishment of the NSC, the multidimensional character of international affairs, and the need to coordinate those issues with domestic concerns, require a supradepartmental agency for defining agendas, coordinating policies, and, on occasion, in matters of extreme sensitivity and novelty (the two often go hand-in-hand), executing policies. It can be argued that there is no bureaucratic forum short of the White House itself capable of playing this role. This, however, is one role the president can and should play. All too often cabinet level officials try to protect their bureaucratic interests even at the expense of national interest. A secretary of state who enjoyed, under the president, primacy in the foreign policy process would go a long ways towards reducing conflicting competition which the "two State Departments" system in the past has permitted.

To meet the foreign policy needs of the twenty-first century, the foreign policy system must encourage greater coordination and efficiency. There have been far too many persons, offices, agencies, and departments involved in the foreign policy process over the last several years. Presidents need to focus on resolving conflicts between America and other nations, not on resolving conflicts between competing sections of their administrations. They need to concentrate on global economic and environmental problems and not dissipate their energies resolving competing and conflicting goals of scores of foreign policy agencies within their own administrations.

ENDNOTES

1. While blaming and finger-pointing between the president and Congress has been a characteristic of the American political system since it was created, a new high was reached during the 1992 campaign. H. Ross Perot, an independent presidential candidate, based much of his campaign on this perceived gridlock. Another independent candidate, Bo Gritz, a former Green Beret, campaigned on the platform that there was still one more hill to be taken, namely Capitol Hill.
2. This is Hoffmann's useful distinction between domestic and international politics in his *The State of War* (New York: Praeger, 1965).
3. Historically, the global stage could be described as state-centric in that nearly all of the actors represented states. Today it is a nonstate-centric stage where the mix of state actors and nonstate actors is incredibly complex.
4. Perhaps the best treatment of one particular relationship is by Alexander L. George and Juliette L. George in *Woodrow Wilson and Colonel House: A Personality Study* (New York: The John Day Co., 1956).
5. President Reagan's reliance on Attorney General Edwin L. Meese III illustrates this point. Meese's influence grew from his long-time association with the President. Meese even served on the NSC, a foreign policy position not usually held by the attorney general.

See James Bamford, "Carlucci and the N.S.C.," *The New York Times Magazine,* 18 January 1987, 26. Robert Kennedy was similarly influential in foreign policy matters though he did not occupy an official foreign policy position.

6. The classic study on this topic is Henry M. Wriston, *Executive Agents in American Foreign Policy* (Gloucester, MA: Peter Smith, 1967). See also Edward F. Sayle, "The Historical Underpinnings of the U.S. Intelligence Community," *International Journal of Intelligence and Counterintelligence* 1 (Spring 1986): 1-27.

7. According to the official U.S. Senate investigation of this affair, U.S. foreign policy pertaining to these matters was in the hands of a "cabal of the zealots"—some in official government positions and others not. Senate, Senate Iran-Contra Committee, *Iran Contra Affair,* (Washington, D.C.: GPO, 1987).

8. James W. Clark, "Foreign Affairs Personnel Management," Commission on the Organization of the Government for the Conduct of Foreign Policy, Vol. 6, pp. 181-222, Appendix P, Washington, D.C.: GPO, 1975.

9. The quoted phrase is from Title I, Section 101(a) of the National Security Act itself. Both formal amendments and informal alterations to the act have occurred since 1947. Other cabinet and subcabinet officials have participated in council meetings and the chairman of the Joint Chiefs of Staff and the director of Central Intelligence have been designated officially as advisers to the council. The best collection of both documents and opinions about the establishment and development of the NSC is Karl F. Inderfurth and Lock K. Johnson, eds., *Decisions of the Highest Order: Perspectives on the National Security Council* (Pacific Grove, CA: Brooks/Cole, 1988).

10. For consistency, we use the term "national security affairs adviser" to describe the person performing this role even though various presidents have bestowed different official titles, as well as duties, on this office.

11. Philip Geyelin, "Cutting the NSC down to Size," *The New York Times,* 22 October 1980, A15. Geyelin is quoting Clark Clifford, who as a young White House staff member drafted the National Security Act of 1947.

12. Geyelin, "Cutting the NSC Down to Size." William Hyland, who has served on the NSC staffs of several presidents, argues that personalities play a greater role in the policy process than do institutions. See his comments in John Korb and Keith D. Hahn, eds., *National Security Policy Organization in Perspective* (Washington, D.C.: American Enterprise Institute for Public Policy Research , 1981).

13. It is widely believed that James Forrestal, Truman's secretary of war and a major force behind the creation of the NSC, used the British War Cabinet as a model for the NSC. He wanted to create institutional barriers to the kind of informality that existed under Roosevelt during WWII. In fact, in its early days the NSC was occasionally referred to as "Forrestal's Revenge."

14. The following headlines are merely typical of every recent president's intentions: "Carter and Brzezinski Stress What NSC Chief Will Not Do," (*The Washington Post,* 24 January 1977) and "Reagan Plans to Reduce Security Adviser's Role," (*Washington Star,* 2 November 1980.)

15. Inderfurth and Johnson, *Decisions of the Highest Order,* 144.

16. It was a cynical friend of Napoleon who described Napoleon's execution of his rival, Duc Enghien, as "worse than a crime, a blunder." Phillip Jacobsen and Richard Owen, "It's a French Knock-out," *The Times (London),* 19 November 1987, 12.

17. Dean Rusk, "Mr. Secretary: On the Eve of Emeritus," *Life,* 17 January 1969, 62.

18. Haig's "talking paper" for his meeting with President Reagan was printed in *The Washington Post,* 11 July 1982, C1, C5.

19. I. M. Destler, "National Security Advice to the US President: Some Lessons from Thirty Years," *World Politics* 29 (January 1977).

20. Dean Acheson, *Present at the Creation* (New York: W.W. Norton & Co., Inc. 1969), 733.

21. Keeping an exact count of the size of the NSC staff is more difficult than one might suppose. If one looks solely at payroll, the staff might seem smaller than it really is since many of the members of the staff are loaned or seconded from other agencies to the NSC. Some writers also become confused between the *professional* staff and the *administrative* or *clerical* staff. Finally, it is easy to mistake members of the White House staff for members of the NSC staff. It is nevertheless possible to generalize and suggest that the staff of the NSC has grown from one professional foreign policy administrator under Truman to over fifty under Nixon and Kissinger. Presidents since Nixon have almost inevitably talked about reducing the size of the professional staff but it has continued to hover around fifty, give or take a few individuals on any given day. The White House, in comparison, has gone from between 200 and 300 for Truman, Eisenhower, Kennedy, and Johnson to between 500 and 600 for Nixon, Ford, Carter, and Reagan.

22. In contrast, Reagan's fifth adviser for national security affairs, Frank Carlucci, had considerable experience in the foreign policy bureaucracy and was seen by the other players as a person with substantive and procedural knowledge. When Carlucci was appointed as secretary of defense, Reagan seemed to resort to his earlier practice by appointing Lt. General Powell as his national security affairs adviser.

23. The best historical metaphor may well be the experience of Henry II of England, whose continuing frustrations in dealing with Archbishop Thomas Becket culminated in a fit of rage during which Henry is reported to have said, "Is there no one who will rid me of this low born priest?" Four of the King's entourage began plotting to get rid of Becket. Shortly after Christmas day in 1170, they traveled to Canterbury and killed Becket. It is widely believed that Henry did not think that he had given orders for the assassination of Becket, but it is clear that he created an environment in which the four knights quite easily thought they were carrying out the King's desires while saving him the difficult act of ordering Becket's murder.

24. Old Washington hands who had worked under both Carter and Reagan used to chide the operating styles of both by saying that, as captain of the ship of state, Carter spent so much time finding out what was going on in every room of the ship that he didn't have time to steer it. Reagan, on the other hand, spent all of his time steering the ship but didn't have an idea about what was going on throughout it.

25. Joseph C. Harsch, "A National Security Council Primer," *The Christian Science Monitor,* 24 February 1987, 15. One anecdote illustrates Kissinger's reputation. When a small group of U.S. senators and a few staff people boarded a jet aircraft at Andrews Air Force Base in January, 1979, at the start of their flight to Moscow to discuss SALT II matters with senior Soviet officials, the pilot announced over the intercom that the aircraft was the one used by Kissinger for his famous "shuttle diplomacy" in the Middle East and that the plane was still configured just as it had been for Kissinger except that the Air Force had removed his scepter.

26. Barry Rubin, *Secrets of State: The State Department and the Struggle over U.S. Foreign Policy* (New York: Oxford University Press, 1985), Chapter 7.

27. Harold Hongju Koh, *The National Security Constitution: Sharing Power after the Iran-Contra Affair* (New Haven, CT: Yale University Press, 1990), 54.

28. Louis Fisher, *Constitutional Conflicts between Congress and the President* (Princeton: Princeton University Press, 1985): 204-20 contains a good introduction to the doctrine of executive privilege.

29. How widely the blanket of executive privilege covers the NSC and its staff has been discussed frequently but has not been settled definitively through the courts. In fact, many NSC-congressional confrontations have been resolved by a variety of personal accommodations and circumlocutions rather than through legal settlement.

30. I.M. Destler, "The Constitution and Foreign Affairs," *News for Teachers of Political Science* (Spring 1985): 1.
31. See, for example, Graham Allison and Peter Szanton, *Remaking Foreign Policy: The Organizational Connection* (New York: Basic Books, 1976).
32. William V. Kennedy, "Reorganizing the NSC is not Enough," *The Christian Science Monitor*, 4 February 1987, 15 .
33. This is suggested in Kennedy, "Reorganizing the NSC is not Enough." See also Ronald H. Hinckley, "National Security in the Information Age," *The Washington Quarterly* (Spring 1986): 125-39.
34. Four past secretaries of state, Rusk, Rogers, Vance, and Haig, unsurprisingly recommended that the "Secretary of State who is responsible to the Congress as well as the President should be the President's primary spokesman on foreign affairs." See William O. Chittick, "The Secretaries on Continuity and Bipartisanship in American Foreign Policy," *International Studies Notes,* Vol. 11, No. 1 (Fall 1984) for a report on a panel discussion among these former officials.
35. This proposal is from Allison and Szanton, *Remaking Foreign Policy,* 78-80.
36. Geyelin, "Cutting the NSC Down to Size."
37. One of the most telling criticisms is made by Duncan L. Clarke in "Why State Can't Lead," *Foreign Policy,* No. 66 (1987): 128-42. Our suggestion is based on significant reorganization and change in the department. These changes would need to bring about greater area and language specialization, a Foreign Service more responsive to presidential initiatives, increased rotation into other foreign policy and national security agencies, and improved morale.

4

THE ROLE OF OTHER EXECUTIVE BRANCH DEPARTMENTS AND AGENCIES

This chapter continues our examination of the institutions which both shape and carry out foreign policy. While the previous chapter focused on the president and the NSC, this chapter examines the roles of the Department of State, the Department of Defense, and the intelligence community. As in Chapter 3, we are here interested both in the changing role these institutions play in the foreign policy process as well as in discussing some suggestions which might improve the foreign policy process in an age of increasing vincibility.

THE DEPARTMENT OF STATE

According to the oversimplified foreign policy model mentioned in Chapter 3, the State Department should be the most influential and prestigious foreign policy agency. It is the oldest of all cabinet level departments and was created to serve the foreign policy needs of a new nation. The secretary of state, at least through World War II, has been not only the president's chief spokesperson on foreign policy matters, he or she is fourth in line to succeed the president. Virtually any government organization chart one can make shows the State Department occupying a central foreign policy role. By intention, by tradition, and by logic, the Department of State has a reasonable claim to be the lead agency in the conduct of U.S. foreign policy.

The Department of State was not only the first executive department created, it may be older than the government it serves. A good argument can be made that the origins of the department go all the way back to the Committee on Secret Correspondence which was appointed by the Continental Congress in 1775. Its name was changed to the Committee on Foreign Affairs in 1777 and in 1781 a Department of Foreign Affairs was established. By 1789 this department was moved as a unit into the newly formed government. After having been given some purely domestic functions to perform, its name was changed to the Department of State. The department has long ceased to perform any of the domestic functions but still carries the name, the Department of State, and is still headed by the secretary of state.

The State Department is both the oldest as well as the smallest cabinet level bureaucracy. It employs less than 1 percent of the federal bureaucracy while the Department of Defense employs over 35 percent. State's budget averages about 1 percent of the budget of the Department of Defense and about 10 percent of the estimated CIA budget.

In the early history of America, the Department of State and its ambassadors had a near monopoly over the conduct of U.S. foreign policy, sometimes exercising more influence in foreign capitals than the president. Early secretaries of state often served as chief counselors to the president as well as the head of a department. At least up to World War II, the Department of State was usually the "lead agency" in nearly every aspect of U.S. foreign relations.

In this early period, presidents adopted the then prevailing diplomatic practice of appointing ambassadors to represent them in foreign nations. Up until the War of 1812, these ambassadors were, more often than not, well-known public officials (Adams, Jefferson, Franklin, etc.). Since then, however, wealthy men and women who make financial contributions to the president's campaign have tended to fill a large number of the most prestigious diplomatic posts. That practice has continued up to the present day for two reasons. First, only independently wealthy people can afford the high representational expenses associated with certain embassies and, second, ambassadorial posts are viewed as rewards to be given to those who have helped the president either politically or financially.

Over the years, a professional foreign service gradually developed but it was not until the Rogers Act in 1924 that a modern corps of professional Foreign Service Officers (FSOs) was formally created. After a brief period of playing a supporting role to the military through World War II years, the State Department reached its high point under President Truman and strong Secretaries of State George C. Marshall and Dean Acheson. Though reorganized many times, the diplomatic corps is still considered the backbone of the State Department and sees itself as the repository of all of these diplomatic traditions.

The department is organized into five geographical areas, as well as several other offices which have special functional responsibilities. State Department personnel are expected to report on the developments in the countries in which they are stationed so that U.S. policy towards those countries will be sound. These reports are sent back to desk officers who prepare policy recommendations that will help shape U.S. foreign policy.

Of the over 28,000 State Department personnel working in about 150 embassies and other U.S. facilities around the world and in Washington D.C., just over 10,000 are Foreign Service Officers. Logically, both the morale and the effectiveness of a professional diplomatic corps depend, to some degree, on the monopoly which it exercises in its field. A fundamental rule of any successful bureaucracy is that authority must be commensurate with responsibility. It is perverse to create an organization charged to deal with foreign relations and then fail to give it sufficient authority to carry out that task. Yet, that is what has happened.

Today the State Department does not play the traditional role just described. Why it does not is crucial to an understanding of the changing role of America in a world of sovereign states, the changing foreign policy process, and increasing American vincibility. There are at least six significant developments that have brought these changes about.

1. The international system has changed dramatically and the way that all nations play their roles within this altered system has had to change. At one time, political and military relations made up the bulk, certainly the most important part, of U.S. foreign relations. Were an ambassador from the previous century to spend a day in one of today's embassies, he or she would be astounded to see important roles being played by representatives of over thirty Washington agencies outside the control of the State Department and to see FSOs providing services to other government agencies. For example, in the U.S. Embassy in London, 44 agencies outside the control of the State Department are represented and only about 16 percent of the personnel are State Department employees (see number 6, below).

There would be an even greater shock at the number and complexity of issue areas on the contemporary diplomatic agenda. The extensive and endless ramifications of contemporary questions would be mind boggling to a nineteenth century diplomat. As an increasing number of experts representing scores of domestic agencies has entered the diplomatic stage, the role of the traditional players, the State Department's Foreign Service officers, has necessarily changed.

2. Changing diplomatic functions have also altered the traditional role of the Department of State. Both of the traditional functions performed by the department have changed dramatically.[1] The first traditional function of the diplomatic corps was to represent American interests to the governments of the world. In spite of the old saying that "an ambassador is an honest man sent

to lie abroad for the good of his country," early ambassadors played an essential role in informing foreign governments of U.S. interests. They were the primary means through which other nations learned of official U.S. policies and positions. Today, other nations find out about American policies through their own diplomatic and intelligence networks or, more likely, through widely available public media. Many American ambassadors abroad have complained that they have learned about U.S. foreign policy developments through various media or from senior foreign affairs officials in the host country rather than from their own superiors in Washington, D.C.

The second traditional function was to gather information about foreign governments and to report that information back to the president and other senior policy-makers. That function has also changed. FSOs continue to write reports for senior policy-makers and those reports, particularly those about low profile matters, can be very significant. But contemporary senior officials have many sources of information and the FSO knows that his or her reports are just part of the stream, particularly when they are writing about high profile issues. As a rule of thumb, if a senior foreign policy official wants to know what to do about long-range problems, State Department reports might be consulted. But in crises, State Department reports are viewed as not very helpful. Since crises seem to drive the machinery of modern government, State Department reporting has diminished in value. That is unfortunate because many future crises could be prevented by paying more attention to contemporary reports.

Contemporary reporting methods and practices also contribute to this problem. FSOs in the field know that their careers depend on both the quality and (unfortunately) the quantity of their reports. This creates incentives to swamp Washington desk officers with embassy reports. In earlier years reports that were not time-sensitive would be sent as airgrams and often were reflective and thoughtful analyses of situations. Today virtually all reports are sent instantaneously, often as "classified" or designated as "action items" in order to attract the attention of the desk officer, and are not as penetrating in their analysis as they should be. Over a million such telegrams pour into the State Department annually, creating a stream of information that senior foreign policy officers have great difficulty assimilating.

In fact, today's foreign policy-makers suffer from a surfeit of information, not a shortage. With hundreds of commercial information-providing agencies and scores of government agencies making information available to foreign policy officials, the primary task of decision-makers today is not to acquire information but to decide on which information they will rely. In previous centuries, decision-makers had to struggle to acquire timely and accurate information. As we move into the twenty-first century, decision-makers must become as skillful and proficient in evaluating the accuracy of the information they receive as past decision-makers were in merely getting that information. To an invincible nation, a well-focused stream of insightful information flowing to policy-makers is a welcome, but unnecessary, luxury. To a vincible nation, it is an absolute necessity.

3. The increasing complexity of foreign relations has led to the development of hundreds of international agencies, some of which have altered significantly the traditional foreign policy role of the State Department. This began with the first large-scale multilateral diplomatic conference in Vienna in 1815 and has continued in the hundreds of standing multilateral diplomatic gatherings of today. This development has not lessened the importance of government-to-government representation but it has diminished the role of the State Department in these representations, since many of these standing multilateral agencies deal with representatives of other U.S. departments and agencies. The Department of Agriculture, for example, plays a significant role in U.S. dealings with the Food and Agricultural Organization, and the U.S. Public Health Service has a great deal to do with the World Health Organization. In Egypt, for example, Agency for International Development (AID) personnel have at times outnumbered State Department personnel.

4. The diminished role of the Department of State also stems from sclerosis within the Department itself—its organizational arteries have become clogged. As with all large bureaucracies, the Department of State has gradually developed certain characteristics and traits which inhibit its effectiveness. A combination of seemingly endless paper work, apparently unbending procedures, and a perceived paucity of new ideas make the State Department appear as an unattractive foreign policy partner to any new president.

Some of these accusations are misplaced. The State Department is better equipped, by tradition, temperament, and role, to view U.S. foreign relations in a longer time frame. It looks beyond crises whereas other agencies (the CIA and the Defense Department) tend to be more current events oriented. This longer run perspective often elicits charges of inflexibility or even "wimpishness" from new presidents and "take charge" NSC staff officials, but is often a vital consideration which is missing in many foreign policy blunders. As one experienced government official has said, "the experienced eye and pragmatic perspective of career specialists—unlikely to view Iranian weapons buyers as 'moderates' to be wooed with a Bible, cake and concessions—are needed to balance White House pressures for quick and dramatic solutions that conform with campaign slogans or popular sentiment."[2]

Nearly every new administration has complained about the difficulty in changing the Foreign Service. It is often believed (not entirely fairly) that the Foreign Service is more interested in looking out for the interests of the nations in which its officers are stationed than for the interests of the United States and that a president who wants policies changed or carried out quickly will have to look beyond the Foreign Service to do it. It is difficult to think of an administration since World War II which has had unbounded confidence in the Department of State and its Foreign Service, at least beyond its first few months. Presidents have criticized the formality of the State Department and the tedious and lengthy reports of its officers.

5. Another cause of the declining role of the Department of State is the deteriorating morale of the Foreign Service. The decline began with Senator Joseph McCarthy's investigations into communist infiltration in the service in the 1950s. These hearings were woefully short on facts but had considerable popular support from segments of the American public. Over half of the senior FSOs at that time were either forced out of the service or left voluntarily. The failure of Secretary of State Dulles to vigorously defend the service was resented deeply. The effects of this period have continued to be felt in the form of low public esteem and difficulty in recruiting top candidates into the Foreign Service.

New entry FSOs face many years of tedious apprenticeships before they assume positions of significance and influence. As with all bureaucracies, new personnel are usually assigned the least desirable postings and tasks. Moreover, the continuing practice of filling prestigious ambassadorial posts as a reward for political loyalty and/or financial largess reduces the already limited number of ambassadorial positions available to the professional service. Early in the Reagan administration the number of political appointees to ambassadorial posts rose from the normal 30 percent to 50 percent.[3] "No president would dream, for example, of appointing a campaign contributor or crony as a military theater commander. But making him an ambassador, and permitting him to bypass the secretary of state, is commonplace."[4]

The growing practice of stationing abroad personnel from other departments and agencies to perform tasks traditionally performed by Foreign Service Officers has not helped morale. It violates the need for a bureaucratic monopoly discussed above.

Attacks on the biennial department budget are another source of low morale. The State Department is perhaps the only major government department with no domestic constituency. Every other cabinet level department has a domestic constituency which will lobby Congress in the department's interest. Many subcabinet level agencies have powerful constituencies. The Veterans' Administration, for example, can unleash a forceful lobbying effort if Congress tries to cut veterans' benefits. No such constituency exists for the State Department; there is virtually no group from whom opposition to State Department budget cuts can be expected. Therefore, the department is an easy target for budget cutting. And as more and more tasks (increased visa processing and more frequent congressional "junkets," for example) are being expected of the department, no new funds have been appropriated to pay for them. The department has been drained of resources without a concomitant reduction of duties.

Since 1985 Congress has cut the international affairs budget by 24 percent, or $5.5 billion, from fiscal year 1985. The cut was ten percent in 1986, 12 percent in 1987 and four percent in the fiscal year that began in October [1988]. If these figures are adjusted for inflation and exchange-rate losses, the reduction from [fiscal year] 1985 increases to 32 percent.[5]

Growing cynicism in the Foreign Service inevitably resulted when the department, in an amazing demonstration of congressional largess, was given additional billions of dollars earmarked for increasing security against terrorism at U.S. facilities abroad, only to see much of the money used for badly needed building renovations that have very little to do with additional security. The justifications given for such efforts were enough to lay to rest for years accusations that the State Department is not very creative.

Senior FSOs stationed around the world also resent the tendency of most new secretaries of state to bring into the department their own senior management team. Although it is not necessarily representative of all senior FSOs, the following segment of a letter written early in the Bush administration by a deputy chief of mission stationed abroad reveals the bitterness that can be engendered.

[If you detect any bitterness,] it's a result of watching Secretary [of State] Baker and his people take over the Seventh Floor [where senior management officials] of the State Department [are located] and the concurrent power setup at the NSC and CIA. The Bush people obviously distrust the career service, and have swallowed right-wing charges that career people subverted Ronald Reagan's policies, and led him down the garden path to accommodation with the Soviet Union. Extremely good people are being cast aside and replaced by twenty-nine year old wunderkind from Treasury or aging used car salesmen from Des Moines. While a few career people will be given important Ambassadorial assignments, the Seventh Floor power and policy structure will be firmly in the hands of people brought in from outside. In an age where the role of an ambassador has been diminished by the speed and ease of communication, squeezing professionals out of the Seventh Floor will do even more damage to our role in the world.[6]

Finally, pay and perquisites have not kept pace with those in roughly comparable careers, particularly international business. Many FSOs are tempted to cash in on several years of training and overseas experience and leave the diplomatic corps for more lucrative international business assignments or for positions that will allow them to keep their families in one home for more than three or four years at a time.

One experienced observer summarized the malaise of the department very succinctly. "Its morale is low after years of budget cuts at home and terrorist attacks abroad, investigations from the outside and ideological purges within. The next president, seeking a more supportive department, must offer more support to it."[7]

6. There has arisen, largely in response to some of the above developments, competing foreign policy agencies. These have weakened the monopoly of the Foreign Service in the foreign policy process.

The increasing importance of the NSC has already been mentioned. Washington-based FSOs who might be "loaned" to the NSC for short tours of duty often remark on the noticeable increase in their influence and sense of significance while with the NSC. In fact, some NSC staffs have been nothing but a miniature State Department located in the White House with geographical and functional subdivisions paralleling the "real" State Department and staffed by FSOs on loan to the NSC. A senior department desk officer for African Affairs within the State Department, for example, will find that he must compete with an NSC staff counterpart (perhaps even a former FSO underling) whose access to the president through the national security affairs adviser is much more direct than is his through the secretary of state. And in Washington D.C., as in all bureaucracies, propinquity is power.

Also, other government departments and agencies have developed their own "foreign services." It is not unusual for a major embassy to have personnel from intelligence agencies, military services, the Department of Commerce, the FBI, the Department of Agriculture, the Department of Justice, the Drug Enforcement Agency, the Bureau of Alcohol, Tobacco, and Firearms, the Secret Service, the Office of the U.S. Trade Representative (USTR), the Department of Treasury, and more.

Theoretically, all of this is forged into a coherent foreign policy through the Country Team concept under the coordination of the ambassador. But in practice, the loyalty of government employees tends to flow to the source of their paychecks and promotions and does not track easily up through interagency committees. The creation of the Department of Commerce's Foreign Commercial Corps took much of the former economic tasks from State and the work of the U.S. Trade Representative (USTR) has eaten into what remained.

Several years of a strong secretary of state, by the end of 1992, increased the role of the department in the foreign policy process and improved the morale of the Foreign Service somewhat. However, both perennial budget problems and wage scales far short of what private citizens in related international professions receive keep discontent close to the surface.

The Future of the State Department

All nations seek rational, focused, and coherent foreign policies; unfortunately few nations enjoy such. A nation which, by dint of its military, economic, political, and cultural predominance, can influence at will the policies of all other nations, perhaps will not rue the absence of such a foreign policy as much as less hegemonic nations. For better or for worse, the United States is no longer such a nation. As the department itself has acknowledged, "interdependence, globalization and the multiplication of issues and actors means that United States' national interests will in the future require [more skillful, energetic, and efficient officers and organizations]."[8] Technological, economic, and political developments have all conspired to end U.S. invincibility, if indeed it ever existed. Should the department be reorganized in some new way to accomplish these goals? Unfortunately, many government functions are personality dependent and not altered by bureaucratic restructuring. As one former senior government official has remarked,

> No table of organization can offset human chemistry, incompetence or excessive zeal. No theoretical model can effectively impose on a president a decision-making system unsuited to his needs, interests and experience.[9]

What could be done to limit the proliferation of foreign policy agencies? As one writer has noted, "the American presidency is cluttered with advisers, not just within the White House but across a wide range of official agencies. Indeed, so many agencies are pressing their advice on the president that the manageability of the highest office in the land may be one of the most significant issues before the American people."[10] In the previous chapter we noted one suggestion which would make the secretary of state the president's primary national security affairs adviser and spokesperson on foreign policy matters, and abolish the national security system as it now exists. Under this suggestion, the actual "council" part of the NSC would continue as at present (a meeting of cabinet level foreign policy officials) but the NSC staff would be headed by the secretary of state or by someone under him, perhaps an undersecretary of state for national security affairs.[11]

This dramatic reorganization would immediately solve the problem of low morale in the State Department but would bring a chorus of criticisms from other foreign policy agencies and departments. Those responsible for such cacophony could be reminded that this would merely restore State to its traditional role and that representatives of other agencies and departments could be represented on a new NSC staff.

While there would be much debate over a proposal to abolish the existing NSC system, there is widespread agreement that in an age of growing interdependence and intertwining of economic, environmental, and security issues, the foreign policy organization to deal with these issues must be at least as integrated as are the problems it faces. Those responsible for the organization and coordination of the foreign policy process must seek ways to enhance relationships between State and the other foreign policy actors, particularly the arms control, information, foreign aid, trade, and other related bureaucracies. As the "Management Task Force—State 2000" asks, "alternatively, what would be the advantages and disadvantages of a partial or full merger of any or all of these agencies with the Department of State?"[12]

Other, less revolutionary, changes might improve the quality of State's work and make it more suitable for the twenty-first century. The department must do more to develop and capitalize on regional and country expertise among its FSOs. Frequently changing assignments, a practice developed to prevent FSOs from becoming too attached to countries in which they were assigned, now works to prevent the development of country and regional expertise. With frequent home leaves and occasional Washington D.C. desk assignments, loyalty to the countries in which they are posted is not a serious problem for FSOs. Yet it is still common to find FSOs who have spent a few years in several different countries but who have not been able to develop a strong regional or country expertise. While there are some exceptions to this among what used to be called Sovietologist and Middle East experts particularly, the department does not do enough to encourage and develop strong regional expertise. A 1961 study found that "only 15.8 percent of all FSOs had spent more than six years in any region and that only 32 percent were in any one part of the world more than three years."[13]

The department also needs to change the texture of its reporting. FSOs currently do laudatory "think pieces" but do less well on operational reporting. Much of this arises from FSOs who do not understand the decision-making climate into which their reports are fed. FSOs who have been seconded to decision-making units write much more usable field reports than those who have always been in the field. Also, there are some bureau assignments which would add valuable depth and breadth to an FSO but which tend to be seen as harmful to one's career development. The Bureau of Intelligence and Research (INR) and the Bureau of Economics and Business Affairs (EB) are both seen as assignments which do not further one's career, but they are assignments which would provide significant additional insight to FSOs.

THE DEPARTMENT OF DEFENSE

Any consideration of the institutions which both shape and carry out U.S. foreign policy must deal with the largest and most expensive department in the federal system—the Department of Defense. In a sense, it is the responsibility of the Department of State to see that other nations have nothing to fight about when dealing with the United States, while it is the duty of the Department of Defense to see that they have too much to fight against.

Organization

The Department of Defense was created through the Unification Act of 1947 out of two existing departments—the Department of War and the Department of Navy. The department was born out of a complex set of compromises between existing departments, military services, and congressional interests. It continues to be marked by interservice rivalries and intense public and private competition for its huge congressionally authorized budget. It is no coincidence that "the Department of Defense, which was supposed to be the nation's sword, looked more like a pitchfork."[14]

With its unique intermixing of civilian and military personnel, the Department of Defense is the most complex of all government organizations. One side of the department is called the Office of the Secretary of Defense (OSD) and is predominantly civilian while the other side, the Military Departments, is predominantly military. While the OSD is fairly integrated, the Military Departments continue to be marked by intense interservice rivalries.

The Military Departments consist of the Department of the Army, the Department of the Navy, and the Department of the Air Force. Theoretically, this is all coordinated by the Joint Chiefs of Staff (JCS), an organization made up of the operating chief of each military department, including the Commandant of the Marine Corps. The Joint Chiefs of Staff has under its command the two Specified Commands (within one military department but under the JCS) and the eight Unified Commands (made up of all military departments).

Many reorganizations since 1949 have attempted to strengthen the authorities of the secretary of defense over the service chiefs. One way of achieving this goal has been to increase greatly the number of civilian personnel and the number of offices within the OSD. In order to avoid complete duplication of functions, these new offices have tended to deal more with strategic planning than with military tactics. It is this which has blurred the traditional distinctions between State and Defense and which warrants including the Department of Defense in a foreign policy textbook.

Some of these new civilian-dominated agencies, particularly the Office of International Security Affairs (ISA), function suspiciously like a "State Department." ISA, in fact, looks much like a miniature State Department with its geographical and functional subsections. Although its mandate is to work with military matters which impinge on foreign policy, in today's world that is a very fuzzy boundary.[15] During the years when Vietnam dominated U.S. foreign policy, ISA's more precise and succinct reports were favored over what were seen as fuzzy and pessimistic reports of State and CIA. Under President Reagan, ISA was divided into two units creating even more duplication.

The Role of Personality

The secretary of defense is a statutory member of the National Security Council and, as such, should participate in the coordination of all U.S. national security policy. The degree to which that occurs varies according to the personal relationships between the members of the council and the forcefulness and effectiveness of the secretaries. The secretaries of defense under President Truman were concerned either with personal problems (Forrestall) or with the problems inherent in forging a new single department and were dominated by Truman's strong secretaries of state, George C. Marshall and Dean Acheson. President Eisenhower's secretary of state, John Foster Dulles, also eclipsed the secretary of defense. In contrast, the administration of President Kennedy was marked by a secretary of state, Dean Rusk, who neither dominated the process nor enjoyed the political infighting associated with it. Thus, President Kennedy's secretary of defense, Robert McNamara, and his staff of young economists known as "whiz kids," prevailed over the State Department throughout the Kennedy and Johnson administrations. In fact, McNamara played an increasingly important role under President Johnson who was less interested in foreign affairs than his predecessor.

During the years of Presidents Nixon and Ford, the foreign policy process was dominated by Kissinger, first as national security affairs adviser and then as secretary of state. While assessments of Kissinger vary, few doubt that he was the central source of foreign affairs and national security ideas and policies.[16] President Carter's defense secretary, Harold Brown, had been secretary of the Air Force under McNamara. His experience and relationship with the president, combined with secretaries of state who did not take well to the "barracuda politics" of Washington D.C., contributed to his strong role during the Carter administration.

President Reagan's series of less well-known and less forceful national security affairs advisers led to debilitating infighting between his secretaries of defense and his secretaries of state. With Haig's resignation and the appointment of George Shultz as secretary of state, Secretary of Defense Weinberger's influence initially increased, but Secretary of State Shultz gradually came to be the dominant foreign policy adviser to the president. That was particularly the case when Secretary of Defense Weinberger resigned and national security affairs adviser Frank Carlucci was made secretary of defense in 1987.[17]

President Bush appointed a strong secretary of state and a secretary of defense who was known as a competent "team player." This arrangement, as mentioned earlier, has diminished the role of the NSC as an initiator of foreign policy and has strengthened the role of the secretary of state. In many respects, the Bush administration, NSC functioned more coherently as a team than did other previous NSC systems.

Beyond Personality

The ability of the Department of Defense to influence foreign policy goes beyond membership on the NSC and strong personalities, however, since other foreign policy actors may enjoy those same endowments. The Department of Defense also enjoys (1) the constitutional role to defend the nation, (2) an effective lobbying system, and (3) a large network of defense-related industries and other support groups which can play a major role in national security affairs.

1. No one should underestimate the seriousness of the constitutional imperative to "provide for the common defence." Where military matters are concerned, many Americans listen very carefully when leading military officers speak. Whether this is justified or not is debatable. Some argue that asking military officials foreign policy questions is like asking a barber whether or not one needs a haircut—the answer is likely to be self-serving. Nevertheless, among other foreign policy officials, the counsel of leading military organizations is taken very seriously, though not always followed.

This influence has led to some suggestions that the military has a disproportionate influence in the foreign policy process. Often, these suggestions stem from specific incidents and cannot be generalized. Richard Betts has concluded that military and civilian foreign policy advisers differ on details of the application of military force but not on whether or not it should be used.[18]

2. The ability of the Department of Defense and its supporters to influence other policy-making bodies, particularly Congress, is very impressive. Military lobbyists rank alongside the National Rifle Association and the Jewish lobby in terms of effectiveness. Few other lobby groups have such a vast supply of personnel and money to devote to this task.

Technically, government agencies are not allowed to lobby Congress. However, the Office of the Assistant Secretary of Defense for Legislative Affairs does much more than merely respond to questions from Capitol Hill. Some of the very brightest military officers work in congressional liaison offices and provide detailed information on any defense-related issue more quickly and more accurately than nearly any other source. The offices also offer on-site investigations on any U.S. defense facility in the world and provide excellent exposure to military personnel and defense-related civilians in congressional districts. All of this is quite legal and there are few congressional staffers or their principals, especially those on defense-related committees, who have not benefitted from (or been coopted by) the information and experiences provided by these legislative liaison offices. The difference between this and lobbying is not very clear.

3. Finally, the financial and political impact of the vast network of defense and defense-related contractors and suppliers gives the Department of Defense considerable foreign policy influence. Although much has been written about what President Eisenhower once called "the military industrial complex," the early literature was too simplistic and not very objective. One

foreign observer commented, "we know that there is no headquarters of the military-industrial complex where they make decisions that they then dictate to the White House, [but, there is a] military-industrial-scientific complex, which is very active in pushing its priorities."[19] That is probably an accurate assessment.

This differs from other lobbying efforts in that the billions of federal dollars spent on defense allows disproportionate amounts to be channeled into advertising, lobbying, and public relations. If American military spending could be isolated and treated as a separate budget, it would rank as the thirteenth largest nation-state in the world.[20]

In 1985, just four out of the scores of defense contractors spent $31 million on advertising alone. This money, as well as the expenditures of the over fifty Political Action Committees (PACs) supported by defense-related industries ($7.2 million in 1984), is all added into the fees charged to the government for developing and delivering weapons systems.[21] In congressional testimony in 1985, Admiral James D. Watkins, then Chief of Naval Operations, said plaintively:

> Today, our big contractors average over four times as much profit as a percentage of assets on their defense contracts as on their commercial contracts. Why is that? What is it in the defense business that would warrant four times the percentage of profit? There is nothing. We are one of the most reliable, prompt-paying customers the world has ever seen. So why do we award that kind of benefit? There is no reason.[22]

The Future of the Department of Defense

Perhaps the most serious challenge to the Department of Defense is to rationalize its force structure for the twenty-first century. Whether or not this can be accomplished under the existing military department structure is problematic. A critical issue associated with the process begun by the National Security Act of 1947 is the relationship between OSD, the CINCs, and the chairman of the Joint Chiefs of Staff, on the one hand, and the separate services, on the other. Again, the trend has clearly favored the civilian authority of OSD relative to the service secretaries and the military authority of the chairman of the Joint Chiefs of Staff and the CINCs relative to the service chiefs of staff. It is true that under President Reagan the service secretaries, especially the Navy secretary, exerted a greater authority than has been seen in the recent past and that the service chiefs of staff continued to see the Chairman of the Joint Chiefs as first among equals. But what Congress came to see as the unwillingness of OSD to force strategic choices and concomitantly to impose programmatic and fiscal discipline on the services, caused it to force by legislative mandate and committee pressures the directive role of OSD. At the same time, the belief in Congress that a number of the military operations undertaken by the Reagan administration, such as in Grenada and the Libyan strikes, betrayed a lack of coordination and effectiveness, caused them to strengthen by legislation the chairman of the Joint Chiefs, the CINCs, and the joint elements of the Defense Department in general. All of this was enshrined in the Department of Defense Reorganization Act of 1986—the so-called Goldwater-Nichols bill.

The Goldwater-Nichols bill consolidated responsibility for certain functions of the military departments in the civilian service secretaries' offices—acquisition, auditing, comptroller, information management, inspector general, legislative affairs, public affairs, research and development (which in areas of military requirements and test and evaluation may be assigned by the service secretary to military headquarters staff). In turn, the bill strengthened OSD relative to the civilian secretariats and military departments in supervising defense agencies and field activities and in defining strategic, program, and budget guidance.

Moreover, the chairman of the JCS was designated as the principal military advisor to the president, the NSC, and the secretary of defense and will be assisted by a four-star vice chairman who will preside in the chairman's absence. Furthermore, the role of the joint staff was clearly strengthened in support of the chairman and his deputy. The staff's authority for education, assignments, and promotion throughout the military has been expanded. Clearly, the chairman is more than first among equals and the status of the joint element in DOD has been enhanced.

The legislation affirmed the CINCs' responsibility for fighting wars and program-related advice and strengthened their command and personnel authority. The legislation specifies that the operational chain of command, unless otherwise directed by the president, runs from the president to the secretary of defense to the unified and specified commanders, thus avoiding the charge of creating a General Staff by putting the chairman of the JCS, in the chain. However, communication between the president, the secretary of defense, and the CINCs is, as directed by the president, to run through the chairman who both assists the president and the secretary in their command responsibilities, including oversight, and serves as the spokesman for the CINCs, especially on their operational requirements. Clearly, the chairman is only a breath away from being in the actual chain of command. Again, practice will determine what this ultimately means.

In a diverse and interdependent world and in a bureaucratically divided government, the clear thrust is toward improving policy coordination and institutional integration. As in much else, however, the balance between the centrifugal and the centripetal forces will shape to a large degree the character of America's external responses in the decades ahead.

INTELLIGENCE AGENCIES

In any human endeavor, policies—the outcome of the decision-making process—are seldom any better than the information on which they are based. As Kenneth Boulding has said, "all behavior depends on the image."[23] That is, all human behavior is a function of the mental image forged through perception and cognition of the behavioral environment and that image is built through the accumulation of information.

It is the critical function of the intelligence agencies to provide information about all kinds of global matters to decision-makers. Foreign policy made in the absence of this information is like a central heating system with a faulty thermostat—that is, it receives only limited feedback from its operating environment and is unable to assess the relevance of its policies. It is like a furnace or air conditioner not knowing whether it is too hot or too cold in the area it is supposed to make comfortable.

The Intelligence Process

The intelligence process begins when foreign policy decision-makers express a need to know something about the foreign policy environment. Although this sounds very simple, it is in fact quite complicated. There are hundreds of foreign policy decision-makers with competing (if not conflicting) geographical and functional responsibilities, each wanting to know something immediately about a different aspect of the international environment but, at times, not quite sure what it is they need to know about it. This results in severe competition between decision-makers to place the information they need to know higher on intelligence priority lists (called National Intelligence Topics) than the information required by others. In a theoretical world of unlimited resources this would not be a problem. But in the real world of scarce resources, the first foreign policy/intelligence battle is the fight to have the information you want ranked high on an intelligence priority list.

Once a priority list is established, the optimum way to collect the information must be set. That is, the intelligence community must decide what sorts of collection techniques (electronic, human, satellite, etc.) are best suited to provide the needed information and which agency can best collect it.

After collection, the information must be evaluated. A fundamental axiom of all intelligence agencies is that facts do not speak for themselves. Even the most apparently self-evident information must be subjected to analysis in order to determine its full meaning and importance. This evaluation is a continual process beginning with the collector who must decide on what to report, on through the formal analytical stage where all bits of information must be viewed as part of a whole, and ending with the intelligence consumer, the policy-maker, who must decide what to read, believe, and act upon.

The analytical process involves such disparate activities as translating, reducing to essentials, collating and processing, evaluating, interpreting, explaining, and, finally, turning the raw intelligence into finished products. The information is then distributed to the consumers of the intelligence process—the decision-makers—and used by them to assess various foreign policy options.

In practice, this ideal process suffers from a number of maladies. To begin with, there are hundreds of policy-makers who continually request timely, accurate, and complete intelligence information. These range from the president, the NSC, and Congress to scores of foreign policy officials and, in some cases, even to private defense contractors. Secondly, these policy-makers are not clear about precisely what it is they need to know. What they think they need to know may turn out to be quite different from what they ultimately find out they really need to know or, as is more often the case, needed to know, since the event is usually history before they come to this knowledge.

For example, few policy-makers wanted to know much about Iran until there was a fundamentalist revolution and an anti-American regime came into power. Central America was low on the priority list until some American officials decided it was being "communized." For years, hundreds of foreign policy decision-makers wanted to know all about Soviet military capabilities but frequently were quite unaware of more significant developments in Soviet ethnic, energy, economic, or agriculture problems. That is why many decision-makers were surprised at the demise of the Soviet Union. Not knowing what it is one needs to know is a frequent human failing.

Secondly, the intelligence cycle just described is not really a cycle. In reality, the distinction between a policy-maker and an intelligence provider is not clear at all. Policy and intelligence fuse together just as the institutions that represent them are inseparable. The NSC, for example, is both a consumer and a provider of intelligence and the same is true at lower operational levels throughout the CIA, the military, and the foreign policy establishment. Thus, the separation between intelligence provider and intelligence consumer, which is supposed to enhance objectivity, does not exist, at least as usually described.

Thirdly, the information policy-makers really need to know is often not available to anyone, not even the targets of the intelligence operations themselves. All nations like to impute to other states a degree of rational and hierarchical decision-making and planning which they do not have themselves and which, if the truth were known, other states probably do not have either. Thus, it is difficult to answer the question most frequently asked by decision-makers, "What are they [Russians, Chinese, Serbians, terrorists, etc.] going to do?" Intentions are much more difficult, if not impossible, to determine than are capabilities, yet they are the most highly desired of all intelligence data. Initially, for example, policy-makers needed to know the numbers and characteristics of Soviet missiles, but ultimately they needed to know what the Kremlin planned to do with those missiles. The truth is that even the Kremlin itself did not know the answer to that question since it depended so much on other external and internal developments.

The entire analytical process is fraught with difficulties. Often varied bits of intelligence do not make a single picture. Incomplete intelligence, deliberately placed false information, an overwhelming volume of information, or poorly trained or careless analysts all make clear and whole intelligence pictures very rare.

Finally, serious problems arise in the intelligence process when the information gets back to those who requested it. By then their need to know may have waned or they may have decided that the information provided is not precisely what they had in mind. Or even worse, new sets of policy-makers may be in office who wonder why their predecessors wanted to know some arcane bit of information, the relevance of which completely escapes them. Unfortunately, intelligence consumers usually value intelligence information on the basis of brevity, timeliness, and accuracy, all too often in that order.

Structure

The intelligence community has been reorganized many times to enhance coordination and prevent unnecessary duplication and redundancy. The National Security Act of 1947, among other things, established the Central Intelligence Agency to be, as the name suggests, the central or coordinating body among all intelligence agencies. The head of the CIA is called the Director of Central Intelligence (DCI) and acts as the intelligence advisor to the NSC and the president. But the DCI has command authority only over the CIA which is just one component of the intelligence community.

In order to facilitate coordination over the entire community, the Intelligence Community Staff (ICS) was created in 1972 and the DCI was formally designated as head of the ICS. Through the ICS, the DCI has some authority to coordinate the allocation of intelligence resources, to supervise the analytical process, and to direct the intelligence product. Nevertheless, the other principal intelligence agencies, the National Security Agency (NSA) and the Defense Intelligence Agency (DIA), fall under the command authority of the Department of Defense. In fact, 85 percent of all intelligence, measured in terms of budget funds, lies within the Department of Defense. This means that, although the DCI has some authority over NSA and DIA, he does not have traditional command authority over them. Moreover, since the DCI is head of both the CIA and the intelligence community, he is not seen as an objective arbiter in the normal bureaucratic competition.

Central Intelligence Agency

Inheriting the remnants of the wartime Office of Strategic Services (OSS), the CIA was created in 1947 to advise the NSC on all intelligence matters and to correlate all national intelligence activities. It is divided into four sections: (1) an operational section (called the Directorate of Operations or the Clandestine Services), (2) an analytical section (the Directorate of Intelligence), (3) a section concerned with scientific and technological matters (the Directorate of Science and Technology), and (4) an administrative section (the Directorate of Administration).

Simply stated, the CIA does three things: (1) it collects information from a wide variety of sources, (2) it analyzes that information and provides a wide variety of intelligence products to a large array of users, and (3) it maintains, and on occasion uses, covert action capabilities to alter the course of political developments in the world. Each of these functions will be discussed below.

1. Collection Intelligence targets fall into one of three categories: (1) the capabilities of other actors—what means they possess to effect developments in a world of competing states, (2) the objectives of other actors—how they plan or wish to utilize those capabilities, and (3) the effects of the policies of one's own nation in the international environment. Information in the first category is the easiest to collect. Technical advances in various surveillance methods have greatly eased the burden of human collectors in finding out about the capabilities of other nations. Seventy-five percent of all intelligence is now classified as technical intelligence, that is, it is intelligence collected through some kind of electronic, satellite, infrared, or other sophisticated technical means.

Information in the other two categories is much more difficult to gather. To know the real objectives of other actors requires human sources placed literally within the policy-making circles of those groups. And to predict the effects of one's own policies requires, among other things, forecasting techniques generally scarce among mortals.

Human intelligence is quite a different matter. This information is collected through a variety of ways, but the CIA will most commonly send an intelligence officer abroad whose task is to identify and recruit foreign nationals who are willing and able to provide information to the United States. Most intelligence officers will be assigned to an embassy in a foreign nation and given some kind of official cover position to publicly justify their presence. For example, a CIA officer may appear on embassy records as a State Department employee.[24] This legitimizes contacting nationals of that nation and provides diplomatic protection to the intelligence officer. Generally, foreign nationals who become agents managed by CIA case officers do so for ideological or financial reasons.[25]

Other CIA officers may be given nonofficial, private sector cover positions and use their contacts to recruit foreign nationals as agents. These CIA officers are said to be in "deep cover"; that is, they have no apparent connection with the U.S. government. In either case, the desired outcome is the same—information is collected from foreign nationals who are in a position to provide it.

CIA officers under official cover who are "caught" managing agents can, at worst, be declared *persona non grata* and asked to leave a country. Those under nonofficial cover can be dealt with under the laws of the nations in which they were caught since they do not have diplomatic protection.

Much has been written about the legality or illegality of this kind of intelligence collecting, but it is really quite simple. First, the domestic laws of the collecting nation always permit (either expressly in statutes which create such agencies or tacitly through the existence of them) the sending of their own personnel abroad for such purposes. The nation recruits them, pays them, protects them, and provides for their retirement. Secondly, positive international law (bilateral and multilateral treaty obligations between states) is generally silent or permissive on the subject of espionage. A few treaties even mention and condone the clandestine collection of technical information. For example, some arms control agreements between the U.S. and the former Soviet Union specifically condone the collection of information about strategic arms needed for verification purposes.[26] Customary international law (traditional and accepted patterns of international interactions) is ambiguous on the subject—most authors view the ubiquity of spying as evidence of its legitimacy while a few view spying as illegal under virtually any circumstances.[27] Thirdly, the laws of all nations prohibit their own citizens from revealing state secrets to other nations. In short, it is legal under the laws of one's own nation to be sent abroad to persuade citizens of other nations to do what their own laws prohibit and international law is either silent or permissive on the subject.

2. Analysis While clandestine collection and covert action receive the lion's share of publicity, the Directorate of Intelligence performs what are perhaps the most critical and significant functions in the intelligence process—analysis and production.[28]

The sheer volume of raw information which comes to CIA analysts, virtually daily, is staggering. It requires an immediate selecting and sorting into related categories and then prioritizing into material which must be viewed immediately or material which can be discarded or saved to be viewed at a later time. Much of this is done under considerable time pressures (policymakers always want the information immediately) and done in an environment where the word "crisis" is used frequently, sometimes even fairly. This is not an easy task. Many headline-grabbing intelligence failures result not from collection problems but rather from inadequacies in the analytic process. Moreover, "the range of issues is breathtaking—from strategic weapons to food supplies, epidemiology to space, water and climate to Third World political instability, mineral and energy resources to international finance, Soviet laser weapons to remote tribal demographics, chemical and biological weapons proliferation to commodity supplies, and many, many more."[29]

All of the forces which prevent any ordinary person from correctly perceiving, understanding, and acting intelligently on everyday information are present in the analytic process in addition to the obvious problems of urgency and significance. Some of these problems are inherent in the human act of interpreting the world around us, others are caused by the analytical process itself, and, finally, some problems occur because of the nature of the information being analyzed.

1. In the first category are all of those potential problems which can occur in the processes of human perception and cognition: existing mental images screen out nonconforming perceptions, pressures to conform to prevailing understandings cause distortions (either because of the unwillingness to challenge prevailing understandings or because of the overeagerness to disprove them), improper and faulty analytical methods, inadequate training (intellectual, methodological, and linguistic) of analysts, or being buried with too much raw information or starved with not enough. All of these are problems common to anyone who interacts in a human environment.[30]

2. In the next category are problems which occur in any decision-making process: personal, business, industrial, etc. It is not easy to challenge old policies and the assumptions on which they are based. Preferences for existing policies (either because they are good policies or because they are the policies of one's superior) can skew the interpretation of new data. Sometimes the desire to please one's superiors is virtually unconscious; other times it is blatant. In the intelligence profession, sharing the ideological preferences of senior policy-makers enhances the tendency to feed them selective information which supports their visions of the world.

As mentioned earlier, analysts are always frustrated by policy-maker's desires to know the intentions of other states—something that the other states themselves may not know. Policy-makers and analysts alike must come to understand that the power of a state is not merely the mobilized capabilities of that government, but the strength and quality of the political, economic, and social base from which that power arises.

3. Finally, some problems are unique to the intelligence process. The data being analyzed is often about nations and groups whose intentions may be quite hostile to U.S. interests. No single factor skews perceptions more consistently and dramatically than does the assumption of hostility. Information about a hostile group or nation will almost automatically cause that information to be seen in its worst light. Sometimes the available information may be meant to deceive or discredit an analyst. Analysts also must work under severe restrictions of compartmentation (a security technique which limits potential damage of a compromised collection system by restricting all infor-

mation from that system to a specified compartment) and classification. These may result in corroboratory information being available to other analysts, but not to the one who needs it.[31]

Of course, the most fragile link in the intelligence process occurs after the collection, analysis, and production stages are complete. It occurs when senior policy-makers decide which of the large array of intelligence products they will read, believe, and act upon.

3. Covert Activities The National Security Act of 1947 also states that the CIA, under the direction of the NSC, shall "perform such other functions and duties related to intelligence affecting the national security as the National Security Council may from time to time direct." Subsequent executive orders have confirmed and defined this general statement which acknowledges CIA authority to undertake what is commonly called "covert actions" or, to use the more recent term, "special activities."[32]

Covert action is U.S. government-sponsored activities to prevent an adverse development (or enhance the likelihood of a desired development) in a foreign nation while at the same time disguising any U.S. involvement. Some covert activities are very spectacular while others are quite mundane. We know more about efforts that failed than we do about the successful ones which, by definition, have remained quiet. Moreover, it is difficult to distinguish between successful and unsuccessful operations since an apparently successful covert action which keeps an unpopular but friendly government in power may guarantee the eventual rise of an anti-American government twenty or thirty years in the future.[33]

In 1961, President Eisenhower created a blue ribbon panel to review foreign intelligence matters, including covert actions. "We have been unable to conclude," they reported, "that, on balance, all of the covert action programs undertaken by the CIA up to this time have been worth the risk or the great expenditure of manpower, money and other resources involved."[34] One writer argues that there have been no successful cases of covert (paramilitary) action in the history of the CIA.[35] This may be an example, however, of the principle that successful cases remain unknown to scholars or the public while unsuccessful cases are publicized widely.

Spectacular covert actions usually involve (1) significant military or financial intervention to embarrass, destabilize, or overthrow an unfriendly government (China [1950s], Cuba [1960s], Iran [1953], Guatemala [1954], and Indonesia [1965], for example), (2) military or financial aid to support a friendly government (Philippines [1950s], Brazil [early 1960s], Vietnam [1950-73], Congo [early 1960s], and Bolivia [1960s], for example), (3) military or financial support and aid to friendly insurgents in a domestic civil war or insurgency (Afghanistan [1980s], Nicaragua [1980s], and Angola [mid-1970s], for example), or (4) financial or political assistance to friendly factions in domestic political contests (Chile [1960s], Greece [1964-74], and Italy [1947-48], for example).[36]

Less spectacular intervention usually involves some kind of financial or political support to friendly political parties, labor groups, popular movements, media, etc. in foreign nations where the democratic process is generally intact but under siege from antidemocratic forces.

The use of covert activities to alter developments in other nations is a singularly dangerous foreign policy tool which must be used very sparingly. In fact, in the absence of similar activities by other nations, it would be easy to argue that, at least in peacetime, the United States should refrain completely from any covert actions.[37] Unfortunately, given the anarchic nature of the international environment, other nations, as well as the United States, engage in these kinds of special activities, thus justifying the covert actions of others.

Six criteria, however, ought to be met before the United States engages in covert actions.

1. The desired goal must be essential to U.S. national interests. Covert actions to accomplish ends which are not absolutely necessary in order to protect U.S. national security interests need to be discouraged. Both executive branch guidelines and the requirement that proposed covert actions must be reported to the two intelligence committees of Congress help to meet this criterion, but constant oversight is necessary to see that the reporting requirements are being met. "Covert action should never become . . . a routine instrument of foreign policy."[38] Few investigators who have examined the record of covert action conclude that the United States should disband all covert action capabilities. Most, however, urge that covert action be used rarely, carefully, and only when essential.

2. The proposed activity must be feasible. It must involve, at the inception of the strategy, available resources which would not be jeopardized by potential public knowledge of the activity or by reasonably anticipated changes in the U.S. domestic political environment.

3. Covert action must be the best, if not the only, means to accomplish the desired goal. All too often policy-makers have turned to covert action, not because it was the best way to accomplish a task, but because it was seen as the most secret and, therefore, the easiest way. As has been pointed out, senior foreign policy-makers often "mistake secrecy for coherence."[39] The prospect of secrecy seduces national leaders into preferring covert action to overt diplomatic or military efforts. They believe that, even if unsuccessful, the U.S. role will be masked. This has proved to be a very foolish assumption.

It is illustrative to review the funding of Radio Free Europe and other such clandestine broadcasting networks in light of this criterion. U.S. policy-makers were alarmed when American clandestine support of these activities was disclosed. Yet, after public disclosure brought covert government aid to an end, open congressional appropriations allowed these broadcasts to the then

Communist bloc nations to continue virtually unchanged. Those who listened to the broadcast probably suspected they were U.S. government supported all along anyway. Often, covert action is chosen primarily because it is hoped it will keep the American public from knowing what is going on.

4. Approval procedures must be spelled out clearly and must require the written approval of senior officials. This is now the case under both executive and congressional guidelines and laws but the Iran-Contra affair revelations in 1987 gave evidence that the procedures were not always followed. It is imperative that findings of essentiality be signed by senior policy-makers. The most intrusive and potentially dangerous of all government foreign policy tools, covert action, should not be authorized by word-of-mouth, by low level officials nor, even worse, by operators in the field.

5. The degree of military force, intrusiveness, and deception must be commensurate with the nature of the threat. The American public will usually support such activities if that is the case. They will not support them if massive clandestine efforts appear to be in response to minor irritants or embarrassments.

6. All covert actions, even those successfully carried out in complete secrecy, must be able to stand the light of public awareness eventually—they must merit widespread domestic support even though the public is not immediately aware of them. Policy-makers must ask themselves continually, "When this action is exposed, will it have sufficient political support to justify it?"[40] When the CIA placed mines in a Nicaraguan harbor in April 1984, it failed to meet this criterion. When the act was revealed, widespread negative reaction from the American public not only stopped the activity but caused considerable embarrassment to the Reagan administration. And to use a contrasting, although much older, example, when the CIA secretly acted to prevent a communist victory in the 1948 Italian elections, the American public was in support of that broad policy objective. As a former chief-of-staff of the Senate Foreign Relations Committee has written:

> Covert Action is not appropriate when its objective is controversial within the US—or would be if people knew about it. In this circumstance, it is worse than inappropriate, it is subversive.[41]

These criteria are not meant to stifle all proposed covert actions. Many of these criteria exist already in one form or another and yet covert actions have continued. Treverton argues that:

> Even now, not every covert action is controversial. For the 40 or so covert actions under way in the mid-1980's, at least half had been the subject of some press account. Yet only several were controversial enough that the original leaks developed into continuing stories. Most

of the rest were open secrets, more unacknowledged than unknown; they were so because most members of Congress thought they made sense, as did most Americans who knew or thought about them—and, no doubt, most of the journalists who reported them.[42]

National Security Agency

The NSA is one of the more shadowy agencies which make up the U.S. intelligence community.[43] In very general terms, the mission of NSA is to protect all U.S. government classified communications and to collect and attempt to read all such communications and transmissions of other governments.

Popular press accounts describe this as a massive effort to eavesdrop on as many critical communication links of other governments as possible.[44] This involves the most sophisticated signals intelligence and cryptology in the world. A 1971 magazine claimed that the NSA operated "the most elaborate computer system anywhere in the world."[45] Today, it is even more elaborate, complex, and extensive. Publications detailing NSA's funding are always unofficial and highly speculative.[46] The only authoritative writing about NSA is that contained in the 1976 reports of the U.S. Senate. While not revealing dollar amounts, the Senate reported that NSA and the other intelligence units under the control of the Department of Defense (DIA and the intelligence branches of the three military services) consumed about 80 percent of the intelligence budget.

Of interest to students of the foreign policy process is the effect of this type of intelligence gathered by NSA. Information gathered through electronic surveillance, photographic surveillance, etc. is called technical intelligence, not because it is intelligence about technical matters but because it is collected through technical means. Like most intelligence this information is considered raw intelligence until it is analyzed, understood, and placed in a larger context. This later product is often called "finished intelligence."

The problem is that there is a variation of Gresham's Law in intelligence which states that raw, technical intelligence drives out finished intelligence. That is, the increasingly available raw intelligence collected through technical means tends to be seen as more immediate, more secret, more accurate, and more important than the same information after it has been turned into finished intelligence. What people say in secret conversations or communications tends to assume greater meaning than the larger context of the exchanges themselves. This is a dangerous tendency not only because of the vulnerability of technical intelligence to disinformation, but also because it assumes that communication between any set of individuals reflects, in fact, the totality of the policies and intentions of the governments for which those individuals work. Anyone who has seen the "inside" of any government's decision-making circles knows this is not true. A foreign intelligence service, for example, could have a hidden microphone on the president of the United States and still not know clearly what America was doing on the stage of world politics. How could they when the president himself or herself may not? The same is probably true of every bureaucratically large and technologically advanced nation.

According to existing practices, only the CIA is supposed to present finished intelligence to senior policy-makers; the NSA is limited to collecting technical intelligence and should not analyze it. In fact, this distinction cannot be maintained since it is impossible for information even to be selected and reported on without some kind of analysis taking place.

Other Intelligence Agencies

There are many other intelligence agencies which play a role in the foreign policy process, but only two of sufficient importance to be mentioned here. The Defense Intelligence Agency (DIA) was created in 1961 under the Office of the Secretary of Defense. It was meant to take over some of the work performed by the army, air force, and navy intelligence units (whose work was often seen as self-serving) and to allow greater control and correlation by the secretary of defense.

In fact, it has not reduced either the scope or size of any of the military service intelligence organizations although it has improved coordination. In its early years, DIA was seen as a fairly incompetent intruder on the intelligence scene, but in recent years the DIA intelligence product has gained greater respect.

The Department of State also has an intelligence arm called the Bureau of Intelligence and Research (INR). Small, underfunded, and more a consumer of intelligence than a collector, INR nevertheless produces some excellent intelligence products. In contrast to the general State Department practice of frequent changes in regional and country assignments, INR leaves people on desk assignments long enough for them to become veritable heavyweights within intelligence circles. INR's Morning Summary is often more preferred by policy-makers than either of the two CIA daily publications.[47]

The head of INR represents the secretary of state on intelligence community committees and acts as his chief intelligence adviser. INR is clearly a case in which money and size are not accurate indicators of significance.

Duplication of Intelligence Activities

With the CIA, NSA, DIA, INR, and other intelligence agencies all collecting, analyzing, and reporting on global developments, it is easy to understand why there is some duplication of efforts within the intelligence system. What is less easy to understand is how much duplication is necessary and how much is wasteful. Clearly, some duplication is necessary in intelligence collection. Neither individuals nor satellites are completely reliable and some corroborating redundancy is necessary. Duplication in the analytical process is less justifiable but quite common. There are several analytical shops located in the Washington D.C. area which are each doing essentially the same thing. For example, the CIA, DIA, NSA, the FBI, and military intelligence, all have offices analyzing information about international terrorist groups and producing finished products (papers, reports, bulletins, briefings, etc.) about those groups. In another domain, the CIA, DIA, and military intelligence all have offices analyzing information about military developments in hostile or potentially hostile nations. In fact, these offices spend a great deal of time arguing about the accuracy of their respective perceptions and judgments. In some community-wide intelligence reports, various means (footnotes, split columns, etc.) have been developed to reflect these different estimates. The ICS argues that each analytical center has areas of specialization and that there is not undue duplication. Observers who have been in each analytical center doubt that judgment.

After organizational efforts to end such duplication have run their course, the remaining redundancy is often justified on the basis (1) that it provides checks on errant analysis, (2) that it offers the president a wider menu of intelligence estimates, and (3) that the competition improves the overall intelligence product. None of these justifications is wholly true.

Rather than providing a check on potentially errant analysis, multiple analytical sources can create a demand for consensus. Senior intelligence officers place pressures on their junior officers to work out their differences with analysts in other offices but this can be interpreted as pressure to conform. Sometimes these pressures may result in better analyses, but at other times they result in sweeping unorthodox (but promising) analysts, new methodologies, and their analyses under the rug.

A wide choice of intelligence estimates may also be a disservice to a president. It forces a president to sort through a wide array of intelligence information of varying quality and accuracy and, in effect, to become his or her own intelligence analyst. For a president with a keen interest and enough time to do this, such a wide menu may be a good thing. President Kennedy preferred this style. For a president with neither the interest, the time, nor the ability to make these choices, it is a considerable disservice. It forces this kind of president (and there are several who fit this description) to make choices based more on the rhetoric and ideology of the competing analyses rather than on their accuracy.

Widespread duplication of the analytical effort also creates an almost inexorable drive towards "worst-case scenarios." This occurs when analysts array the range of possible event outcomes and then decide to put forth the worst possible case—that is, the most damaging series of events that could possibly occur.

The logic that drives this tendency is impeccable. Faced with competition from other analytical centers, no individual analyst or agency wants to be left with mud on their faces. That is, they do not want to be accused of predicting a benign future when in fact the future turns into a mess. Thus, the safe thing to do is to protect oneself by being on the pessimistic side. If things turn out better, one merely breaths a sigh of relief and says "at least we were prepared for the worst." If the worst comes to pass the analyst merely says, "I told you so."

In the absence of widespread competition, an analyst might be more willing to stick to moderate and statistically more likely interpretations and predictions. If something worse occurs, there are not too many people in the bureaucratic jungle waiting to dance on your grave.

But in the presence of competition there is a strong urge to protect oneself by projecting worst-case scenarios. This results in community-wide worst-case projections and interpretations which, in themselves, turn into self-fulfilling prophecies.[48] Policies based on these worst-case scenarios have a way of evoking counterpolicies from other nations which then appear to justify the original bleak analysis. This phenomenon operates not only with predictions about future developments but also when analysts must interpret the meaning of ambiguous data—there is an inexorable urge towards worst-case interpretations. There is an enormous amount of pessimism built into the analytical process.

FOREIGN ECONOMIC POLICY INSTITUTIONS

U.S. foreign economic policy is partially shaped and conducted by a wide variety of executive branch agencies and departments. There are over sixty executive agencies or departments involved in the process, including: the U.S. Trade Representative (USTR), the Department of Commerce, the Department of the Treasury, the State Department, the Department of Agriculture, the Council of Economic Advisers, the National Security Council, and the International Trade Commission. Furthermore, depending on the issue involved, the Defense Department, the Department of Justice, the Labor Department, the Interior Department or numerous other departments and agencies may play a role in the process.

As each executive unit competes for policies that reflect its own interests and the interests of its varying constituencies, the policy-making process becomes complex and usually inefficient. Furthermore, there are often several agencies involved in one certain policy or issue which, without coordination, often results in a disjointed process, making it difficult to pursue consistent and sound policies. Although the USTR has taken a role to coordinate the various agencies, it has seldom succeeded.

As foreign economic policy becomes increasingly important in a modern and interdependent world and as it is used not only to enhance the world economy, but also for political and strategic purposes, the United States must take greater strides to coordinate its institutional departments and agencies and to produce a long-term, sound, and consistent policy. This and other foreign economic-related issues, however, will be discussed in Chapters 12 and 13.

TOWARDS THE TWENTY-FIRST CENTURY

It should by now be clear that there is not a foreign policy of the United States—there are instead foreign policies, each pursued by some foreign policy agency, bureau, or department. And it is not uncommon for these policies to be contradictory.[49] In addition to the traditional foreign policy processes and institutions of the federal government just described, there are foreign policies of U.S.-based multinational corporations, foreign policies of state and even local governments, and foreign policies of a variety of interests groups. These policies are based on multiple sources of information or, occasionally, on no information at all. This process is supposed to be correlated by the president through the National Security Council system, but the success of that correlation varies with the skills and styles of different presidents and with the complex intermixture of the personalities of other senior foreign policy officials. Sometimes this process works quite well and other times it breaks down completely. Paradoxically, even effectively correlated policy may fail when it is unleashed on the global stage and, at times, even poorly correlated policy can be successful.

This process is played out on both the domestic and the global stage in a very competitive environment. While the most frequent metaphors used to describe this competition are chess, poker, prize fights, etc., perhaps more accurately it resembles a large billiards table with every player possessing his own cue stick and all shooting at will. Thus, foreign policy targets may change even after the cue ball has been struck and others may strike your target ball while you are sizing up the situation. The players continue to play not only because the stakes are significant, but because they really cannot get out of the game.

Several specific suggestions have been made throughout this chapter on ways to improve the foreign policy process in preparation for the twenty-first century. With the exception of the suggestion to make the secretary of state the president's national security affairs adviser and to abolish the NSC staff system, none of these suggestions would require major organizational overhauls. And even that proposal could be accomplished by changing existing laws. The rest would require merely the changing of procedures and operating principles.

But as is usually the case, the most significant changes must be made in the minds of the men and women who shape and conduct foreign policy and, even more importantly, in the minds of the American public. America is a much more mature nation than it was through the two world wars and through the conflicts in Korea and Vietnam. And the world in which it now acts is a vastly different world. All Americans must become even more aware of these changes. Other nations change, our own nation changes, and no nation can reach its full potential by choosing to ignore these changes.

The economic interdependence of the world is treated in other chapters of this book, but the world is also politically more interdependent than it has ever been. Political developments in far distant parts of the world can dramatically affect American society, and developments within the United States significantly affect not only the interests of other international actors but also the very foreign policy process itself. The next chapter will discuss some of the fundamental changes which are occurring within American society and culture that may have serious consequences for American foreign policy in the twenty-first century.

ENDNOTES

1. The consular function is not discussed here, but remains an important role performed by the foreign service.
2. Theodore C. Sorenson, "The President and the Secretary of State," *Foreign Affairs* 66 (Winter 1987/88): 238.
3. "The Foreign Service & the National Interest: A Conversation with Malcolm Toon," *Foreign Service Journal,* April 1982, 22-27.
4. Sorenson, "The President and Secretary of State," 235.
5. See correspondence from former Secretary of State Shultz in *Foreign Affairs* 66 (Winter 1987/88): 426.
6. Personal letter in possession of the authors.
7. Sorenson, "The President and Secretary of State," 239.
8. This phrase is from a preliminary document ("The Future Operational Context for Foreign Affairs") prepared by the Management Task Force—State 2000. This group was created in response to a March 24, 1992 letter from Secretary of State James Baker to Under Secretary for Management John F. W. Rogers.
9. Sorenson, "The President and the Secretary of State," 243.
10. Norman Cousins, "Uncluttering the Presidency," *The Christian Science Monitor,* 5 January 1989, 19.
11. Duncan L. Clarke presents a well-reasoned argument that the State Department cannot play the role we recommend it play in, "Why State Can't Lead," *Foreign Policy,* n.s. 66 (1987): 128-42. Clarke's points are all well taken, but, we believe, based on practices and procedures that can be changed.
12. U.S. Department of State, Under Secretary of State for Management, Management Task Force—State 2000, "Primary Research Questions," 13 July 1992, 1.

13. Barry M. Rubin, *Secrets of State: The State Department and the Struggle Over U.S. Foreign Policy* (New York: Oxford University Press, 1984), 84.
14. James MacGregor Burns, J. W. Peltason, and Thomas E. Cronin, *Government by the People*, 10th ed. (Englewood Cliffs, NJ: Prentice Hall, 1978), 456.
15. Appearing almost as an act of revenge, the State Department has a Bureau of Politico-Military Affairs to deal with that fuzzy area in which foreign policy impinges on military matters.
16. Marvin and Bernard Kalb in *Kissinger* (Boston: Little, Brown, 1974) give a fairly favorable assessment of Kissinger while retired Admiral Elmo R. Zumwalt, Jr. in *On Watch: A Memoir* (New York: Quadrangle/New York Times Book Co., 1976) is much more critical.
17. Caspar Weinberger, who was known as "Cap the Knife" for his budget cutting policies during his service in the Nixon administration, was knighted by the British government on his retirement in honor of his support of the British during the Falklands/Malvinas controversy. The British press then dubbed him, "Cap the Knight."
18. Richard K. Betts, *Soldiers, Statesmen, and Cold War Crises* (Cambridge, MA: Harvard University Press, 1977), 5.
19. Vitaly Churkin, quoted in *Newsweek (International Edition),* 14 December 1987, 10-11.
20. The Center for Defense Information, *The Defense Monitor,* 16 (No. 3 1987): 4.
21. *The Defense Monitor,* 16 (No. 3 1987): 4.
22. *The Defense Monitor,* 16 (No. 3 1987): 7.
23. Kenneth Boulding, *The Image: Knowledge in Life and Society* (Ann Arbor, MI: University of Michigan Press, 1961), 6.
24. This is a point of some irritation within the Foreign Service among those who resent having their status "tainted" by offering cover to some CIA officers. They believe it causes foreign nationals to view all Foreign Service officers as employees of the CIA.
25. Accurate and objective books on the techniques of clandestine intelligence collection, for obvious reasons, are not very plentiful. For a very critical view written by a former CIA employee who turned Marxist see Phillip Agee, *Inside the Company* (New York: Stonehill Publishing Co., 1975). Another book by a former employee, who remained loyal, is David A. Phillips, *The Night Watch* (New York: Atheneum, 1977). Halfway between is the book by another former employee, John Stockwell, *In Search of Enemies: A CIA Story* (New York: W. W. Norton and Co., 1978).
26. In order to avoid giving the impression that these treaty arrangements officially sanction this kind of espionage (which they do), the euphemism "NTM" is used frequently to refer to this activity. NTM stands for "national technical means" of collecting verification information.
27. Michael J. Barrett provides an excellent brief summary of the status of spying in international law in his "Honorable Espionage," *Journal of Defense and Diplomacy* 2 (February 1984): 19 ff. As Richard A. Falk says, "traditional international law is remarkably oblivious to the peacetime practice of espionage." (Falk is quoted by Barrett on page 19.) It is clear, however, that no spy can claim any special status under international law—that is, international law does not offer any protection to those involved in espionage other than that provided by their official cover positions.
28. The best discussion of the core of this process, what is called estimative intelligence, is found in Harold P. Ford, *Estimative Intelligence: The Purposes and Problems of National Intelligence Estimating* (Rev. ed. Lanham, MD: University Press of America, 1993). See especially Chapter 9.
29. Robert M. Gates, "The CIA and Foreign Policy," *Foreign Affairs* 66 (Winter 1987/88): 218.
30. The best discussion of how these problems occur in international politics is in Robert Jervis, *Perception and Misperception in International Politics* (Princeton, NJ: Princeton

University Press, 1976). His "What's Wrong with the Intelligence Process?" *The International Journal of Intelligence and Counterintelligence* 1 (Spring 1986): 28-41 also discusses some of the inherent limits of intelligence.

31. There is a growing body of literature which addresses the analytical problems discussed in the previous two paragraphs. Among others, see Richard K. Betts, "Analysis, War, and Decision: Why Intelligence Failures are Inevitable," *World Politics* 31 (October 1978): 61-89, Allen E. Goodman, "Dateline Langley: Fixing the Intelligence Mess," *Foreign Policy,* n.s. 57 (1984-85): 160-79, and the seminal work by Robert Jervis, *Perception and Misperception in International Politics.*

32. In the absence of legislation specifically authorizing the broad range of CIA activities suggested by the National Security Act of 1947 and specifying procedures under which these activities can be reviewed and conducted, Presidents Ford, Carter, and Reagan have issued executive orders to accomplish the same purposes. Respectively, these orders are numbered 11905, 12036, and 12333. Essentially they have the same effect as law but fail to provide stability and continuity since an executive order of one president may be rescinded by that of another. They also fail to bestow quite the same legitimacy as would stem from legislation. The Senate Select Committee on Intelligence, after working for several years to create an inclusive "charter" for all intelligence activities, abandoned the inclusive approach and passed a truncated version of a charter covering basic principles and procedures. See the National Security Act of 1980.

33. To some extent, this is what happened in Iran in 1953 when the CIA helped unseat Prime Minister Mohammed Mossadeq and returned the Shah to the throne. There followed twenty-five years of close cooperation between Iran and western oil firms, but no one knows to what degree the CIA-masterminded coup created a base for growing anti-Americanism which came to a head under the revolutionary government of Ayatollah Khomeini in 1979. The same argument could be made about the then "successful" CIA intervention in Guatemala in 1954 when a CIA-assisted Guatemalan army led by Colonel Carlos Castillo Armas overthrew a Guatemalan President not favored by the United States, Jacobo Arbenz Guzman. Did that involvement have any effect on a rising tide of anti-American feelings manifest in Central America over the next thirty years? For a slightly one-sided view of the Iran intervention see Kermit Roosevelt, *Countercoup: The Struggle for the Control of Iran* (New York: McGraw-Hill, 1979). For the Guatemalan intervention see Richard H. Immerman, *The CIA in Guatemala: The Foreign Policy of Intervention* (Austin: The University of Texas Press, 1982). The best summary of covert action as a tool of U.S. foreign policy is in Gregory F. Treverton, *Covert Action: The Limits of Intervention in the Postwar World* (New York: Basic Books, 1987).

34. The report is cited in Arthur Schlesinger, Jr., "A Democrat Looks at Foreign Policy," *Foreign Affairs* 66 (Winter 1987/88): 270.

35. Paul Kattenburg, "Dilemmas of Covert Action." Paper read at the Annual Meeting of the International Studies Association, Anaheim, CA, 22-25 March 1986.

36. The countries mentioned as examples under each category are drawn entirely from public media and scholarly writing and are not officially confirmed by U.S. government sources with the exception of the examples drawn from the publications of the Senate Select Committee to Study Governmental Operation with Respect to Intelligence Activities. This committee's *Covert Action in Chile,* Staff Report, 94th Congress, 1st Session, December, 1975 is particularly good. The ongoing publications of the congressional intelligence committees are also useful. For scholarly speculation the best record is Treverton, *Covert Action,* 1987.

37. In fact, the CIA resorts to covert activities relatively infrequently. According to the Deputy Director of the Agency, less than 3 percent of all CIA personnel are involved in covert activities and over 95 percent of the national intelligence budget is allocated to the collection and analysis of information. See Robert M. Gates, "The CIA and Foreign

Policy," *Foreign Affairs* 66 (Winter 1987/88): 216. These data are entirely accurate but just slightly misleading. The percentage of personnel involved in covert activities, for example, ought to be compared only with the percentage involved in analysis, not with other members of the clandestine corps who may become involved in covert activities when needed and who are continually involved in sensitive clandestine collection operations. Also, the budget percentage given includes all national intelligence operations, including very expensive collection techniques. Here again, the percentage of the CIA budget devoted to analysis would be a more interesting figure.

38. Schlesinger, "A Democrat Looks at Foreign Policy," 270.
39. Bert A. Rockman, "Mobilizing Political Support," in *National Security and the U.S. Constitution,* ed. George C. Edwards III and Wallace Earl Walker (Baltimore: The Johns Hopkins University Press, 1988), 27.
40. Treverton suggests in "Covert Action and Open Society," *Foreign Affairs* 65 (Summer 1987): 1010, that policy-makers should ask, "What happens if—or more likely, when—it becomes public?"
41. Pat M. Holt, "The Congressional Impetus to Tie a 'President's Hands,'" *The Christian Science Monitor,* 7 January 1987, 12.
42. Treverton, "Covert Action and Open Society," 1003.
43. Aside from the authoritative, but brief, mention of NSA in publications of the congressional committees, particularly in the six volumes published by the Senate Select Committee to Study Governmental Operation with Respect to Intelligence Activities in 1976, little is known about the NSA. Students must look to less authoritative works such as, James Bamford, *The Puzzle Palace: A Report on America's Most Secret Agency* (New York: Penguin Books, 1983).
44. See "Eavesdropping on the World's Secrets," *US News and World Report,* 26 June 1978, 45-49, for example.
45. See "The New Espionage American Style," *Newsweek,* 22 November 1971, 31.
46. See for example, Victor D. Marchetti and John D. Marks, *The CIA and the Cult of Intelligence* (New York: Alfred Knopf, 1974), 80.
47. Allan E. Goodman, "Does Intelligence Matter?" Paper prepared for the International Studies Association, Annual Convention, 22-25 March 1986, Anaheim, CA, 7.
48. In July 1988, the commander of the *USS Sides,* part of the *USS Vincennes* battle group in the Persian Gulf, suggested that the *Vincennes* might not have shot down the Iranian civil airliner had it not been for worst-case scenarios presented by military intelligence analysts. "All of us," he wrote, "were done a grave disservice by an intelligence system that covered itself by forecasting every possible worst-case scenario. Crews of ships reporting to the Middle East Force in the summer months were noticeably on edge" as a result. Cited in Stan A. Taylor and Theodore J. Ralston, "The Role of Intelligence in Crisis Management," in *Avoiding War: Problems of Crisis Management,* ed. Alexander George (Boulder, CO: Westview Press, 1991), 403.
49. Throughout the Balkan crisis in 1992, for example, the State Department would announce intentions to escalate the possibility of military intervention only to see the chairman of the Joint Chiefs of Staff, General Colin Powell, give an interview in which he announced that the U.S. had no interest in military intervention.

5

THE SOCIAL
AND CULTURAL
BASES OF U.S.
FOREIGN POLICY

While chapters 2, 3, and 4 dealt with constitutional and bureaucratic processes, this chapter addresses some of the important social and cultural forces which shape American foreign policy. We believe that these basic forces are becoming more diverse and that American society is becoming more fragmented. And, in a more diverse and fragmented society, we believe it is more difficult to define and articulate the national interests which a foreign policy should promote.[1]

We attempt to discuss in this chapter some fundamental social and cultural forces which influence both the public and policy-makers. We are interested in what gives rise to the values which define and articulate the national interest and which lead to specific foreign policies.

Setting foreign policy is a political process that occurs within a social setting.[2] To focus solely on the constitutional guidelines for decision-making or on the administrative and bureaucratic context in which the decisions are made ignores the very fabric of society and culture into which those processes are woven. This political process occurs when foreign policy leaders make choices which define both the goals and interests of America and the means to attain those goals in a global setting. Our argument is that the political processes which set foreign policies are shaped by these social and cultural forces. It is the resultant foreign policies that set standards by which relations with other nations become something more than random or accidental.

SOCIAL AND CULTURAL FORCES

Culture is deeply held, latent, generalized predispositions, conditions, and attitudes which shape the cognitive process. It consists of

> habits of mind and feeling, assumptions which precede beliefs
> and emotions which lie behind motions. Culture, in short, is the ideal-
> ized and generalized accumulation of the past, the abstraction lying
> behind government, religion, foreign policy and economic or
> military behavior.[3]

Society is a particular manifestation of culture. It is more changeable, more observable, and its structure is more easily defined, and, society is important to the study of foreign policy because "ultimately, foreign policy is a reflection of American society itself."[4] In some of his very influential writings, James Rosenau combines many of these variables into one category and calls them "those unique aspects of a society's history, capabilities, institutions, and values" and "those nongovernmental aspects of a society which influence its external behavior."[5] For our purposes, we will discuss the following aspects of the social and cultural milieu: the geographic and demo-graphic conditions of a nation, the national value system, the role of public opinion in articulating national interests, and the role of education in estab-lishing national values.

Geography

Foreign policy scholars are becoming increasingly interested in the relation-ship between geographical conditions and foreign policy.[6] And while this is not the place for a detailed discussion of a very complicated subject, both objective geographical conditions and perceptions of those conditions play a significant role in establishing both the ends and the means of foreign policy. Lest we be accused of geographic determinism, we hasten to add that the effects of geography change over time and that, in some cases, subjective perceptions of geographic conditions are as important as the objective condi-tions themselves. The changing values of certain geographic conditions have wrecked havoc with the foreign policy means and goals of many states. And some states have forged successful foreign policies in spite of adverse geo-graphical conditions.

Such variables as size, natural resources, topography, climate, and loca-tion are but a few of the geographical conditions which shape foreign policies. And the relationships between these geographical conditions and political power are complex. Size, for example, does not necessarily translate into power. Coupled with such other factors as highly developed communications and transportation systems, moderate climate, friendly topography, etc., a large land mass is significant and will enhance a state's power and influence its foreign policies. Without this convergence of other benign or favorable conditions, however, size may be detrimental to national power. In either case, the existence of these conditions becomes a fairly constant foundation which shapes foreign policy.

We must say "fairly constant" because the implications and perceptions of these geographical conditions change over time. And these changes affect foreign policies. British foreign policy, for example, was influenced significantly by its large and accessible coal deposits in a time when steam engines were used to drive the locomotives and ocean vessels which were so essential for economic development and world trade. When changing technology made steam power inefficient, British foreign policy had to chart new courses to reflect these changes. And as combustion engines became the primary source of energy worldwide, the foreign policies of oil rich, as well as oil deficient, states changed dramatically, as did the foreign policies of other states in relation to them. Should further technological developments make fossil fuel uneconomical, the national interests and subsequent foreign policies of the currently oil rich states would change precipitously.

Even the foreign policy effects of such geographical constants as insularity are altered by changing technology. The English Channel was seen by Hitler as offering considerable protection to his western front during World War II. Today, the channel would be little more than a temporary annoyance to a continental invasion.[7]

Geographical conditions influence foreign policy only as those conditions are perceived by the public. The English viewed insularity as a source of great protection up to World War II even though the island had been invaded successfully by Celts, Romans, Anglo-Saxons, Danes, and Normans over its history. On the other hand, American continentalism, even in an age of ICBMs, is probably a much stronger deterrent to invasion than military might and has not always been seen as such by the American people.

Clearly, U.S. foreign policy has been helped by favorable geographic conditions: the absence of overwhelming internal geographical obstacles made national unification possible; the presence of two ocean borders offered considerable external protection; the availability of relatively free land encouraged immigration and brought to America from other nations ambitious, industrious, and risk-taking peoples who cherished political freedom and economic opportunity; climate and other factors have given rise to a superlative agricultural system; and having only two land borders has kept America free of concern about land invasion, a luxury certainly not enjoyed by most European states.

In the twenty-first century, traditional geographic concerns (size, population, resources, etc.) will be less important than they have been in the past and new and different transnational geographic concerns will take their place. The newer problems of growing concern are, for example, industrial pollution and its effects on forest, rivers, estuaries, and animal life; the search for new supplies of culinary water (this could be a serious problem, particularly in the American West which is receiving the largest share of population growth and where there is already a shortage of groundwater); new and environmentally safe sources of energy; and acceptable means for waste disposal, a problem that has already crossed national borders.

Strategic resources, those defined as essential for national security, have attracted a lot of attention in recent years. In fact, in 1982 Secretary of State Haig talked of potential "resource wars" in which America might have to invade other countries merely to protect access to such resources. Two considerations, however, make this kind of talk virtually nothing but scare-mongering. First, the United States has stockpiled vast amounts of these resources to insure availability even in the face of changing supplies. Unfortunately, in an effort to make the current account balance look better, recent government actions have resulted in a depletion of some of these stockpiles. American foreign policy through the last decade of the twentieth century must pay careful attention to the stockpiling of strategic minerals.

Secondly, in most cases, the United States would be more damaged by a "resource war" than it would be by the loss of a particular, even strategic, resource. Carefully pursued foreign policies, domestic conservation, and increased research and development into alternative materials are all easier and more likely to succeed than are resource wars.[9]

There is one other geographical development which is likely to have profound effects on U.S. foreign policy in the twenty-first century. The United States has always been a Euro-centered society. By and large, up to World War II, the U.S. strategic world map placed Europe at the center of national security concerns. Even two major wars in Asia (Korea and Vietnam) did not alter that worldview significantly. In the twenty-first century all of Asia must be enveloped more thoughtfully into U.S. geopolitical thinking. This coincides with a westward shifting economic, demographic, industrial, and political center inside the United States. The American global strategic map must be broadened considerably, particularly to include the Pacific Basin. These areas will be as significant to U.S. national interests in the twenty-first century as Europe has been in the past. Millions of new Asian-Americans, and their descendants, will make this easier to do.

Demography

Demography is the study of populations and, as with geographic factors, has been of greater interest to students of international politics than to students of foreign policy. This can no longer be the case if we are to understand the social and cultural forces which drive foreign policy. Both global population developments as well as the changing texture of the domestic population are of interest to foreign policy analysts.

The widely heralded global "population explosion" has been much more complex than anticipated. In many industrialized states, low or negative population growth rates have caused concern for some. According to one demographer, falling birthrates in industrialized states may signal the "gradual decline in Western power as well as a growing number of economic problems. . . . Western values [may] become more and more meaningless in the future."[10] Even some developing states have made unpredicted progress in slowing population growth. On the other hand, some of the very poorest of the developing states still maintain population growth rates that cannot be sustained with available food and other resources.

In other words, the global population growth rate has not been as much of a problem as differential national and regional growth rates have been. Some parts of the world are nearly stable or are growing at very low rates while other parts are growing rapidly and are unable to provide basic services, food, education, and employment for their citizens. European states are growing at an average of .34 percent per year and will stabilize at zero population growth by the year 2010. It has been widely believed that North America was growing at 1.04 percent annually and would stabilize about 2030. However, more recent data suggest that the U.S. population will continue to grow up through the year 2050, largely as a result of immigration and the higher birthrate of immigrants.[11] China is growing at 1.5 percent per year and will stabilize about 2070, the rest of Asia with its 2.17 percent annual growth will not stabilize until 2085, South America at 2.38 percent per year will not achieve zero population growth until 2090, and Africa, growing at 3 percent per year will not stabilize until 2100. At that point, the population of the earth should be somewhere between 8 billion and 15 billion, depending of course on a number of other developments.

According to Daniel Bell, the much talked about population time bomb has fizzled somewhat at the global level but is still a serious problem when one considers differential growth rates between various countries, the increasing numbers of young people in developing societies, and the appearance of urban agglomerations, the very size of which will make certain cities virtually ungovernable in the twenty-first century.[12]

At the international level, the growing disparity between what are called the industrialized democracies and the developing countries continues to be a problem of major dimensions. In 1950 the industrial democracies accounted for just under 25 percent of the world's population, in 1993 they accounted for about 12 percent, and by the mid-twenty-first century they are projected to account for only 8 percent of the total global population. What the World Bank calls the "low income economies" of the world made up 53 percent of the total world populations in 1980, 58 percent in 1990, and are projected to be 62 percent of the world's population in 2025.[13]

This population growth rate in developing societies presents at least three serious challenges. The first is the need to produce or acquire sufficient food. "Each year 40 million people die from hunger and hunger-related diseases. This figure is equivalent to more than 300 Jumbo jet crashes a day with no survivors, almost half of the passengers being children."[14] This presents a foreign policy challenge which the United States must face in the twenty-first century and it also creates a condition which shapes U.S. foreign policy attitudes. American farmers must produce additional food, the government must find new and more efficient ways to share the American food surplus, the American people must become more sensitive to the food and nutrition needs of other societies, and, as we have learned in the case of Somalia, American forces may be necessary to insure the actual delivery of food. Much of this can only be done by working more cooperatively through the United Nations and other multilateral agencies.

Second, societies with rapidly growing populations must find better ways to educate their populations. Today, over 90 percent of the illiterate people in the world live in developing countries. In many of these nations, less than half of the children under sixteen are enrolled in schools. And the number of children under sixteen is growing faster than either schools or teachers can be produced. Even worse, those who could most efficiently teach literacy to their families, the females, are less literate than males. In Asia, male literacy is 56 percent while female literacy is 34 percent and in Africa the male/female literacy disparity is even greater—35 percent for males and 15 percent for females.

These data have profound implications for U.S. foreign policy since literacy and education are two of the most significant forces behind economic development. If increased economic opportunity is to be the cure for political instability, then education must be expanded for all. Current rates of population growth in many developing countries make this a difficult task. If the per capita income within developing nations does not grow faster than it has been growing, then perpetual political instability and localized crises of all kinds will be on the American foreign policy agenda throughout the twenty-first century.

Finally, developing societies are unable to provide employment for the rapidly growing number of fourteen- to sixteen-year-old children as they enter the labor force in increasing numbers each year. With slowly growing economies and rapidly increasing populations, the employment prospects for young people in developing societies is very bleak. Between 1988 and 2005, just under 2 billion children will enter the work force in developing societies. This is on top of the already tens of millions of unemployed adults in 1993.

For a brief glimpse of the challenge this might present to future U.S. foreign policy, one need only look at neighboring Mexico which is expected to have approximately 3.5 million unemployed persons by the year 2000.

This mass of humanity, usually crowded into urban slums of enormous size (32 percent of the people in developing countries live in slums and that figure is growing at a rate of 4.5 percent each year), most of them hungry and out of work, make an ideal breeding ground for political unrest and instability. Perhaps even more significant is the growing number of homeless people in every society. A UN Commission on Human Settlements reported in 1988 that "one billion people, a fifth of the world's population, are homeless or live in slums—and the number will rise to three billion within 12 years unless governments make a number of fundamental changes in their existing approach to the problem."[15] Illegal immigrants seeking employment opportunities and refugees fleeing political unrest created by these conditions are already significant domestic considerations for U.S. foreign policy and will become even more important in the future.

Most of these demographic developments will be played on the global stage. And while they will require carefully established and skillfully executed U.S. foreign policies in order to lessen global instability, it is to demographic developments within the United States that we must look to see the impact of changing social and cultural conditions on U.S. foreign policy. Here the changes are more subtle and their effects are more difficult to predict, but it is here that significant changes are occurring.

America has always been known as the melting pot—a nation of immigrants. Immigration to America grew steadily through the nineteenth century. Most believed it reached its peak in the first two decades of the twentieth century "when the annual inflow reached 1.3 million and accounted for 30 percent of the population growth."[16]   However, a Census Bureau report described as "striking and dramatic" released on December 3, 1992, indicated that in the six decades up to the year 2050, legal and illegal immigration could be as high as 1.4 million annually.[17] During the first wave of immigration, 90 percent of all immigrants came from Europe. Even up to 1950 almost 80 percent of all immigrants to America came from Europe and that dropped to 40 percent in the 1960s. In the 1980s, only 8 percent of all legal immigration came from Europe.

In 1989, however, 60 percent of all legal immigrants came from Latin America and there were over 22 million Hispanics living in the United States. That figure, of course, does not count the undocumented or illegal entrants. The Census Bureau's mid-range estimate is that there is an annual flow of approximately 200,000 undocumented entrants into the United States, most from Latin American countries. Some people estimate that there was a stock of around 10 to 12 million illegal immigrants living in the United States in the mid-1980s; however, the 1980 Census reported just over 2 million. The

Department of Justice claims that the number of illegal aliens rose from approximately 2 to 3.5 million in 1980 to between 4 or 5 million in 1987.[18]

All of this means that by the middle of the twenty-first century, "the [U.S.] population will include 82 million people who arrived in this country after 1991 or who were born in the United States of parents who did. This group of immigrants and their children will account for 21 percent of the population."[19] The effect of this on the fabric of American society is seen most immediately in those regions where much of the immigration has been centralized. Of the over 8 million immigrants who arrived in the United States during the decade of the 1980s, 11 percent made Los Angeles their home. This created a city in which "40 percent of all Angelenos were foreign born; 49.9 percent spoke a language other than English at home; [and] 35.3 percent spoke Spanish."[20] It has been estimated that the city of Los Angeles receives approximately 700,000 immigrants each year.[21]

All of these numbers will be added to the already more rapidly growing Hispanic and Asian segments of the American population to create a vastly changed texture of American society for the twenty-first century. According to the U.S. Census Bureau, from 1992 to 2050 the U.S. population will grow by 50.2 percent, the white (non-Hispanic) segment will grow by only 29.4 percent, the black segment by 93.8 percent, the Hispanic segment by 237.5 percent, and the Asian segment by 412.5 percent.[22]

This changed social texture will alter existing definitions of the national interest as America's traditional Euro-centered values are challenged by different values from other cultures of the world. American policies towards those nations from which an ever increasing number of Americans will have come, and to which they continue to have various ties and interests, must reflect those changes.[23] International trade, global capital flows, and tourism are but a few of the foreign policy concerns that are sensitive to these kinds of changing cultural and demographic conditions.

Early immigrants provided much of the energy and drive that was needed to propel America into major power status by the twentieth century. The new immigrants may well play that same role in the future. Sagging American productivity, a diminishing number of native-born Americans entering the annual job force, and a worsening dependency ratio (the number of people under sixteen and over sixty-five per 1,000 workers) may all combine to present opportunities to the new immigrants and their offspring as well as a source of growth to the nation.

The composition of American society is changing in another way—it is becoming an older society. In 1800 half of the population was under sixteen; in 1900 a third was under that age and by 2000 less than a fifth will be under sixteen. Viewed from the other end of the scale, in 1992 1 percent of the population was 85 or over while in the year 2050 4.6 percent will be 85 or older. In 1992 45,000 Americans were over 100 years old; in 2050 there will be a million centenarians.[24] This aging of America is heightened as those born during the baby boom period move out of the labor force between 2010 and 2030 and the much smaller number of persons born during what is called the baby dearth period move into the labor force. The resulting smaller labor force relative to the under sixteen/over sixty-five population will bring about an increase in federal expenditures for pensions and health care for the elderly that will expand to 13 percent of the total GNP, about twice current U.S. expenditures on defense.

Two areas account for most of this increase. The Social Security system paid out under $22 billion in 1965, $65 billion in 1975, $186 billion in 1985, and $230 billion in 1989. The trend is essentially the same for federal programs to support health care for the elderly—Medicare. Begun in 1966, two years later Medicare expenses grew to $4.6 billion, in 1975 this figure had risen to $12.9 billion, it reached $32.1 billion in 1980 and in 1989 was $102 billion.

The public policy issues these figures raise are important but will not be discussed here. However, a society in which a smaller number of nonwhite Americans are paying for the retirement benefits of an increasing number of aging white Americans is a society with a high potential for social cleavage. As one prominent economist says: "Young black and Hispanic workers may well question the equity of paying income and payroll taxes to support older people, particularly the dominant group of white retired workers, when they already have lower average incomes, higher poverty rates, and lower expectations that they eventually will receive equal program benefits."[25]

This has implications for U.S. foreign economic aid and trade policies as well as for a wide range of U.S. international involvements, especially national defense, which annually requires billions of dollars from American taxpayers. It may alter fundamentally the economic base of America as money for the care of the elderly drains available funds for rejuvenating the economic infrastructure and as care and service industries proliferate while basic industries wane. Successful American foreign policies over the last 200 years have depended more on economic strength than on military strength to a much greater degree than most realize. American military might has been but a particular manifestation of the true strength of the nation—its economic system. "Economic strength is central to foreign policy, both in terms of resources and in terms of . . . [how others see a nation]. Diplomatic skill cannot wholly compensate for material weakness."[26] It is difficult to imagine a future America playing both the military and the foreign aid roles it played in the twenty years after World War II in the face of these problems.

All of these demographic developments may contribute to increasing social and cultural fragmentation as Americans become more and more differentiated by age, gender, country of origin, and income levels. The Los Angeles riot of 1992, the most costly and violent urban riot in U.S. history, had a complex variety of racial overtones.

National Values

Just as behavior is shaped by perceptions, perceptions themselves are shaped by values. We use the word "values" to characterize the very basic ideas and ideals of a society, the abstract and deeply held notions on which a belief system is constructed. This foundation becomes the glue which holds a society together—its source of cohesion and legitimacy. Political leaders are able to fashion policies only if those policies are in harmony with these national values, which themselves are but an aggregation of individual values. Questions about American national interests can be answered only by reference to national values. It is these values which define the national interest and national security. Some have argued that while traditionally security was sought through an increase in military might, the 1970s ushered in an era in which security had to be expanded to include international economic considerations and that in the twenty-first century our definition of national security must be broadened to include international environmental, economic, and other concerns.[27]

These values are transmitted to subsequent generations through a process known as political socialization. They are subtle, latent, and often unrecognized—that is precisely why they are so powerful. Rosenau calls them "culturally derived premises" around which national goals are organized and "action scripts" which maintain cohesion in a society.[28]

The exact content of a nation's value system is difficult to define precisely because it is so deeply seated and so fundamental. It influences processes even more than it influences specific institutions and policies. And while not every American shares equally all aspects of this value system, it is, nevertheless, sufficiently widely shared to give legitimacy to the political process. Since this value system does not lead inevitably to one best policy on any public issue, there can be fairly wide disagreements on political and economic policies among people who share the same basic value system.

No single ideology totally encapsulates this value system, but most writers correctly identify liberal democracy as its widest inclusive conceptualization.[29] Combined with some related economic ideas, liberalism can be said to stand for three fundamental principles: liberty, security, and opportunity. That is, virtually all Americans place great value in being able to believe as they wish (liberty), in being physically protected (security), and in being able to enjoy the fruits of their labors (opportunity). These ideas are epitomized in the Declaration of Independence which is perhaps the best single statement of the American value system.

American historical experiences have brought additional values to the original core. These related and intermingled values are: rationalism, natural rights, pragmatism, activism, messianism, nationalism, exceptionalism, and a belief in limited government. Again, the periphery of this core is challenged frequently and, occasionally, successfully, but the heart has remained fairly constant throughout American history.

The precise means by which these basic social values influence policies are not entirely clear. Obviously it has to do with the way that values shape perceptions and drive the cognitive process. Early studies which concentrated almost solely on what was called "national character" were interesting but resulted in too many overgeneralizations and stereotypes. More recent research into modal personality (widely shared personality attributes) and into the way cultural values shape business practices and policies, however, have suggested that there is a relationship between national value systems and ways of doing business as well as between values and foreign policy.[30]

One of the more fundamental questions which must be addressed by those who forge U.S. foreign policy in the twenty-first century is whether or not a dramatically altered American society still espouses the values which animated the founding of the nation. While it is difficult to measure these changes, public opinion researchers have discovered some changes already. Based on the premise that self-perception is one of the better windows into social values, a number of studies have reported some fundamental changes in how Americans see their role in the global community. Rosenau and Holsti discuss the breakdown of the fundamental consensus that has guided foreign policy, at least from 1945 up to the Vietnamese war.[31] Kegley and Wittkopf write about an American society which has moved beyond consensus.[32]

Sociologists report similar results, though on slightly different questions. Riesman suggests there is growing egocentrism among Americans and Lasch talks about increasing narcissism.[33] Other political scientists, again using different methodological approaches and addressing slightly different questions, also suggest that there are some fundamental changes in American values which have implications for U.S. foreign policy.[34] And none of these studies had access to 1990 and subsequent census information.

Precisely what is causing these changes is not understood clearly. Some critics blame television and mass media, others point accusing fingers at churches or other primary social institutions. Some argue that the political socialization process itself is breaking down—that parents no longer inculcate fundamental liberal democratic values as part of family life. Each of these accusations is probably true, plus many others. Indeed, there is sufficient blame for all social institutions to share. Similarly, probably no single explanation is sufficient in itself.

How many of these developments are cyclical and how many signal irretrievable changes in American social values is, again, not clear. If the family is both the fundamental basis of a society and the primary mechanism for political socialization, then some of the changes may be very long lasting. Demographic data send a clear message in this respect.

Not only is American society becoming older, more diversified in its racial, linguistic, and national origin characteristics, it is also becoming more characterized by single parent, usually female, households. As recently as 1970, 71 percent of all American households were married-couple families. In 1989 that figure was 57 percent and by 2000, one expert predicts it will be approximately 50 percent.[35] An increasing proportion of single family households are headed by women, particularly black women, whose wages are typically lower than those of men.[36]

> By most objective measurements, the vast majority of these families hold a disadvantageous position in society relative to other family groups. They are characterized by a high rate of poverty, a high percentage of minority representation, relatively low education, and generally have little equity or stature in American society and constitute a group with unusually pressing social and economic needs.[37]

The impact of the family on international politics and foreign policy has not received a great deal of attention.[38] But the changes in social values stemming from these demographic developments are likely to be as significant as those which were brought about by the changes of the industrial revolution when the family ceased being the basic unit of economic production and, instead, became the basic unit of economic consumption in society.

We can only speculate on how the changing demographic characteristics mentioned above will affect American values and, subsequently, U.S. foreign policy. Will the increasing Hispanization and Asianization of America change social values as well as global outlooks? A more realistic consideration of Latin America and Asia as part of an American global strategy is long overdue. And what effect will the aging of America have on social values and, subsequently, on foreign policy? Clearly, the economic costs of an aging population will not make it easier to pay for the economic excesses of the last three decades. And pressures to alter the massive trade deficit will make it very tempting for the United States to solve its economic problems at the expense of other nations. The 1992 election demonstrated the popular appeal of protectionist rhetoric. It will be very difficult to get rid of a multi-billion dollar merchandise trade deficit without causing debilitating and destabilizing crises in our major trading and alliance partners on whom we increasingly rely for trade as well as for strategic support.

The core question is: Do all of these changes mean that American society is becoming more fragmented? It was suggested in Chapter 1 that nations are becoming less homogeneous at the same time that the international system is becoming more homogeneous. A vastly fragmented American society will ask more and more frequently; whose foreign policy is the United States pursuing?

That is, on behalf of which segment of American society is U.S. foreign policy being pursued? Which of the many and diverse groups across American life are benefitted and which hurt by particular foreign policies? The fundamental assumption of a democratic society is that the government, at least to the best of its ability, will seek the interests of the widest groupings of its society.

But as America becomes marked by more and more groups with wider and wider interests and as the interests of groups within American society become more commingled with the interests of other groups outside of the United States, it is virtually impossible for foreign policies to be blessed with collective legitimization. What has been said about Great Britain applies with greater force in the United States: "In a society which is marked by a greater variety of groups and cultures, by more political information and disinforma- tion and by an increasingly questioned idea of legitimacy, the interaction of British and foreign groups has grown, with diverse effects on policy."[39]

Jewish groups within the United States have exercised significant influences on both U.S. foreign policies (policies towards the Middle East, for example) and on domestic policies (immigration laws, for example) for many years. Certainly domestic pressure groups representing Hispanics and Asians will attempt to further the interests of their own cross-national links as well.

It should be stressed that the potential effect of these demographic changes on national values is neither intrinsically good nor bad. There are both positive and negative effects which might result. But, at a minimum, increased fragmentation, greater social cleavages, and more widely disparate value systems will alter the fundamental core of American values. That change will affect ways of thinking about the role of America in the twenty-first century and could contribute to the increasing vincibility about which we have spoken.

Public Opinion

We have said that foreign policies grow out of the values of a society and that national interests are the widest possible aggregations of individual and group interests. This section explores how those interests are aggregated and how decision-makers come to believe that certain policies are in the national interest. It is difficult to determine just what American social values are at any given point in time. In a democratic society it is assumed that elected officials will reflect national values and enact laws and pursue policies consistent with them.

It goes without saying that this is not always the case, but it is generally the case. When decision-makers range too widely from the elastic and permis- sive boundaries of public opinion, those officials are either defeated in elec- tions or, in cases of flagrant abuse, removed by legal procedures. In some cases, Congress, which because of its more frequent electoral stands is usually more sensitive to public opinion, reacts (or overreacts) to return foreign policy to within the boundaries of what the public will allow. "Strengthening Congress's hand in foreign policy has one decided advantage: It accords a larger role to American public opinion. . . . History suggests that the most effective and durable foreign policy is generally that which has the broadest public support. This point goes to [the] heart of a democratic system."[40]

Since measurements of public opinion are frequently accepted as barometers of national values and beliefs, it is natural to assume that if one wants to know what the American public wishes its foreign policies to accomplish, one would consult public opinion polls. As usual, however, conventional wisdom is a bit misguided.[41]

In the first place, the American public is relatively unconcerned about foreign affairs.[42] That inattentiveness can be explained, at least partially. Public concern is usually measured by opinion polls which ask about specific foreign policy positions; yet, Americans tend to be more concerned about general principles and less concerned about the details of policies. That is why general values about foreign affairs tend to be quite stable in America while attitudes toward specific policies are much more volatile. For example, at least since the end of World War II, Americans have held as a core value that the United States has had a vital role to play in global affairs. Particular manifestations of that value in policies have changed over time but the basic value has remained fairly constant, at least up to the present. Scholars keep reporting the presence of different varieties of internationalism, but the core commitment to a global role has been quite constant.

Drawing conclusions from public opinion polling is problematic for another reason: Public opinion polls are very time sensitive. A national poll immediately following a series of television news reports on famine in Africa would find greater interest in certain aspects of foreign affairs than a similar poll would find in the absence of such television coverage. So to say that Americans are disinterested in foreign policy matters may be a bit oversimplified.

Moreover, the growing interdependence about which so much has been said may have given Americans a greater global consciousness. The lives of Americans are touched by foreign developments much more continuously than they were in previous decades. The oil shocks of the 1970s made this quite obvious to Americans, but it is much more than that. The "financial invasion of the United States" has touched directly the lives of millions of Americans.[43] Thus, Americans today may be more interested in foreign affairs than they were in earlier times. Both income and spending are affected as many Americans now see jobs either lost or created by the actions of foreign firms or nations and as they realize that more and more of the things they want to purchase are affordable primarily because they come from abroad.

Sometimes what passes as indifference about foreign affairs is rather the notion that the public should defer to national political leaders on such matters.

This general indifference about policies gives foreign policy leaders considerable latitude. That latitude increases as public attentiveness wanes. But when public attentiveness heightens, the leader's latitude lessens. That is why attempts by foreign policy leaders to "educate" the public often backfire. Such attempts may merely heighten interest and, hence, lessen decision latitude.

Knowing just what public opinion is on any specific topic is also not as easy as it seems. Media headlines are quick to report that some public opinion poll suggests that Americans want either more or less money spent on foreign affairs, for example. But those who work with these polls know how extremely sensitive their measuring devices are to wording and tone. That is why it is possible to find reports of divergent opinions among the public on the same issue—that is, the results depend on how the questions were phrased, how the samples were drawn, the skill of the pollsters, and the statistical knowledge of the analysts. The questions, "Do you approve of the way Bill Clinton is handling foreign policy?," "Do you approve of the way President Clinton is handling foreign policy?," and "Do you approve of the way the president is handling foreign policy?" will yield different results from among the same population. Thus, the obscurity of public opinion is made clear about as easily by intuition as by statistical manipulation.

A close adviser to President Kennedy once said that public opinion was both a sword and a compass to a president.[44] The metaphor is too limiting. Public opinion can also be a shield to a president, particularly in international negotiations. Presidents, while negotiating with foreign or domestic leaders, may appeal to limits beyond which he or she cannot yield based on public opinion. It is also a restraint. Many foreign policy leaders have confessed to feeling constrained by what they think the public will allow.

The essential point, however, is that public opinion polling has become increasingly important to public policy; indeed, one can argue, "opinion polls are at the core of presidential decision making."[45] This was not the case prior to the 1980s. In the twenty-first century, if the goals of foreign policy consistency and continuity are to be met, foreign policy officials will pay increasing importance to polls. They must also become more sophisticated in their understanding of how public opinion is formed, measured, and, manipulated.[46]

In sum, public opinion is not always a clear reading of the American value system nor an unambiguous guide to foreign policy action for decision-makers. However, it becomes more of a political factor when it is marshalled and focused towards specific goals. Traditionally, the two primary means of marshalling and focusing U.S. public opinion are the mass media and interest groups.

Mass media in the United States is very pervasive. Virtually every home has at least one television set and more than one radio. Three television sets were sold for every baby born in the United States in 1987.[47] Nearly every

American home also receives a daily newspaper and occasional magazines. Some social critics describe American society as "sheep-like" in its willingness to have its foreign policy attitudes manipulated.[48] Yet in spite of the pervasiveness of the mass media, its influence on foreign policy is quite limited for several reasons.

American mass media is not particularly attentive to foreign affairs. Perhaps this merely reflects the inattentiveness of the public at large; but, except in special interest magazines, elite newspapers, and specific television networks and programs, the mass media does not widely report foreign affairs and that which they do report is dealt with very superficially. Graber reports that foreign news stories make up only 11 percent of all stories in American newspapers.[49] The average time devoted to an international story on U.S. television network news broadcasts is less than two minutes. By contrast, in Britain, the average time is over five minutes, even on commercial television channels.

Even though the coverage of international news is quite limited, some suspect that it nevertheless manipulates foreign policy beliefs. In the sense that the mass media is able to choose particular foreign policy goals and enlist the American public behind them, this is not the case. On the other hand, the mass media does dictate the foreign policy agenda. By and large, the American public becomes concerned only about those issues deemed newsworthy by the mass media, particularly the television networks. Given sufficient time on national television, virtually any foreign development, even an innocuous one, could dominate the foreign policy agenda for some segment of the American public. This interest could then be transferred onto the national foreign policy agenda. In other words, the ability of the mass media in the United States to report news is not nearly as important as its ability to select what is news.[50] It is not the ability of the mass media to tell the American public what to think that is worrisome; it is its ability to choose what the public should think about that causes some observers to call mass media the fourth branch of government.

The irony of this is that political leaders then use mass media-generated issues as their reading of public opinion. In reality, the international significance of an event is mediated by such considerations as viewer interest, available visuals, and general commercial attractiveness. Some critical international issues which do not meet these criteria are virtually ignored by the mass media. The American public tends to be quite independent and does not react well to the mass media telling it how to vote. More newspapers endorsed Gerald Ford than Jimmy Carter in the 1976 presidential election, but the majority voted for Carter.

Finally, it is wrong to think that the mass media is a monolithic entity controlled by a few people who, in turn, control the minds of the American people. Ownership of the American mass media is fairly diversified, especially in its editorial content, and it is neither centralized nor coordinated. There has been a trend towards concentration in recent times but the dictates of commercialization shape mass media far more than does centralized control.

Other than the mass media, public opinion in America is also focused and marshalled by various interest groups. In fact, public opinion used to be the primary weapon by which interest groups shaped political outcomes. The information revolution—the wide availability of information to the public through a wide variety of media—has changed that.[51] The public is no longer dependent on interest groups for its information about either foreign policy or attitudes towards foreign policy.

Since World War II, few public interest groups concerned themselves with foreign policy. That is no longer the case as an increasing number of both public interest groups (some registered as PACs—Political Action Committees) and lobbyists have foreign policy interests.

Sometimes the foreign policy effects of these groups are unintended. In 1977 a bill to combat international terrorism was defeated, in large part, by the lobbying efforts of the National Rifle Association, one of the nation's most powerful lobby groups. The defeat of the bill had foreign policy implications, but the campaign against it was based solely on narrow domestic considerations. The bill would have required that U.S. manufacturers of black powder (the most commonly used explosive in terrorist bombs) include within the powder two inert identifying materials which would allow the powder to be detected by chemically sensitive monitors and to be traced to manufacturer and sales distribution channels even after use in a terrorist bomb. But the NRA, whose muzzle-loading enthusiasts also used black powder, decided that the effects of these inert materials on bullet velocity and trajectory would be undesirable and they launched a successful effort against the legislation.

Multinational corporations also have lobbied effectively for various changes in trade legislation. American automobile companies successfully ended a U.S. trade embargo on Cuba via Argentina and the efforts of multinational corporations on ending U.S. trade restrictions with the People's Republic of China were very successful.[52] American tobacco companies have been successful in marshalling the resources of the government to force some Asian nations to eliminate trade barriers which restricted the importation of American tobacco products.

The American Israel Public Affairs Committee (AIPAC) is one of the more effective and more interesting of the new breed of pressure groups whose primary interests are abroad. AIPAC supports legislation which it believes is in the best interest of Israel and works to defeat any policy or politician which, in its judgment, does not have the interest of Israel sufficiently in mind. Yet it does not have to register under the Foreign Agents Registration Act since its financial support comes from American sources. This is significant since AIPAC is able to point to Arab interest pressure groups and call attention to their registration as "an agent of a foreign power," a singularly ominous epithet.

Seeing the success of pressure groups and lobby efforts, nearly all foreign nations have now decided not to leave diplomacy solely to their foreign offices and have hired Washington D.C. law firms or lobby groups to represent their interests within Washington, particularly within the halls of Congress. More and more American legislators, state as well as national, are being wined and dined in foreign places in an attempt to influence foreign policy towards those countries.

In sum, public opinion is increasingly difficult to gauge in a more fragmented American society. Groups with narrow interests may mold the thinking of national leaders on special causes and the mass media more and more defines what the American public will think about. National leaders both use and abuse public opinion and, all things considered, the electoral process continues to be the best gauge of public values and subsequent foreign policies.

As discussed in Chapter 2, the democratization of foreign policy has enlisted public opinion in the foreign policy process as presidents have used all of their powers of persuasion to convince the American public that a particular policy was in the national interest. But there is also an ominous side of this coin. Once the American public is convinced of a particular policy, adapting that policy to changing political realities is difficult. United States-Soviet relations illustrate this phenomenon. The American public has been conditioned so thoroughly to the Cold War mentality that even conservative presidents like Ronald Reagan and George Bush ran into right-wing criticism at home as they sought to come to terms with a dramatically changed Soviet Union. As the tense but stable terra firma of the Cold War began to shake, many Americans began to wonder where they could find stable ground again.

Education

Education influences foreign policy in two ways—one very fundamental yet difficult to assess and the other more obvious. There is a complex yet fundamental relationship between education and national power. None of the traditionally considered elements of national power mean anything in the absence of an educated populace able to marshall latent national capabilities and turn them into economic, political, and military strengths. The rise of America to international political prominence in the early twentieth century was not inevitable. America was endowed with many natural resources and other capabilities of power, but something else was required. That something else was an educational system based on the principle that ability and talent could lead to economic success—in other words, an open society. In an open society, even the least fortunate feel that they can rise to a more comfortable existence through education and effort. Only when opportunity does not exist does a society become cynical, revolutionary, or passive. England offers a classic example of what can happen when a nation neglects its educational system. "The relative decline of Britain as a great industrial nation was already apparent by the 1870s, and pronounced by the 1880s; and it has, of course, continued ever since. It was produced by a number of factors, but by far the most important was the backwardness of the English educational system."[53] Most of the early great inventors and scientists who produced the substance of the British industrial revolution and who were responsible for Britain's subsequent rise to great power status came from families of religious dissenters or from lower classes and were not allowed to attend the elite public schools. But, being barred from this educational system, including Oxford and Cambridge, resulted in their learning science and engineering and gaining the all-important belief that they could distinguish themselves through merit. These attitudes were not passed on to their children who became accepted into the upper classes and admitted to the elite school system. Therefore, British entrepreneurial skills declined, British inventiveness lessened, and Britain entered the twentieth century with nothing like the relative power it had enjoyed in the previous two centuries.

A nation's system of education is critical because it is one of the primary means by which national values and attitudes are passed from generation to generation. And it is these national values and attitudes which create the foundation for consensus and legitimacy, two qualities which allow national officials to become national leaders.

Secondly, an educational system contributes to a successful foreign policy through the global mental images it creates. If generation after generation of America's children are taught that America is the hub of the global wheel, that the interests and desires of all other groups and nations must revolve around that hub, and that, in short, American is invincible, then America is destined to become less and less effective in dealing with the modern world which, as we have said many times before, is characterized by vincibility. In other words, the quality and level of international education in America must improve.

Examples of declining interest in foreign language study and of abysmally low scores in tests about basic foreign matters are reported almost daily in America. There is an almost endless number of studies showing that Americans, even those in college, cannot identify key nations on unmarked maps, cannot answer fundamental foreign policy questions (for example, which two nations are involved in talks to control strategic arms?), and have little conception of who is involved in most international quarrels. We discuss several of these reports in Chapter 13.

Perhaps the most extensive study of the quality of international education in America was the 1980 effort sponsored by the American Council on Learning and conducted by the Educational Testing Service. That study reported that college seniors could answer correctly only half of 101 fairly basic questions concerning global issues.[54] Most of these studies are not comparative, but are nevertheless alarming. However, in a six nation comparative study in 1985, McWilliams reported that American students scored lower on a common foreign affairs test than students in West Germany, Brazil, India, and Canada.[55] In a study conducted by the National Endowment for the Humanities in 1986, 30 percent could not identify Great Britain on an outline map of Europe, 33 percent could not identify France, and only a third could identify America's enemies during World War II.[56]

Former Congressman and presidential candidate Paul Simon has written a great deal about the status of foreign language education in the United States. Simon asserts that the United States is the only major "nation in which one can go through grade school, high school, college, and even in some cases get a Ph.D. without ever having had a single year of foreign language instruction."[57]

The Office of Education's Center for Statistics reports that "the only academic field to lag behind the over-all growth rate was foreign languages, which declined by about 4 percent" between 1972 and 1982. And the number of earned degrees in modern foreign languages conferred by institutions of higher education has declined since its high mark in 1969. By 1986 it had reached its lowest point in twenty years.[58] Even in schools where there is wide participation in language instruction, all too often language is not well used as a window into foreign cultures. Too many students learn how to conjugate French verbs but learn nothing about France. All foreign language instruction ought to be used to broaden understanding about peoples, cultures, the national interests of foreign nations, their histories, their foreign relations, and their roles in today's world. More will be said about the impact of education on economic competitiveness in Chapter 13.

In sum, America is more and more involved in global affairs, more and more interpenetrated by global developments, more and more affected by global forces, yet, at least as measured by educational data, Americans know less and less about global matters. And it is not merely being able to locate Nicaragua on a map or knowing that Korea is divided into North and South that is required. Adequate international education must go beyond that in two ways. First, it must teach an understanding of the changed, fragile, and interdependent world in which we live. The notion of an isolated, fortress America is antithetical to the needs of the contemporary world. "Every $1 billion in exports means 25,000 more jobs for Americans. Half the earnings of America's 23 largest banks come from overseas. And exports now account for 9 percent of the nation's output."[59] American students need to learn that the challenges of the twenty-first century will have as much or more to do with economic relations, trade, environment, Third World relations, etc. as they will with military matters.

A broadly defined concept of civic responsibility is also necessary in today's world—a civic responsibility that extends across national boundaries. This is not a plea for the kind of nationalistic indoctrination that leads to chauvinism or worse, nor is it a plea for sentimental internationalism. But most Americans get stuck on debating whether the United Nations, for example, is good or bad when they should be discussing ways that the UN, and other multilateral agencies, can be used to further the American goals of order, stability, and justice in all aspects of global life and for peoples of all nations.

Above all, two generations of Americans who have grown up thinking that a tenuous nuclear confrontation between the United States and the Soviet Union is the only possible international system must see that subsequent generations learn otherwise. New generations must be prepared for alternative international systems with different but equally precarious problems. The Soviet Union may have been consigned to "the dust bin of history," as recent presidents have reminded us, but it has left a lot of smoldering ashes in its wake. America in the twenty-first century must deal with worsening squalor and poverty in some Third World countries and with growing economic strength in others, with allies whose interests may diverge increasingly from traditional American interests, with transnational problems which will threaten all nations equally, and with a rapidly changing international political system. Unfortunately, there is some evidence to suggest that the next generation of political leaders is increasingly unconcerned about, at least, some international developments. A survey conducted by Peter Hart Research revealed that "forty per cent of young Americans can think of no circumstances under which they would fight for their country and only one in three young men would go to war to defend Britain or other European allies." In his analysis of these data, William Greider says that Americans born within the twenty-five year span from 1945 to 1970 reflect "a profound shift in political attitudes, unlike anything that has existed since the isolationist climate preceding World War Two." He describes them as "isolationist, pacifist, and above all, politically apathetic." Other significant findings are that only a third follow news on any regular basis and half want nuclear disarmament to receive the highest priority (followed in order by stopping terrorism and ending world hunger).[60]

TOWARDS THE TWENTY-FIRST CENTURY

United States' foreign policies do not spring, as did the Greek goddess Athena, fully armed from the head of a decision-making Zeus. They are developed in response to a deafening variety of international events and challenges, they are mediated through a complex, bureaucratic decision matrix, and they grow from a social and cultural foundation made up of several very basic national conditions. In this chapter we have suggested that new and different transnational geographic concerns will modify the foreign policy agenda; that demographic changes may alter the focus of American foreign policy as well as limit its scope and range; that the consensus that springs from national values will be more tenuous; that public opinion will be at the same time more important and yet more fragile and difficult to interpret; and that Americans must learn more about the broader world in which they live.

We have reached a situation in America in which ". . . the number of interest groups has become so many, the divisions between them so deep, and the attachment to any central core of agreed-upon values so weak that that system tends to fragment and not function effectively."[61] The seriousness of this problem is exacerbated by the increasing vulnerability America faces.

Vincibility imposes a changed approach to foreign policy. That approach must understand the changes we have discussed in this chapter. It requires foreign policy officials to understand that the America whose interests are being defended in a fragile twenty-first century global society, is not the same America of the twentieth century. Figuratively, relatively, and symbolically, America's geographic condition has changed. Her people are less European oriented, more fragmented, older, and less willing to spend vast sums on global problems. The very values and interests which foreign policies are meant to protect may well be changing and ways to measure those changes must be sought and used. And all of this is occurring in a domestic society which is woefully ignorant, not only of these changes, but of the larger global environment in which foreign policies operate. Foreign policy officials must strive to create a vision which unites this diverse population, which shapes national values rather than merely reads them, and which educates and energizes Americans about their challenges in the twenty-first century.

ENDNOTES

1. For an excellent summary of several alternative approaches to the question of what shapes foreign policy, see Charles E. Hermann and Gregory Peacock, "The Evolution and Future of Theoretical Research in the Comparative Study of Foreign Policy," in *New Directions in the Study of Foreign Policy,* ed. Charles Hermann and others (Boston: Allen & Unwin, 1987), 13-32.
2. Christopher Farrands uses the phrase "foreign policy is a social process" in his "State, Society, Culture and British Foreign Policy," in *British Foreign Policy: Tradition, Change and Transformation,* eds. Michael Smith and others (London: Unwin Hyman, 1988), 51.
3. J. Martin, "American Culture: The Intersection of Past and Future," in *America Now,* ed. J. G. Kirk (New York: Atheneum, 1968), 187.
4. Howard J. Wiarda, *Foreign Policy Without Illusion* (Glenview, IL: Scott, Foresman, 1990), 15.
5. James N. Rosenau, *The Scientific Study of Foreign Policy* (London: Francis Printer, 1980), 527 and 128-29, respectively.

6. See, for example, Valerie Hudson and others, "Why the Third World Matters, Why Europe Probably Won't: The Geoeconomics of Circumscribed Engagement," *Journal of Strategic Studies*, 14 (September 1991): 255-98.
7. Even here, however, it is interesting to note the foreign policy implications many raised when the channel tunnel between England and France was begun in 1987.
8. In 1987 a peripatetic New York barge loaded with rubbish was denied access at several Caribbean ports.
9. See Jock A. Finlayson and David G. Haglund, "Whatever Happened to the Resource War," *Survival*, 29 (September/October 1987): 403-15.
10. Timothy Aeppel, "'Birth Dearth' Effects Begin to Show in some Developed Nations," *The Christian Science Monitor*, 2 March 1987, 6.
11. Robert Pear, "New Look at the U.S. in 2050: Bigger, Older and Less White," *The New York Times*, 4 December 1992, A1 citing a 3 December 1992 Census Bureau report.
12. Daniel Bell, "The World in 2013," *New Society*, 18 December 1987, 36.
13. Comparisons over time are always difficult because of the changing criteria for categories. These statistics merely calculate the population of "low income economies," (even though the states in that category change some over time), as a percentage of the global population as reported in the annual editions of the World Bank's *World Development Report*.
14. Norman Myers, ed., *The GAIA Atlas of Planet Management* (London: Pan Books, 1985), 49. Most of the data in this section are from this atlas.
15. *The Times* (London), 8 April 1988, 7.
16. Sidney L. Jones, "Demographic Trends in America: Squaring the Population Pyramid," *The Washington Forum*, 30 September 1987. This pamphlet, written by an economist who has been both an assistant secretary of the Treasury for Economic Policy and an under secretary of Commerce for Economic Affairs, is one of the more significant collections of data and analysis to be published in recent years. Unless otherwise indicated, we have relied on it for much of our data in this section. We have updated his figures when updates were available from Department of Commerce, Economics and Statistics Administration, Bureau of the Census, *Statistical Abstract of the United States, 1991* (Washington, D.C.: Government Printing Office, 1991), Section 1.
17. Pear, "New Look at the U.S. in 2050," A1.
18. Department of Justice, Immigration and Naturalization Service, *Statistical Yearbook of the Immigration and Naturalization Service, 1988* (Washington, D.C.: Government Printing Office, 1989), xliv. The passage of the 1986 Immigration Reform and Control Act (IRCA) altered dramatically the accounting for undocumented entrants. The Justice Department asserts that after IRCA legalized many undocumented entrants, the number of illegal aliens was reduced to 1.5 to 3 million. The best discussion of these changes is found in Frank D. Bean, Barry Edmonston, and Jeffrey S. Passel, eds., *Undocumented Migration to the United States: IRCA and the Experience of the 1980s* (Washington, D.C.: The Urban Institute Press, 1990). Passel suggests (page 18) that, at least up to 1986, there was an average of 250,000 illegal aliens entering the U.S. annually. That figure would suggest a stock of at least 1.5 million by 1986.
19. Pear, "New Look at the U.S. in 2050," A1.
20. Jack Miles, "Immigration and the New American Dilemma: Blacks vs. Browns," *The Atlantic* (October 1992): 41.
21. This is an estimate made by Vernon Briggs of the Federation for American Immigration Reform and cited in Jack Miles, "Immigration and the New American Dilemma," 60.
22. Reported by Pear, "New Look at the U.S. in 2050," A10.
23. See Bill Richardson, "Hispanic American Concerns," *Foreign Policy*, No. 60 (1985): 30-39 and the other articles in that journal on the topic of "New Ethnic Voices."

24. Pear, "New Look at the U.S. in 2050," A10.
25. Jones, "Demographic Trends in America," 25.
26. Farrands, "State, Society, and Culture," 54.
27. Jessica Tuchman Matthews, "Redefining Security," *Foreign Affairs* 68 (Spring 1989): 162-77 and Theodore C. Sorensen, "Rethinking National Security," *Foreign Affairs* 69 (Summer 1990): 1-18.
28. James N. Rosenau, "A Pre-Theory Revisited: World Politics in an Era of Cascading Interdependence," *International Studies Quarterly* 28 (September 1984): 272-73.
29. See Louis Hartz, *The Liberal Tradition in America* (New York: Harcourt, Brace and World, 1955) for an early statement of this thesis and Kenneth M. and Patricia Dolbeare, *American Ideologies* (Chicago: Markham, 1971) for a later treatment.
30. See Douglas Ashford, *British Dogmatism and French Pragmatism* (London: George Allen and Unwin, 1982) and C. Lammers and D. Hickson, eds., *Organizations Alike and Unalike* (London: Routledge and Kegan Paul, 1979). Martin Sampson III has attempted a specific study of the way Japanese and French values influence their respective foreign policies in his "Cultural Influences on Foreign Policy," in *New Directions in the Study of Foreign Policy,* ed. Hermann and others, and has examined Britain in his "Cultural Effects on Foreign Policy Decision Processes and Outputs: Britain," Unpublished paper prepared for the Annual Convention of the International Studies Association, Anaheim, CA, March, 1985.
31. Ole R. Holsti and James N. Rosenau, *American Leadership in World Affairs: Vietnam and the Breakdown of Consensus* (Boston: Allen and Unwin, 1984).
32. Charles W. Kegley, Jr. and Eugene R. Wittkopf, "Beyond Consensus: The Domestic Context of American Foreign Policy," *International Journal* 38 (1982-83): 77-106.
33. David Riesman, "Egocentrism: Is the American Character Changing?" *Encounter,* September 1980, 19-28 and Christopher Lasch, *The Culture of Narcissism: American Life in an Age of Diminishing Expectations* (New York: Warner Books, 1979).
34. See, for example, Richard Rosecrance, ed., *America as an Ordinary Country: US Foreign Policy and the Future* (Ithaca, New York: Cornell University Press, 1976) and Thomas L. Hughes, "The Twilight of Internationalism," *Foreign Policy,* No. 61 (1985-86): 25-48.
35. Jones, "Demographic Trends in America," 93-95.
36. Jones, "Demographic Trends in America," 93-95.
37. Arthur J. Norton and Paul C. Glick, "One Parent Families: A Social and Economic Profile," *Family Relations* (January 1986): 16, cited in Jones, "Demographic Trends in America," 93.
38. See one attempt by Stan A. Taylor, "The Family: The Forgotten Element in the Study of International Relations," *Family Perspective* 16 (Spring 1982): 53-76.
39. Farrands, "State, Society, and Culture," 60.
40. "President, Congress, and Public: A Shared Foreign Policy Role," *The Christian Science Monitor,* 4 March 1987, 15.
41. Ronald H. Hinckley, in his *People, Polls, and Policy-Makers: American Public Opinion and National Security* (New York: Lexington Books, 1992), provides perhaps the best summary of the complicated relationship between polls and policy-makers. He summarizes much of the research in this growing field. We have relied on several of his insights in this section.
42. See, for example, Lloyd Jensen, *Explaining Foreign Policy* (Englewood Cliffs, NJ: Prentice Hall, 1982), 139-50 and the studies cited by him.
43. See Earl Fry, *The Financial Invasion of the United States: A Threat to American Society?* (New York: McGraw-Hill, 1980).
44. Theodore C. Sorenson, *Decision-Making in the White House: The Olive Branch or the Arrows* (New York: Columbia University Press, 1963), 45-46.

45. Richard S. Beal and Ronald H. Hinckley, "Presidential Decision Making and Opinion Polls," *Annals,* American Academy of Political and Social Science, No. 472 (1984), cited in Hinckley, *People, Polls, and Policy-Makers,* 4. Hinckley argues persuasively that polling will be increasingly important in policy-making and Ole R. Holsti, in "Public Opinion and Foreign Policy," *International Studies Quarterly* 36 (December 1992): 455, argues that the impact of public opinion has increased "during recent decades."

46. See Hinckley, *People, Polls, and Policy-Makers,* 134-38 for examples of the uses of public opinion.

47. Department of Commerce data reported in *Harper's* (November, 1988), 14.

48. See William Lederer, *A Nation of Sheep* (New York: W. W. Norton, 1961).

49. Doris A. Graber, *Mass Media and American Politics* (Washington, D.C.: Congressional Quarterly Press, 1980), 244.

50. See Paul A. Smith, "Media and the Making of U.S. Foreign Policy," *Washington Quarterly* 7 (1984): 135-41.

51. See Hinckley, *People, Polls, and Policy-Makers,* 6.

52. Thomas N. Gladwin and Walter Ingo, *Multinationals Under Fire* (New York: John Wiley and Sons, 1980).

53. See the more extensive commentary on this by Paul Johnson, *A History of the English People,* rev. ed. (New York: Harper & Row, 1985), 300-306. Some argue that the "English disease" has been cured, but others think it is too early to tell.

54. Thomas S. Barrows and others for the Council on Learning, *What College Students Know and Believe about Their World* (New York: Change Magazine Press, 1981).

55. Wayne C. McWilliams, "What University Students Know About Foreign Affairs: A Six Nation Study," unpublished paper presented at the Annual Meeting of the International Studies Association, Anaheim, CA, March 1986. Japanese students in this study scored lower than other national groups. This, however, is not consistent with other studies and McWilliams believes the anomaly is explained by an inadequate sample of Japanese students.

56. Reported in Richard Wood, "For Americans, the World is Terra Incognita," *The Christian Science Monitor,* 28 February 1989, 19. A Gallup Poll revealed similar results: 57 percent of American adults could identify France and only 34 percent could locate Greece. More remarkable was a survey of 5,000 high school seniors which revealed that 25 percent of the students in Dallas could not name the foreign country which bordered on Texas. These data were reported in John Dillin, "Education's New International Wave," *The Christian Science Monitor,* 1 March 1989, 8.

57. See his *The Tongue-tied American* (New York: The Continuum Publishing Corporation, 1980) and "Is America Tongue-tied?" in *Standard Education Almanac: 1984-85,* ed. Gerald L. Gutek (Chicago: Professional Publications, 1984), 10-13. The quote is from the latter article, page 11.

58. Department of Education, Office of Educational Research and Improvement, Center for Statistics, *Digest of Education Statistics: 1985-86,* by W. Vance Grant and Thomas D. Snyder (Washington, D.C.: Government Printing Office, 1986), 42-43.

59. Dillin, "Education's New International Wave," 8.

60. Charles Brenner, "Apathy Dulls Senses of America's Sixties Rebels," *The Times* (London), 19 March 1988, 5.

61. Howard J. Wiarda, *Foreign Policy Without Illusion* (Glenview, IL: Scott-Foresman/Little Brown Higher Education, 1990), 15.

PART II

INTERNATIONAL SECURITY AND NATIONAL DEFENSE

I n Federalist Paper Number 23, Alexander Hamilton argued that securing the international position of the United States was a prime motive for a renewed union under the proposed Constitution: "The principal purposes to be answered by Union are these—The common defense of the members—the preservation of the public peace as well against internal convulsions as external attacks—the regulation of commerce with other nations and between the States—the superintendence of our intercourse, political and commercial, with foreign countries." Domestic order, international commerce and comity, and national defense were linked in his mind to each other and to the national union. If this were true in 1787, it is at least as valid today.

Having considered the context of policy-making and the general issue of the external representation of U.S. interests in a changing global system, we now turn to the conditions of external security since World War II and the American defense response. The transformation of America's role in the world by mid-century was a strategic shift of historic proportions not only in terms of the traditional American international approach to the outside world but of the very shape of global politics. Nothing short of the political collapse of Europe and of Japan, as well as the rise of an antagonistic central power that spanned two continents and embraced global ideological pretensions, could have so thoroughly changed the peacetime foreign and defense policies of the United States. Having essentially transfigured at the conclusion of World War II its domestic order and international role to meet the opportunities and dangers of a world that seemed smaller than ever before, the United States found itself at the end of the twentieth century once again redefining its security posture and national persona.

In many respects, the Cold War and its defense requirements were simply an extension of the experiences of World Wars I and II. Both of those conflicts were general in character and went to the heart of the very structure of international relations. They involved mastery of Europe and Asia and therefore the international pattern of power itself. Moreover, these conflicts were driven or legitimized with reference not only to the balance of power but to the object of government itself. World War II was not only a contest between Germany, Italy, and Japan, on the one hand, and the United States and its partners, on the other, but a struggle with nazism, fascism, and militaristic and racial imperialism. And even if the United States and Britain were allied with another totalitarian regime, there was on the part of many the hope, undoubtedly naive, that the very association with the Soviet Union would not only establish collective norms of security as represented in the United Nations, but also bring about the progressive democratization of the USSR itself.

The final disappointment of this hope, and the power vacuums that World War II yielded, effectively perpetuated the frame of mind that saw the stakes of conflict as global and the modality of conflict as a great crusade. The United States' role after World War II was most definitely not seen as the normal interaction of a great power in international affairs but as a war, however cold it might at times seem. The issues were considered transcendent and the threat mortal. In effect, the United States did not see itself as a normal power in normal times but as an extraordinary state in extraordinary times.

The Soviet Union's strategic withdrawal from Eastern Europe and its collapse as a unitary state, as well as the redistribution of power internationally, confront the United States for the first time since its emergence as a great power with the prospect of interdependency in a world more of gray hues than of stark colors. Paul of Tarsus once declared, "For if the trumpet give an uncertain sound, who shall prepare himself to the battle?" As the century turns over, the United States may be less certain than in the dramatic days following World War II as to the nature and direction of the threat in the international arena, and more tentative in sounding the trumpet both to the American people and to potential friends and foes. In this section, we will examine the nature of the world that called forth the U.S. policy of containment and the strategies that served that policy. This in turn will provide a valuable framework in which to comprehend the range of choices that face the American people in the uncertain global climate of the twenty-first century.

6

GEOSTRATEGIC FOUNDATIONS OF NATIONAL DEFENSE

We now turn, over the next four chapters, to an analysis of national defense and U.S. military strategy. We shall examine the political presuppositions undergirding the defense policies of the U.S., the broad strategic concepts that have evolved since World War II, and the contemporary problems posed by international terrorism that strike at the very heart of state sovereignty and the security of its citizens. Chapters 8 and 9, particularly, illustrate the theme of increasing vincibility that is woven throughout this book.

National defense remains the fundamental duty of any government—that is, the maintenance and prosperity of the state in the face of immediate or potential threats. Many things contribute to the welfare of the state and a great number of them will be secured in our external relations through cooperative or at least nonmilitary activities. Defense policies are, however, precisely oriented toward challenges that might call forth military responses. Whether or not and the degree to which such responses are appropriate or counterproductive depends on an accurate evaluation of the situation confronting the nation, including the costs, risks, and benefits of the military approach as compared with alternative options. National strategy is thus more than the application of military means to political objectives. It is the exercise of the whole range of national power in whatever combination is judged effective and proper. Hence, although the next several chapters will be oriented toward the military aspects of national strategy, it should not be forgotten that defense policies and military strategies are but parts of broader national policies and strategies.

STRATEGY AND NATIONAL CULTURE

Strategy, in its broadest terms, involves more than the threat or application of force.[1] It entails an intertwined set of concepts through which we seek to relate ends to means. It reflects all of those interests, values, assumptions, principles, and guides to action that go under the name of policy. Moreover, it is important to understand that international conflicts of interest are endemic and one cannot divide time into clearly defined periods of peace and periods of war. The spectrum of conflict is continuous, and any point on the spectrum requires that we bring to bear the relevant panoply of national capabilities from psychological to economic to cultural to military.

It is also evident that any national strategy must harmonize with the *strategic culture* of the people it seeks to serve. By strategic culture, we refer to generally shared attitudes in the society concerning the nature and requirements of external security, the conditions of peace, the causes of war, and the utility and restrictions on force. Here we would emphasize two aspects of the strategic culture that bear directly on U.S. strategy development. One concerns problems of *intelligence* and *expectations* and the other concerns problems of *implementation*.

The first aspect of our strategic culture to highlight is the tendency to project into the international sphere attitudes derived, first, from our domestic situation and, second, from our peculiar historical security environment. On the domestic side, for over a century our national agenda has focused less on constitutional issues—that is, the structure and limitations of political power—than on bargaining issues, that is, the distribution of benefits within the system. Furthermore, we have pursued our national politics in an environment of remarkable prosperity. Secondly, our historical external security position has been rare for a great power. One nineteenth-century observer stated it well—weak neighbor to the north, weak neighbor to the south, fish to the east, fish to the west. In contemporary terms, the United States does not define its security position in terms of a hostile state or states on its borders ready and willing to threaten it through direct military intervention.

In contrast to this domestic and security environment, most other states of the world have been less favorably situated. On the contrary, many states are struggling to answer the most fundamental questions of who rules, under what restrictions, and how power is transferred—and this is being played out under conditions of much greater scarcity than we have experienced. Moreover, most other states have been shaped by different historical imperatives and have thus been more conscious of the tenuousness of their national existence.

It has been said that perception is 90 percent projection. To a very large degree, the United States, like other states, interprets the world through the spectacles of our own national experiences and situation. However, given the distinctive character of American development, some have called it insular, we interpret threats and offer political solutions that at times seem to underestimate the deadliness of many struggles in the world and to overestimate the possibility of political or negotiated settlements. It is this particular character of our strategic culture that colors our expectations and shapes our interpretation of intelligence.

A second problem in the American strategic culture concerns the unwillingness in peacetime to take war seriously enough. Obviously, the American people have spent billions on defense, raised and trained forces, and devised plans. But the key aspects of war and perhaps of international conflict generally are uncertainty, risk, and probabilities. The conditions of deterrence and the requirements of victory are dependent on time, space, and circumstances. A single strategic option, a fixation on one region or theater, and a narrow range of options may meet the desire to limit expenditures and to be as nonprovocative as possible. But it is clear that the maintenance of peace and stability, as well as the specific requirements of deterrence, demand that one be able to pose a range of threats to would-be adversaries. Furthermore, the flow of conflict in peace or war is inherently uncertain. If this be true, then those states whose power makes them in some sense regulators of the international security environment need to insist on a much broader range of contingency planning, operational options, and military exercises. To be effective in implementation, therefore, strategy must not only link, in some general sense, resources to ends, but it must also provide the conceptual base for developing and exercising a variety of power instruments and military operations.

As a people, Americans must therefore always be conscious of those distinct aspects of their strategic culture that both provide the undergirding strength of their policies and strategies and bias their perspectives of what is and of what is possible. Wise statecraft requires not only that external policies be shaped in terms of fundamental national character but that national predispositions be so understood as to allow compensation for the defects inherent in that character. This was in fact the approach the American founders took to the drafting of the U.S. Constitution. As James Madison noted in Federalist Paper Number 10:

> Liberty is to faction, what air is to fire, an aliment without which it instantly expires. But it could not be a less folly to abolish liberty, which is essential to political life, because it nourishes faction, than it would be to wish the annihilation of air, which is essential to animal life, because it imparts to fire its destructive agency.

Hence, in the constitutional construction of 1787, the object was to secure the public good and private rights against the danger of such a faction, and at the same time to preserve the spirit and the form of popular government."[2]

In similar fashion, the strategic culture necessarily propels Americans to see violent conflict as abnormal, differences subject to compromise, individual rights prior to community claims, and domestic politics as primary. Much of what the American people have accomplished both within and beyond their borders is founded on these perspectives. But, as the founders sought to correct the "defects" of popular government, so latter-day Americans must seek to ensure that they do not simply see the world in their own image and develop national strategies and defense policies that may meet the requirements of domestic consensus but be irrelevant or perhaps dangerous in the international environment.

Three basic relationships have shaped American national strategy and defense policy and provide the key to its course into the next century: (1) the relation between the geopolitical position of the United States and changing technology; (2) the relation between the values and institutions of the American Republic and the changing threats and opportunities in the international environment; and (3) the relation between the general state of the American economy and the public's propensity to support foreign policy and defense expenditures.

Beyond these critical relations lies the relative global distribution of power and influence. In the early days of the Republic it was plausible for President Washington to look forward to the day when the United States could "defy material injury from external annoyance" and "choose peace or war, as our interest, guided by justice, shall counsel."[3] And in the twentieth century, it was reasonable, if more risky, for the United States to defer engagement in the general wars sweeping Europe and Asia. The issue that confronted the United States with great force after the Second World War was the continuing appropriateness of this detachment.

The political and material collapse of the principal powers of Western and Central Europe, as well as of Japan, and the rise of Soviet power in Eastern and Central Europe and the Pacific ultimately impelled the United States into a strategy that required the construction and forward deployment of a large military force unprecedented in its peacetime history. Moreover, it became involved in a number of interventions and limited wars directly linked to its concerns about the expansion of Soviet power and to the options made available to successive administrations by the existence of large peacetime forces.

The collapse of the Soviet empire in Eastern Europe in 1989 and the subsequent disintegration of the USSR itself by late 1991, raise again the question of the proper role of the United States in world affairs and the implications for national strategy and defense. To understand both from whence the United States has come and where it will go in national defense and military strategy, Americans must once again reflect on the most fundamental relationships of geopolitics and technology, of domestic politics and international challenges, and of the American economy and the defense budget.

GEOPOLITICS AND TECHNOLOGY

Despite its continental dimension, the United States has often been described as an "island nation" or since Alfred Thayer Mahan, the great naval strategist, as a "maritime power."[4] The description arises out of a *particular combination of geopolitical and internal political factors.* The United States achieved by the late nineteenth century secure borders on its north and its south with states incapable of launching a direct invasion across those boundaries. The continent itself is separated from the great powers of Eurasia by vast expanses of water. At the same time, the political unity and common market forged through common institutions, territorial expansion, and civil war reduced the vulnerability of the nation not only to external invasion but to political and economic manipulation. Abraham Lincoln in the Civil War grasped, as did George Washington at the time of the American founding, the critical link between internal unity and a foreign policy detached from external threat.

If the United States can be characterized as secure from invasion and relatively detached from direct intimidation, it is also a fact that increasingly in the twentieth century a large number of its economic interests and political connections lie across those same oceanic expanses that undergird its security. To the degree that those interests and alignments, especially in Eurasia, have themselves been threatened by successive would-be hegemons—Germany, Japan, and the Soviet Union—or by regional conflicts, the crucial issue for the United States has been less invasion of its own continental base than the projection of its political influence and military power across the oceans in order to defend friendly regimes, organize defensive coalitions, and sustain U.S. and allied forces.[5] *Diplomatically,* this has translated into a search for mechanisms whereby divergences of interests may be minimized and strategic consensus forged with those states whose resources, location, attachments, or values bear upon U.S. interests. *Economically,* the U.S. geopolitical posture and economic regime have favored commercial linkages with those same states. *Militarily,* these same circumstances have favored mobile forces, military alliances, forward bases, and control of the lines of communication between the continental U.S. and the external world. All of these attitudes constitute the very essence of what has been described as a maritime power.

To appreciate the full dimensions of this historic posture, it is only necessary to contrast this position with those states often described as *continental powers* and to compare it with the situation of other modern *island nations,* such as the United Kingdom and Japan.

A continental power is first of all a state that *can* conceive of a powerful state directly on its borders. Threats are not distant or hypothetical and delay in reacting to such threats may endanger the existence of the state itself. Depending on the geographical expanses of the country, such states may, in the event of invasion, be able to trade space for time, such as Russia has historically done. Very often, however, the location of the population and the relative ease of access to the capital, such as in Germany and France, or the diverse character and fragile unity of the people, such as in pre-World War I Austro-Hungary, dictate policies of watchfulness and engagement. Given these circumstances, such powers tend to develop two controlling concepts: *reason of state* and the *primacy of foreign policy.* Reason of state asserts that the security of the state—its integrity, order and well-being—is a preeminent value from which flows all other secular values. The government thus possesses an extraconstitutional authority to exercise whatever means are necessary to preserve or perhaps even to enlarge the effective power of the state. The notion of the primacy of foreign policy derives from this reasoning. For if national security is both fundamental and fragile, the executive should be constitutionally unencumbered in this realm.

By contrast to the orientation of continental powers toward the concepts of reason of state and the primacy of foreign policy, the United States has seldom felt the pressure of sudden and overwhelming invasion so as to accept in any unqualified way either the extraconstitutional notion of reason of state or the certain subordination of domestic politics to foreign policy. Whether it was in the Korean and Vietnam Wars or American intervention in the Persian Gulf and on the Arabian peninsula, the constitutional struggle over the appropriate roles of the presidency and Congress and the ubiquity of domestic politics continued. Although calls for unity and rallying around the president carry weight in American politics, they rarely subordinate "normal" constitutional and political processes.

If the traditional U.S. posture can be contrasted with "continental power," so it can also be compared with other recent examples of maritime power. Both the United Kingdom and Japan fall into the latter category and both of them have been not only figuratively but genuinely island nations. There are important parallels between the United States and those nations. All were in some sense secured by oceanic barriers and all established such internal unity as to broach no major challenge within or on their borders. This political unity was the precondition for an enormous expansion of economic power and ultimately the ability to project influence and force across the oceans. The enclosure acts, consolidation of power under the Tudors, the Cromwellian revolution—all provided the basis for a truly United Kingdom and the Industrial Revolution. Similarly the 1867 Meiji restoration in Japan and the 1861-65 Civil War in the United States removed the last important vestiges of division and decentralization in those respective countries and impelled them toward the exercise of power far beyond the confines of their state.

If there are similarities, there are also crucial differences. The English Channel and the Sea of Japan were, as technology advanced, increasingly in the nature of moats rather than oceanic expanses, although even today they constitute formidable tank traps. More important, the energy and resource bases of Japan and the United Kingdom make them in an advanced technological and commercial society inextricably linked to broader external markets. Interdependence is not a new discovery for these states: It has been a fact of their existence since emerging as great powers. Moreover, both the United Kingdom and Japan consolidated power so as to leave intact no other state rival on its frontiers. The United States shared the continent with two large sovereign states—Mexico and Canada—and an unstable amalgam of ministates in the corridor linking North and South America, as well as the islands of the Caribbean.

This latter circumstance undergirds philosophically the tenets of the Monroe Doctrine, whatever the historical origins and evolution of that doctrine. The doctrine was stimulated by the collapse in the Napoleonic Wars of Spanish and Portuguese control in the Americas and by the British desire to make permanent this circumstance. Salient to American considerations were hostility to the recolonization in any form by the European powers and hope that continuing vestiges of such control in the Americas would decline.

Over time as the states (particularly of Latin America) became independent, there was concern that the weakness of those new states, including their growing indebtedness, would invite intervention of the several European states and make them instruments of extra-American ambitions. Ironically, it was fear of weakness adjacent to its borders that prompted periodic U.S. intervention and may even be a driving force today despite the presumed obsolescence of the Monroe Doctrine.

The appearance of a direct threat on U.S. borders arising from extra-American intervention or links would complicate America's ability to project power across the oceans. Moreover, the political or economic collapse of the states south of the U.S. could lead to a demographic surge across the southern frontier that could dramatically alter the American sense of integrity. The U.S. security conception does not include a fear of an invasion by a great power across the frontiers, but it does encompass concerns for the independence, political orientation, and socioeconomic stability of proximate states. The latter concerns are rooted in the fear that the weaknesses of those societies might thrust across U.S. borders dispossessed and alienated populations and that these states could be manipulated by hostile Eurasian powers so as to divert U.S. attention from the defense of its interests in other parts of the world.

Technology has changed many things in the U.S. international posture, but perhaps less than might be expected in its basic geopolitics. The thermonuclear age is characterized by a capability to deliver massive destruction over great distances with a high degree of confidence that enough invading missiles will survive sufficient to destroy the target. This does signal one enormous change in the American security posture: The United States as an organized political entity can be utterly destroyed. Yet, it is still difficult to conceive of a direct invasion. It is possible to destroy the United States: It is a complicated problem beyond belief to occupy it. And the guarantee that it will not be destroyed lies not in successful defense but in the ability to retaliate in kind. If a secure retaliatory capability and the will to use it remain intact, it is assumed that the nuclear threat, while real, will remain distant. Concern about nuclear proliferation and terrorism in the post-Cold War era may yet stimulate a massive sense of insecurity among the American people. Yet, although many claim that the U.S. perception of threat has fundamentally changed, its behavior would suggest that, in fact, little has changed in its security consciousness. Political debates on the structure of security in Europe after the Cold War and the objectives of the Iraqi government in the Middle East and the Persian Gulf could have been carried on within the same terms of reference at almost any time in the nearly five decades since World War II.

On any comparative examination, it should be clear that the American security culture is special. There remains a remarkably modest sense of direct threat. The typically insular concept that war or peace is primarily a matter of American choice prevails. In Europe, in Southeast Asia, in Central America, or in the Persian Gulf, most Americans see the decision to engage and the consequences of the decision as centered in the United States. The country is engaged at distant points around the globe and is expending billions of dollars in that enterprise—and yet the citizenry and a vast number of its representatives appear disengaged. The international changes wrought by World War II explain the *engagement;* the stability of the U.S. geopolitical posture and the accompanying insular mentality explain the sense of *disengagement.*

The fundamental geopolitical posture of the United States in the Americas has remained relatively constant over the last hundred years and continues to shape the American security consciousness. On the other hand, drastic shifts in the identity, character, and capabilities of the great Eurasian powers and the collapse of traditional colonialism have altered the challenges and opportunities within the broader global geopolitical structure.[6] These latter transformations have moved U.S. perspective and policies toward international entanglements beyond anything the founders could have envisaged—or probably countenanced. As previously noted, if much in the American situation reinforces a sense of security detachment, so these latter trends have favored engagement in international society, extrication from which can now only be at a stunning cost.

The roots of the transformation reach back into the nineteenth century. The period after the Napoleonic Wars was from the American point of view one of international quiescence. However, by the 1860s major forces were unleashed that would ultimately define the twentieth century. The rise of united Germany and Japan, the transformation of Russian power, and the growing inadequacy of the Hapsburg power, to mention but a few key changes, opened a period in which the nature of the state actors, their interlinkages, and their power relationships were the central issues, eventuating in what A.J.P. Taylor characterized as the struggle for mastery in Europe. But it went far beyond Europe. The new restlessness and power politics led to a scramble for control or influence in Africa, in the Middle East, in Asia—and even in Latin America. For example, in 1875 less than 10 percent of Africa had been colonized but by 1895 only 10 percent of Africa had not been colonized. During the U.S. Civil War, the French and Austrians meddled directly in Mexican politics and by the turn of the century Germany was seeking to extend its influence in a number of Latin American states. The potential for and the extent of conflict were seen as growing and even welcomed by certain partisans of social Darwinism. Clearly, many in the United States saw cause for alarm; some saw opportunity.

The completion of the American westward expansion, the acquisition of Alaska, and the conclusion of the Civil War coupled with the period of massive industrialization after 1870, raised the capabilities of the United States to unprecedented heights even as the international environment seemed more threatening. The historian Thomas S. Bailey well summarized the situation:

> By 1890 we were the number two white nation in population, still trying to catch up to the Russians. We had bounded into first place in total manufacturing, including top rank in iron and steel—the standard indices of military potential. In addition, we held either first or second place in railroads, telegraphs, telephones, merchant marine, and in the production of cattle, coal, gold, copper, lead, petroleum, cotton, corn, wheat, and rye. The armies and navies were not there, but we had the means of creating them when we needed them—and did.[7]

As will be discussed below, the reaction to the twin transformation of the international and the domestic environment was contradictory—the sense of fundamental security and growing capabilities coupled with a consciousness of the impingement of a fluid, increasingly global external environment, introduced into American foreign policy an incoherence of objectives and approaches that could be said to have endured until after World War II.

Looking back from the vantage point of the 1990s over the last one hundred years, the turbulence of power is almost overwhelming: United Germany, reaching for the pinnacle of power, twice defeated and then divided between adversary alliances in the center of Europe, and in 1990 reunited in new form; the Austro-Hungarian and Turkish empires fragmented into their component parts; the British empire but the congeries of memories; the Russian empire transformed into the Soviet imperium which at its height achieved greater territorial extent and political centralization than could have been dreamed by the czars, but by the early 1990s withdrawing from Eastern and Central Europe and fragmenting into its component parts; Western Europe altered from the scene of great power rivalry into a common market still of uncertain inspiration and political vision; Japan, the short-lived military master of Asia, now the economic dynamo of the world; China, once divided, humiliated, and exploited, struggling to complete its revolution of political centralization and economic modernization; the emergence of 150 new or renewed states, moved by contrary dreams of justice and power; and a technological revolution that has brought these slivers of Babel into uneasy contact with, and often suspicious reliance on, each other. Despite all the remarkable changes that have taken place in the United States in the same period, one can be excused for seeing this spot in North America as an island of tranquility in a turbulent sea—and one can also understand why it is so difficult for Americans to relate either intellectually or emotionally with much of the outside world and to better understand the forces which are eroding comfortable assumptions.

If the geopolitical shape of the world has undergone profound changes, so too has the *technological configuration.*[8] In many critical ways, technology defines the meaning of geopolitical relations. The very concepts of time and space are altered by the technical characteristics of a civilization, especially the technology of conflict. The importance of different resources from wood to coal, iron, oil, and uranium are determined by scientific and technical developments. The development of nuclear weapons is the most obvious change in the strategic environment and the one most mentioned in any discussion of U.S. strategic policy during the Cold War—but there are other inventions that are equally, perhaps more, decisive.

It is worth emphasizing that no local destruction today could be any more thorough than that inflicted by the Romans on Carthage: the utter destruction of the population, the city, the vegetation, and the reproductive vitality of the soil. The contemporary difference lies in the territorial expanse of the destruction—it is possible to speak today of planetary holocaust—and the enormously heightened certitude, speed, and accuracy of the attack. The ability to successfully penetrate American airspace and deliver on designated targets a destructive nuclear blow has changed the U.S. strategic environment. For the moment, the improbability of such an attack, whatever the crisis or political circumstances, is vouchsafed not by the ability to construct an adequate defense but by the capability and policy to launch a retaliatory strike on the aggressor. Nuclear peace is, to slightly paraphrase Winston Churchill, the sturdy twin of mutual terror—or, if you will, assured retaliatory capabilities. If this is the case, the technical dilemmas and possibilities confronting U.S. security policy are of other kinds.

To put the issue succinctly: the problem of *projecting U.S. forces* across the oceans so as to defend U.S. interests and allies remains the *principal defense problem;* but the technical requirements are vastly more complex. On the positive side, technology allows the United States to move troops and material across the land and seas and through the air in numbers, logistical support, and speed unprecedented in history. It allows the penetration of firepower, not only nuclear but conventional, through the enemy's defenses and on target with a high degree of accuracy. On the negative side, potential enemies possess comparable capabilities and have the added advantage of being in the area of the conflict—hence having a less severe problem of maintaining their lines of communication and sustaining their forces. Moreover, the expense of much sophisticated technology and the projected enormous attrition involved in the clash of such forces mean that the cost of such conflicts and the pressure on the industrial bases would be enormous. Even when the major combatants are not in direct clash, the use of force against lesser adversaries, given the proliferation of sophisticated weapons, is tremendously risky and expensive. Witness the U.S. involvement in the Persian Gulf in 1987-88 and again in the same region in 1990-91. In sum, technology has, at one and the same time, reduced the barriers of time and distance but increased the costs and risks of vaulting those barriers.

As the United States entered the 1990s the most salient factors bearing upon its geopolitical posture were the *changes in the character of the former Soviet power,* the continuing *rise of diverse power centers* around the world, and the *proliferation of sophisticated weapons.* Perhaps most immediately dramatic were the changes associated with the collapse of the Soviet Empire and the fragmenting of the Soviet Union with the subsequent reordering of U.S. relations with the successor states of the USSR.

The years 1989 and 1990 saw the virtual collapse of the Warsaw Pact and the beginning of the withdrawal of Soviet forces from Eastern Europe. At the same time there intensified within the Soviet Union a struggle among diverse populations and political jurisdictions for greater autonomy or even independence as well as the virtual breakdown of the Soviet political economy. As we will examine in greater detail in the next chapter, the fundamental premises undergirding U.S. foreign policy and military strategy after World War II were the control of Eastern Europe by the USSR and the permanent mobilization of Soviet forces for general war. The change in these situations was accompanied and probably driven by a crisis of economics and political legitimacy—a crisis that impelled the Soviet leadership toward a more inward-looking policy and the search for alternative political-economic arrangements. The August 1991 attempt to overthrow the government of Gorbachev was in large measure driven by the desire to halt the reconstitution of an association among the Soviet republics. Ironically, the failed coup opened the door to the successful "constitutional coup" in December by which the Russian leader, Boris Yeltsin, replaced Gorbachev and the momentum toward a definitive break among the Soviet republics was accelerated. To the degree that U.S. policy and the forward positioning of U.S. forces were driven by the immediacy of a Soviet threat, these changes necessarily drove policy-makers toward the most fundamental reconsideration of U.S. policy and strategy since the end of World War II.

Given the still remarkably insular position of the United States, it was to be expected that many would argue that the end of the Cold War not only justified the drastic reduction of U.S. military forces but would reduce the military aspect of U.S. policy generally. This was sometimes called the *demilitarization* of foreign policy to be replaced by the *economization* of foreign policy—that is, reliance on positions and instruments of economic power to achieve one's global objectives. Of course, the trade-off was not seen as absolute but a change in the relative balance. Moreover, it was felt that, as Russia and the other successor states of the former Soviet Union were either turning inward in order to transform the bases of their national wealth or seeking favorable economic arrangements with the outside world, so the United States needed to bring about adjustments in its own political economy. This necessitated not only drastic cuts in military-related expenditures but also a recognition of the diminished utility of military force in the face of the types of external threats we were likely to face in the rest of the decade.

The invasion of Kuwait by Iraq on August 2, 1990 and the unprecedented transport of U.S. forces to the region gave a new dimension to the debate. Many believed the U.S. involvement in the area only confirmed the need to reduce the military aspects of U.S. policy whereas others argued that the exercise demonstrated the continuing relevance of U.S. military force and a strategy that allowed quick forward deployment. In any case, it was clear that, with the passing of the certainties of the Cold War, a renewed debate was opened over the implications of geopolitical insularity and political-economic interdependence for U.S. policy and most particularly for its military posture and strategic thinking.

As the position of the Soviet Union underwent radical alteration, the intensified attention of policy-makers and commentators to the changed balance of global power grew apace. The rise of the economically powerful and increasingly self-confident states of Japan and united Germany, as well as the independent aspirations and power bases of states as diverse as China, India, Iraq, and Iran, signal that the United States is finally fully in the "post-post-World War II" world. Moreover, the Cold War sense of common danger that held many divergent states together has passed, allowing historical grievances and contemporary parochial ambitions to undermine old solidarities. The fragmentation and ethnically driven strike in Yugoslavia may only be a harbinger of conflicts among peoples awakening from the imposed quiescence of the Cold War. Accompanying this fragmentation has been the spread of weaponry whose numbers and sophistication are truly awesome, particularly in areas of high tension such as in the Middle East and South Asia. At the same time, however, new or revitalized forms of international association have seized the imagination of many statesmen—the halting movement of the European Community toward greater political cohesion, the North American Free Trade Area, more active and cooperative East-West associations, and the United Nations.

It is the relative balance between these forces of *disintegration* and *integration* that must concern the United States. It is possible to project a relatively benign, if not peaceful, world in which the great cooperative political-economic designs that united Western Europe, Japan and a number of other Asian states, and North America, could be extended to cover Eastern Europe and many of the states in the so-called Third World or the South. If this happens, forms of both cooperation and conflict are likely to be more diplomatic and economic in character and less shaped by military considerations. On the other hand, the inability of the states of Eastern Europe, including the states of the former Soviet Union, to find new forms of political integration and economic growth; bitter and ultimately protectionist economic competition among the advanced industrial states; the failure of the less-developed states to achieve self-sustaining per capita economic growth; and the inflaming of religious, ethnic, and national rivalries among state neighbors—any or all of these possibilities could lead to a period of instability and even chaos that could make the reliance on military force no less salient in the future than it has been in the past. It is the uncertainty of global trends that both gives the edge to the current debate over U.S. policy and strategy and makes that debate so inconclusive. As noted earlier, if the general geopolitical posture of the United States has remained relatively constant, alterations in the principal states and the balance of power among them, as well as the increasing economic interdependence of the United States, will provide most Americans with a sense *both* of continuity and of change that will be difficult to disentangle.

POLITICAL CONSENSUS

Successful foreign policy execution depends on the correct fit between the political assumptions, guidance, and instruments chosen and the actual challenges and opportunities in the external world. At the same time, the policies and strategies chosen must receive the concurrence, passive or active and in varying degrees, of the relevant political elites and institutions, the politically attentive public, and the general body of the citizenry. It should be clear that if the geopolitical circumstances of the nation and hence the attitudes shaped thereby are substantially different than much of the outside world, there may be a persistent tension between the requirements for external action and the requirements for internal consensus. This tension is exacerbated if the founding assumptions of the Republic reinforce a sense of being exempt or apart from the historical political forces and attitudes that have animated most states. Moreover, the public view of the extent of the nation's material capabilities and the percentage of those capabilities that should be devoted to national security will also shape the direction and intensity of external engagements.

A glance at the back of a dollar bill will reveal the logo in Latin: *novus ordo seclorum*, the new order of the ages. The founders of the American Republic believed that there were certain true propositions about the nature of man—his way of thinking, his passions, his aspirations—that should be explicated as the foundations of a government that would be both stable and democratic in character. It was believed that these insights and the special circumstances of the new nation allowed the formulation of a science of politics and a form of government both distinctive and paradigmatic for the world.[9]

Born of the Enlightenment, the new American Republic was heavily influenced by the natural rights tradition. As Thomas Jefferson eloquently argued, governments are instituted not to confer but to secure rights that belong to people simply by virtue of their humanity. These rights include the security of one's life and property and rather extensive parameters within which individuals and groups may pursue their private visions of happiness. It was assumed that religious feeling, moral education, the juxtaposition of interests, and the constraining influence of local sentiment and institutions would shape a civic consciousness robust enough to allow the widest exercise of individual liberty while maintaining public institutions sufficiently stable and competent to secure union, justice, defense from attack, and the general welfare.

The scope of government was neither to define nor to impose a model for a morally complete or "saved" individual but, more modestly, to provide a free but orderly environment within which individuals might realize their interests. The founders designed forms of government both to create and to maintain such an environment and to contain the natural excesses that might arise from such a milieu. The pattern established is well known: a democratic polity in which the danger that an overbearing majority might pose to the rights enunciated in the Declaration of Independence is mitigated by the fragmenting but intermixing of powers. A divisive and general struggle between two classes would thereby be replaced by conflicts of limited and specific interests and would force the widest possible consensus within and across the institutions of government as a condition of public policy.

It was the embodiment of these ideas in the Constitution that defines the American version of limited government. The critical question for any inquiry into national security policy is whether or not this constitutional formula was to be applied to the conduct of foreign affairs as it was to domestic policy-making. The answer at the founding was clearly "yes" but the historical evolution of the Republic has in practice made it an open question.

The founders at best severely qualified any notion of presidential prerogative and rejected what would effectively be an executive-reserved sector in foreign policy and national security. There were three basic reasons underlying this decision:

1. Such unfettered authority in the area of foreign policy and national security could ultimately be extended into the domestic sphere;
2. There was no threat to American security so massive or so immediate as to require such a surrender of power to the executive;
3. The founders asserted the primacy of domestic concerns which in practice implied the primacy of Congress in the political arrangements.

The aim of the American constitutional order, therefore, was to provide to the individual, whether alone or joined with others, the widest possible sphere within which personal and private interests and values might be pursued. Institutions are so arranged and so endowed with power to resist encroachments on the Republic and the liberties of its people both from external foes and from internal ambitions. The conditions which favored this constitutional balance included the unity of the states composing the Republic, an integrated and relatively self-sufficient economy, the absence of a great power threat on its borders, and the protection afforded by the oceans. The joining of wise institutions and favorable geographic and material conditions provided an unprecedented opportunity to construct a government "of the people, by the people, and for the people." Abraham Lincoln well understood how the unity and integration of the Republic were critical to this objective. Not only insularity but unity undergird the survival and prosperity of the Great Experiment in democratic republicanism.

Moreover, there was widespread concern among many of the founders and shapers of American institutions throughout the nineteenth century that the federal power itself be limited in its ability to engage the United States in foreign quarrels or to pursue ambitions that would alter the central character of American society. If it is inexact to characterize nineteenth century foreign policy in the United States as isolationist in some absolute sense, it is correct to see that policy as governed by norms of nonalignment and by limitations on what we today might characterize as power projection. Both the challenges of expanding to its continental dimensions and the desire to retain the basic character and spirit of free and limited government forbade extensive "foreign" (i.e., transoceanic) adventures. These views undergird the suspicions of the Jeffersonians and the Jacksonians about a National Bank, the credit potential of which could finance foreign engagements, and about a vast naval capability that could be an instrument of these engagements.

One cannot understand many of the recurrent controversies in foreign policy and national security areas unless these founding biases are clearly recognized. The definition of the new Republic and the character of its external relations were fundamentally linked: who Americans are and how they present themselves to the world.

This brief recitation of the concepts and conditions that underlay U.S. foreign policy in its first century makes clear how much began to change by the last decade of the nineteenth century. The end of the European peace after the defeat of Napoleon; the rise or transformation of powerful state actors, in the first instance, Germany and Japan (and indeed the United States); the increasing political and economic global context of state ambitions; techno-logical changes; the "socialization" and "politicization" of heretofore rela-tively quiescent populations around the world—these and other trends decisively altered the environment within which the *novus ordo seclorum* was to be developed. The threats to and then the collapse of the Eurasian balance and the interconnectivity of the world's economies inexorably brought the United States from nonalignment to continuous engagement.

The struggles within Europe and Asia that jeopardized American move-ment throughout the world and appeared to threaten the immunity of the continent, ultimately drew the United States into two world wars. Both conflicts were initially seen as momentary exceptions to the policy of nonen-tanglement. But the resultant collapse of the formerly great powers of Eurasia and the extension of Soviet power into Eastern and Central Europe, as well as its link to a new communist giant in China, converted America's episodic involvement in the outside world into a continuous one. The United States became a coalition builder of the states surrounding the new Soviet empire and the driving force behind the new balance of power. In effect, the United States assumed the classical role of regulatory power.

As indicated above, however, the remarkable immunity of the United States from direct invasion and occupation and its overwhelming superiority over the allies that it was organizing, served to reinforce the classical American perception of itself as an extraordinary state apart from states. Even in their engagement, the Americans were substantially detached. Moreover, the great struggles in which this people had engaged were all in a sense polarized and suffused with a moral interpretation that only such conflicts of hegemony and equilibrium can generate. World War I, World War II, the Cold War—all strengthened the sense that the issue was that of 1776 and 1787, the creation and preservation of the *novus ordo seclorum,* and that the battle of Gettysburg for government of the people, by the people, and for the people had now been writ large. Thus was strengthened the ancient vision of a nation both immune from the material threats to other peoples and endowed with high moral purpose and thus was fulfilled the picture painted by Alexis de Tocqueville of a land which "had been kept in reserve by the Deity and had just risen from beneath the waters of the Deluge."[10] The circumstances of the nation may have been altered but the fundamental integrity and position of the Great Republic endured.

The Cold War, which early centered on the reconstruction and defense of Western Europe and of Japan, however, quickly gave way to the tasks of supporting new regimes caught up in strife which obscured the distinction between domestic and international conflicts. The relevant model no longer seemed to be that learned in the period prior to World War II, but rather that of the sixteenth-century state-building struggle among the Italian city states, where terror and deceit were the hallmarks. The searing experience in Vietnam and the inherent moral-political ambiguity of U.S. involvement in internal and regional conflicts throughout the non-Westernized, nonindustrialized world shook not only the post-World War II consensus on appropriate policies and strategies, but the entire self-conception of American power and purpose.

The end of the Cold War with its polarizing and moralizing tendencies only serves to exacerbate this sense of moral and political ambiguity about external engagements, especially armed engagements. Many have forgotten how intense the opposition has been in this century to a policy of foreign entanglement, a posture of large standing armed forces, and a strategy of forward deployment. Only the utter collapse of the traditional states of Western and Central Europe, as well as the defeat of Japan, accompanied by the rise of a foe mobilized for war, in occupation of half of Europe, and ideologically antithetical, impelled the United States to abandon its posture of nonalignment and limited armed forces.

The collapse of the Soviet challenge and the restoration of other power centers have in effect led the United States back into "normal" times—that is to say, times in which a multitude of clashing interests and shifting coalitions supersede the relative moral and political clarity of the Cold War. But, precisely because of this transformation, the rationale in the minds of many Americans for alliance commitments and military engagements has disappeared.

The diminished sense of direct threat either to physical security or to political identity and the complexity inherent in regional quarrels, tend to drive the American polity back toward policies of nonentanglement and particularly to diminish support for military interventions. The shifting public and congressional support for the Bush administration's handling of the 1990 Iraqi invasion of Kuwait reflected in part these sentiments.

Public support was high for the initial deployment of U.S. forces to forestall any invasion of Saudi Arabia and President Bush received high marks for organizing an international coalition within the United Nations to condemn Iraq and to impose economic sanctions. Indeed, it was the first time since the founding of the United Nations that there had been such unity among the permanent members of the Security Council in the face of a military challenge. However, the decision of the president to substantially increase U.S. combat forces in Saudi Arabia, thus providing the United States the option of forcefully liberating Kuwait, and the successful United States' initiative to receive approval for the eventual use of force from the Security Council, encountered the opposition of the Democratic majority in Congress and of wide sections of the public at large.

A CBS News/New York Times poll completed on January 5-7, 1991 showed 46 percent of Americans thought the United States should commence military operations if Iraq did not pull out of Kuwait by January 15 and 68 percent felt that U.S. representatives should try to meet Saddam Hussein before that date. The actual congressional vote of January 12 authorizing U.S. military engagement in the Persian Gulf was 250 to 183 in the House of Representatives and 52 to 47 in the Senate, with the majority of Democrats opposing immediate military action.

Opposition was not only based on the prudential ground that the use of military force would be both costly in American lives and counterproductive in terms of Middle East stability, but on the moral ground that the reactionary or unprincipled nature of the regimes involved in the quarrel dictated that the U.S. abstain from the use of force. Moreover, to the degree that Iraq should be forced to disgorge Kuwait and that U.S. economic interests should be secured, these goals, many felt, would best be accomplished through the continuance of the economic sanctions and the search for a negotiated settlement. Undergirding all these arguments, however, was the profound sense on the part of the opponents that, with the passing of the Cold War, the need to maintain a strong interventionary capability had also passed and U.S. objectives should be met in other ways. It is worth noting, in this regard, that had the U.S. possessed in 1990 the forces that were being projected by the congressional leadership for the end of the decade, the United States would have been incapable of mounting the operation that it did. Ironically, a force that had been largely developed on the basis of a Soviet threat provided the precondition for a major regional intervention. And it was found that the stress of such an operation required not much less. Rather than resolve the quarrel over the future shape and direction of the U.S. military role, the Iraqi affair only became one more point of contention.

This quarrel was only magnified by the constitutional division of power between the presidency and Congress.[11] Congress has always been sensitive about its constitutional prerogatives. In times in which it was agreed that the nation faced a substantial threat, including the height of the Cold War, it has been reasonably deferential to presidential judgment. The protracted and inconclusive character of the Vietnam War and suspicions generated by what many consider to be the devious styles of Presidents Johnson and Nixon led, as discussed in an earlier chapter, to a series of attempts by Congress through legislative mandates and hearings to place increased limits on presidential initiatives in foreign affairs and military interventions. Moreover, the fact that the White House was largely in the hands of the Republicans since Johnson and the Congress was dominated by the Democrats gave a partisan overlay to this struggle. The end of the Cold War further diminished the willingness of Congress to defer to presidential judgment. The search for a new consensus on national defense and military strategy is hence further exacerbated by this institutional and partisan division.

Whether the overwhelming command of both the White House and the Congress by the Democrats after the 1992 elections will moderate this radical division over the long run may be an important issue for the remainder of the decade. The early experience of the Carter administration with a Democratic Congress would not be a happy precedent but the expected consensus-building character of the Clinton presidency and the substantial change in the makeup of Congress may open up greater possibilities for harmony. Whether this harmony will be forged on the basis of a continuing, vigorous political-military role in global affairs or a more insular posture remains to be seen. But, it is clear that whatever consensus is achieved will be decided not only on the basis of geopolitics and strategic concepts but on the requisites of the economy, public budgets, and constituent demands.

One wag noted that, when Adam and Eve were driven from the Garden of Eden, Adam remarked to Eve: "Dear, I believe we are entering a period of transition." The transition that the United States now finds itself in may not be of the same cosmic level, but it is likely to be protracted and contentious. When the new consensus emerges, it must first include an acceptable reinterpretation of the meaning of the U.S. geopolitical posture and political tradition within the changed context of global politics. But, as we shall see in the next section, it must also be sensitive to the economic limits and possibilities of the economy.

POLITICAL ECONOMY AND DEFENSE

Two interrelated issues bear upon the question of the level of resources that will be devoted directly to national security matters: first, the relation between power potential and mobilization capability; and, second, the relation between national economic growth, governmental budgets, and public expectations.

The first relationship—power potential and mobilization capability—points to the nation's propensity to sacrifice. This propensity is not simply determined by the size of the gross domestic product but the people's sense of threat and of priorities. Drawing from what has been said earlier, it is apparent that Americans do not have a strong sense of external threat; neither geopolitical position nor political conceptions have historically sustained an abiding orientation toward national security matters. Nor have our institutions directed us in a consistent way toward external affairs. A heavy emphasis on the private market and personal choice, divided government, and the primacy of a Congress oriented toward local constituency concerns all reflect and reinforce the attitudes born of geographical position and of the founding political philosophy. On these grounds alone, the national security budgets, including both foreign and defense policy items, are subject to enormous variability, with a boom or bust quality that makes consistent policy difficult at best.

Beyond these general propositions is the special circumstance that has arisen since World War II in the relationship between economic growth, the composition of the total national budget, public expectations, and the defense portion of the budget.[12] Beginning in 1985, downward pressures again began to build on the defense budget after the most expansive military build-up in U.S. peacetime history. In the second Reagan administration, the critical issue was whether or not there would be sufficient funds to sustain the forces acquired as a result of the budgetary expansion in the late seventies and early eighties while continuing force modernization, research, and development. Anyone knows that once you have bought a larger home, the income required to maintain it also increases. So it is with national defense: Any major expansion of forces requires a continuing, higher level of funding for readiness and for research if further modernization is to take place. And, of course, there is a rather deadly game of "keeping up with the Joneses" in all this, for potential adversaries are also changing and building their forces. However, at the beginning of the Bush administration the terms of the debate changed dramatically.

The collapse of the Warsaw Pact and Soviet willingness to withdraw and reduce forces allowed and impelled a search for a generally reduced U.S. defense establishment. The debate by the early nineties centered not on whether or not there would be substantial force reductions but on the exact size and nature of the cuts. Prior to the Iraqi invasion of Kuwait there was developing in Congress a serious constituency for cuts in the defense budget of up to 50 percent within five years. At the same time, the Bush administration was preparing a new strategic perspective based on the premise that once Soviet forces withdrew from Eastern Europe, it would take Moscow at least two years to mobilize for a major invasion. Most planners believed that the disorganization within the Soviet polity and the uncertain evolution of that state made the time horizon for mobilization even longer. Even if one could not with certainty predict the long-term relation between the U.S. and the Soviet Union, the probability of military conflict between those states had been dramatically reduced and one could see no other state or group of states on the horizon which would be capable over the next five to ten years of launching a general war. Regional and local conflicts and even civil anarchy in Eastern Europe were certainly possible and even probable but world war style conflicts seemed remote. On this basis the administration calculated that active ground forces could be reduced substantially, as well as limiting air and naval forces. If the demands of the Iraqi challenge demonstrated the continuing need for the ability to project and sustain even very "heavy" (main tank and armored) forces at distant points, there was still a growing consensus driven by the reduction in East-West tensions and in funds that large cuts were possible and desirable.

As part of administration rethinking, the Pentagon drafted a five year plan which called for a 500,000 reduction in the armed forces from 2.1 million to 1.6 million and recommended a new organizational structure for the military. The plan proposed that the military be organized under four operational commands—an Atlantic force, a Pacific force, a Strategic force, and a Contingency force. This plan would reduce substantially the number of principal commands and draw from all the services in varying combinations depending on the theater or mission. The end result would be a cut in Army active divisions from 18 to 12 plus 8 reserve divisions, 2 of which would be "reconstitutable" (i.e., partially staffed reserve units that could at times of tension be brought relatively rapidly to full strength); a reduction of Air Force active and reserve tactical air wings from 36 to roughly 25; a cut of deployable Navy carriers from 14 to 12; and a reduction of the Marine Corps from 196,000 troops to about 150,000. It should be noted, however, that if these cuts to a "base force" did materialize over the period of 5 years, it would have only meant a 10 to 15 percent cut in inflation-adjusted dollars. The reason given for what will appear to many as relatively modest budgetary cutbacks was signalled above—the cost of maintaining new and technically sophisticated weapons and supporting military research and development, education, and training is increasingly higher even with fewer troops and equipment. More important, the strategic concept undergirding the Pentagon study was that the United States would continue to be the major "regulatory" power providing a stable presence throughout the world. Indeed, many European and Asian states appeared anxious in the early nineties that as the world underwent uncertain change, a precipitous withdrawal of U.S. forces would encourage those states most prepared to exploit instability. However, this line of reasoning clashed with the desire of many in Congress and the public at large both to solve the problem of the federal budget deficit and to expand domestic programs by massive cuts in defense. Moreover, Democrats in Congress argued that the White House and Pentagon figures were based on the collapse of the Soviet Union but not on the subsequent disintegration of the Soviet Union itself.

If one took into account the latter, it was argued, the "base force" could be substantially lower than that projected by the Bush administration. The principal adversaries of the Bush administration position were Congressman Les Aspin and Senator Sam Nunn, respectively chairmen of the House and Senate Armed Services Committees. In the winter and spring of 1991-92, Les Aspin particularly enunciated an alternative strategic perspective that pointed toward more substantial force reductions. The ideas were close to and probably influenced the campaign positions of Governor Bill Clinton and provided the foundations for his policy as president.

This clash of interests and assessments touched, however, not only the question of the nature and requirements of the newly emerging international security environment. The broader issue was the degree to which the defense budget was part of the budgetary problem and therefore the extent to which it could be part of the solution without utterly decimating the U.S. defense posture.

Some retrospective economic discussion will put the problem in relief. In the 200 years after the beginning of the Industrial Revolution, annual real economic growth among the industrializing/industrialized nations was around 2 percent of gross domestic product (GDP), which translates into an impressive (by preindustrial standards) doubling of the economy every 35 years. After World War II, however, the average real growth was 4 to 5 percent—and the doubling of the economy every 15 years. Not only was a consumption economy generated but, both in terms of public and private expenditures, that economy became the established norm. Private and public spending increased and credit expanded based on the expectation of the continuation of this higher growth figure. Because resources were relatively abundant the public faced few difficult choices as between public spending and private discretionary spending or between guns and butter. In a real sense, spending advanced across the entire spectrum. And most remarkably, the growth of the economy was so great that the United States had smaller government relative to the size of the economy, but more programs.

However, once the growth rate declines, a major problem presents itself: Government needs a higher percentage of money to sustain programs or it must cut programs. But the American public has retained the older expectations that expansion of the economy can pay for increases in social-welfare programs, national security budgets, and private discretionary spending. It is the combination of lessened economic growth and older expectations (i.e., the propensity to sacrifice has not increased), as well as of declining productivity (some believe because of inadequate education and infrastructure), that result in the budget deficits.

There are broadly four categories within the federal budget: entitlements, defense, interest on the debt, and "everything else," from roads to dams to forests to embassies to education. What is remarkable is that, if "everything else" were canceled, it would hardly impact on the budget deficit. As for interest payments, one cannot afford to destroy the good faith of the federal government, with all the consequences for political and economic stability, by failing to pay the interest on the national debt. That leaves entitlements and defense—and herein lies the rub.

Entitlements include a host of programs from social security to medicare/medicaid and are designated as entitlements because they are virtually on automatic; they do not require periodic reauthorization by Congress and the funding includes built-in cost-of-living adjustments (COLAs). The great expansion in these benefits took place in the Johnson and Nixon years and are geared to expectations of a 4-5 percent real growth economy. This explains why defense has declined from 50 percent of the budget and 9 percent of the GDP in the Eisenhower years to 27-28 percent of the budget and less than 5 percent of GDP, despite the defense buildup in the later Carter and early Reagan years. To take some recent comparisons, in 1979 defense spending represented 4.8 percent of the GDP and in 1986 it reached 6.5 percent of GDP, but in 1991 it declined once again to below 5 percent of GDP. The most important comparison may be, however, that in 1965 entitlements represented 5 percent of GDP and in 1993 they represented over 9 percent. Consequently, defense and entitlements have reversed places in the last 20 years. Moreover, if one looks at real defense spending in the entire period from 1957 to 1993, real growth in defense spending averages out at about 1 percent a year—considerably below growth in entitlements. It should be further understood that while defense continues to decline both as percent of GDP and of the federal budget while entitlements grow, federal government receipts increased from 517 billion dollars in 1980 to 1.05 trillion dollars in fiscal 1990. Still the deficit grew from 74 billion dollars in fiscal 1980 to well over 300 billion dollars a dozen years later.

The point is *not* that, since defense spending is already declining, there can be no further cuts. The point is that the growing gap between revenues and expenditures is decreasingly attributable to the defense budget. On the other hand, there may in fact be a political limit to how far taxes can be increased to cover the deficit and meet increasing demands. Although President Bush and Congress finally cut a "deficit-reduction" deal just prior to the 1990 November elections, the process was so painful and the public so outraged at the tax increase portions of the package that further tax increases will not come early or easily. More troubling, even after the presidential- congressional deal, government spending continued to escalate while there was in fact no decline in the rate of increase in the deficit. Moreover, personal income taxes had already climbed from 244 billion dollars in fiscal 1980 to over 470 billion dollars in 1989 and virtually every source of government revenue had increased. At the same time, with state and local governments facing increasing demands and deficits, taxes on that level are also being raised. Hence, although many commentators speak of the American public as being undertaxed in comparison to the publics of other advanced industrialized nations, it is not a politically winning notion and continues to constrain the Clinton administration. Lastly, it should be observed that the combination of consumer demand, credit, oil prices, and the relative openness of the American market, among other factors, exacerbate the trade as well as the budget deficit, despite increases in American exports.

From this discussion and the earlier discussion of the changing social and cultural bases of U.S. foreign policy, it appears that these forces and trends may be systemic in character—that is, they are built into social and demographic patterns—and, it may be prudent to expect that, absent a major international crisis and absent a willingness to increase taxes substantially and to rein in entitlement benefits, the domestic pressures on the defense budget are likely to be persistent and *not necessarily related to any real assessment of what is strategically required in the international environment.*

In summary, beginning in the 1860s vast changes in the structure and process of domestic and world politics began to change both the character of American power and the stage upon which that power would be exercised. In a sense, that particular drama played itself out for over 100 years and by the middle of the twentieth century the United States occupied center stage and performed according to a script crafted in the experiences of two world wars and the challenges posed by an ideologically alien and imperial Soviet Union. By 1990, however, the cumulative effect of political, economic, and cultural trends and transformations both within and outside the country began once again to alter American power and the context of that power.

In response to these changes, some speak of the resurgence of isolationist sentiment in the United States. And, indeed, there may be profound forces in the country that incline the people toward detachment and disengagement. But the character of the American external role is being defined by other, more complex forces that involve both the habits of the past and the realities of the present—geopolitical attitudes and institutional constraints, economic structures and cultural expectations. We have highlighted some of those forces that have defined the American security posture in the past and will shape it in the future. As we now turn in the next chapter to an assessment of the elements of national defense and military strategy since World War II and the probable directions of change, we must always keep in mind those fundamental factors.

ENDNOTES

1. Robert S. Wood, "The Conceptual Framework for Strategic Development of the Naval War College," *Naval War College Review,* 20, No. 2/Sequence 318 (Spring 1957): 4-16.
2. James Madison, "The Federalist No. 10," in *The Federalist,* ed. and intro. by Jacob E. Cooke (Middletown, CT: Wesleyan University Press, 1982), 58 and 61.

3. Washington's Farewell Address, 17 September 1796, in Norman A. Graebner, *Ideas and Diplomacy* (New York: Oxford University Press, 1964), 73-76.
4. Alfred T. Mahan, *The Influence of Sea Power Upon History, 1660-1783* (Boston: Little, Brown and Co., 1890).
5. See Colin S. Gray, *The Geopolitics of Super Power* (Lexington: The University Press of Kentucky, 1988).
6. For a thoughtful analysis of the relations between transformations in the political, economic, and social elements of the international environment and the policies of states, see Richard N. Rosecrance, *Action and Reaction in World Politics* (Boston: Little, Brown and Company, 1963).
7. Thomas A. Bailey, "America's Emergence as a World Power: The Myth and the Verity," *Pacific Historical Review* 30 (1961), 1-16.
8. For useful studies of the relationship of technology to strategy and policy, see "New Technology and Western Security Policy," Parts I, II, and III, *Adelphi Papers* 197, 198, and 199 (Summer 1985) and Elizabeth J. Kirk, ed., *Technology, Security, and Arms Control for the 1990s* (Washington, D.C.: The American Association for the Advancement of Science, 1988).
9. For an analysis of the roots of American foreign policy, see Robert S. Wood, "Henry Kissinger and the American Conception of Foreign Policy," Chapter 2 in Louis J. Mensonides and James A. Kuhlman, eds., *America and European Security* (Leyden: A.W. Sijthoff, 1976). Also see Felix Gilbert, *The Beginnings of American Foreign Policy to the Farewell Address* (Princeton: Princeton University Press, 1961), and Paul A. Varg, *Foreign Policies of the Founding Fathers* (Lansing: Michigan State University Press, 1963).
10. Alexis de Tocqueville, *Democracy in America,* Phillips Bradley, ed., 2 vols. (New York: Vintage Books, 1957), Vol. 1, 302.
11. For a more extensive analysis, see Robert S. Wood, "The Constitution, Congressional Government, and the Imperial Republic," in Howard E. Shuman and Walter R. Thomas, eds., *The Constitution and National Security* (Washington, D.C.: National Defense University Press, 1990), 97-113.
12. For a provocative examination of the relationship between the defense portion of the budget, the national economy, and the rest of the federal budget, see James L. Payne, "Wrong Numbers," *The National Interest* 14 (Winter 1988/89): 60-71.

7

THE COLD WAR
AND NATIONAL
DEFENSE

Speaking on the Battleship *Missouri,* where he had just accepted the Japanese surrender on behalf of the Allied forces, General Douglas MacArthur said:

> A new era is upon us. Even the lesson of victory itself brings with it profound concern both for our future security and the survival of civilization. The destructiveness of the war potential, through progressive advances in scientific discovery, has in fact now reached a point which revises the traditional concept of war.
>
> Men since the beginning of time have sought peace. Various methods through the ages have attempted to devise an international process to prevent or settle disputes between nations. From the very start workable methods were found insofar as individual citizens were concerned, but the mechanics of an instrumentality of larger international scope have never been successful. Military alliances, balances of power, leagues of nations, all in turn failed, leaving the only path to be by way of the crucible of war. We have had our last chance. If we do not now devise some greater and more equitable system, Armageddon will be at our door. The problem basically is theological and involves a spiritual recrudescence and improvement of human character that will synchronize with our almost matchless advances in science, art,

literature and all material and culture developments of the past two thousand years. It must be of the spirit if we are to save the flesh.[1]

The renunciation of war as a rational instrument of state policy in MacArthur's statement arose not only from the glimpses of Armageddon provided by the atomic bomb unleashed on Hiroshima and Nagasaki, but the human carnage and social disruptions that had racked the world since the onset of the First World War. It is estimated conservatively that nearly 60 million soldiers and civilians lost their lives directly or indirectly as a result of the two world wars with millions of others wounded and incapacitated. With war comes famine and revolution—and the collapse of norms of civilized behavior. Millions thus died in the revolutions and civil wars, as well as from the disruptions caused thereby to husbandry and culture.[2]

MacArthur could well have echoed the sentiments of another general from ancient Greece, Thucydides, who recorded in his day the evaporation of order and decency in the midst of war, famine, and revolution:

> . . . there were the savage and pitiless actions in which men were car-
> ried not so much for the sake of gain as because they were swept away
> into an internecine struggle by their ungovernable passions. Then,
> with the ordinary conventions of civilized life thrown into confusion,
> human nature, always ready to offend even where laws exist, showed
> itself proudly in its true colours, as something incapable of controlling
> passion, insubordinate to the idea of justice, the enemy to anything su-
> perior to itself; for, if it had not been for the pernicious power of envy,
> men would not so have exalted vengeance above innocence and profit
> above justice. Indeed, it is true that in these acts of revenge on others
> men take it upon themselves to begin the process of repealing those
> general laws of humanity which are there to give a hope of salvation
> to all who are in distress, instead of leaving those laws in existence,
> remembering that there may come a time when they, too, will be in
> danger and will need their protection.[3]

In the face of such devastation and such disorder, it is easy to understand the contradictory feelings that moved the American people in 1945: either demobilizing and withdrawing back into "normalcy" (i.e., disengagement and nonalignment) or joining one's forces with others in a collective security organization that would define and suppress aggression. These sentiments either of isolation or of universalism, however different, were shaped by the same horror and were identical to those expressed at the conclusion of World War I. Whatever one's position, most Americans concurred with the observation to Congress in 1943 of Secretary of State Cordell Hull that we needed to find a world order in which "there will no longer be a need for spheres of influence, for alliances, for balances of power, or any other of the special arrangements through which, in the unhappy past, the nations strove to safeguard or to promote their interests."[4]

Given these conditions and attitudes, could one have predicted that forty-five years later the United States would still be the principal mover in the most extensive, integrated, multinational alliance in history, the North Atlantic Treaty Organization, and that the country would have political-military commitments around the globe, have intervened dozens of times with military forces in far-flung places, and have fought two wars in Asia? Moreover, the United States was maintaining the largest standing military force in its history and in the 1980s undertook the largest peacetime military buildup in American history. There was certainly no return to "normal" nonalignment or isolation here!

But what of the desire of many Americans at the conclusion of World War II to construct a universal collective security organization that would transcend the world of alliances and of independent, national assertions of force? The United Nations, as the League of Nations that had preceded it, was to be the expression of this vision. Like its predecessor organization, the United Nations provided at best a supplemental—not an exclusive—framework for resolving issues involving the threatened or actual use of force. Indeed, in the great violent struggles since World War II, the United Nations appeared to be either incidental or irrelevant. If there was no move back to an idealized age of disengagement, so there was no move forward to an era of collective peace. The world of balances and of alliances, whose passing had been pronounced by Secretary Hull, seemed lively enough.

What had transpired that so disappointed expectations and that seemed so distant from MacArthur's call to devise new forms of conflict resolution? The change in expectations and the development of new policies and strategies came about largely from 1945 through 1952—perhaps the most momentous period in the reconstruction of the American national security posture. Those who were players in the drama of this period saw it as a decisive moment in the life of the nation and, indeed, the transforming experience of their own lives. Dean Acheson, secretary of state to President Harry Truman, captured these sentiments in the title of his memoirs, *Present at the Creation*.[5]

THE FOUNDING OF CONTEMPORARY
AMERICAN SECURITY POLICY

The United Nations was premised on the expectation that the grand alliance of Great Britain, the Soviet Union, and the United States would survive the conclusion of the Second World War. It was not assumed that this would be easy. Several major problems confronted the victorious states:

- the political evolution of the traditional colonial territories in Asia, the Indian subcontinent, Africa, the Middle East, the Pacific, and the Caribbean;
- the reconstruction of the states devastated by war;
- the restoration of a global economy shattered by depression and war;
- the search for a political-military framework to forestall the retreat of the United States back into relative isolation;
- and, in the event, most crucially, the accommodation of Soviet territorial aspirations legitimized, the Russians believed, by military hardship and the ultimate victory of their arms—and universalized in terms of their ideological pretensions.

Any one of these problems was perplexing but their interconnection made the resultant issues knotty beyond belief. The wartime agreements among the allied powers were largely centered on the disposition of the defeated states, but it was hoped that the establishment of an international organization would provide the framework for resolving the myriad of problems arising from the troubled decades after World War I.

FROM VICTORIOUS
COALITION TO COLD WAR

In February 1945 at Yalta in the Crimea, the Soviet leader, Joseph Stalin, promised to support self-government and free elections in Eastern Europe and to accept participation in the United Nations on the basis of a formula allowing the veto in the Security Council to be applied only to enforcement actions and not to peaceful attempts to settle disputes. Moreover, the Soviets agreed upon the conclusion of the war against Germany to enter the war against Japan, for which the Soviets were granted in a secret protocol the restoration of those territories lost in the 1904 Russo-Japanese War plus the acquisition of the Kurile Islands. It was agreed in principle to divide Germany into a number of independent states and to provide for some form of German reparation payment to be rendered in the removal of capital equipment rather than the transference of funds. Adjustments in the Polish frontiers were accepted, to the benefit of the Soviet Union, and a joint American-British-Soviet commission was established to resolve the contentious issue of the character of the Polish government. On balance, the American administration felt that, whatever the ambiguities of the agreement, a basis had been laid for post-war cooperation.

For many Americans the Yalta agreement signaled a peacetime security system in keeping with Secretary of State Hull's vision. The victorious powers would join their forces to halt aggression and would concert together to establish a global order sensitive to the security needs of those great powers and to the aspirations of peoples everywhere. And, yet, even as the agreement was being signed and in the months thereafter, there was growing evidence that the security concepts of the Soviet Union, on the one hand, and the Western states, on the other, were going to diverge, most significantly over the nature of the political regimes in Eastern Europe and the disposition of Germany. When the new president, Harry Truman, met in July 1945 with the British and the Soviets at Potsdam in Germany, the difficulty of agreement was more evident, even if the assumption of peacetime cooperation remained.

At Potsdam, the British and Americans expressed their concern with Soviet highhandedness in Bulgaria and Romania, whereas the Soviets complained of British administration in Greece. Commissions of experts were set up to resolve these issues and the wartime allies turned to the easier of the peacetime agreements—treaties with Italy, Romania, Bulgaria, Hungary, and Finland. It was agreed that a Council of Foreign Ministers of the three powers plus France and China would draft treaties for these countries, but that only those signatories of the respective surrenders participate in the peace agreements, thus effectively excluding France from Eastern Europe since that latter country had been liberated rather than having participated throughout the course of the conflict as a co-belligerent. The exception to this rule was to be Italy. Moreover, as a result of an earlier agreement at Yalta, France was also to be an administering power in Germany in territories taken from the American and British zones of occupation.

As to the more difficult issue of Germany, it was agreed at Potsdam that Germany would be disarmed, demilitarized, and de-Nazified. Decentralization of Germany would be promoted in order to prevent a central German government, but there was now an implicit understanding that some cohesion would bind the German nation. If the final disposition of the German political system was left vague, the issue of frontiers was no clearer. However, the British and Americans did undertake to support the transfer of part of East Prussia with Konigsberg to Russia while the territories east of the Oder-Neisse line were to be under temporary Polish administration. The latter understanding grew out of the Soviet desire to redraw the boundaries of Poland so as to extend its own western frontier and to compensate Poland at the expense of defeated Germany. Although the western powers were sympathetic to some recasting of the borders, they were unwilling to resolve definitively the question until the final character of the Polish government was determined. Moreover, the large Polish population in the United States made the issue a particularly sticky domestic concern. In any case, it should be clear to the reader that agreement was forged at Potsdam largely by postponing final resolution of the issues dividing the allies.

If, in the late spring and summer of 1945, the Allies were attempting to shape the peace of Europe, the Pacific war was moving to a conclusion. On July 26 the United States, Britain, and China issued a joint ultimatum of unconditional surrender to Japan. This was rejected by the Japanese government but the dropping of the atomic bomb on Hiroshima on 6 August followed by another on Nagasaki on 9 August induced the Japanese to accept the ultimatum. Moreover, on 8 August the Soviet Union declared war on Japan and invaded Manchuria, thus acquiring title to the territories promised by the Yalta agreement. Both the European and the Asian theaters of war were quiet. Peace had descended upon the world. And the American people clamored to "bring the boys home." General, if vague, accords had been achieved with the wartime allies, the enemies had surrendered, the new international institution was about to be launched—and the pressures for withdrawal of American forces and demobilization were overwhelming. And so began the, as it proved, near-impossible task of translating the words of the wartime Allied agreements into concrete form acceptable to all the parties and to do it in conditions in which U.S. forces were being withdrawn from the point at which they touched those of the Soviet Union, central Europe.

The question of the origins of the "Cold War" has not only divided the Soviet Union and its cohorts from the Western states but has been the occasion for heated controversy among western historians themselves. In retrospect, however, it is possible without unnecessary heat to discern the fundamental basis of that great post-World War II struggle and hence the origins of the American security system. The Soviet conception of security in the years after World War II required that the states in Eastern Europe be so arranged as to accept Soviet dictation on their external alignments. Given the ideological predispositions of the Soviet regime and the character of Stalin's rule, this meant that the internal regimes of the eastern European countries would necessarily be dominated by Moscow-controlled Communist parties. And this in turn implied that, since free elections would not produce this outcome, what the West believed was a commitment at Yalta to self-determination in Eastern Europe, was never met. Moreover, since the only conditions under which Germany might be united under a common constitution would be in accord with the Soviet conception of security or, conversely, in accord with the western definition of free elections, this meant that the "temporary" division of the country for purposes of military occupation congealed into political boundaries. The decision of Britain, France, and the United States to institute a currency reform in their sectors in order to lay the basis of economic recovery in western Germany, and the division of the four powers over the control of Berlin, were met by a Soviet blockade of Berlin—a blockade that the West overcame by an airlift to West Berlin in the winter and spring of 1948-49. The

Republic in their own zone. And even though the United States had offered in 1947 a plan to reduce the barriers among the European states and to extend aid for the reconstruction of all the European states (i.e., the Marshall plan), it is clear that the Russians believed that such "intervention" by the United States in the affairs of Eastern Europe could only complicate, if not defeat, their efforts to shape the character and external orientation of those states. In effect, Europe was moving toward division with separate security systems inexorably following.

The political events outlined above insured that the unity of the wartime allies in the Security Council of the United Nations could not provide the foundation of U.S. security policy. The authority given to the five permanent members of the United Nations—China, France, Great Britain, the Soviet Union, and the United States—to protect their own vital security interests by halting any forceful action by the United Nations judged inimical to any of them (i.e., the veto), was quickly transformed from an occasional assertion of power to a normal routine characterized by stalemate. The world was rapidly moving toward alliances, spheres of influence, and balances of power—the most significant manifestations of which were to be the North Atlantic Treaty Organization and the Warsaw Pact Organization.

POLICY, STRATEGY, AND
THE NORTH ATLANTIC TREATY

The agreement on 4 April 1949 by twelve states to the North Atlantic Treaty represented the definitive collapse of the efforts to organize a security system including both West and East Europe.[6] Moreover, it signaled the most significant change in American alliance policy since the founding of the Republic. The progressive integration of the signatories to the treaty within a common defense organization "entangled" the United States in a permanent, peacetime alliance founded on traditional concepts of the balance of power. The dangers of withdrawing into isolation seemed to most Americans as patent and the inability to maintain the World War II grand coalition within the framework of the United Nations was manifest. NATO was the military response to what was perceived as the potential political and military domination of the Soviet Union over a shattered and divided Europe. If the eastern part of Europe had slipped under Soviet control, the extension of the latter's influence into Western Europe would decisively shift the global balance of power against the United States.

The North Atlantic Treaty Organization was grounded on three factors:

1. the inability of the United States and the Soviet Union to agree on the political shape of Germany and of Eastern Europe;

1. the inability of the United States and the Soviet Union to agree on the political shape of Germany and of Eastern Europe;
2. the asymmetry in the strategic positions of the United States and the Soviet Union;
3. the need to rearm Germany as part of the defense of Europe.

In simple terms, the ability of the United States and the Soviet Union after World War II to agree on a neutralized Germany would probably have been a minimum precondition for any collective security system and disarmament arrangements. Moreover, the manner in which the Soviets acted within their zone of control in Eastern Europe was to determine how the West would judge Soviet proposals for Germany. In the event, Soviet pressures on Turkey to cede territories and to allow bases in the Turkish Straits, support for guerrillas in Greece, resistance to withdrawal from northern Iran, the suppression of political opposition in Eastern Europe culminating in the coup d'état in Czechoslovakia in 1948—all these moves by the Soviet Union heightened suspicion that any arrangement for Germany would be exploited by the U.S.S.R. to extend its unilateral influence over all of Germany. At the same time, the reduction of American, British, and Canadian forces in Europe from about 5 million troops in 1945 to 880,000 in 1946, whereas the Soviet armed strength amounted in 1946 to more than 6 million troops still on a wartime footing, created a growing sense of anxiety as to the ability of the states of Western Europe to seize their own destinies.

Political stalemate joined with strategic asymmetry to suggest the need for a shift away from the traditional American antipathy to peacetime competitive alignments. To restate a central theme from the previous chapter, the United States is separated by vast expanses of air and water from its interests and potential friends in Europe and Asia. The requirement to secure those friends and interests demands an air and naval capacity to traverse with certainty those expanses and to find states willing and able to cooperate once having arrived. With the collapse of the traditional Central and Western European powers and of Japan in World War II and the rise of the Soviet Union straddling both Asia and Europe, the United States for the first time since becoming a Great Power directly confronted a potential adversary with no intervening state to bear the initial brunt of defense.

The American response to this problem was two-fold:

- first, to strengthen the political institutions and economies of the states lying on the periphery of the Soviet Union through direct military and economic aid, as was extended to Greece and Turkey under the 1947 Truman Doctrine or to Europe generally under Marshall Plan recovery assistance;

■ second, to employ its superiority in atomic weapons to deter any direct invasion by the Soviets of their neighbors.

Indeed, on the latter point, NATO was initially very much an American nuclear guarantee of Western Europe. It was assumed from the very invention of atomic weapons that their possession directly deterred any attack on the United States, but now, in order to counterbalance Russia's geographical advantage and large conventional forces, the threat to use those weapons would be extended to Western Europe to deter an attack by those superior Soviet conventional forces. Hence, the distinction in strategic analysis between *direct deterrence* and *extended deterrence.*

NUCLEAR DETERRENCE
AND CONVENTIONAL FORCES

With nuclear weapons constituting the foundation of Western European defense, the last prop was kicked out from under the American 1946 proposal for the elimination of nuclear weapons to be supervised and maintained by a United Nations commission whose work could not be subject to the veto (the Baruch Plan). The Soviet desire to develop their own atomic weapon doomed the plan from the start in any event, although the Soviets excused their opposition on the grounds that the U.S. planned to retain its (monopolistic) stockpile until international controls were in place and that, in any case, the veto-free international control commission would be subject to Western domination. In fact, the Soviets very much wished their own capability as they well understood that their conventional preponderance in Europe could be neutralized by American technological advantage, visible in the atomic bomb.

It was clear that, given American strength in air and sea power, the U.S. could strike directly at the Russian homeland whereas Soviet power could only be brought to bear in Europe. A threat to occupy Western Europe from this perspective might not deter the United States from using its nuclear monopoly to impose its political will on the Soviet Union or even from attacking directly. Only a comparable capability sufficient at a minimum to threaten nuclear devastation in Western Europe could counterbalance U.S. advantage. The successful testing of its own air-delivered atomic bomb in 1949 brought this capability within reach and caused the NATO powers to develop a second defense pillar to supplement extended deterrence—the *forward strategy or defense.*

If the U.S. nuclear capability was the ultimate guarantor of the states of Western Europe, there was still the problem that Soviet land forces could move swiftly west overwhelming NATO defenses. This raised the problem of having to liberate a devastated Europe even if the United States attacked the Soviet

Union directly. The issue was further complicated if the Soviet Union itself possessed nuclear weapons which, even if their delivery capacity was insufficient to reach the United States, could utterly destroy Western Europe. Indeed, the ability to do so might be used to deter the United States from employing its capability to attack the Russian homeland. It became evident to a number of western strategists that, to forestall this dilemma, NATO needed sufficient conventional forces to prevent a breakthrough across the border separating West Germany from East Germany and Czechoslovakia (the "Central Front") or at least to prevent the attack from sweeping to the Rhine before a nuclear response was possible. Moreover, since U.S. striking power was not yet intercontinental but was located on air bases in Europe itself, it was important to prevent these bases from being overrun. At the same time, with the Soviet nuclear capabilities likely to grow in size and range, it was important psychologically to ensure that U.S. ground forces be engaged on the first day of battle so that the link between North America and Western Europe was patently clear.

This line of reasoning led to two important conclusions—that U.S. forces would be permanently located in Europe, particularly Germany, and that an adequate enough conventional force was needed to prevent a sudden Soviet breakthrough. As the planners thought through the latter proposition, it became clear that West Germany would have to be rearmed.

FROM NORTH ATLANTIC TREATY TO NORTH ATLANTIC ORGANIZATION

Two events in 1950 led even more inexorably to the decision to rearm West Germany—the completion of the document known as NSC-68 and the invasion by North Korea of South Korea on 25 June.

NSC-68

The successful testing in 1949 by the Soviets of an atomic device raised serious doubts in the United States about exclusive reliance on its atomic capability to deter attack on itself and its friends. The question arose whether or not to begin work on another deterrent agent—the hydrogen bomb. President Truman asked the State and Defense Departments under the leadership of Paul Nitze to consider this question within the broader context of an evaluation of Soviet intentions and the shape of the U.S. defense budget and structure.

George Kennan, a former envoy in the Soviet Union and later head of the Policy Planning Staff in the State Department, had already in 1947 laid the political foundation for the policy of containing the Soviet Union:

> . . . the main element of any United States policy toward the Soviet Union must be that of a long-term, patient but firm and vigilant containment of Russian expansive tendencies . . . the Soviet pressure against the free institutions of the western world is something that can be contained by the adroit and vigilant application of counter-force at a series of constantly shifting geographical and political points, corresponding to the shifts and manoeuvres of Soviet policy.[7]

The report to President Truman accepted as National Security Council Directive 68 (NSC-68) on April 1950 extended this analysis and provided a rationale for both the hydrogen bomb project and a major expansion of the defense budget from 6 or 7 percent of the gross national product to 13.8 percent.[8]

The paper called for a rapid military buildup in conventional forces and suggested that the nation could afford as high as 20 percent of the GNP for military purposes and the government could increase spending from 15 billion dollars to as high as 50 billion dollars a year. Clearly a major military dimension was being given to the containment policy—one which, even though Kennan himself thought was excessive, was accepted by senior members of the administration. The real issue in their minds, however, was whether Congress and the public were prepared to accept such a substantial change in the nation's peacetime military posture. The Korean War proved to be the event that brought for the moment such acceptance.

The Response to the Korean War

The attack of North Korean forces across the 38th parallel on the morning of 25 June 1950 was quickly seen by the administration as a direct assault on the whole structure of global peace and perhaps the initial phase of a campaign that would eventually include an attack into Western Europe. It was also seen how difficult it was to bring to bear nuclear weapons in such a sudden ground assault. One of the great ironies of the Korean War was that its most dramatic effects were felt in Europe. Very early, and particularly after the entry of the new Chinese Communist government into the fray, it was decided to limit the scope of the Korean War while strengthening forces in Europe, where it was felt the real prize and danger lay. The organization of the North Atlantic Treaty was finally put in place and the integration of the allied forces under a political committee and unified commander was developed. The U.S. defense budget did increase from 22.3 billion dollars in fiscal year 1951 to 44 billion dollars in fiscal year 1952 and to 50.4 billion dollars in fiscal year 1953.

The implications of these events for NATO seemed clear—the need for a much larger ground force forward deployed to prevent any sudden breakout of Soviet forces. Indeed, at a NATO Council meeting in Lisbon, Portugal, in May 1952, the ministers agreed to raise NATO forces sufficient to fight a relatively protracted conventional war. Not that a nuclear defense was abandoned but the "threshold" of the nuclear response was raised, giving time to the aggressor to reconsider and to the defenders to prepare their ultimate response. There was no intention of matching Soviet forces on the battlefield. But it was considered critical to prevent the Russians from engineering a *fait accompli* on the ground while threatening the nuclear devastation of Europe. It was felt that if such a *fait accompli* could be prevented by forward-deployed conventional forces, the Soviets could not then threaten nuclear strikes against Europe without incurring nuclear retaliation from the United States. Hence, conventional forces would perpetuate the U.S. nuclear advantage even as that advantage decreased in the face of nuclear developments in the Soviet Union.

A major problem, however, remained: French forces were engaged against a national and communist rebellion in Indochina and would shortly face a major insurgency in Algeria. There was a limit to how many U.S., Canadian, or British forces could be forward deployed—all of which brings us back to the issue of German rearmament. It was impossible to conceive of the defense of Europe without a substantial German contribution.

Germany and the Defense of the West

If there was one issue calculated to cause anxiety in both West and East Europe, it was the rearmament of Germany. Twice in this century German armies had swept both east and west. It was only with great exertion, tremendous suffering, and the intervention of forces from North America and the British Empire that Germany was finally defeated. Moreover, the very unification of the various German states in the last half of the nineteenth century had thrust the new state into the position of predominance on the continent and rivalry with Britain globally. Hence, if the western half of Germany were now to be rearmed in order to contain the Soviet Union, some framework needed to be found in order to reassure Europeans, west and east, that German armed forces could not be used to undertake by force the reunification of Germany and the recasting once again of the map of Europe.

The formula hit upon was a French proposal to create a European Defense Community (EDC)—a European army composed of corps in which no more than two divisions could be of the same nationality. This allowed the use of German soldiers while preventing the creation of a German general staff or army. EDC would be formally linked to NATO under whose command it would serve in the defense of Europe. The EDC Treaty was signed in May 1952.

Unfortunately, the EDC never got off the ground and the treaty itself was rejected in August 1954 by the French National Assembly whose fear of Germany and whose concern for a renewed German predominance made even the EDC unacceptable. The fury of the Eisenhower administration and the diplomacy of Anthony Eden, the British Prime Minister, finally produced another mechanism which the French really had no choice but to accept.

Revising the 1948 Brussels Treaty which bound together Belgium, France, Luxembourg, the Netherlands, and the United Kingdom in a mutual assistance pact aimed more at containing Germany than Russia, Eden proposed including both West Germany and Italy in the Treaty and reconstituting the pact as the Western European Union (WEU). The union itself would have no direct role in formulating a common strategy but would be linked to NATO and provide the channel whereby German forces would be placed under NATO command. History has many ironies. This is certainly one of them. The EDC was rejected by the French National Assembly because it was considered too weak to contain German energies, but the WEU substitution was less integrated and the original pact on which it was premised was in fact anti-German! In any case, WEU was signed in October 1954 and on 9 May 1955 the Federal Republic of Germany became a member of the North Atlantic Treaty Organization, beginning the process by which West Germany became the contributor not only of the probable battlefield but of the bulk of the ground forces.

Well before Dwight Eisenhower assumed the presidency in 1953, the basic outlines of the U.S. strategic approach were becoming clear, but the final adherence of the Federal Republic of Germany to the North Atlantic Treaty completed the process. Issues would now center on how to maintain the alliance, how to respond to changes in Soviet strength, and how to relate to other threats a force and a strategy aimed at containing the Soviet Union.

STRATEGIC DEBATES
AND POLITICAL EVOLUTIONS

By 1955 the critical elements of the U.S. defense posture were well defined:

1. deterrence by the threat of nuclear retaliation of a direct Soviet attack on the American homeland (i.e., *direct deterrence*);
2. the extension of the U.S. nuclear deterrent to cover external military threats to the Western Hemisphere, Western Europe, and Japan (i.e., *extended deterrence*);
3. in order to signal commitment and to prevent any immediate breakthrough of a sudden, massed Soviet attack, the deployment of U.S. ground, air, and naval forces—both nuclear and conventional—around the periphery of the Soviet sphere (i.e., *forward defense*); and

4. the development of bases and of mobile, interventionary forces designed to intimidate enemies and to reassure friends, to inflict limited damage, and to secure air and sea lines of communications (LOCS), in order to sustain distant friends and interests against threats external or internal to the states concerned (i.e., *power projection*).

The major issues facing U.S. leadership thereafter were to maintain the cohesion of allied partners and to respond to the changing dimensions of the military threat at a cost politically sustainable by democratic publics during peacetime. During the Eisenhower administration, this translated into a policy more reliant on nuclear than on conventional force in areas both vulnerable to direct attack and vitally important to the United States—e.g., Western Europe (a position sometimes designated by the use of Eisenhower's Secretary of State John Foster Dulles' phrase—*"massive retaliation"*). In other areas both less important and less subject to direct Soviet or Chinese intimidation, the Eisenhower administration employed navy, marine, and airborne forces for limited intervention (e.g., Lebanon, 1958) or political, economic, or sub-rosa intimidation, as well as support for friendly indigenous forces (e.g., Iran, 1953; Guatemala, 1954).

By the late 1950s short-range nuclear weapons were added to the arsenal of longer-range missile or airplane-delivered nuclear weapons. With the introduction of such battlefield weapons, the "nuclearization" of NATO was virtually complete. The muster of Western conventional armies would compel a Soviet Union intent on invasion to mass sufficient forces in order to punch through the West's defensive lines; but, once the Soviets had brought their forces together, they would be vulnerable to destruction by a nuclear barrage. And, of course, there still remained the longer- range attack aircraft or missiles that could threaten the Soviet Union with direct nuclear attack. Hence, at every level of warfare, the West would dominate and hence render deterrence virtually complete (a concept often referred to as *"escalation dominance"*).[9] If one coupled this posture in Europe with superiority over the global air and sea lanes, as well as the ability to intervene with limited force in crisis contingencies (i.e., limited external incursions or civil disturbances), you have a national security posture that allowed the United States to maintain the central balance of military force with the Soviet Union and to assist friends and defend interests against more limited challenges. This posture not only provided the military basis for building political-military coalitions with states in Latin America, Europe, Southwest Asia, Southeast Asia, and East Asia, but it accomplished this at acceptable political and economic costs. Indeed, inflation in the United States during the Eisenhower years was very low and economic recovery in Europe and Japan very rapid.

By the late Eisenhower administration, however, voices of criticism were being heard. These critiques centered on two issues: the credibility of the American nuclear deterrent and the flexibility of its military power.

Credibility and Nuclear Deterrence

The development of long-range bombers and missiles by the Soviets, as well as the acquisition of their own battlefield nuclear capabilities, cast in doubt the certainty of our escalation dominance. If they could do to us both on the battlefield and on our own territory what we could do to them, could they force us, by their own nuclear deterrent threat, to forego the use of either battlefield nuclear weapons or of direct strikes on the Soviet Union? Under these circumstances, the only use of nuclear weapons might be to prevent their use by the other side. If this is so, however, it restores the political and military impact of the geopolitical and conventional superiority of the Soviet Union in Eurasia.

Speculation on the meaning of emergent nuclear parity between the United States and the Soviet Union led to two principal, and dissimilar, conclusions. One line of thought argued that it was not nuclear deterrence as an instrument to prevent attack or invasion that was in doubt but extended deterrence. That is, the question was posed whether or not the United States would risk New York to save Bonn or London. The implication of this question was that one might deter a direct strike or attack on one's own country *if* your own state possessed nuclear weapons; but it is not credible that any country would risk nuclear armageddon on behalf of another. This argument undergird the claim by the French in the late fifties for an *independent nuclear deterrent*. The British, as a result of the World War II military and technological collaboration with the United States, had already acquired such a deterrent with American acquiescence and, in the critical area of delivery systems, assistance. The French claim was, however, particularly disruptive as it was posed in such a way as to call in question the defense of West Germany and the central front; for, if French logic were correct, how would the latter be protected without putting nuclear weapons directly in the hands of the Germans themselves—something neither the eastern nor western states would welcome.

The response to this challenge was twofold: (1) attempts to find formulas to increase the control by the NATO partners of nuclear weapons and (2) the French decision to leave the integrated structure of NATO and develop its own independent nuclear deterrent.

Proposals to "put more fingers on the nuclear trigger" took many forms, ranging from multilateral nuclear-armed, sea-going surface or subsurface forces to increased consultation on the conditions under which nuclear forces might be used. Ultimately, a Nuclear Defense Affairs Committee and a Nuclear Planning Group were developed, as well as the assignment of nuclear forces to the NATO command, although those forces still remained under the ultimate control of the state owning them, the United States.

In any case, many argued that the whole concern over the credibility of extended deterrence was overdrawn. At worst, nuclear parity would make a nuclear response uncertain; but the consultative mechanisms, doctrines, and deployment of nuclear forces in NATO still made their use in the event of conflict a high probability and thus a credible risk for the Soviets in their calculations. Moreover, it was argued, the desire by the French for their own nuclear deterrent had less to do with strategic logic than the political logic of autonomy and national self-assertion. Nonetheless, the issue of the credibility of the American extended nuclear deterrent remained a concern thereafter.

Flexible Response

A second response to the issue of nuclear parity related to the flexibility of U.S. forces—a concern that centered both on the NATO theater and elsewhere.

In 1959 General Maxwell D. Taylor published a book critical of what he saw as the inability of the Eisenhower defense structure and doctrine to respond to the range of threats facing the United States.[10] He felt that between limited interventionary forces and nuclear forces, there were too few responses and too little thought as to how to threaten or use military forces along the whole range of contingencies. Even on the nuclear level, he argued, there was too little sophistication in the types of response possible.

With the development of submarine-launched ballistic missiles (SLBMs), the United States acquired a capability relatively secure from preemptive attack or discovery. Although this system was not accurate or powerful enough to destroy "hardened" missile sites nor could one be sure that it would locate and destroy all the adversary's aircraft or ships, it was secure enough to deliver a devastating strike against populations and industrial capabilities even after absorbing a surprise Soviet nuclear strike. This secure, *countervalue* (i.e., against populations and industrial/economic infrastructures) force provided what became known as an *assured destruction second-strike*. But, in addition to this retaliatory force, the increasing accuracy of land-based intercontinental ballistic missile systems (ICBMs) allowed the United States to threaten military targets as well (i.e., *counterforce*). And, in addition to these long-range weapons (strategic nuclear forces), the U.S. continued to develop short-range nuclear weapons for use in circumstances ranging from the battlefield (500 kilometers or less) to theaters of military operations (as developments continued, anywhere from 500 to 5500 kilometers!). There was hence a technical basis for developing nuclear doctrines that would cover employment from the battlefield to intercontinental exchanges.

Although the basis of this formidable array of nuclear weapons, as well as the general concepts of nuclear deterrence, were well established in the Eisenhower administration, the administrations of John F. Kennedy and Lyndon B. Johnson in the 1960s expended considerable effort to link explicitly these systems and concepts to the doctrine of "flexible response"—that is, the linking of defensive and retaliatory forces to whatever level of challenge an adversary might mount. It was felt that such flexible responses would allow the president to choose options appropriate to the political, technical, and military requirements of different situations. However, the issue mentioned earlier remained: As the adversary acquired comparable capabilities, how credible was an American threat of nuclear defense or retaliation in circumstances less than a direct onslaught on the United States itself? Indeed, one heard talk in the Kennedy administration of mutual assured destruction—the possession by both sides of a secure, second-strike capability against the homeland of the other. It was felt that such a mutual capability would be "stable" in that neither side need fear a devastating surprise attack since, even should such an attack materialize, an equally devastating response was guaranteed.

Again, however, such a mutual posture might provide a high level of confidence that one's homeland was secure against attack; but could one have the same level of confidence that this protection would cover attacks, whether conventional or nuclear, against one's allies? This concern drove the desire to develop and maintain nuclear systems for use on the battlefield and in the military theater of operation directly subject to threat or attack. Even here, uncertainty that one could contain nuclear use to the area of battle or that such use would even guarantee a favorable outcome on the battlefield, led to the desire to extend flexible response to improving conventional or nonnuclear forces—hence *raising the nuclear threshold,* that is deferring the moment when the decision to use nuclear weapons would have to be made.

It was thus in the area of conventional, nonnuclear forces that the Kennedy and Johnson administrations expended much of their intellectual and material efforts—and thus, in a sense, returned the United States back to the budgetary assumptions of NSC-68. Moreover, the expansion of a whole range of nonnuclear forces was explicitly linked with a variety of contingencies and policy options, many of which were not in the European area or in defense against a traditional invasion across a well-recognized international boundary. It was felt that the Soviet Union and China were seeking to extend their influence by supporting insurgencies, subversion, infiltration, and civil wars in so-called *wars of national liberation.* Moreover, such conflicts were taking place in former colonial areas where political, economic, and social institutions had not yet been fully developed. It was felt that U.S. policy must not only provide military training and direct assistance, therefore, but aid in developing such institutions—i.e., "nation-building." In a real sense, this line of reasoning provided the intellectual underpinning of the Vietnam War.

Nuclear Sufficiency and the Nixon Doctrine

If the Korean War led Eisenhower to search for a less costly and divisive national security posture, the Vietnam War had a similar impact on the Nixon, Ford, and Carter administrations. The inability of the United States to force the government of North Vietnam to forego its ambitions to unite Vietnam under its auspices and the apparent inability of the South Vietnam government to command the necessary unity and tenacity to prevail against the North, caused serious rethinking of the assumptions underlying our policies in the sixties. In the nuclear area, this translated into a doctrine of *nuclear sufficiency*—a rather vague idea that basically entailed the search for a stable nuclear balance at lower levels of force.

Perhaps more relevant to the lessons of Vietnam, in the area of conventional force policy, this rethinking was expressed as a doctrine that placed greater responsibility on individual states and regional associations subject to externally supported insurgencies (what was known as the Guam or *Nixon Doctrine*). Moreover, the definitive break between the Soviet Union and China and the willingness of the United States to seek accommodation with China, led to more multifaceted power relationships and finally laid to rest policies arising from the notion of monolithic communism.

Strategic Arms Limitations Talks (SALT)

During the Nixon and Ford administrations, strategic nuclear agreements with the USSR and a political accommodation with the People's Republic of China were reached. A dominant policy thrust of the Nixon and Ford administrations was to ground U.S.-Soviet relations on a more stable and predictable nuclear balance. Limits were accepted on ICBMs and SLBMs but not numbers of warheads or such systems as manned bombers and short-range nuclear weapons. The limits on ICBMs were those in existence or under construction on 1 July 1972 and the limits on SLBMs were those in existence or under construction on the date the agreement was signed (26 May 1972). But since the parties had the right to substitute on a one-for-one basis pre-1964 ICBMs with SLBMS (i.e., the "freedom to mix") and since the agreed figures represented more missiles and submarines than either one possessed at the time of signing, the deployed, *modern* systems actually increased after the agreement. Moreover, since the agreement allowed each missile to carry multiple, independently targetable reentry vehicles (MIRVs), there was actually an increase in offensive deliverable warheads in the years following the 1972 agreement. At the same time, however, there were limits placed on the deployment and development of antiballistic missile (ABM) systems, thus effectively enshrining the concept of mutual assured destruction. Although technological limitations on an effective ABM system undergird the treaty, many saw the doctrinal merit of foregoing any development that might threaten to upset either side's ability to maintain an assured, second strike capability. The nuclear stalemate on the strategic level at least was seen as the foundation of a "stable" U.S-Soviet relationship.

The 1972 Strategic Arms Limitations Talks did not reduce the nuclear threat but they did strive to establish agreement that would define some upper limit to that threat. In late 1974 President Ford reached an accord with Chairman Leonid Brezhnev at Vladivostock extending the ABM agreement and placing a limit on each side of 2,400 strategic nuclear delivery vehicles (ICBMS, SLCM, and heavy bombers), of which 1,300 could be equipped with MIRVs. At the same time, construction of new ICBM launchers was banned, as was the conversion of light to heavy ICBMs (launchers with such powerful rocket boosters as to be able to carry warheads with enormous explosive yield).

Although in 1977 the new Carter administration sought to substitute deep reductions for the limitations of the Vladivostock accords, it eventually returned to the framework established by the Nixon and Ford administrations and accepted the initial 2,400 ceiling on strategic nuclear delivery vehicles with the ceiling to be reduced to 2,250 by 1981 and with sublimits on MIRVed systems and air-launched cruise missiles. A ban on increases in heavy ICBM launchers was accepted as was one on constructing additional fixed ICBM launchers. Limits were established on the number of warheads that various systems could carry. Hence, despite some limited reductions and an accord on further reductions in the future, the SALT II treaty did not substantially alter the high level of nuclear threat. Moreover, Soviet activities in Cuba, Africa, and the Middle East and its 1979 invasion of Afghanistan provided the occasion for the Carter administration to withdraw the treaty from Senate consideration—an agreement probably unable to be ratified in any case given Soviet activities. Nonetheless, despite candidate Ronald Reagan's criticism of the treaty during the 1980 presidential election campaign, the newly elected Reagan administration chose to abide by the terms of the agreement while it sought other bases for U.S.-Soviet relations.

Malaise and Renewal:
From Defense Stagnation to Defense Buildup

If there was an attempt in the Nixon, Ford, and Carter administrations to find a basis for American-Soviet accommodation, particularly on the nuclear level, so economic pressures and the internal political divisions generated by the Vietnam War led those administrations toward less intense defense commitments. Throughout much of the seventies, this meant reduced defense budgets and a transfer of more responsibilities to both allies and threatened states. Accommodation with China and the inability of a victorious Vietnam, despite its incursion into Cambodia (Kampuchea), to sustain the momentum of military conquest, foreshadowed a relatively stable period in Asia. Moreover, the rising tide of economic prosperity propelled by Japan and some of the lesser Asian states undergird this stability. And in a prosperous Europe there was a commitment to increased military spending. In a real sense, therefore, there were a number of forces at work that allowed the United States to reduce or to freeze some of its forward defense commitments. It was Soviet adventurism in Africa and its invasion into Afghanistan, as well as the collapse of the Shah in Iran and the rise of Islamic fundamentalism, that by the end of the Carter administration led once again to a reassessment of the adequacy of the U.S. security posture.

If after 1968, U.S. ICBM and SLCM deployments remained constant and by the mid-seventies Soviet ICBM and SLCM deployment leveled off, both sides expanded throughout the seventies and into the eighties the number of their reentry vehicles, the Soviets most dramatically in the ICBM area and the United States in the SLBM area. At the same time, the USSR developed during the seventies four new ICBMs and two new SLBMS along with three new ballistic missile submarines. During the same period it developed and deployed the long-range Backfire bomber and the SS-20, a 4,000 kilometer-range ballistic missile system. In 1970 Soviet spending on strategic forces exceeded that of the United States by 2 to 1; by 1980, the figure had risen to 3 to 1. More generally from the mid-sixties to the mid-seventies, American defense spending declined about 8 percent whereas Soviet spending increased by 3 to 4 percent annually.

If these development, deployment, and spending patterns are coupled with developments in Soviet military doctrine and in foreign policy activities, one can understand the motive force for the defense reassessment in the latter years of the Carter administration and the beginning of the Reagan administration. Soviet involvement in Africa, Afghanistan, the Middle East, and Latin America created a general foreign policy anxiety in the West, but the Soviet conception of military security converted this anxiety into a hardening of positions. Under Brezhnev, the Soviets evolved a doctrine of total security that required the ability to launch a rapid and massive offensive land and air strike into Western Europe and to neutralize the U.S. nuclear capability either by direct attack (in the case of U.S. land-based missiles) or by the threat to devastate U.S. allies in the event of a sea-launched retaliatory strike at the Soviet Union. Even if Soviet leaders saw or presented this approach as a prudent, defensive posture in order to forestall a Western threat, it could not but stimulate Western fears and renewed defensive efforts. The deployment of intermediate-range ballistic missiles (the Pershing II) and of land-based cruise missiles (GLCMs) in Western Europe was not only a counter to the deployment of Soviet SS-20s in the East but a response to the whole offensive-minded approach of the Warsaw Pact. Moreover, increases in Western defense spending and the largest peacetime military buildup in American history from the last two years of the Carter administration through the mid-eighties were clearly driven by the apparent momentum in Soviet foreign and defense policy.

In addition to heightened tensions in East-West relations in the late seventies, there were other changes in the American national security environment that increased frustrations in a nation already divided from the Vietnam years. Tremendous increases in oil prices, as well as actual shortages, coupled with an inflation-ridden and stagnant economy to generate a rising tide of anger among the American public. A kind of xenophobia began to grip the country—a growing belief that many of our woes derived from ungrateful allies or rapacious erstwhile friends. Moreover, the inability to reach accommodations with the new regimes in Iran and Nicaragua and, indeed, the hostile stances taken by those governments toward the United States proved particularly nettlesome. In many senses, the culminating event of the Carter administration was the seizure of the U.S.embassy in Teheran and the taking of American hostages. The apparent helplessness of the government to settle this dispute, as well as divisions in the administration on the proper course of action, contributed to the sense of "malaise" in the country which Carter chronicled but could not transcend.

Given these circumstances, the early Reagan years can be seen as a period oriented toward national reassertion: the defense buildup; the development of more offensive-minded military strategies and doctrines (such as the *forward maritime strategy* and the tactical *air-land battle* concept); the willingness to assert military force or offer military assistance whether in Central American, Libya, Grenada, the Eastern Mediterranean or the Persian Gulf, Afghanistan, and elsewhere; and the reigning in of inflation and then concentration on economic growth.

If, however, the Reagan years can be seen as a time of national renewal, it is equally true that by the end of that administration, a fundamental reassessment in our relations with the Soviet Union and the outside world was again taking place. Perhaps a period of economic growth and military expansion was necessary to provide a sense of strength to confront the increasing complexity and diversity of the outside world. But it is also true that significant changes seemed afoot in the Soviet Union and other external areas. The Bush administration that was seen as continuing the basic directions set by the Reagan administration clearly saw itself in a time of transition and was saddled with the always difficult problems of sorting out what should be constant and what should be changed in U.S. postures and policies.

COLD WAR ASSUMPTIONS:
CONTINUITIES AND CHANGES

The post-World War II American security system was founded on six assumptions or perspectives related to:

1. the proper external role of the United States;

2. the requisites for West European reconciliation and recovery;
3. the bases for East-West detente and understandings;
4. the relationship between regional and civil conflicts around the world and the central balance of power between the Soviet Bloc and the West;
5. the trade-offs between strategic or defense requirements and economic arrangements; and
6. the Soviet conception of security.

The United States in World Affairs

As considered earlier, the devastation of World War II, the virtual political collapse of the traditional power centers in Europe and Asia, and the enormity of the military and territorial position of the USSR in Eurasia, as well as uncertainty as to the extent of Soviet ambitions—all these factors suggested that the protection of American interests, including the maintenance of a stable balance of power, depended on the transformation of America's security posture from episodic to continuous engagements. If historically the balances among the various Great Powers allowed the United States to defer action in order to assess the nature and direction of the struggles among those Powers, the devastation of war and of political and economic chaos removed from the United States any buffer between itself and the outside world.

West European Reconciliation and Recovery

If an all-consuming involvement in world affairs was the condition of American life after World War II, it was also the object of postwar American statecraft to reduce the intensity of this involvement. In the first instance, this meant the reconstruction of the devastated states of Europe and Asia and the reconciliation between the former enemy states and the weakened victorious or liberated states. In Europe, this object led to the creation of a number of security and economic arrangements, most notably NATO and the European Community. In Asia, the principal foundation of security, reconstruction, and reconciliation became the U.S.-Japanese bilateral relationship.

If a stable multipolar world was to be reconstituted after World War II, it required some mechanism for renewed German and Japanese strength and ambitions. The need to contain Soviet power and ambitions required the military or economic contributions of the defeated enemy states. Moreover, their geographical location insured they would be on the front lines of containment. But no one could in the long run see these states as simply providers of services; resurgent national identity and revitalized ambitions were sure to reemerge. The issue thus became how to channel and transform German and Japanese power so as to reinforce cooperation and trust in Europe and Asia rather than stimulate once again the security anxieties born of earlier competition and war. The North Atlantic Treaty Organization and the U.S.-Japanese Treaty were thus not simply instruments for the containment of the Soviet bloc but frameworks of Western power. They bound Germany, Japan—and, in a real sense, the United States—in a broader political and institutional web.

Key to the security and economic arrangements binding the Western Powers to each other were three desiderata:

1. economic liberalization;
2. democratic legitimization; and
3. mutual defense without crushing costs and permanent mobilization for war.

The experience of the 1930s had convinced the United States that there was a link among substantially open and free international markets, democratic processes, and the peaceful resolution of international disputes. The general principle of the post-World War II General Agreement on Tariffs and Trade (GATT) was that there should be a progressive, multilateral reduction of barriers to international commerce. And, although the United States supported the development of a European common market in order to join in peaceful association erstwhile competitors and enemies, it insisted that over time the general level of protection must be reduced not only among the West European states but among the signatories of the GATT accord. As will be evident in the chapters to follow, it has not always been easy to maintain this position. Nonetheless, the general notion of economically interlinked societies as an underpinning for Western unity and strength has been fundamental to the U.S. security conception, as has been the progressive democratization that it believed would accompany such linkages. And, indeed, the U.S. occupation regimes in West Germany and Japan after the war consciously moved those societies toward democratic processes.

The economic growth, democratic consultation, and burden-sharing among the Western Powers that ensued after World War II allowed those states to reach a relatively high level of peacetime defense expenditure without stifling economic growth or the expansion of the welfare state and *personal* discretionary spending. In effect, the Western societies did not become garrison states. It was this posture that undergird the Western negotiating position with the Soviet Union and Eastern Europe.

Positions of Strength and East-West Detente

The United States and its allies believed that the West could not effectively negotiate with the Soviet Union unless it occupied a "position of strength" defined not only by its military power but by its political stability, economic prosperity, and alliance unity. At the same time, there was a belief that the Soviet empire in Eastern Europe was "unnatural" or "inorganic" in that there was no legitimizing order, including Marxist-Leninism, that could permanently override the national sentiments or, indeed Western attachments, of the several East European states. At some point, the USSR would very likely find the cost of maintaining what for all intents and purposes was a permanent military occupation, increasingly difficult to bear in both political and economic terms. A Western position of strength and an empire increasingly troublesome to the Soviets might at some point provide the occasion for a more acceptable East-West settlement. In fact, this premise was central to the containment essay of George Kennan in 1947.

The frame of mind just outlined was reflected in NATO in what became known as the "Harmel exercise." On the initiative of Foreign Minister Harmel of Belgium, the members of the NATO alliance resolved "to study the future tasks which face the Alliance and its procedures for fulfilling them in order to strengthen the Alliance as a factor for durable peace." In December 1967 the Ministerial Meeting of the North Atlantic Council approved the Harmel Report on the Future Tasks of the Alliance which linked the Western position of strength with East-West detente and settlement. The report stated that

> the Atlantic Alliance has two main functions. Its first function is to maintain adequate military strength and political solidarity to deter aggression and other forms of pressure and to defend the territory of member countries if aggression should occur. In this climate the Alliance can carry out its second function, to pursue the search for progress towards a more stable relationship in which the underlying political issues can be solved. Military security and a policy of detente are not contradictory but complementary. Collective defense is a stabilizing factor in world politics. It is the necessary condition for effective policies directed toward a greater relaxation of tensions.[11]

This perspective rationalized the search for arms control and political understandings in a number of East-West forums—including the Conference on Security and Cooperation in Europe (CSCE), the Mutual Balanced Force Reduction Talks (MBFR), the Conventional Stability Talks (CST), and others. It also is the intellectual foundation for the "two-track approach" (defense and detente).

Until the late 1970s the United States retained a significant advantage in Europe of theater nuclear forces—ground- and air-delivered nuclear weapons. By the end of that decade, however, the Soviet Union clearly reversed this advantage by the deployment of a mobile, MIRVed intermediate-range ballistic missile (the SS-20) capable of hitting targets all over continental Europe and the British Isles, even from bases in the Soviet Union. Coupled with older SS-4 and SS-5 missiles, the Soviets achieved in Europe superiority in theater-wide nuclear weapons. The

NATO deterrent, heavily concentrated in short-range battlefield nuclear weapons, was being steadily eroded as the Soviets sought "total security" through preeminence in every category of weapon. If "escalation dominance" was ever crucial to flexible response, the whole structure of Western strategy was now suspect.

Responding to these developments, the NATO Nuclear Planning Group decided in December 1979 to modernize the U.S. theater nuclear posture by replacing 108 Pershing I intermediate-range ballistic missile systems with the longer-range, high-accuracy, terminally guided Pershing II and adding to the Western arsenal 464 new ground-launched cruise missiles (GLCMs). At the same time, however, in keeping with the "two-track" approach, modernization was to take place concurrently with efforts by the United States to negotiate with the Soviet Union reductions in theater or intermediate-range nuclear systems.

Despite strong public antipathy to any nuclear modernization, the West began intermediate nuclear force (INF) deployments in December 1983, coupled with the offer to forego deployment of both the Pershing II and GLCM should the Soviets dismantle all SS-4s and SS-5s as well as the SS-20s. The Soviets steadfastly refused and further argued that French and British national nuclear systems should be counted in any negotiated reduction or balance. By the mid-1980s INF negotiations had essentially stalemated and finally, to protest the Western deployments, the Soviets simply walked out of the talks. The two-track approach had allowed modernization while maintaining the unity of the West but it apparently failed to bring about any negotiated reduction with the East. It appeared to be the same story as well in talks over long-range strategic nuclear missiles.

The Reagan administration took the position, as had President Carter at the beginning of his term, that it was insufficient to limit strategic delivery vehicles. One had to reduce the total number of delivered weapons or warheads, for, since the beginning of SALT, total destructive power had in fact increased. Reagan called for strategic arms *reduction* talks (START). At the same time, however, he argued that the foundation of a new arms regime should be not primarily or indefinitely the protection of a mutually-assured destruction capability but the construction of a strategic defense capable not only of defending missile sites and military facilities but populations.

This proposition stirred raucous debate in the United States and the West as to whether or not such a nuclear "umbrella" was technically and economically feasible and if the attempt to develop and deploy such a system would undermine stability while violating the terms of the SALT I antiballistic missile agreement. The stability argument was animated by the belief that, if one side could appear to be developing and deploying such a defense, there would be an increased incentive on the other side to launch a preemptive attack since the combination of a strategic defense with a powerful offense would ultimately render the latter state vulnerable to blackmail or attack. More likely, even if preemption was not likely, there would be stimulated an heightened arms race as each side sought to develop more or different offensive weapons to defeat the strategic defense. And, in any case, argued the critics, a foolproof system was beyond our science and wealth, but the attempt would increase danger without delivering improved security.

The Reagan administration argued that if the development of a strategic defense system were ultimately coupled with an agreement to reduce nuclear offensive systems, there would be less concern for preemption or surprise while moving away from a patently immoral posture of holding each other's populations hostage. Moreover, the Soviets themselves were exploring defensive alternatives. Hence, the West should seek a cooperative venture in this area. And, as in the Pershing II and GLCM deployments, unless the West demonstrated resolve, the Soviet would never have any incentive to negotiate seriously. As to the technical and economic argument, only substantial intellectual and financial investment would determine the validity of that objection—but, argued Reagan, the promise was sufficient to make the attempt. Although by the early nineties, most analysts believed that a strategic defense would always be more limited in its effectiveness than Reagan had hoped, the basic controversy continued.

More importantly for our present consideration, what of the Soviet reaction? Initially it was identical to their response to the Pershing II and GLCM deployments: START discussions stalemated. The deterioration of the health of Leonid Brezhnev in the spring of 1979 had led to a prolonged "succession crisis" in the Soviet Union. After his death in November 1982, he was rapidly succeeded by Yury V. Andropov and in February 1984 by Konstantin U. Chernenko—both of whom died in office. Finally in March 1985, Mikhail S. Gorbachev came to power. In a period of twenty-eight months four men successively occupied the office of General Secretary. In some respects, the stalemate in U.S.-Soviet relations was related to this difficult succession. At the same time, however, it was becoming evident to the Soviet leadership that the entire system was threatened with an immense crisis: economic growth had slowed; U.S.-Soviet relations had worsened markedly since the invasion of Afghanistan, a war that was going badly; West Europe and Japan's ties with the U.S. had been strengthened; and Soviet Third World activities were costly and problematical in benefits. Gorbachev had a mandate to do something, if no clear guidance as to what. In a few years, he moved to consolidate his position and undertook radical steps to reform the economy, to strengthen support for the regime, to reduce the cost of empire while retaining influence, and to improve the international environment so as to allow greater concentration on internal restructuring *(perestroika)*. With almost breathtaking suddenness, given the glacial character of U.S.-Soviet relations previously, agreements were reached with the United States and dialogue began.

On 8 December 1987 in Washington, President Reagan and General Secretary Gorbachev signed the INF Treaty. The Treaty provided for the elimination of all U.S. and Soviet ground-launched INF missile systems in the range of 500-5,500 kilometers (about 300-3,400 miles), along with all related facilities, within three years of the Treaty coming into force. All facilities for production, storage, repair, or deployment for these missile systems were banned and the most stringent joint verification regime in history was accepted. Moreover, as to START, by February 1988 the two sides had agreed in principle to reduce by 50 percent to equal levels strategic offensive arms. Although there were differences over the modalities of such reductions and the Soviets were still insisting that the U.S. forego further development and deployment of strategic defensive systems and bring sea-launched cruise missiles under restriction, dialogue continued and formal agreement by early 1993 seemed likely.

On 7 December 1988 Gorbachev announced at the United Nations that within 2 years the Soviet Union would unilaterally: (1) reduce their forces by 500,000 troops; (2) withdraw and disband six tank divisions from East Germany, Czechoslovakia, and Hungary, along with assault landing troops, their weapons and equipment; (3) reduce Soviet forces stationed in those countries by 50,000 troops and their armaments by 5,000 tanks; and (4) reduce all Soviet forces globally, including those in Europe, by 10,000 tanks, 8,500 artillery systems, and 800 combat aircraft, and by an unspecified number of troops in the European part of the Soviet Union. Moreover, he claimed that Soviet force structure and military doctrine would be reoriented toward "defensive defense" rather than "offensive defense"—i.e., Soviet forces would be so structured and deployed as to repel attack without posing an offensive threat to the West. In talks held in Moscow in May 1989, Gorbachev further informed Secretary of State James A. Baker that the Soviets intended to propose at the Conventional Stability Talks in Vienna cutbacks of more than a million troops on each side and a 55 percent cut in NATO's strike aircraft and helicopters. In the same talks he announced the Soviet intention to eliminate unilaterally 500 warheads from its battlefield nuclear force. This latter initiative represented only a modest 5 percent reduction in a theater force of more than 10,000 nuclear warheads, including missiles, air-launched weapons and nuclear artillery. This compared to a U.S. deployment on the continent of 4,000 nuclear warheads. If a small military gesture, however, the move had enormous political impact.

For, after the INF agreement, NATO decided to modernize its battlefield nuclear weapons—specifically the Lance system—in order to maintain a European nuclear deterrent against the still offensive Soviet conventional capability. The antipathy toward nuclear weapons, especially in Germany where those weapons would be used, combined with a kind of "deterrence weariness" on the part of many of the West Europeans, notably the West German public, made modernization far less attractive to those publics and more difficult for their governments. Gorbachev's initiative appeared to offer hope for a substantially reduced threat. Even though defense analysts argued at the time that the rhetoric needed to be tested and that the force reductions promised could stabilize Soviet predominance at a lower level of cost to them, confidence in Gorbachev's sincerity was itself becoming an important driving force. This attitude chagrined NATO's political and military leadership. The fear was that any reduction in Western strength and unity would remove from Gorbachev one of the major incentives for agreeing to a stable, long-term East-West security regime.

This latter fear returns us to the critical post-World War II assumption that detente and stable arms agreements are in large measure a function of the Western position of strength. The consistently firm position of the West on the deployment of the Pershing II and GLCMs, as well as Reagan's uncompromising stance on the strategic defense initiative, did appear to cause a reappraisal by the Soviet leadership, and they did return to the talks. It is equally true, however, that a change of Soviet leadership and the general problems of the Soviet system impelled the USSR toward accommodation. But, it may be argued, the general policy of containment and the Western position of strength, not only militarily but economically, were in fact part of the consistent challenges that finally forced a Soviet reevaluation of its policies. Like all issues of causality, this question is likely to be debated for some time. The issues facing the Bush administration in the early months of 1989, however, were whether the object of containment had been met and a general settlement was possible.

By May 1989, Bush was able to pronounce that the objects of containment had been met and by the latter months of that year the events in Eastern Europe and the Soviet Union convinced the administration that a definitive break in the Cold War was taking place, requiring a complete reevaluation of the United States' own strategic assumptions.

The Central Balance and Parochial Conflicts

A fourth major assumption undergirding the post-World War II security system was that regional and local conflicts were critically related to the maintenance of the central balance of power with the Soviet Union. Critics argued that U.S. policy was so dominated by issues of containment that it gave too little attention to the regional or local causes and consequences of conflict and too much attention to whether or not the U.S. or the Soviets would be advantaged by developments in those areas. This criticism has considerable merit but it may also miss a critical point. With the collapse of major power centers after World War II, except for the United States and the Soviet Union, and given increasing Soviet desires to become a—some would say *the*—major global power, all issues were almost inevitably infected with the East-West competition. And, indeed, in some areas U.S. and Soviet interests appeared exclusively driven by this competition as there were few apparent material interests at stake. It was felt that many events in the world could *hurt* the U.S. but only the Soviet Union had the ability to *kill* the United States and erode its international freedom of action. It was thus through this prism that successive American administrations looked at world politics.

But it was also clear that should new power centers emerge and should the Soviet Union define its global position in less competitive terms, then this U.S. strategic assumption would come under more serious scrutiny. Indeed, in successive administrations, there were movements toward reducing the Cold War element in U.S. calculations. By the 1980s it was becoming evident that the world was tending toward greater multipolarity and that other threats could impinge on U.S. well-being, quite apart from the Soviet Union.

The crucial variable was the outcome of developments in the Soviet Union. Early in the Bush administration, Secretary of State Baker advanced the thesis with the Soviets that both greater internal freedom in the USSR and autonomy in Eastern Europe as well as cooperation between the U.S. and USSR were important if East-West relations were to be put on a permanently peaceful basis. And Gorbachev gave indications that he was prepared for his own purposes to accommodate greater pluralism in the East and to pursue cooperative ventures with the U.S. elsewhere. Both the sincerity and durability of Gorbachev's pretensions became crucial concerns as the United States and the West reevaluated their security assumptions. The rush of events from the autumn of 1989 onward resolved for all intents and purposes this concern. Political and economic forces both in the Soviet Union and Eastern Europe were clearly sweeping before them leaders, plans, and strategic calculations.

Security Requirements
and Economic Relations

A fifth assumption in the post-World War II American security system was that the security of the West against Soviet blandishments and threats required a willingness of the Western states to transcend their own quarrels and to maintain a high level of unity in facing the Soviet Union. In concrete terms, this meant that economic disputes were never to be pushed so far as to undermine that unity. Moreover, the United States was willing in the 1950s to support a high level of economic integration among its European allies, potentially limiting U.S. exports, in order to establish the economic preconditions for West European stability and unity, as well as burden-sharing in the NATO alliance. A similar attitude prevailed toward Japanese economic development. It should be emphasized that these positions were relatively easy so long as the U.S. retained its economic preeminence, but, as that began to erode in the late sixties and early seventies, public and congressional support for this posture began to erode—so much so that, by the late eighties, if one asked an audience what constituted the greatest threat to U.S. security, the answer was more likely to be Japanese or European economic competition than the Soviet Union. Again, as the Soviet threat was perceived by many in the late eighties as diminishing, crucial assumptions about the trade-off between security requirements and economic arrangement were inevitably challenged.

The Soviet Conception of Security

At every point in our discussion of the major assumptions undergirding the American security system after World War II, the question of how the USSR defined its security system has understandably arisen. To conclude this section, it would be well to draw together all these threads and address explicitly the sixth assumption, that of the nature of the post-World War II Soviet defense posture.

Stated quite simply, after World War II the Soviet Union believed that the extension of the Soviet security zone into Eastern and Central Europe was fundamentally important to its defense and to its influence. The conquests of war and the legitimization of ideology consecrated in their mind this position. But, Soviet leadership believed that effective control in Eastern Europe required the utter suppression of political autonomy within those states and the imposition of Stalinist controls. This position in itself required a substantial forward deployment of Soviet forces. When combined, however, with a growing commitment to a concept of total security and an offensive military doctrine, as well as global political pretensions, the result is a militarized and mobilized society that could only generate anxiety among its neighbors.

If anything, the sense by the West of Soviet threat grew under Brezhnev. Khrushchev, at his ouster in 1964, bequeathed to Brezhnev a military force of about 3,300,000 troops, 140 divisions (of which 26 were foreign deployed) and 35,000 tanks. When Gorbachev took office, he inherited a force of 5,500,000 troops, 208 divisions (40 of which were foreign deployed) and over 50,000 tanks.12 There is nothing comparable in peacetime history or contemporary events to rival this military buildup.

Soviet military doctrine went apace with this force buildup. Should the Soviets have determined to undertake military action, they intended to do so with a massive and rapid strike into Western Europe, concluding the conflict in a matter of days or weeks. The level of permanent mobilization required even to contemplate such a strike is formidable. It provided the NATO rationale not only for its own conventional modernization but its insistence that it reserved the right to initiate nuclear strikes in the event of a Soviet breakthrough. In an important sense, Brezhnev achieved his object of total security: No one ever gave serious thought of "marching to Moscow!"

On the other hand, the fears that this buildup generated led to a remarkable degree of Western unity and in the late seventies and early eighties a reactive military buildup in the West. Perhaps more importantly, the Soviet economy was throttled by this buildup and, ironically, the consequent weakening of the economy undermined their technological and defense industrial base.

As the United States entered the decade of the nineties all of the critical assumptions of its post-World War II national security policy were being reevaluated. And so too were the Soviets evaluating their own assumptions. And, as ever, the two giants were bound together. On 12 May 1989, at the end of a protracted examination of the premises and context of U.S. external policy undertaken by his administration, President Bush delivered a major foreign policy address that indicated once again how closely the two states were bound. Containment, he declared, had met its objectives but now the time had come "to move beyond containment, to a new policy for the 1990s, one that recognizes the full scope of change taking place around the world and in the Soviet Union itself." The goal of the United States was now to move beyond containment of Soviet expansionism: "We seek the integration of the Soviet Union into the community of nations."[13]

But the call for a transformation of policy was initially cautious. The critical factor would be the continuing evolution of the Soviet Union. President Bush asked for five commitments from the Soviet Union: (1) a reduction of their forces to the point where they would be seen as genuinely defensive; (2) respect for political autonomy and self-determination in Eastern and Central Europe; (3) cooperative diplomatic initiatives to resolve regional disputes around the world; (4) a "lasting political pluralism and respect for human rights" within the USSR itself; and (5) joint ventures with the U.S. in addressing global problems affecting all societies, i.e., drugs, environmental dangers, etc. A statement of these objectives indicates how close the United States was to the original thrust of George Kennan's containment article. Within a year the Bush administration believed that every one of these desiderata were being met in one degree or another and the United States faced a major reevaluation of its national defense requirements and the elements of its military strategy.

In the very midst of this reevaluation, one constant in post-World War II planning disappeared—the Soviet state itself. The August 1991 attempted coup against Gorbachev not only decisively undermined his authority but it removed virtually all political incentives to reconstitute the former Soviet republics into a new union. The forces of fragmentation unleashed by the collapse of the Soviet Union swept through Eastern and Central Europe. The Czechoslovakian state peacefully divided in two and Yugoslavia splintered violently into pieces. Ethnic strife convulsed Russia and the former states of

THE COLD WAR AND NATIONAL DEFENSE 187

the Soviet Union. Refugees flowed into Western Europe, especially the newly united Germany, creating in that state an upsurge of ethnic antagonisms and nationalist extremes in a country already beset with the enormous costs of political integration. Outside Europe itself, regional and domestic conflicts coupled with the end of the Cold War order to magnify ambitions and fuel conflict in places as diverse as Somalia and the Persian Gulf. It was this "new world order" that provided the backdrop and a motive force for new defense planning in the last two years of the Bush administration and the beginning of the Clinton administration.

ENDNOTES

1. Douglas MacArthur, *Reminiscences* (New York: McGraw-Hill Book Company, 1964), 276.
2. "World War I" and "World War II," *The Encyclopedia Americana* (Danbury, CT: Grolier Inc., 1987), 358-60, 529-30.
3. Thucydides, *The Peloponnesian War,* trans. by Rex Warner and introductory notes by M.I. Finley (Middlesex, England: Penguin Books, Ltd., 1954), 244-5.
4. U.S. Department of State *Bulletin,* 9 (20 November 1943): 343.
5. Dean Acheson, *Present at the Creation* (New York: W.W. Norton & Co., Inc., 1969).
6. The original signatories included Canada, Belgium, Denmark, France, Iceland, Italy, Luxembourg, the Netherlands, Norway, Portugal, the United Kingdom, and the United States. Subsequently, Greece and Turkey formally acceded to the Treaty on 18 February 1952. The Federal Republic of Germany was invited to accede to the Treaty following the signature of the Paris agreements in October 1954 and formally joined NATO on 9 May 1955. Spain formally became a member of NATO on 30 May 1982.
7. "The Sources of Soviet Conduct," *Foreign Affairs* 25 (July 1947): 576.
8. "NSC-68: United States Objectives and Programs for National Security," in Thomas H. Etzold and John Lewis Gaddis, *Containment: Documents on American Policy and Strategy, 1945-1950* (New York: Columbia University Press, 1978), 385-442.
9. A seminal work in the development of U.S. thought on nuclear deterrence and escalation dominance was Henry A. Kissinger, *Nuclear Weapons and Foreign Policy* (New York: Harper, 1958).
10. Maxwell D. Taylor, *The Uncertain Trumpet* (New York: Harper, 1959).
11. The Future Tasks of the Alliance: Report of the Council—Annex to the Final Communique of the Ministerial Meeting, December 1967 (Brussels, Belgium: NATO Information Service, 1967).
12. For an excellent analysis of the meaning of the proposed changes in Soviet forces and military doctrine, see Phillip A. Karber, "The Military Impact of the Gorbachev Reductions," *Armed Forces Journal International* (January 1989): 54-64.
13. "Transcript of Bush's Remarks on Transforming Soviet-American Relations," *The New York Times,* 13 May 1989, 6.

8

NATIONAL
DEFENSE AFTER
THE COLD WAR

It is a melancholy fact that, even if one senses that the structure of power and the patterns of conflict are so changed as to make former strategies not quite adequate, the actual direction and end of the transition are still opaque. The shape of national defense and military strategy is likely to remain tentative and our assessment of the past is more satisfying than our comprehension either of the present or of the future. Several issues may be stated, however, that will define the character of U.S. security policy now and in the future:

- the character of the threats confronting the nation;
- the range and nature of possible forceful responses and the relation of those responses to nonmilitary instruments of policy;
- the utility of force in meeting probable threats;
- the distribution among would-be allies of the costs and benefits of any strategy;
- the latitude that domestic opinions and internal political calculations give to the political and military leadership; and
- the potential for strengthening or developing, formally or informally, international conflict-limiting codes of behavior.

THE THREAT

In broad terms most states have two concerns about their external environment: the shape and character of the central balance of power and the specific and concrete challenges to their foreign interests. Great Powers in one degree or another also have the wherewithal to address directly these concerns. The second concern might be seen as comparable to the fears of a resident in the early American West about an attack of a rapacious outlaw gang on his family or property. Using the same analogy, the first concern addresses the broader issue of the existence and effectiveness of laws, courts, public-minded citizens, U.S. marshals, sheriffs, and the like to establish a condition of law and order whereby all gangs may be discouraged, contained, and punished.

As a number of statesmen have noted ever since the beginning of the modern state system, oftentimes it is the Great Powers that ultimately provide both the conditions of law and order and the greatest challenges to those conditions. When the Great Powers are united in their desires to maintain certain standards of international behavior, severe challenges may arise from lesser states, but the ability to contain them at less cost is much greater than when the principal states have utterly contradictory calculations and ambitions. In a real sense, it was this insight that shaped the construction of the United Nations Charter: If the five permanent members of the Security Council could coordinate their interests in terms of the normative principles of the Charter, then relatively nonviolent change could take place within a broad environment of international peace and security. It was precisely the absence of this precondition that undermined the United Nations' most basic goal after World War II and led to the construction of the alliance systems and military arrangements that characterized the Cold War. Moreover, local and regional quarrels among lesser states were not contained to the hoped-for degree but often became elements in the grand struggle between East and West.

As a result of the breakdown of the World War II grand coalition and the subsequent Soviet-American competition, concern for the central balance of power became for the United States the overriding issue. If a framework of power and legitimacy could not be achieved for all the Great Powers then a system of countervailing power needed to be constructed—one which would bring together the material and moral power of the associated states in concert against "the Threat." Even five years ago any book or article published in the United States on "the Threat" would almost inevitably imply the Soviet Union and, when security threats from another direction were the object of the analysis, there was almost always a section on the Soviet involvement or dimension of the particularlistic threat in question. When the issue is a continuing threat from another Great Power and this other power is armed and mobilized for a comprehensive threat to one's power position or survival, the stakes are mortal and the primary strategic issue becomes one's ability to deter or to fight a general war.

U.S. defense policy and military strategy can thus be seen as oriented since World War II by the need to deter or to resist a threat to such vital interests as to raise the prospects of fighting a global conflict. As noted several times before, this perspective meant that even lesser threats would be evaluated in terms of their relationship to the central balance between the East and the West. Moreover, engagement in local or regional conflicts would always raise the concern that U.S. or Western forces not be "maldeployed"—that is, so positioned that the Soviets and their clients could make advances elsewhere. As early as the Korean War, the Truman administration feared that U.S. involvement on the Korean peninsula would be exploited by the Soviets to extend their forces into Western Europe.

It is the collapse of the Soviet Union and of its Eastern European empire that largely defines the U.S. security perspective today. The substantial alteration in a Great Power and the fragmentation of empire are in many respects as troublesome as a direct challenge from a would-be global hegemon. In other words, uncertainty as to the shape and character of the new political arrangements introduces not only a sense of hope but of dread as to both the turmoil of the transition and the nature of the world that will emerge from the chaos. If implication in a general conflict has been reduced, the danger is magnified of being swept up in a vortex of regional conflicts and civil strife, the very meaning and importance of which are problematical. At the same time, the weaponry that defined the Cold War struggle remains. Agreements to reduce and control these are crucial and accords on cooperative arrangements with the erstwhile enemy remain central. As one faces new dangers, the old dangers still have remarkable potency. Even in the midst of geostrategic revolution, there is a constancy of anxieties and concerns.

The agreement over forces in Europe and over strategic nuclear forces gives substance to this continuing concern. Even as the Soviet Union and then Russia and the former members of the U.S.S.R. went through stunning turmoil and transformation, the leaders of the respective sides attempted to formalize the arms regime in Europe and in the general area of nuclear weapons. On 19 November 1990 the United States and the Soviet Union joined with 20 other states that made up the North Atlantic Treaty Organization and the Warsaw Pact in a Conventional Forces in Europe agreement (CFE) to limit or destroy many categories of nonnuclear weapons in Europe in the area stretching from the Atlantic Ocean to the Ural Mountains. This included, for instance, a reduction of total tanks on each side from 133,700 to 66,600 (33,300 on each side); a reduction of armored vehicles from 140,500 to 50,000 on each side for a total of 100,000; a cut in artillery pieces from 131,650 to 33,700 on each side for a total of 67,400; a cut in helicopters from 8,500 to 3,500 on each side for a total of 7,000; and a reduction in combat aircraft from 32,100 to 11,950 on each side for a total of 23,900— perhaps the most ambitious arms control treaty in history. Technical difficulties over the inclusion of the Treaty-Limited Equipment (TLE) of naval, infantry, coastal defense units, and strategic rocket forces, as well as the political difficulties of the breakup of the Soviet Union, delayed ratification among all the 29 states until the end of 1992. Nonetheless, the dynamic of reduction was clearly evident. In May 1990, Presidents Bush and Gorbachev had earlier agreed to a common ceiling in Central Europe of 195,000 Soviet and American forces on each side. But with the union of the two German states as well as the continuing political evolutions in Eastern Europe and budgetary concerns on both sides, negotiations began on the heels of the agreements of 19 November looking toward further accords.

By the time that Bill Clinton was sworn in as president on 20 January 1993, the interaction between political transformations in the former Soviet Union and Eastern Europe, on the one hand, and the continuing arms talks, on the other, had decisively altered the strategic situation in what used to be called the "central front" of Europe. The Intermediate Nuclear Force Agreements (INF) and the Conventional Forces in Europe Agreements (CFE) were in force. In addition to these formal treaties, discussions on confidence-building measures were also under way and included provisions for observation flights over Europe (Open Skies) and for limits on the number of armed military personnel in the CFE treaty area (Personnel Strength in Europe).

In addition to the various arms agreements, a remarkable change in alignments had also taken place by early 1993. Today all the states of Europe plus Canada and the United States are joined together in one European political-security arrangement, the Conference on Security and Cooperation in Europe (CSCE), whose origins were in the Nixon administration's push for detente and whose operations were heretofore characterized by Cold War rhetoric. The conference that originally convened in Helsinki in July 1973 was premised on the relative stability of the post-World War II political arrangements in Europe, East and West, and was aimed at moderating the divide by reducing tensions, expanding East-West human and material transactions, and improving respect for human rights. The Final Act of August 1975 reflected the hopeful but conservative assumptions of the initial meeting, effectively recognizing the political and territorial arrangements that emerged from World War II but extending East-West detente and affirming standards of human dignity. The conferences that followed in the subsequent years focused on the problems of implementation and the gaps in compliance.

When the conference convened in November 1990, however, seven weeks after the unification of Germany, the political structure of Europe was being radically transformed, and the Charter of Paris signed by thirty-four participants defined a far more ambitious agenda—beyond detente and even entente. There was much talk about the CSCE becoming the focal point for a European-wide collective security organization.

Until November 1990, the CSCE was but a periodic conference in which the representatives of the member states discussed compliance with the commitments undertaken at Helsinki—and often became a propaganda forum in the Cold War contest. At the Paris Summit, however, the leaders of the CSCE proclaimed in the Charter of Paris for a New Europe the end of the "era of confrontation and division" and agreed to create a number of permanent institutions: a Secretariat in Prague, a Conflict Prevention Center in Vienna, and an Office of Free Elections in Warsaw. They further agreed to hold annually a Council of Foreign Ministers and a Parliamentary Assembly. They also provided for an *ad hoc* Committee of Senior Officials.

A central element of the Charter of Paris was the area of security. The charter reaffirmed the achievements of the Treaty on Conventional Armed Forces in Europe and the Negotiations on Confidence and Security-Building Measures. It states that

> the changing political and military environment in Europe opens new possibilities for common efforts in the field of military security. . . . Following a period for national preparation, we look forward to a more structured co-operation among all participating States on security matters.

Bound by rules of unanimity and having no habit or established machinery of cooperation, the CSCE has made a largely ineffectual attempt to resolve the Yugoslavian conflict. While the fifty-two member states agreed in May 1992 to consider in principle broader roles in assuring and guaranteeing peace in Europe, the Russian government initially refused to join in an otherwise unanimous vote to condemn Yugoslavia, now consisting of Serbia and Montenegro, and to suspend that state's membership in the conference until such time as it ended its assault on Bosnia and Hercegovina. Although the Russian government, amid much criticism from Russian nationalists, did later reverse itself and vote for sanctions in the UN Security Council, the CSCE itself continues to play little effective role in ending the ongoing strife in the former states of Yugoslavia. Nonetheless, there are attempts, however feeble thus far, to strengthen the collective security role of this inclusive organization.

NATO Secretary-General Manfred Woerner made the observation that NATO now provides the only truly functioning security system in Europe. Although NATO has not been notably effective in the Balkan conflict either, it has been committed since May 1992 to considering peacekeeping and enforcement roles outside the treaty-defined area. It is thus conceivable that NATO could be called upon to act as an agent for such an operation for the CSCE or the UN or both. What is extraordinary in all this is that a number of East European leaders are exploring the possibility of NATO membership and even Boris Yeltsin has spoken of Russian membership.

It should be clear why the extension of NATO membership eastward might be appealing to those states, for it might provide a framework both for effective U.S. involvement in the European evolution and for a controlled German resurgence. It should be equally clear why there may be some reluctance on the part of even those in the West who hope that NATO will be maintained. First, there is a desire to retain a clearly Western capacity that could be expanded to meet a renewed Eastern challenge, and there appears to be little public support either in the United States or West Europe for increased formal security commitments. In any event, what the NATO leaders did at the November 1991 Heads of State and Government meeting was to establish a formalized relation between the NATO member-states and the former communist states of Central and Eastern Europe, without directly incorporating them into NATO. The new arrangement is called the North Atlantic Cooperation Council (NACC) and the initial invitation to join was extended to Czechoslovakia, Poland, Hungary, Bulgaria, the Baltic states, and Romania; it was later extended to include the successor states of the USSR. It is intended that these states participate in some form in the annual ministerial meetings of the North Atlantic Council and that periodic meetings at the ambassadorial level take place as circumstances might warrant. It should be noted, however, that for the moment, like the CSCE, this new organization is more a series of conferences and consultations than formal mechanisms for collective security. But, of course, this is a long way from the Cold War!

In addition to the changes in the political-military arrangements in Europe, President Clinton was also bequeathed an altered strategic nuclear environment. The START I treaty ratification was virtually completed by the Clinton inaugural and Presidents Bush and Yeltsin signed the START II Treaty on 3 January 1993. A number of other accords were in process. As a result of the dissolution of the Soviet Union, the number of states party to the treaty expanded from two to five, and now includes Belarus, Kazakhstan, and Ukraine. Russia assumed the former Soviet Union's status of nuclear weapon state and Belarus, Kazakhstan, and Ukraine became parties to the treaty as nonnuclear weapon states until all nuclear weapons and strategic offensive weapons were removed from their territories. Political maneuvers among the former member-states of the Soviet Union, political problems within those states, and disagreements over the disposition of those nuclear weapons outside of Russia all delayed the ratification process until the end of the Bush administration and the beginning of the Clinton administration. Under the START I agreement, both sides are limited to 1,600 strategic nuclear delivery vehicles (SNDVs), i.e., missile launchers and bombers, and 6,000 accountable weapons, with a sublimit of 4,900 deployed ballistic missile reentry vehicles and, within the 4,900 warhead limit, 1,100 deployed mobile ICBM warheads. The Russians are also allowed 154 heavy ICBMs carrying a total of 1,540 reentry vehicles, which are counted within the 1,600 SNDV and 4,900 ballistic missile warhead limits. As bombers are discounted in the agreement, the actual number of warheads on both sides is over 6,000 with the United States deploying 8,556 and the Russians 6,163.

Beyond START I, however, the terms of a START II Treaty were already well advanced by mid-1992 as a result of unilateral steps and bilateral proposals by the two sides. Many of these measures effectively eliminate weapons systems from the arsenals and reduce the alert status of many forces. Moreover, Presidents Bush and Yeltsin announced on 17 June 1992 understandings that were to form the basis of a START accord, which reached fruition at the January 1993 Moscow Summit. In this capstone of a stunning four years of unilateral steps and mutual agreements, it was agreed that START I and START II would be independent of each other and are to be enforced simultaneously. In addition, if ratified, the second START treaty will eliminate all land-based missiles with multiple warheads on both sides and all of the "heavy" SS-18s on the Russian side. The United States will retain its seaborne multiple-warhead missiles and it is virtually assured that the Russian nuclear deterrent system will increasingly be at sea.

Although the changed political environment generated proposals that a few years ago would have been beyond imagination, the difficulty of translating those proposals into agreements and advancing the ratification process were subject not only to technical problems but to dynamic political changes in Russia itself. Indeed, by the end of 1992 President Yeltsin was under considerable attack by the conservative Congress of Deputies which was asserting an ever greater veto power over Yeltsin's reforms in the political economy and in foreign affairs. Russia was no longer an enemy but it was clearly not yet a reliable partner—and the future orientation of that still considerable power center remains uncertain.

In the face of these changes, then, how is one to define "the Threat"? There are two broad answers and a general concern. First, the U.S. cannot be unconcerned with the general balance of power. Second, there will be specific threats to U.S. interests from various regional powers that may require the threat or use of military force. But, finally, there is a generalized worry that tremendous political and economic instability could yield such chaos as to stimulate the rise of militaristic or ideological regimes that might ultimately upset either regional balances or the general balance of power.

THE CENTRAL BALANCE AND GENERAL WAR

As long as there are nation-states with distinct geopolitical positions and independent armed forces, the general relationship prevailing among those states will continue to provide the environment within which political, socio-economic, and cultural interactions will take place. Therefore, even in times of lessened threat, one must ask the question whether there might arise a state or group of states whose political and economic evolution could radically threaten the general interests of the United States. As in the past, such a challenge is most likely in Eurasia. Hence, one hears discussions about the future aspirations and power potential of Germany, Japan, China, and even such supranational entities as the European Community. In the longer term, there are sometimes expressed concerns about such states as India. Most of these concerns are so speculative as to provide little substantive basis for current defense planning. Clearly the United States has an interest in maintaining an international environment that will favor the peaceful evolution of these states and entities, but there appears to be no immediate basis for assuming that their evolution could unfold in such a way as to pose a threat comparable to that of Napoleonic France, Imperial or Nazi Germany, Imperial Japan, or the Soviet Union after World War II.

Yet there does remain in this regard a continuing anxiety for defense planners—the still massive armed forces of Russia, its general power potential, and the uncertainty of the evolution of that state. Most assume that the U.S. and its traditional allies can substantially reduce the posture that would allow them to engage with very short warning in general war. The issue then becomes an evaluation of how rapidly forces might have to be reconstituted in the event of a general challenge to the central balance of power. This is not only a question of military capabilities, but also of the general economic and technological base as well as political judgment and support.

It is a fact that governments and their peoples, especially democratic polities, are slow to recognize a growing military threat and to make the painful shift of priorities that such a recognition would require. The reluctance to accept and confront a threat in a timely fashion has, however, often converted what might have been a major crisis or limited confrontation into a general war. In an era of nuclear and advanced conventional weapons, general conflict could be catastrophic. Indeed, in most periods, even hegemonic states have not sought such general conflicts, but have found themselves engaged in such wars because they assumed that they could limit the terms of the fight. One reason for this calculation was a perception that other states could not or would not adequately resist.

Some have assumed that the presence of nuclear weapons, especially if they are in such numbers and safe deployments as to render minimal the possibility of a surprise attack leading to their total destruction, is adequate to maintain a general deterrence posture and thus inhibit the activities of future would-be hegemons. The problem, however, remains as it has since the early days of the nuclear age: The presence of a mutually assured destructive nuclear capacity on both sides to a dispute may inhibit the use of such weapons on each side and the temptation to attack each other's homeland. The result is that aggressive ambitions will be pursued in areas beyond the territories of one's opponent and perhaps without using weapons of mass destruction but more conventional forces. As a result, even with the end of the Cold War, there is a desire to maintain both a range of force and an industrial base that could be so deployed and reinforced as to inhibit in the early stages the rise of a prospective hegemon. And thus the question becomes "how much is enough?" It is on this question that the defense debate will continue to center in the next several years and, as in the past, it is likely to be linked to an evaluation of Russia's prospects through the 1990s and well into the twenty-first century.

Russia *is* changing but in what ultimate direction is not certain. Gorbachev determined that his primary goal was to strengthen the economy and public support for changes in the political economy without so destabilizing the regime as to fragment utterly the Soviet Union or provoke civil war. His reluctance to engineer radical changes in the economy coupled with the opening of the political system ultimately antagonized the bloated bureaucracy and management of the old regime, without giving hope to the populace that the precipitous decline in the economy was being reversed. Long before the amateurish coup of August 1991, any popular base had evaporated. Boris Yeltsin, the first popularly elected leader of Russia, finally pushed aside Gorbachev but saw himself and the genuine reformers he brought to power stymied by the same bureaucratic resistance and the rising anger of a populace that saw the cost of change but no glimmer of better times. Yeltsin finds himself in a double-bind. By 1993, he was forced to make major accommodations with the nationalistic and antimarket forces that continue to dominate most of the levers of power. This means pressures to defer, if not kill, free market reforms and to limit political cooperation with the West. At the same time, financial and political support from the outside world requires a relatively benign international environment and most particularly a generally cooperative relationship with the West. To the degree that Yeltsin bends towards the reactionary forces within Russia, he raises concerns in the West and, indeed, among the former members of the Soviet Union and the Warsaw Pact. But, too great an accommodation to the concerns of the outside world is portrayed by his opponents as appeasement and a betrayal both of the Russian and the Soviet legacy.

The crucial question facing the West is also twofold. First, should Yeltsin or his successors succeed in the bold attempt at internal modernization and relegitimization of the state, will a more powerful political-military threat to the West ultimately emerge? While this may be a distant concern, there are so many developments that must take place and so many possibilities in U.S. relations with Russia that it provides little guidance for current defense thinking. Second, should the attempt at reform falter and forces of disruption increase, will the Russian state react with such severity as to repress internal dissent that a new Cold War will ensue? It is this possibility that many commentators see as more likely than the first. But, even if it came to pass, the Russians would be in the short-run oriented toward internal consolidation, allowing whatever longer-term adjustments in the security posture of the other states that might be warranted.

REGIONAL BALANCES
AND LOCAL CONFLICT

If the "Russian Threat" seems less immediate or ambiguous, other challenges, many always present but not always salient, are pressing upon the United States. A Soviet Union permanently mobilized for war, utterly repressive of autonomy in Eastern Europe, and driven to establish global preeminence, presented a threat so compelling as to constrain, if not eliminate, ancient quarrels, local antagonisms, and national egoism among those states joined together to contain Soviet pretensions. With the transformation in the character of the Soviet posture, the willingness to dampen these quarrels, antagonisms, and egoisms is disappearing.

Within Europe itself—East and West—the historical forces of division are reappearing, if under new guises, and the psychological distance between Europe and the United States may increase, as may the distance between those states and Asian powers such as Japan. The great states may be less willing to subordinate their economic fears and quarrels and the lesser states may lose the leverage granted by the superpowers' need to insure their sympathy and support in a bipolar struggle.

If tight alliances may loosen and loose coalitions fragment, so too may the world witness the even more dramatic assertions of power by frustrated nationalists, rapacious regional states, and fanatical ideological and religious fundamentalists. If the Cold War was at times described as an international civil war, so the progressive multipolarization of conflict among diverse claimants to power may make this designation even more apt—with, however, a more chaotic and anarchical flavor. It is in such turmoil that terrorism flourishes, weapons proliferate, respect for political boundaries diminishes, and moral or legal restraints, always fragile, steeply erode. Like the "worst-case" analysis of possible "futures" in Russian behavior and among erstwhile allies, this apocalyptic picture is not inevitable. But this outcome is credible enough to complicate planning for military force and for strategic responses.

The Iraqi invasion of Kuwait in 1990 and the subsequent response by the United States and the world community brought new emphasis to the concern for both political frameworks and military structures within which such regional challenges can be met. It did bring home how difficult it will be in this new security world for the United States to unilaterally confront a significant regional military threat. If the United States had the capacity to project quickly into the Persian Gulf and Saudi Arabia the bulk of the military forces, it acted within a universal frame of legitimacy and with international financing. At the same time, the American public found even this international support inadequate. The demands for greater military contributions from other states in such conflicts are in fact likely to grow and, therefore, the prospects for many replays of this intervention less likely. Moreover, the principles invoked and the UN mechanisms activated by the Bush administration for U.S. intervention in the Persian Gulf are also likely to inhibit or at least raise substantially the political costs for unilateral U.S. interventions, such as in Grenada or Panama.

The collapse of Yugoslavia and the onset of war between Croatia and Serbia and the subsequent genocidal assault on Bosnia and Hercegovina alarmed many Europeans as they saw the European "zone of peace" violated and feared that potential Serbian action against the Albanian populace in the province of Kosovo could spill over into Macedonia and other states in the region. In any case, the civil strife in Yugoslavia and the general political-economic troubles in the former Soviet Union and Warsaw Pact states were creating a refugee problem not seen since World War II. Actions by the United States, the European states, and the United Nations proved ineffectual in stopping the drive of Serbia toward a "Greater Serbia" through a policy of "ethnic cleansing," i.e., to kill through armed action, to execute, or to drive out non-Serbs from those areas claimed by the Serbian nationalists.

At the same time that Yugoslavia exploded into violence, the collapse of all public order in Somalia and the struggle among armed bands led to such massive starvation and suffering that the world community felt impelled to intervene. But, as in all things, the world community is effectual only to the degree that it is animated by a Great Power willing and able to take action. Hence, in late 1992 the Bush administration intervened in Somalia with American armed forces with the intent of establishing safe zones where humanitarian assistance could be given without disarming the armed bands which would have directly involved it in the civil strife. This "limited" intervention raised troubling questions about the future role both of the United Nations and its state members in enforcing international norms of behavior, not only among but within states. Humanitarian assistance to those in distress because of natural disasters and with the concurrence of a recognized national authority is one thing, but the attempt to render assistance in a situation where the suffering is the direct result of policy by the parties to a civil strife is something else again. The issue becomes not only of an American "policeman" role but of the responsibilities of the organized international community as represented in such universal organizations as the United Nations and such regional organizations as NATO or the European Community. What are the genuine requisites of international security and of American interests?

These turns of events led to agonizing reappraisals both in the United States and Europe, as well as within the United Nations generally, over the security requirements and defense policies needed in the post-Cold War era. As Americans were disappointed that the victorious conclusion of World War II did not at last allow a withdrawal from a major international security role, so the United States may find once again that there is less "peace dividend" than was once expected with the end of the Cold War.

THE STRATEGIC RESPONSES AND THE UTILITY OF FORCE

Under all circumstances, the threat or use of force is a blunt instrument. Policy-makers and theoreticians alike have tried to portray force as a tool for the signaling of intentions, of bargaining, of shaping expectations, and of altering calculations and plans. And there are persistent attempts to calibrate the kinds and levels of violence—threatened or delivered—to achieve these outcomes. Moreover, there are learned reflections and policies aimed at integrating such forceful instruments with mechanisms of diplomatic, economic, and ideological suasion. These approaches *are* products of a more sophisticated and effective strategy, but the record of the failure of force to achieve policy objectives is nevertheless sobering.

Force works best, whatever the wisdom of the policy, if it is aimed at occupying or defending territory, at crushing or protecting regimes from direct assault, at deterring direct armed actions by posing overwhelming defensive or costly retaliatory force. The successful military strategy aims at isolating the enemy, at penetrating his defenses at his weakest point or at blunting his strength by sheer attrition, at economizing one's own forces—and all this is done best if the prime object of the war is the destruction of the war-making ability of the other side, whether or not victory demands that the objective inevitably be pursued to its consummation. In such a clash, political direction, and hence limitation, is not surrendered but the relative clarity of the direct clash of arms often gives the military commander great latitude.

Such "clarity" is, however, the trait most absent in recent conflicts, and global trends indicate even greater ambiguity. Erosion of political boundaries, the intertwining of state and nonstate actors, the willingness to attack directly the innocent and ignore any distinction between combatant and noncombatant, the use of highly personal and nontraditional forms of combat (e.g., the destruction by design of commercial aircraft)—all these and similar characteristics of modern conflict make it difficult at best to design strategy and render problematical any particular form of forceful response.

Military strategy at its most basic is a plan of action relating military assets to political objectives. It is a set of interrelated concepts about the employment of force under specified circumstances and for specific ends. The adequacy of a strategy thus depends on its ability to guide the acquisition, structuring, and use of force to achieve, in concert with other elements of power, a state's objectives.

As we have seen, the fundamental strategy of the Cold War flowed from the political objectives of maintaining the Eurasian balance of power and of insuring that the Soviet Union did not advance its interests through military intervention and violent subversion. The policy developed to achieve these objectives was called "containment." Although other interests and other objectives called forth on occasion military responses, in a real sense these responses were treated as part of the general problem of containing the Soviet Union.

U.S. strategy and forces were geared to these objectives and this policy. The strategic concepts developed in service of containment were, as we discussed earlier, centered around deterrence, power projection, forward defense, and the management of regional and local threats in such a way as to maintain the basic anti-Soviet strength of U.S. armed forces and the alliances and coalitions organized to meet the "Soviet Threat." On the basis of the containment policy and strategy, important decisions were taken as to the size, types, and dispositions of forces: The United States raised large armies heavily armored and positioned on forward defense lines in Germany and Korea; it developed fighter aircraft that could contend for control of the battlefield; it fielded naval capabilities that could destroy enemy submarines, aircraft, and missiles so as to have command of the sea and the waters adjacent to critical land theaters; it developed penetrating missiles and bombers that could threaten military and industrial targets deep inside the territory of the enemy with either nuclear or conventional bombardment; and it maintained industrial and research capabilities in order to expand and sustain forces rapidly and to maintain a technological edge over any putative enemy.

It was sometimes said during the Cold War that the U.S. had neither a policy nor a strategy. Such statements were almost always politically motivated or driven by the fact that the critic did not particularly like the policy or strategy or felt that both were inadequately sustained by the forces available. In retrospect, it is becoming evident how clear and crisp the policy and strategy were and how straightforward was the view of the threat and the military mission that sustained the forces proposed and acquired. At least they seemed clear and straightforward when compared with the situation that now prevails!

With the passing of the general bipolar struggle of the Cold War and hence the necessity to orient one's forces and strategy toward the deterrence and, if necessary, conduct of general war operations, there comes also the passing of the comprehensive strategy that issued from that struggle. There is nothing in the current international environment that would sustain such a comprehensive and integrated strategy. If the threats that might require the exercise of military force are multiple and parochial and if the very character and dimensions of the state actors are undergoing radical change (who can be confident what the basic regime characteristics of Russia, or for that matter of a number of other key states, will be in even five years?), then one can at best define a strategic perspective but not a full-blown military strategy.

It is, however, a reasonable estimate that the United States will continue to need to project military forces across the oceans and airways that separate it from Eurasia, but that there will be far fewer heavily armored ground forces forward deployed. It is also evident that less attention will be given to maintaining in readiness such heavy forces generally within the continental United States, but that those forces that are not eliminated and that would be most relevant to the conduct of general war will be placed in the reserves. There will be attempts to maintain political agreements and military infrastructures in the territories of erstwhile allies in the event that the international climate again turns toward general struggle, but there will be fewer dedicated U.S. bases abroad.

All of this means that the United States should move toward the retention and development of those sea and air forces that can both move rapidly into threatened areas and be able to sustain themselves for a period of time without the full infrastructure that has been available in Europe, Korea, Japan, and the Philippines. It will be important to have sea and air lift to move large numbers of forces, if that is required, and the capabilities integral to the sea and air forces moved into an area to defend themselves against both relatively sophisticated weapons (such as missiles and submarines) and less sophisticated threats (such as mines and terrorist attack) that are daily proliferating. Moreover, these forces will need to be visible enough in peacetime to contribute to their deterrent effect and thus reduce the necessity of the test of arms.

As to the general nuclear deterrent, this will in the future be driven as it has in the past by the size and capability of the Russian force. If there is a substantial reduction in nuclear delivery capabilities and warheads, the United States will rely increasingly on those nuclear forces that are most mobile and secure. In the first instance, this favors submarine forces but it will probably also favor bomber forces. Land-based mobile forces are less likely to constitute a substantial portion of the American arsenal as the public finds unacceptable such a deployment mode. Air bases are stationary and sea forces roam over the seas but land-based mobile forces are seen as cutting through the "front yard" of Americans.

It is likely that the issue of the strategic defense initiative (SDI) will remain. For, if the numbers of offensive missiles are decreased and the technology of defense against missiles is increasing, then the viability of a strategic defense increases. Moreover, the missile threat emanating from other countries besides Russia, such as Iraq, Iran, and other Third World states, might be seen as making a strategic defense more attractive and perhaps extending the technology to the local battlefield. It is also likely that concern for defense against missiles will extend to air defense in general. It is probable that any serious move in these areas will require not only greater public support at home but some general framework of understanding with the principal state powers, including Russia. It can thus be said that at least the discussion of this issue is unlikely to abate!

Congressman Les Aspin and Senator Sam Nunn, respectively chairmen of the House and Senate Armed Services Committees, spoke widely and often during the early nineties about the requisites of the new national defense. With the election of Bill Clinton in 1992 and the appointment of Aspin as Secretary of Defense, a major effort was made to realize their vision. In most respects, there was more continuity with the Bush administration than change. But there was more emphasis on U.S. basing rather than forward basing of U.S. forces and thus more concern with the ability to respond rapidly and with as self-contained forces as possible. This meant greater attention to air and sea lift and more "balanced," i.e., self-reliant, forces. All this was more a matter of degree than of quality from the previous administration. One issue did, however, surface near the end of the Bush administration that laid the basis for major disputes throughout the Clinton administration: the definition of roles and missions of the military services.

The post-World War II missions of the Army, Air Force, Marines, and Navy were determined by the Key West accord in 1948 and in effect laid the basis for the assignments given to each service during the Cold War. Senator Nunn and presidential candidate Clinton argued during the 1992 campaign that the original accord allowed too much duplication and that over the years, for instance, the United States acquired four separate air arms and two light infantry forces. Most military officers, notably Chairman of the Joint Chiefs of Staff General Colin L. Powell, however, contended that many of the forces were in fact not duplicative but complementary capabilities. It is argued by those officers that, even if certain military efforts may receive greater attention in the post-Cold War era, such as UN or humanitarian operations, and that, even if certain support or logistic efforts may be consolidated, the basic distribution of missions and current service capabilities should remain substantially the same. It was clear by December 1992 that the contest over the organization and budget of the Defense Department under the Clinton administration would be largely determined, as it had been at the beginning of the Cold War, by the outcome of the debate over the respective roles and missions of the separate military services.

Beyond the question of the relative balance among military missions and the respective roles of the services, both the outgoing and incoming administrations were concerned with the implications of what has been called the "military technological revolution." This latter phrase points to the belief that there are changes in technology, especially in the information and communication systems, that will alter both the objects and the character of conflict. It is felt by military planners that the very shape of U.S. military forces may change so as to allow decisive attacks on the key elements through which national leaders and military commanders control their forces. Strengthening the national economy and maintaining scientific-technological dominance are considered by both the new and old defense teams as the critical precondition of such military forces. Debate over future defense postures thus automatically becomes intertwined with debates over economic and science/technology policies.

The United States will most likely be the chief "regulator power" over the next ten years—that is to say, it will continue to possess such political unity, economic strength, and global military capability as to be the prime state mover in the forging of political understandings, institutional mechanisms, and collective military enterprises. Former President Bush once spoke of the need to construct a new world order after the passing of the Cold War. Despite the declining gap between U.S. strength and that of the European Community and Japan, as well as other lesser power centers, the United States is still likely to be seen as the most capable of providing both reassurance and deterrence in regions that are undergoing vast political transformations and social disruptions. It will inevitably be drawn into attempts to construct regional and global understandings and stable balances. The visibility and credibility of its armed forces, as well as seemly restraint in their employment, may be the key to such activities.

Yet there are severe political and economic limits to U.S. force, both domestically and internationally. U.S. power may therefore be catalytic and necessary but it is unlikely to be self-contained and sufficient. It is the American ability to cooperate in common or convergent causes with other states and in terms of general norms of international behavior that will both justify the existence of its military forces and animate its strategic vision.

ALLIANCES, DOMESTIC POLITICS,
AND THE DISTRIBUTION OF
STRATEGIC COSTS AND BENEFITS

Even when the Soviet threat was the clearest to Western leaders and publics, there were disagreements on how the cost and risks of the alliance would be distributed. The Federal Republic of Germany always abutted the largest concentration of Soviet force and provided the probable battlefield. Nuclear weapons could implicate all the member states of NATO in a general war but Germany would inevitably be the scene of battle in a general conflict between the East and the West. This geopolitical fact drove the strategy of forward defense and of flexible response. Forward defense would seek to hold the line against a Warsaw Pact onslaught and flexible response would both guarantee a nuclear riposte before the utter loss of German territory and insure that the battlefield would be extended not only throughout Europe and across the oceans but into the Soviet Union itself. Even strategies that sought to raise the nuclear threshold still aimed at extending the battlefield onto the flanks of Europe, into Asia, and across the world's oceans. Such was the implication of the U.S. maritime strategy.[1] Equalization of risk, it was felt, was key to alliance solidarity and effective deterrence.

If risks were to be generalized, so there have been in NATO and in the U.S.-Japanese relationship almost permanent discussions on how the financial and force burdens would be shared. Particularly as Western Europe and Japan recovered from the devastation of World War II and then prospered, there was a growing feeling in the United States that more of the budgetary implications of common defense needed to be faced by the alliance partners. The United States had always devoted a higher percentage of GDP to defense than its cohorts and this at times became the basis for growing recrimination.

In addition, there have always been discussions as to the national composition of alliance forces. A balanced allied force would seem to dictate that each nation would "specialize" in those areas in which it had a natural advantage or in which geographical position dictated a certain posture. For instance, early technological advantage on the part of the United States suggested that it concentrate on the aerospace dimensions of military force and its geographical position dictated heavier attention to seapower. On the other hand, European partners, given their proximity to the threat and their relative economic base, would concentrate on ground forces and theater weapons such as mines or air defense. Many argued, however, that this approach reinforced America's global strength and preeminent political position, whereas the Western European states and Japan were confined to regional horizons. Moreover, it was felt by some that U.S. bases abroad were used not simply to bolster the common defense against Soviet attack but to pursue other major objectives, such as the defense of Israel or the U.S. position in the Mediterranean or the Indian Ocean.

These issues have been the stuff of strategic debate since the fifties. What happens, however, when the Soviet threat evaporates? It was already becoming evident by the late 1980s that Western publics were less prone to bear increased burdens of defense and were more inclined to shift burdens to their partners. At the same time, as the *common* threat diminished, parochial interests and hence parochial definitions of threat were becoming more important. Alliance partners had never evaluated problems in Central America, the Middle East, Southwest Asia, the Persian Gulf, Africa, and the Pacific in the same way. A common estimation of interests and of threats and hence a unified strategy were thus going to be more fleeting. There is now less inclination to accept the strictures of integrated defense and more desire to seek less a balanced alliance force than balanced national forces—the latter objective, however, being constrained by the various publics' desire to devote more of the national treasury to public domestic or private discretionary spending. The latter constraint dictates greater cooperation among traditional or would-be alliance partners whereas the perceived diminishment of a common threat tends toward fragmentation.

A major challenge facing traditional allies and partners in the 1990s is thus either the establishment of a new political and strategic consensus or the definitive recognition that, as the *raison d'être* for an alliance has changed, so the alliance itself must be eschewed or transformed into something entirely different. Both the level of external commitment, including types and numbers of forces, and the distribution of the risks, costs, and benefits of cooperation need to be determined. The outcome of this determination is unclear, but one thing seems almost certain: The United States will be compelled to accept a higher level of genuine consultation and strategic constraints, and traditional or new partners must assume greater responsibility for their defense than at any period since 1945.

INTERNATIONAL CONFLICT-LIMITING CODES OF BEHAVIOR

Both general and cold wars are not conducive to the development of norms of restraint, and even less so cooperation. But, if a bipolar struggle between the "children of light and the children of darkness" has given way to a more multidimensional and multipolar world, the bases for formal or informal codes of restraint may not have been strengthened. On the contrary, the resurgence of national calculations and the ability of subnational or transnational political movements to escape state control have intensified hatreds and loosened moral inhibitions. Are there any grounds for optimism, therefore, that, in the words of Douglas MacArthur, states may yet find "some greater and more equitable system"?

The apparent desire of the post-World War II Cold War combatants to lessen the burdens of defense and to resolve pressing domestic social, economic, and political issues too long deferred, may signal a willingness to cooperate together on global or regional issues that might divert them from these tasks. The proliferation of weapons, especially long-range missiles and chemical weapons, not even to mention nuclear devices, must be a major concern of the advanced industrial states. In some sense, these states may be hoisted upon their own petard, for they have for their own political or economic reasons been major contributors to this proliferation. The growth of regional ambitions and the instability of many Third World governments may force some reconsideration. For, if a benign environment is the immediate agenda for the major states, then they cannot neglect the growing frustrations and armaments of much of the rest of the world. Even if the Great Powers' forces and their military doctrines become less provocative, the world could become a "greater Balkans" and a single spark could cause a conflagration unsought and unwelcome.

If one cannot be too optimistic that new modes of restraint and cooperation will be found, there is nonetheless hope that the strategic reassessments taking place both in the East and in the West may yield a "more equitable system." In any case, the dimensions of the tasks facing the United States are growing, but the intertwining of its interests and capabilities with other states is also growing. Strategic choices premised on unilateral calculations are increasingly unsatisfactory—and perhaps unsustainable in a world of ambiguous threats and limited resources. It is thus the quality of American political judgment and the range and depth of its diplomatic posture which will determine the wisdom of those choices—and, more to the point, their relevance. For it is possible to spend vast sums spread over many units in the Defense Department and aimed at a multitude of threats only to discover that the enormous expense is still low in proportion to the policy and to the challenges of the external environment. Writing in December 1896, Alfred Thayer Mahan, America's great naval strategist, saw the problem in relation to the issue of preparing for war, but it applies equally to using one's defense posture to secure peace and sustain a stable evolution in the international sphere as the United States prepares to enter the twenty-first century:

> Preparation for war involves many conditions, often contradictory one to another, at times almost irreconcilable. To satisfy all of these passes the ingenuity of the national treasury, powerless to give the whole of what is demanded by the representatives of the different elements, which in duly ordered proportion, constitute a complete scheme of national military policy, whether for offense or defense. Unable to sat-

isfy all, and too often equally unable to say, frankly, "this one is chief; to it you others must yield, except so far as you contribute to its greatest efficiency," either the pendulum of the government will swing from one extreme to the other, or, in the attempt to be fair all round, all alike receive less than they ask, and for their theoretical completeness require. In other words, the contents of the national purse are distributed, instead of being concentrated upon a leading conception, adopted after due deliberation, and maintained with conviction.[2]

TOWARD THE TWENTY-FIRST CENTURY

As the Cold War was winding down, there was much talk in the United States and elsewhere about the "peace dividend," the redistribution of funds from the defense to the domestic portion of the federal budget or from the public to the private sector. It became immediately obvious, however, that, while defense would account for a lesser portion of the gross domestic product and the federal budget, there would be no real bonanza either for private or public domestic spending. The size and composition of the national debt placed severe limits both on tax reductions or expanded public services.

At the same time, there was a growing consensus that future public spending decisions needed to be geared more toward long-term investment in the expansion of aggregate supply, that is, in increasing the rate of growth in total goods and services of the American economy. From this perspective, both defense spending (and hence external commitments) and public transfer payments (and hence entitlements) would be scrutinized from the broader perspective of their relationship to the goal of a growing economy.

From the point of view of the policy objective of domestic economic growth, therefore, one could predict that the United States would seek to limit those external commitments that might reverse or substantially slow the reduction in the defense budget that was projected in the late Bush and early Clinton administrations. This scenario suggests either that external threats to U.S. interest will be sufficiently moderate so as to allow a continuing reduction in defense spending or that, whatever the threats, attention to them can or will be postponed.

But herein lies the rub. A world shaken by violent political change and uncertainty as to the requisites of international security will not be one conducive to the stable conditions necessary for long-term economic growth. The Cold War, for all its massive defense commitments and periodic descent into open conflict, was characterized by a remarkably stable security framework. The key issue facing the United States over the next decade, therefore, will be the creation or transfiguration of international security arrangements that will favor peaceful change or at a minimum contain the wider effects of violent change. Central to this will be the reliability and effectiveness of American armed might.

If the goal of economic growth requires both an adjustment in American spending patterns and a secure international system, then one can predict that the American defense posture will stabilize at levels anywhere from 30 to 50 percent of those at the height of the Cold War. At the same time, there will be increased attempts to restructure those forces so as to respond to technological opportunities, particularly in information and communications, and to political opportunities toward renewed defense cooperation with erstwhile allies and enemies alike. Ironically, this attempt to stabilize the cost of defense while exploiting technology and reinforcing alignments was the hallmark of the Eisenhower administration in the early days of the Cold War. The early days of the post-Cold War order may see similar efforts.

ENDNOTES

1. For an examination of the U.S. maritime strategy, see Robert S. Wood, "On Warfare at Sea and Naval Forces," in Edward A. Kolodziej and Patrick M. Morgan, eds., *Security and Arms Control—Volume 2: A Guide to International Policymaking* (New York: Greenwood Press, 1989), 187-207.
2. Alfred Thayer Mahan, *Interest of America in Sea Power, Present and Future* (Boston: Little, Brown, 1897), 175.

9

NATIONAL DEFENSE
AND THE CHALLENGE
OF TERRORISM

Few international problems illustrate the vulnerability, interdependence, and disappearing invincibility of all nations more starkly than the problem of international terrorism. In a sense, a nation is vincible to the extent that its policies do not alter significantly the problems it faces—terrorism is such a problem. It ebbs and flows, to a considerable degree, regardless of what a nation does to combat it. While it is a global problem, we discuss several aspects of terrorism here in order to call attention to the foreign policy challenges terrorism presents to the United States. We also make some suggestions as to how terrorism can be dealt with more effectively as we move into the twenty-first century.

WHAT IS TERRORISM?

Definitions of terrorism are very slippery and quite controversial. In a sense, the definitional problem will never be solved to everyone's satisfaction since terrorism, in some respects, is completely subjective. "Terror" comes from the Latin word *terrere* which means to cause to tremble, and an event that causes one person to tremble may cause another to celebrate. We define terrorism as a type of premeditated violence that is motivated by political, economic, social, or ideological goals. It is capricious in that it is generally directed against randomly chosen innocent persons or against governmental or institutional targets and it is designed to "get the attention of a much wider audience, thereby advancing the terrorists'. . . goals."[1]

Terrorists strike randomly—there is no logic to the choice of targets although there is considerable logic in both tactics and strategy. If terrorists are to be successful, they must convince a target nation that any of its citizens or facilities, anywhere in the world, could become a victim of their acts at any time. And it is not the immediate victims of their acts which terrorists wish to affect. The real target of a terrorist act is usually some policy or practice of a government, most often a liberal democratic government which attempts to protect fundamental civil rights, particularly the freedom of speech.

Terrorists seldom strike at the policies or practices of authoritarian or totalitarian governments for two reasons. In the first place, a government without a due process of law will often deal with terrorists in a very summary and irrevocable manner. Secondly, a government without a free press cannot be relied upon to permit the transmission of the news of a terrorist attack to the broader society.

For this transmission of terror from individual victims to society to occur, terrorism depends completely on publicity. Again, this explains why most terrorist acts are directed against liberal democratic societies where freedom of the press is valued and can be relied on to permit media coverage. Fear of being caught and executed is less of a deterrent than is the fear that the terrorist act may not make the evening news.

Much of the definitional anxiety which surrounds terrorism grows from the dubious practice of expecting more from language than it is capable of giving. A single phenomenon, the use of political terror, for example, must be capable of being described by the same word whether one approves or disapproves of the cause for which it is used. Thus, the old adage, "one man's terrorist is another man's freedom fighter" is inappropriate. A freedom fighter is one who fights for the principle of freedom in a principled way and according to the moral values associated with the general concepts of freedom and liberty. A terrorist is one who fights for a principle in an unprincipled way. Those who fight for freedom fight for a moral cause and must do so in a moral manner— that is, according to accepted rules of warfare as developed over the last several centuries. Those who ignore these rules and who capriciously kill civilians for whatever cause are not freedom fighters—they are terrorists.

TYPES OF TERRORISM

1. State Terrorism. State terrorism is terrorism conducted by the state, usually to intimidate segments of the population into accepting government programs and policies. The state-sponsored terrorism of Mussolini, Hitler, and Stalin are examples of this kind of terrorism.[2] It is coercive intimidation and differs from the legitimate enforcement of state policies in democratic states in that the use of force in democratic states is subject to the voice of the people through democratic procedures. Strictly speaking, state terrorism conducted against the citizens of a state can occur only in totalitarian or authoritarian states where limited democratic procedures exist which can prevent it or where segments of the population are not treated as full citizens.

The occasional use of force to gain compliance with duly enacted laws in a democratic society, when necessary, should not be referred to as terrorism no matter how much one may disagree with the laws or with the methods of enforcement. Liberal democratic states have a right to enforce compliance with the law as long as fundamental democratic principles are followed in that society. On the other hand, the use of capricious violence to coerce or intimidate citizens in a state in which those citizens have little or no say about the content of the laws, who will enforce them, or the methods by which they are enforced, is terrorism. It is terrorism because, in an authoritarian, tyrannical state, the regime, by definition, is a minority which uses force to gain compliance with its will.

State terrorism is as much a foreign policy challenge to the United States as are any other forms of terrorism. America must use all possible legal and diplomatic means to alter the terroristic practices of such states and even the regimes themselves. Friendly states and alliance partners which use state terrorism are a special problem. Especially in this case, however, the United States should use all legal and diplomatic means to put an end to such practices, to demand respect for human rights, and to encourage adherence to democratic principles. Failure to do so ignores the fundamental principles on which America was founded and will do more foreign policy harm, in the long run, than can be offset by cozying up to dictators and despots who dabble in state terrorism.

2. *Revolutionary Terrorism.* This kind of terrorism attempts to change the status quo; it is revolutionary because it attempts to overthrow an existing order. It is often confused with guerrilla warfare but is quite different in several ways. Guerrillas usually direct their attacks against political and military officials whereas terrorists make no distinction between innocent victims and government officials. Guerrillas usually attempt to destroy one system of government in order to establish a different, usually radically different, system of government whereas most (but not all) terrorists have only fuzzy political programs to put forward even should the government against which they are fighting collapse.[3] Guerrillas, particularly urban guerrillas, will often use terroristic tactics to support their long-range goals, but this does not necessarily make them terrorists nor does it condone terrorist activity. Guerrilla warfare is distinguished by its use of irregular (that is, nonuniformed and nontraditionally organized) forces which can blend into the urban or rural landscape in which the conflict is being conducted. Guerrillas capture and exchange prisoners of war and usually adhere to other norms of warfare. Terrorists capture media attention and hostages and accept no rules of war. In most cases, guerrillas do not use indiscriminate or capricious violence to intimidate a larger population. They fight to destroy the morale of an organized army and to gain popular support for their cause.

Whether or not one approves of guerrilla warfare depends on one's view of the legitimacy of the government which is under siege. Again, liberal democratic theory holds that force may be appropriate when aimed at the officials of authoritarian or tyrannical regimes. That was, after all, the meaning of the Declaration of Independence phrase, "When in the course of human events. . . ." But while liberal democratic theory may allow for the legitimate use of force for revolutionary purposes, it does not condone terrorism. A political philosophy based on moral assumptions about the worth of individuals, human rights, and the centrality of prescribed political procedures can never be used to justify terrorism.

While it is the aim of liberal democratic states to create a society in which all political authority is exercised by consensus and within the bounds of political and social legitimacy, it is nevertheless essential to democratic theory to distinguish between legal and illegal uses of violence. Violence used by individuals or groups to coerce or intimidate a democratic government into yielding to their demands is an illegal use of violence.[4]

Acts of violence between states during times of war are usually not classified as terrorism, however terrifying they may be, as long as basic rules of war are followed. These rules have been elaborated philosophically in the rich tradition of the "just war" theory and in positive law through the various Hague and Geneva Conventions and other treaties between states.[5] The continuing concern, more than forty years after the end of World War II, to bring to justice either Allied or Axis officers responsible for acts which went beyond the accepted norms of war, attests to the wide acceptance of these principles.[6]

By this logic, it is *what* is done and not *who* does it that identifies revolutionary, if not all, terrorism. Even though some terrorists "have motives more respectable than their methods," terrorism must be condemned no matter how sympathetic one may be with the cause.[7] Certainly, it is not a question of the interests of which superpower are being served that distinguishes terrorism from other categories of international behavior. Calling terrorists freedom fighters does not alter the nature of evil. On the other hand, legitimate freedom fighters, using guerrilla warfare against repressive and authoritarian regimes, but refraining from terrorism, deserve the support of all who cherish liberty.

3 . International Terrorism. There is a third category of terrorism which can be called international terrorism. It may be revolutionary if it attempts to overthrow other governments; on the other hand it may attempt merely to embarrass or discredit the foreign policies of other nations. This terrorism is directed against the persons or property of other states, for political purposes, and may occur anywhere in the world, usually wherever it can do the most effective damage with the least risk. It may be sponsored by another state but it can be conducted by terrorist groups without the awareness or approval of other states. A state which sponsors international terrorism may or may not be practicing state terrorism within its own borders. State sponsorship is not necessary in order for international terrorism to occur, but it does help. Terrorists may operate out of the territory of another state with or without the knowledge or assistance of that state.

It was in response to state-sponsored international terrorism that President Reagan ordered the air attack on Libya during the night of 14 April 1986. President Reagan claimed to have evidence of "approximately thirty directives from the Libyan government to its foreign missions, exhorting them to kill Americans."[8] The final straw came on 5 April 1986 when a bomb which exploded in a West German disco known to be frequented by U.S. servicemen killed two people and injured 100. President Reagan again claimed to have solid evidence of both the message from Libya to go ahead with the bombing of the disco and subsequent confirmation of the event.[9] Ten days later U.S. aircraft bombed five targets in Benghazi and Tripoli. Assuming the evidence of Libyan involvement to be accurate, these Libyan-sponsored acts were examples of international terrorism—in this case, the state sponsorship of terrorist attacks upon the persons or property of other states.

Some international terrorist groups try to disguise any state sponsorship. The ordeal of Kuwait Airways flight KU422 is an example of this. On 5 April 1988, flight 422 was hijacked while en route from Bangkok to Kuwait. It was flown first to Mashhad in Iran where the original seven hijackers were joined by others who brought with them additional weapons and explosives. This group of hijackers claimed to represent the Lebanese-based but Iran-backed Hezbollah or "Party of God" group. The hijackers who boarded while in Iran could not have done so without at least the complicity of the Iranian government. The governments of Egypt, Saudi Arabia, and Jordan accused Iran of complicity and Yassir Arafat, the head of the Palestinian Liberation Organization (PLO), said, "According to my best information, they [the Iranians] are behind the whole operation."[10]

No better example of international terrorism exists than the Lod Airport massacre on 30 May 1972. Three terrorists from the Japanese Red Army (JRA), recruited by the Palestinian Front for the Liberation of Palestine (PFLP), trained in the use of explosives in Japan and North Korea, given additional training in Lebanon, carrying false passports made up in West

Germany, and concealing Czechoslovak weapons, boarded an Air France flight in Rome and flew to the Lod Airport in Tel Aviv where they killed twenty-five and injured seventy-six innocent travellers. Many of these victims were Puerto Rican Christians who were making a spiritual pilgrimage to the Holy Land. To one degree or another, the political authorities of nine international actors were involved in that episode.

International terrorism is distinguished neither by its revolutionary aims nor its state sponsorship; rather, it is terrorism conducted across international borders or against persons or property from outside the boundaries of the state in which the attack occurs.

TERRORISM THROUGH HISTORY

Violent acts have caused terror from the beginning of time; however, the use of terror as a capricious and systematic political weapon perhaps began with an extremist wing of the ancient Jewish Zealots, known as the *sicarri* or dagger men, who operated against Roman occupation forces in Jerusalem in the first century.[11] These early terrorists would stab a knife *(sicarri)* into Jewish collaborators, Roman occupiers, or anyone who opposed violent resistance to Roman rule. These murders would occur in crowded public places and were meant to coerce or intimidate others into accepting the Zealot approach.[12] The Assassins, literally "hashish-eaters," were a group of extremist Muslims who, after receiving orders from their superior, "The Old Man of the Mountains," would selectively assassinate Christian leaders during the times of the Crusades.

These two early examples of political terrorism actually predate both the word "terror" and the concept of terrorism which came into use at the time of the First Republic of France. In order to preserve the new Republic, a Committee of Public Safety was created which introduced military conscription in order to defeat the foreign threat and terrorism in order to defeat the domestic threat to its existence. Thousands of French citizens were guillotined on the basis of very meager evidence in an attempt to coerce or intimidate the population into compliance. The period from 1793 to 1794 was called The Reign of Terror.

In the nineteenth century, some European anarchists began to advocate terrorism as a means of destroying states. The Russian anarchist, Bakunin, broke with Marx at the 1876 meeting of the First International partially because of Bakunin's willingness to encourage terrorism. Bakunin advocated individual acts of terror ("propaganda by the deed") as a means of destroying bourgeois governments. One of his followers, Kropotkin, believed that anything illegal was good for their cause while another follower, Nechayev, founded the first modern terrorist secret society. Gavrilo Princip was encouraged by the Black Hand, a secret Serbian group, to assassinate Archduke Franz Ferdinand, heir to the Hapsburg Empire, on 28 June 1914. It was this act of terrorism that precipitated World War I.

It is, however, from the cradle of both civilization and terrorism, the Middle East, that contemporary terrorism has emerged with vengeance. Following the traditions of the ancient *sicarri,* two extremist Zionist groups, the Irgun Zvai Leumi and the Stern Gang, conducted occasional acts of terrorism in the British Mandate of Palestine in the 1930s and 40s in an attempt to influence both Arab and British governments to yield to Zionist pressures. Both groups were outside of the Haganah, the official Jewish defense organization, and both were forcibly disbanded by the police of the newly created Jewish state of Israel in 1948.[13] Much contemporary terrorism, from the various alphabetical splinter groups of the Palestinian movement to the sectarian terrorism of Islamic Jihad and the Hezbollah, follows in this stream of Middle Eastern terrorism.

In 1989, Ayatollah Khomeini, the leader of the Iranian government, called on all Islamic people to kill a British author who wrote a book which defamed the founder of the Islamic faith. Over 5 million dollars was offered to any successful assassin. Among other things, this barbaric act was meant to deter others from blaspheming the faith and from angering the Ayatollah. In effect, it was international terrorism.

Throughout the 1970s and early 80s, terrorist activities continued in Latin America, Europe, and the Middle East, mostly in the form of kidnapping (of business and government leaders), bombings, skyjacking, assassinations, and murders. Three groups, the Baader-Meinhof gang in Germany, the Red Brigades in Italy, and the Japanese Red Army, particularly caught the attention of the media and the public for their nihilistic beliefs and ruthless activities. As these groups, and others, were either eliminated or reduced in numbers, there was a subsequent reduction in the incidence of terrorist attacks in the 1980s and 1990s. For example, terrorist attacks in Italy dropped from over 2,500 a year in 1979 to 100 a year in 1986.[14]

Terrorist activities conducted by the Palestinian Liberation Organization (PLO) or on behalf of Palestinian causes have also gradually decreased as the PLO has become convinced that it could gain greater support for its cause through nonviolent means. "Since 1973, they [the PLO] have made numerous denunciations of 'reckless and irresponsible' acts of international terrorism . . . and . . . have frequently threatened punishment for hijackers and others who engage in international terrorist activities."[15]

Much of the international terrorism in the later half of the 1980s was sparked by the complete disintegration of civil government in Lebanon and the use of that territory as a safe haven for many terrorist groups, including those acting in support of the objectives of a Fundamentalist Islamic regime in Iran.

If there is any one common thread running through this very brief review of the development of terrorism, it is that modern terrorism has virtually always been a weapon of the weak used against the strong. Equal, or nearly equal, powers appear to prefer to wage war, relatively inferior movements or groups seem to prefer rural or urban guerrilla warfare or other forms of limited conflict, but vastly inferior movements or groups opt for terrorism. A small terrorist cell of perhaps no more than five or six persons, armed with nothing but smuggled pistols, can capture global attention and hold it for as long as they can hold hostages in a hijacked airliner.

CAUSES OF TERRORISM

There are as many causes of terrorism as there are terrorist groups, but there are some obvious categories.

1. Territorial terrorists are those whose entire existence is tied up with territorial objectives. They want sovereign control over some territory which is occupied by another power or they want to be joined to a larger, usually contiguous, "homeland." In any event, their goal is territorial; their struggle is for political power. The various Palestinian groups wish to have a Palestinian homeland, the Provisional IRA wishes to drive the British and their supporters out of Northern Ireland, the South Moluccan terrorists in the Netherlands wish to create a Republic of South Molucca in a remote part of Indonesia, the Croatian terrorists wanted an independent Croatian state separated from Yugoslavia, the Basque terrorists (the ETA) want a separate Basque state created in the Pyrenees, and so on. These are the most effective terrorist groups and are likely to be around for the longest time because they have linked their cause to the most powerful forces in the world—ethnicity and nationalism.

2. Ideological terrorists conduct their activities in support of some vision of a future economic or political condition. These visions may be more or less articulated. The less articulated visions are virtually anarchic or nihilistic in their ambitions and have no apparent plans for the future or their plans are very unclear and undeveloped beyond a desire to cause the collapse of a regime or government. Others engage in loose ideological rhetoric about some future utopia, socialist nirvana, or fascist heaven on earth, but most have no constructive philosophy and advocate violence for its own sake. To some extent, these groups have been nourished by a stream of intellectual thought which began with Blanqui and Nechayev and was joined in more recent times by Sorel, Sartre, and Marcuse, each of whom celebrated violence and terrorism as an end in itself.

Among the better known examples of this category are (or were) the Baader-Meinhof gang, which operated in Germany from 1970 until its principal leaders all committed suicide in prison in 1977; the Red Brigades, which operated in Italy throughout the 1970s until increasing police counterterrorist measures brought most of its members to justice; and the JRA, one of the smallest and richest terrorist groups. The latter group never had more than approximately twenty members and it is believed that they once received several million dollars for one skyjacking. They have also been known to sell their services to the highest bidder.

Governments have been quite successful in recent years in dealing with these kinds of terrorist groups. Direct Action in France, the Baader-Meinhof gang in Germany, the Fighting Communist Cells in Belgium (the CCC), the JRA, the Red Brigades, and others have been either defeated or neutralized by a combination of forceful police action, shared intelligence, and laudable cooperation and coordination between the various security and police organizations of several countries.[16] With some notable exceptions, these groups operated primarily within their national boundaries, against a variety of both domestic and international targets, with minimal cooperation and consultation between them. Nevertheless, they shared common themes of anti-Americanism, anticapitalism, and antinuclear forces.

European governments have had less success in dealing with nonindigenous terrorist groups, particularly groups which have state sponsors. Terrorist groups receiving support from Iran, Syria, or Libya and operating within Europe have been very difficult for European governments to defeat since their state sponsors have provided them with virtual diplomatic protection.

3. Single issue or narrow issue terrorist groups are those whose operations have a single, usually narrow, focus. It is difficult to give a complete list of these groups since they can arise overnight in response to some event and never be heard of again once they have thrown their bomb, fired their rockets, released their hostages, destroyed their targeted airship, etc. It is entirely possible for a small number of malcontents to form a secret and small terrorist cell, invent a name, and embark on some terrorist scheme almost within a few days. Other groups or even governments may decide to support them in various ways, but, once the specific or limited objective is gained, the members will usually disappear into the human landscape.

For example, in October 1977, two men and two women hijacked Lufthansa flight 181 soon after it took off from Palma, Majorca. The leader of the small group was a Palestinian who six months earlier had murdered a Yemeni diplomat in London. The terrorists demanded the release of eleven members of the Baader-Meinhof gang who were being held in West German jails awaiting trial. After five days of exhaustive shuttling around the Mediterranean, the group directed the aircraft to Mogadishu, the capital of Somalia in Eastern Africa. Members of West Germany's counterterrorist force, GSG-9, eventually stormed the aircraft and killed three of the terrorists and wounded the fourth. The imprisoned Baader-Meinhof gang leaders were so distraught by this failure that five of them attempted suicide in jail, four successfully.

On 29 May 1981, a terrorist group which called itself "In the Heart of the Beast," threw a bomb into the headquarters of a U.S. Army Intelligence Group in Giessen, West Germany. They claimed the act was done to call attention to the hunger strikes of jailed terrorists in West Germany. No one was injured and the group was not heard from again.

The terrorist hijacking of Kuwait Airlines flight KU422 in April 1988 was for the sole purpose of forcing the Kuwaiti government into releasing seventeen terrorists imprisoned in Kuwaiti jails for various acts of terrorism committed in Kuwait. The Kuwaiti government refused to negotiate with the terrorists and, after the brutal murder of two passengers, the terrorists were allowed to slip away into the night and return to Lebanon. Three of the British hostages who were released identified Imad Mugnieh, a Lebanese who was responsible for several terrorist actions all aimed at the release of "relatives" who were in Kuwaiti jails after being arrested in 1983.

Terrorist groups have arisen in opposition to environmental degradation, the killing of certain animals, abortion policies and practices, nuclear energy, economic modernization, and almost any cause of which one can think. A few terrorist incidents were conducted in 1987 and 1988 in an attempt to discredit the ability of South Korea to host the 1988 Summer Olympics. Some of these groups have formed linkages with one another but most have had a short lifetime.

4. Sectarian terrorist groups are difficult to classify. So often their motives are entwined with either territorial claims or single issues of religious and political significance. For example, many terrorist attacks since the 1977 Islamic Fundamentalist revolution in Iran have been conducted by groups variously known as the Hezbollah ("the Party of God"), Islamic Jihad, Shi'ites, or other splinter groups. Some of these groups believe that their terrorism has Allah's blessings, while others merely use religion to mask avarice, adventurism, or nationalism.

It is not always clear which terrorist group is responsible for any given attack. On 12 April 1985, a terrorist bomb exploded in a Madrid restaurant frequented by American servicemen. Immediately following the attack, responsibility was "claimed" by both the Islamic Jihad and a Basque separatist group, the ETA. Both the Red Army Faction and the French Direct Action groups claimed responsibility for the detonation of a car bomb outside the headquarters of the U.S. Rhein-Main airbase near Frankfurt which killed two Americans and wounded twenty other U.S. and West German citizens.

Some writers have listed other categories of terrorist groups including state-sponsored groups and ideologically motivated groups. In fact, many of the groups in the above four categories may be sponsored by states and all have constructed some sort of belief system to rationalize their actions.

WHAT DO TERRORISTS WANT?

1. Political Goals. Ultimately, terrorists want to intimidate a society or its government into yielding to their political demands. These demands and goals vary widely. The Palestinian Front for the Liberation of Palestine (PFLP) wants Israel to grant a Palestinian homeland or they want to force the United States into ending its support of Israel.[17] Sometimes it is very difficult to understand how terrorist actions support their professed political goals. What aspect of the Palestinian cause, for example, was furthered when four Palestinian gunmen hijacked the Italian cruise ship *Achille Lauro* off the coast of Egypt in 1985 and murdered one elderly American? At other times the political goals sought by the terrorists are internal to the terrorist group and, apparently, not related to the target at all. While the victims of much Middle Eastern terrorism may be innocent travelers, the target is often to affect some obscure or arcane power struggle between the almost endless factions with their alphabetic or enigmatic sounding names. The goal is often to embarrass, discredit, or prove ineffective one potential leader or another or one group or another.[18]

Outside of the Middle East, other groups, of course, have different political goals. The IRA want the British out of Northern Ireland, the Kanaks want the French out of New Caledonia, the ETA want the Spanish to grant Basque independence, and so on. The goals of the nihilist groups have been less clear. The Baader-Meinhof gang wanted to bring about a collapse of the West German government while the Red Brigades wanted to embarrass and weaken the Italian government. In the latter case, there is some evidence that they wanted to force the Italian government to resort to repressive practices in an attempt to stop the Red Brigades who would then point to the repression as evidence of the authoritarian character of the Italian government in hopes of gaining more popular support for their cause.

The goals of some terrorists are much shorter-term and much more pragmatic. Groups who take hostages may do so to obtain the release of their fellow terrorists detained in prisons. Some hostages are taken or held merely as a means of forcing the nations from which the hostages come to be cautious and prudent in dealing with the terrorists. West German officials admitted that their unwillingness to extradite one of the terrorists involved in the hijacking of a TWA jet in 1985 stemmed from their fear over the possible consequences of such an action on the West German hostages who were being held in Lebanon.[19] It is widely believed that some of the Iranian-supported terrorists who held Americans hostage in Lebanon for such a long period of time, harbored a hope that this would somehow deter the Americans from taking military action against Iranian interests in the long-running Gulf War between Iran and Iraq.

2 . Publicity.   Since terrorism attempts to intimidate a wider population than its victims, publicity is always an immediate terrorist goal. Indeed, publicity is the mother's milk of terrorism. Terrorism without publicity is like the Goodyear blimp without helium. Traditional military operations, even various forms of unconventional warfare, measure success in terms of territory gained, the number of opponents killed, or the degree to which the enemy's ability to maintain the struggle has been weakened. Terrorists measure success by the number of column inches, the size of headlines, and the amount of airtime on television which their acts receive.

It was the Russian anarchist Bakunin who first identified terrorism as "propaganda by the deed." By committing daring, brutal, and extravagant acts of violence, terrorists believe they can publicize both their cause and their group to peoples and governments of the world. This serves multiple purposes: it lets their own supporters know they are active and vigorous, it inspires others into joining them or emulating their actions, and it sends a message to the target of the act that worse things may happen if they do not yield to the terrorists' demands. "As one of the leaders of the Algerian Front de Liberation Nationale (FLN) put it, 'It was more effective propaganda to shoot a couple of French businessmen in the middle of Algiers than to shoot a hundred or so soldiers in a lonely gully.'"[20]

The requirement for publicity is so powerful that some have suggested that a sure cure for terrorism would be to deny all terrorism any publicity in any form. While true, this is a case where the cure would be worse than the disease. To fight terrorism by denying freedom of the press would be to let in through the back door what you were trying to keep out of the front. On the other hand, there is great need for self-discipline and self-restraint in the media. In America, the heads of the major commercial television networks have worked out procedures and principles to govern the coverage of terrorist incidents. These agreements are meant to protect the integrity of the press while at the same time prevent the media from becoming an arrow in the terrorists' quiver. The media is used frequently as a whipping boy by advocates of hard-line approaches to defeat terrorism. They are charged with playing into the hands of the terrorists by heightening public sympathy for their cause. But, "indeed, recent work suggests that the disproportionate amount of mass media attention on terrorist tactics and their aftermath, rather than precipitating social conditions, goals, and objectives, has provided *TV attention but not legitimacy.*"[21] In other words, the terrorists may be getting the coverage they desire, but it is not having the effect they want it to have.

3. Money.   It should not be forgotten that some terrorist acts are nothing but a form of violent fund-raising. The record of terrorists' successes in collecting ransom money is very incomplete since neither governments nor private corporations like to talk about such payments. Government payoffs may eventually become a matter of public knowledge but payments from private citizens and corporations are kept very quiet. Even if the amount demanded is made known by the terrorists, the amount paid will be kept secret. "Estimates of ransoms paid by all businesses between 1971 and 1981 vary between 150 million dollars and 250 million dollars, with roughly 50 per cent being paid out by U.S. firms. In El Salvador alone between spring 1978 and spring 1980 it has been estimated that as much as 50 million dollars may have been paid by foreign businesses."[22] These data do not report any ransoms paid by governments. For example, the "Federal German Government disclosed that it had paid [in 1972] $5 million in ransom for the release of the hostages and airliner" hijacked by five Palestinians who called themselves members of the "Organization for Victims of Zionist Occupation."[23]

4. Revenge. On the night of 14 April 1986, the Reagan administration carried out an air attack on the Libyan cities of Benghazi and Tripoli in response to what the administration claimed was certain evidence of Libyan involvement in a number of terrorist attacks over several years against U.S. persons and property. This raid was a demonstration of the administration's strategy to make life more difficult for states which sponsor international terrorism. It was believed that, among other things, the raid would deter further terrorist attacks, at least those sponsored by the Libyan government. It is difficult to evaluate this strategy since there were additional motives behind the air raid and because one would need access to classified materials to know what evidence has been gathered since the raid to support any claims of success. However, it is clear that a few spasmodic terrorist attacks occurred immediately after the raid primarily for revenge or to punish those who supported the air raid. For example, on 17 April 1986, two British hostages and one American hostage, Peter Kilburn, were murdered in Beirut, allegedly in response to the U.S. air strikes on Libya, which were launched from U.S. military bases in Great Britain. On the same day, four rocket-propelled grenades were fired at the British ambassador's home in Beirut by Omar Al Mukhtar, a terrorist group known for its affiliation with Libya. Eight days later a staff member of the U.S. Embassy in Sudan was shot near his residence, allegedly by supporters of the Libyan government, and in August a British air base in Cyprus was attacked by a terrorist group which called itself the United Nasserite Organization and which said the attack was in response to the British support for the U.S. air strike against Libya. Libyans also attempted to blow up a U.S. officer's club in Ankara, Turkey and the terrorists arrested for attempting to blow up the U.S. Embassy in Togo claimed they received their explosives from the Libyans.

Probably no single event has unleased more revenge and retaliation than the Israeli invasion of Lebanon in 1982. Among other unintended consequences of that strategy, the PLO leadership was undermined and new waves of attacks by previously unknown groups were unleased. In fact, the most significant terrorist attack ever carried out against the United States was carried out in revenge for the Israeli invasion. In June 1983, a Shi'ite terrorist group loaded a truck with the equivalent of 12,000 pounds of TNT (the largest conventional explosion ever seen by the FBI Bomb Squad) and drove it into the U.S. Marines camp at the Beirut Airport. The resulting explosion was responsible for the deaths of 242 people. In the almost endless conflict between the Palestinians and the government of Israel and between the pro-British terrorists and the pro-IRA terrorists in Northern Ireland, revenge and retaliation are so frequently mentioned as motives for attacks that original causes have become obscured. It is revenge which gives terrorism its own dynamic and, like blood feuds of old, makes it almost impossible to end.

HOW SUCCESSFUL HAVE TERRORISTS BEEN?

On balance, terrorism has not been particularly successful. Some terrorists groups have been partially successful in reaching some of their short-range political goals and some groups have been very successful in securing money with which to finance their activities. Beyond that, it is difficult to put together a very long list of significant success stories.

The various terrorist groups around the world that have advocated anarchy or nihilism have been singularly unsuccessful. The claim to be fighting for a worldwide revolution made by the small JRA was almost ludicrous. The fates of the other European terrorist groups have not been encouraging, although in 1988 there was a brief revival of the Red Brigades, the Italian group which many thought had been ended in the mid-1980s. Anarchic terrorist groups have often sought to evoke such repressive countermeasures from a government that the terrorists could use the resulting repression as a rallying point for wider public support of the terrorists' cause. In fact, European governments have avoided such repressive responses and have fought terrorism through moderate means usually consonant with liberal democratic values. It is even possible to argue that the actions of the Baader-Meinhof gang and the Red Brigades ultimately strengthened, rather than weakened, the governments of West Germany and Italy.

One must look beyond the stated goals, however, in order to assess success or failure. The bomb which destroyed the U.S. Marine base in Beirut on 23 October 1983 killed 242 people and played a significant role in the decision to withdraw the American contingent from the Multinational Force that was meant to further stability in Lebanon. While an American withdrawal was what the Islamic Jihad (the Shi'ite group which claimed responsibility) wanted, the political environment for the Islamic Jihad in Lebanon worsened in the subsequent years. The pro-Iranian groups may have traded U.S. influence for Syrian influence, a trade that was not necessarily in their interests.

International terrorism has not fared much better. One could argue that the Serbian Black Hand society, in providing a weapon for the assassination of the Austrian Archduke, did provoke, at least partially, World War I. But that was not the goal of the assassination and the subsequent war did not further Serbian interests in any way. Jewish terrorism in Palestine may have been part of the reason that Great Britain decided to withdraw from its League of Nations' mandate responsibility over that territory, an event that led to the creation of the Jewish state in 1948. But it would be difficult to argue, however, that after over forty years of a Jewish state, the earlier terrorism or the subsequent state terrorism against the Palestinians have succeeded in bringing about either peace or security for Israel. As one retired Jewish military office has said, "Our people [need to learn] that peace is a major security asset, that peace is worth territory and [that] more peace is worth more territory."[24]

The same is true in regard to years of Palestinian terrorism. While the PLO may have gained considerable notoriety in its early years through acts of terrorism, its recent diplomatic successes have resulted more from moderation than from violence. This relative moderation has brought more international support for the Palestinian cause than was gained through its earlier terrorism and is vitiated only by continuing terrorism from a variety of PLO splinter groups. It is perhaps one of the minor ironies of history to see the head of the PLO, Yassir Arafat, probably at one time the most widely recognized symbol of terrorism in the world, condemning terrorism and acting as a mediator between extremist Arab groups and other Arab governments.

Across the globe, it is difficult to find many "successes" of terrorism. The British are still firm in their commitment to remain in Northern Ireland and terrorist actions by the Provisional IRA and others have done more to bring the Republic of Ireland and Great Britain together in a common resolve to prevent terrorism than it has to further the separatists' cause. The same can be said for virtually all liberationist and separatist terrorist movements.

It is also difficult to find examples of governments that have been brought down by terrorism. Terrorism has not been as effective as guerrilla war in hastening the retreat of colonial empires or in defeating repressive regimes. The Tupamaros were partially responsible for bringing down a fairly moderate Uruguayan government in 1972, but the new government was more repressive than the one it succeeded and was clearly less kind to the causes supported by the Tupamaros than was the collapsed government.

The Reagan administration's arms for hostages deal with Iran may have been a fairly significant terrorist victory. It violated a long-standing U.S. policy of not negotiating with terrorists and may have been a factor in encouraging France and West Germany to enter into agreements with terrorists regarding French and West German hostages in Lebanon.

Some of the more dramatic successes of terrorists have been those which were unintended. It is unlikely that terrorists have set out to raise the price and lower the ease of international travel. Yet the elaborate, expensive, and bothersome security measures at virtually every international airport in the world have been brought about by terrorism. Similarly, the increased costs of embassy and personnel protection for all Western governments, particularly the United States, have been enormous. From the early 1970s, when attacks on U.S. embassies and diplomats began to make headlines, through 1985, the United States allocated 3.3 billion dollars on the most extensive rebuilding program in history. There is not an American embassy in the world that has not been affected by this program. In 1986, Congress passed the "Omnibus Diplomatic Security and Antiterrorism Act of 1986" which allocated over1 billion dollars for additional diplomatic security and authorized 12 billion dollars to be appropriated for reward money.[25]

If terrorists have sought to detract from the esthetics of American diplomatic facilities, they have succeeded. Large cement obstacles and other types of barriers (thinly disguised as landscaping) now surround nearly all U.S. embassies to prevent car bombers from easy access to courtyards and buildings. These, along with newly designed buildings, give the impression of a "fortress America" in spite of attempts to avoid this image. Visiting an official in some of these facilities reminds one of visiting an errant uncle in a state penitentiary. The protection of Americans serving in U.S. diplomatic missions is paramount, however, and few would disagree with the need for these security measures. For the first 142 years of the Foreign Service, only 81 officers were killed in the line of duty, all but 4 by earthquakes, plagues, and other such natural causes. In other words, from 1776 to 1967, the Foreign Service lost 1 officer through violence every 40 years. Since 1967 they have lost an officer through violence about every 90 days.[26]

In the face of a fairly limited picture of successes, why do terrorist acts continue to occur? In the first place, terrorism is one of the safest crimes to commit. Though they usually do not obtain their political goals, the terrorists at least go unpunished. A very small percentage of international terrorists is caught, even fewer are convicted, and even less serve their full sentence.[27] This is closely related to the continuing existence of safe havens for terrorists. Every diplomatic intervention to eliminate such places ought to be pursued. Nations which harbor terrorists ought to be subjected to the most severe international economic and political sanctions.

A second answer lies in the amount of publicity that terrorists continue to receive for what they see as just, but intractable, causes. In spite of empirical evidence that media attention does not necessarily create a favorable image of the terrorists or their causes, publicity continues to be one of the primary goals of all terrorists.[28] No matter how small the group, no matter how obscure the cause, a dramatic terrorist gesture will capture headlines and media coverage for days at a time. In no other way can the powerless and weak become major actors on the stage of world politics. Artificial crises are created and fellow supporters gain inspiration when they see such acts.

Additionally, kidnapping and hostage-taking continue to be a source of money for terrorist groups, particularly small terrorist groups without state sponsors. And, as mentioned earlier, terrorist hostage-taking continues because it has proven to provide at least a limited type of leverage over Western policies.

TERRORISM AND U.S. FOREIGN POLICY

In the case of state terrorism, the United States must decide whether the practice is sufficiently egregious as to warrant military intervention against the offending state. In a sense this was the U.S. response to Nazi and Fascist state terrorism in the 1940s, although it required the Japanese attack on Pearl Harbor to bring about U.S. involvement. During the Cold War, the United States attempted politically and diplomatically to influence the human rights policies of the Soviet Union but judged military intervention either impractical, ineffective, or imprudent.

Friendly states which practice, to one degree or another, state terrorism are just as difficult to influence. It is easy for the United States to condemn such practices, but there is a big difference between rhetorical diplomacy and successful coercive diplomacy, particularly where friendly states are involved.

In the face of international terrorism against U.S. persons and property abroad, the United States must rely on the police and army of the countries in which the attacks occur to bring the terrorists to justice. In duly constituted states, the United States must respect the principles of political independence and territorial sovereignty and not take unilateral actions. Those states may request various kinds of American aid in combatting terrorism (as Italy did at the height of the Red Brigade terrorism), but the United States cannot act in the absence of that request. When U.S. F-14 fighters forced an Egyptian airliner carrying the terrorists involved in the *Achille Lauro* episode to land in Italy, it damaged good relations with both countries, something that is needed in any long-run fight against terrorism.[29] Calls for American aid to governments under siege by terrorists must be weighed carefully and judged according to the circumstances of each case.

In sum, terrorist acts committed against U.S. persons or property within the territorial sovereignty of another state must be dealt with according to the laws of that state. The United States may use all available legal and diplomatic means to influence the ways that the host governments respond, but it may not use force unless invited to do so by the host governments.

Acts of terrorism committed in international territory or within territories where there is no effective sovereign power are a different matter. Responses to terrorist acts committed in international territories (the high seas, international air space, etc.) are covered in a variety of bilateral and multilateral treaties and other international agreements. Most of these agreements permit the use of force to prevent, capture, and punish such actions, as long as certain restraints are followed. The response must be proportional, it must be relatively immediate, and it must be minimal to the task. When the offending terrorist acts are sponsored by another sovereign state, but committed in international territory, international law permits a variety of kinds of responses (reprisals, retortion, etc.) even up to the use of force under certain circumstances.[30]

A state which is unable to exercise effective control of its territory, as was Lebanon in the 1980s or Somalia in the early 1990s, presents a special case. It is possible to argue that the absence of effective sovereign control within a territory places it in the category of international territory. International territory is territory over which no single government exercises sovereignty and by that definition it may be possible for some nations to acquire the characteristics of international territory. If that argument is persuasive, then the use of force could be supported, at least to the extent that it can be justified by international law governing reprisals and retortion in reaction to attacks in international territory. Unfortunately, international law is so ambiguous on topics such as these that the determining considerations turn out to be either prudence and effectiveness or authorization by an international institution such as the UN.

President Carter's failed attempt to rescue the hostages in Teheran in April 1980 is a case in point. Following the successful models of the Israeli and West German military assaults on hijacked aircraft, the United States developed special military units whose primary responsibility was to combat terrorist hostage-taking. After several reorganizations, this group came to be called the Delta Force in the early 1980s. Given the legal and ethical ambiguities involved, few would have challenged President Carter's use of this force to rescue the American hostages in Teheran had it succeeded. Unfortunately, it failed and a host of legal and ethical questions was raised.

President Reagan talked a great deal about the use of force against terrorism early in his administration. The air was filled with strong antiterrorist rhetoric pledging swift and effective military retaliation under certain circumstances.[31] In 1985, President Reagan signed National Security Decision Directive 138 which was designed to give the government an offensive, rather than just a defensive, posture. The act enabled the government to launch preventive and retaliatory strikes against terrorists abroad when evidence was clear and certain. Reagan's Secretary of State, George Shultz, said that "a pure passive strategy" was no longer adequate in coping with terrorism.[32] The air strike against Libya was one of the fruits of that policy emphasis.

U.S. ORGANIZATIONAL
RESPONSES TO TERRORISM

The American government has pursued a variety of organizational schemes in order to enhance its terrorist fighting abilities. International terrorism first attracted the interests of organizational tinkerers during the administration of President Richard Nixon with the Lod Airport massacre in May 1972 and the Palestinian attack on the Israeli Olympic team in September 1972. President Nixon created a Cabinet Committee to Combat Terrorism chaired by the secretary of state.

In 1976, the Department of State designated an Office for Combatting Terrorism to be a crisis center to coordinate U.S. responses to terrorism and to provide assistance to other agencies and to other governments. In 1977, President Jimmy Carter disbanded the Cabinet Committee and assigned its functions, as well as some aspects of crisis management, to a Special Coordinating Committee of the National Security Council. President Ronald Reagan created a very sophisticated information and crisis management center within the NSC and most of the Reagan administration's actions against international terrorism were coordinated through the NSC.

Organizational tampering has been required most seriously in two related areas—incident management and intelligence. What is called in Washington the "lead agency" question arises when two or more agencies become involved in dealing with an incident and questions involving jurisdiction, authority, and procedures arise. In the complex American system of government, many perplexing jurisdictional questions are possible: for example, is the incident within the jurisdiction of federal authorities or state governments? Does it involve foreign groups which might involve the CIA or domestic groups which would involve the FBI? If force is needed, should it be from military or police agencies? And, what role should the functional agencies (the Federal Aviation Administration [FAA], for example) play in the crisis? This can become very complex and confusing, especially since one can imagine a single terrorist incident which raises every question. A bewildering array of bilateral and multilateral agreements have been worked out between U.S. agencies in an attempt to anticipate and overcome jurisdictional problems. One agreement gave the FBI jurisdiction over an airline hijacking as long as the aircraft door was open, while the FAA assumed responsibility when the doors were closed. The early Cabinet Committee and the later interagency committee chaired by the State Department were both attempts to overcome these kind of problems.

Intelligence has been both a jurisdictional problem and an operational problem. Various intelligence agencies have argued about jurisdiction over intelligence collection. There are fifteen agencies that make up the U.S. intelligence community and nearly every one of them has some responsibility for intelligence about terrorism. Cabinet-level committees attempt to work these problems out, but the operational problem of actually collecting intelligence on terrorist groups has been overwhelming. By their very nature, these groups are small and made up of people who have worked together many years. These conditions make it difficult for intelligence agents to penetrate terrorist groups.[33] Terrorists with state sponsors are an easier intelligence target because the flow of communications between the terrorists and the sponsoring state can be monitored. It is widely believed that President Reagan's evidence of Libyan involvement in several terrorist incidents in Europe came through the interception of communications between Libya and the terrorists.

The use of human agents presents all kinds of legal and ethical problems. Terrorist groups have been known to require new recruits to commit a serious crime (robbery or murder) in order to prove their good faith. Both ethical standards and federal law prevent this and make it very difficult for intelligence agencies to turn their officers into undercover agents.

Interstate Agreements

Multilateral or bilateral policy initiatives were the earliest efforts of the American government to combat international terrorism. Working through the International Civil Aviation Organization (ICAO), the United States and other members entered into three agreements, the Tokyo Convention (1963), the Hague Convention (1970), and the Montreal Convention (1971). In spite of a rather tortuous history of gaining sufficient ratification to become effective, these Conventions, along with greatly enhanced airport security measures, have reduced dramatically aircraft hijacking from almost one incident per month in the later 1960s and early 70s to only one or two a year in the late 1980s. Such hijackings still occur but are usually carried out with the collaboration of ground crew, sophisticated nonmetallic weapons, or the collusion of some state sponsor.

In response to the spate of aircraft hijackings between the United States and Cuba that occurred in the 1960s, a bilateral treaty was signed between the United States and Cuba in February 1973. This treaty covered the seizure of both aircraft and ships and was significant for two reasons. First, United States-Cuban relations were very strained and it was a remarkable achievement that an agreement of any kind could be reached. It is a testimony to the ability of hostile states to work cooperatively when both can see advantages to such cooperation. Secondly, it was a significant agreement because it effectively put an end to the growing epidemic of what was called "skyjacking" merely through an agreement not to harbor those who commit the act.

The U.S.-Cuban agreement was denounced by Castro in 1976, although both governments continued to adhere to it in practice. The agreement, among other things, committed both states to the principle known in international law as *aut dedere, aut judicare*. That is, governments agree to either prosecute or extradite those who fall under the terms of the agreement. Similar language has been written into many subsequent multilateral and bilateral agreements concerning terrorism.

The Nixon-Ford administrations pursued policies of multilateral or bilateral agreements to deny terrorists any possible safe harbors or sanctuary while the Carter administration attempted to address the root causes of terrorism by focusing on human rights around the world.[34] President Carter hoped that by redressing the deep-rooted human rights grievances that spawned political radicalism, he would eliminate some of the need to resort to terrorism. To some extent, President Carter did not have enough time to test this approach. On 4 November 1979, 400 "students" seized the American embassy in Teheran and held 100 hostages, including 62 U.S. citizens, most of whom had diplomatic protection, for a year. The event paralyzed the Carter administration and was a major factor in Carter's defeat in November 1980.

DEALING WITH TERRORISM
IN THE TWENTY-FIRST CENTURY

1. Flexibility. Just as capriciousness is a hallmark of terrorism, so flexibility must be the hallmark of counterterrorism. Single-headed policies against a hydra-headed phenomenon are ineffective. U.S. policies to counter international terrorism must be as flexible as the problem is multiple. The government must have a vast array of possible weapons to use in its struggle against terrorism and the terrorists must not know precisely what to expect. The key must be flexibility to choose from a wide array of possible responses. Even though there is no evidence that military reprisals actually result in the reduction of terrorism, it would be foolish either to abandon such capabilities or to renounce the policy. Similarly, preemptive strikes, even though they may actually result in an immediate escalation of international terrorism just to prove that the strike was ineffective, should be retained as a potential policy and as a real capability.

Perhaps the most effective means of reducing international terrorism is the creation of multilateral treaty obligations that will deny terrorists safe haven anywhere in the world. There is some evidence that diplomatic, legal, political, and economic actions can have an effect on regimes that support terrorism and can reduce terrorism without the threat of war.[35] States who otherwise did not want to, signed the various aircraft hijacking agreements because they were faced with losing all international air traffic if they did not.

Anything that promotes inflexibility should be avoided. Public statements that the government will always do something or that there are things it will never do are not particularly helpful. Specific threats of retaliation if certain lines are crossed may only tempt some groups to increase their activities up to the newly announced line and may encourage other groups to cross the line just to test United States' will.

2. Root Causes. One of the most serious mistakes the United States could make in its fight against international terrorism would be to abandon efforts to settle some of the root causes of terrorism. Of course, it is utter nonsense to assume that merely by changing the direction of its foreign policy the United States could put an end to terrorism. It is impossible to conceive of any foreign policy, no matter how liberal or how conservative, that would end forever all animosity towards the United States throughout the world. Dissatisfied groups and individuals lie within the sinews of every society and will always find some cause for which they are willing to fight and die. And they will always find some way to blame the United States for their misery. Neither an end to capitalism nor socialism will end dissatisfaction, rebellion, and terrorism.

Nevertheless, it cannot be forgotten that much international terrorism has resulted from certain international developments which more astute and prudent foreign policies might have avoided. In 1985, just under half of all terrorist incidents in the world occurred in the Middle East and approximately one-third of the 25 percent which occurred in Western Europe involved Middle Eastern groups and causes.[36] Had the issues which led to the creation of the state of Israel and to the displacement of Palestinians been resolved differently, approximately 60 percent of all terrorists incidents over the last twenty years might not have occurred.[37] One author writes that

> The hapless British soldiery in Mandate Palestine were subject to attacks, both during and after World War II, from Jewish terrorist organizations . . . as well as from less organized Arab extremists. Indeed, one might argue that the whole melancholy history of Palestine did much to legitimize the modern phenomenon of terrorism in the Middle East, and that in that sense the more activist elements of the PLO are merely following in the footsteps of the man who later became the Prime Minister of Israel and denounced the PLO in its entirety as a bunch of thugs and murderers.[38]

A great deal of modern terrorism is of domestic origins—the Sikhs, the IRA, Quebec's FLQ, the ETA, the Croatians, and on and on. But surely the problems arising from the Middle East were international in their very origin and continue to be an international problem. The tragedy of contemporary Lebanon, from a once peaceful and prosperous nation to the seething source of much contemporary terrorism, begins with the displacement of thousands of Palestinians by the Israeli expansion of its 1948 borders. With the defeat of Arab forces in the 1967 war, many Palestinian groups decided terrorism was their only alternative. It was this resort to terrorism which prompted the Jordanian government to drive the Palestinians out of Jordan and which took the Palestinians into southern Lebanon. The use of Lebanon as a base for Palestinian activities, coupled with the already fragile constitutional arrangement of the Lebanese government, led to a breakdown of civil authority in Lebanon which was the pretext for the Israeli invasion of Lebanon in 1982. It was this invasion and the subsequent removal of both Palestinians and Israelis from Lebanon which created the anarchic and "baronial" conditions in Lebanon out of which terrorism grows. The very phrase "Lebanese government" became an oxymoron. Subsequent American administrations must recognize this and must be more evenhanded, more firm, and more flexible in seeking solutions to Middle Eastern problems. Middle Eastern stability is in the national interest of the United States and policies to achieve stability should not be deflected by minority domestic interest groups no matter how vocal.

The increase of terrorism in Latin America is alarming and its root causes must be addressed. State Department figures revealed a 31 percent increase in terrorism in Latin America in 1986. There has always been enough anti-Americanism in Latin America to spark terrorists' acts against U.S. interests, but the growth of terrorism associated with illegal drug activities has spawned a whole new category of terrorism known as narco-terrorism. The increasing cost of terrorism has forced some groups, in Latin American and the Middle East, to trade in illegal drugs to finance their activities.[39] Cocaine cartels have undermined legitimate governments in half a dozen Latin American states and have invented new kinds of state-sponsored terrorism. This, along with continuing repression in some near-authoritarian Latin American governments and the increasing frustrations associated with the international debt problem will combine to promote anti-American terrorism in Latin America in the 1990s. Attention to these root causes would reduce terrorism significantly.

3. Multiple Sources of Terrorism. It is always tempting for government officials to declare that most terrorism is sponsored by Libya, by Russia, by Syria, by Iran or by some combination of those states. The demands of political life almost force otherwise clear-thinking individuals to come up with simple solutions to very complex problems. Such solutions appear to make counterterrorism much easier since they suggest that the United States has only to deal with the few governments which sponsor it. Unfortunately, the situation is far more complex than this.

There is a great deal of collaboration between most major terrorist groups. They share information, weapons, and ideas; they help one another with logistics and even use some of the same training facilities. But they do not carry out one another's tasks (although they will sell their services), they do not issue orders or commands to one another, and they are suspicious of further or deeper connections. They fear that increased cooperation would make all groups vulnerable were one group to be penetrated or compromised. Moreover, they have nationalistic ambitions and are not particularly interested in internationalist ideologies. According to Danier Hermsand, a terrorist expert at the French Institute of Military Studies, "A few attacks, and everyone starts screaming 'Euroterrorism.' It doesn't prove anything. As soon as you look, this ideal of a European terrorist network disappears."[40]

During the first term of President Reagan's administration it became an act of faith to ascribe Soviet support to nearly all acts of international terrorism. Again, there is no question that the Soviet Union, had it wished to, could have done more to discourage some terrorism, particularly that sponsored by Soviet client states. But, "concentration on the alleged Soviet role tended to blind many observers to the hydra-headed and complex nature of terrorist violence across the world. The picture was distorted in that it obscured the deep indigenous roots of many groups using terrorist methods, and the complex variety of ideologies, political aims and state sponsors involved."[41]

Attempts to paint all terrorism with a red brush were not very helpful. There is no doubt that the Soviet government was anxious to profit from any misfortunes that might have weakened Western nations or alliances or even Western client states, just as the West was anxious to use instability in the Soviet bloc for its own purposes. There is also no doubt that the Soviet Union could have prevented Czechoslovakia, East Germany, and North Korea from facilitating training, giving financial support, and supplying weapons to certain terrorist groups. But, although latter admissions by Russian and East European leaders confirmed the key role played by the Communist bloc in terrorist activities, the Soviet Union had less to do with international terrorism than some thought.[42]

Philosophically, terrorism does not fit comfortably in the writings of Marx, Lenin, or other communist writers. Essential to communist theory has always been the notion that revolutions would occur in states when objective conditions were ripe and that it should not be forced by "adventurism." The early communists were critical of the Russian anarchists of the 1880s because they believed that such activities would discredit the communist movement and merely result in more repressive measures by the czarist government. Modern disciples (Che Guevara, for example) have also believed that terrorism committed by communist guerrillas turned the people against their movement and evoked unnecessary and repressive measures from the police.[43] Mao Tse-tung was a master guerrilla war strategist but a severe critic of terrorism. Pragmatically, by the mid-1980s, the appearance of supporting international terrorism tended to detract from the dramatic changes in its foreign policy initiated by Soviet leader Gorbachev.

4. Military Reprisals. A military response should always be a last resort and selected only after a careful evaluation of all possible responses. It must be proportionate to the seriousness of the threat posed by the terrorists themselves and it must be structured carefully so as to minimize as much as possible the possibility of any injury to nonterrorists. The government must resist the temptation to use its maximum weapon, military reprisal, prematurely. As Max Beloff has written, "we have weapons [for fighting terrorism] that are too big for the targets."[44] One of the most frequently made mistakes in thinking about responding to terrorism is to accept the Israeli and South African policies of immediate and disproportionate military reprisals to any and all terrorist attacks as effective means for combatting terrorism. Israeli military retaliation particularly is often held up as a model for U.S. policy by those who forget that it has not worked for Israel and it will not work for the United States. "Israel is still plagued by terrorism, both within its borders and outside them. . . . Washington should respond militarily only when it is warranted, when it will work, and most important when an attack is consistent with long-term security concerns."[45] The Israeli military reprisal of invading Lebanon in 1982 unleashed increased waves of terrorism in its aftermath. Military reprisals may satisfy desires for retribution and revenge but they are not the best way to end or even reduce terrorism.

5 .. Multilateral Agreements. International terrorism is susceptible only to international efforts. The United States must seek closer cooperation with other Western democracies for ways to deal with terrorism. This will involve concerted diplomatic action against states which allow diplomatic facilities to be used as a cover for terrorism. The Italian practice of x-raying all diplomatic parcels should be followed by other governments.[46] Above all, intelligence agencies and police will need to cooperate more closely and share information more fully.

INTERPOL has not been particularly effective in the fight against terrorism because of its constitutional ban against unleashing activities against political crimes. That ban was lifted in 1984 and INTERPOL has become more active in exchanging information about terrorists. It is especially important that there be greater cooperation between intelligence agencies of Western democracies.

There are other areas where interstate agreements are necessary. The FBI has learned that in dealing with domestic criminals, access to bank and other financial records was essential. It became easier to arrest and convict criminals for violations of financial regulations than for the commission of crimes of violence. The same is true with terrorists. Interstate agreements making it easier to gain access to bank records of terrorists and streamlined ways of checking compliance with tax and other financial regulations need to be explored. All of this should be done only on demonstration of sufficient evidence to judicial officers. This can be done fairly easily within nations, but interstate agreements facilitating this are quite sparse.

As the EC eliminated, in 1993, passports for EC travel, compensatory policies were being established to allow at least the checking of identification cards in order to control the movement of terrorists within EC nations. It is particularly frustrating for the CIA or the FBI to provide adequate information to European governments to allow them to identify suspected terrorists only to have them slip through Europe undetected.

The 1990s may be the most propitious time in recent history to secure new and more effective international agreements to fight terrorism. Russia, up to recent time either supportive or indifferent to much international terrorism, has begun to show greater interest in such international agreements. The changing domestic climate within Russia has brought about new ways of thinking about terrorism. Even under the old Soviet regime, over sixty of its citizens were killed by terrorists while outside the Soviet Union in the last half of the 1980s and there have now been confirmed the earlier reports of terrorist incidents within the Soviet Union itself. With the fragmentation of the former Soviet Union and ethnic strife within Russia, these developments may in fact continue.

The Russians have acknowledged that they have much to learn about combatting terrorism from the United States and have, it appears, given up the practice not only of training but of providing safe havens for international terrorists in order to gain U.S. cooperation. Even a concerted effort by both governments to control more tightly the distribution of surface-to-air missiles (American Stingers and Soviet SAM-7s) would be a significant step forward.[47]

There are few more important tasks to be accomplished in the fight against terrorism that the need to review and revise, where necessary, both bilateral and multilateral agreements requiring either prosecution or extradition. The case of West Germany and the Hamadei trial illustrates the need for these kinds of arrangements. Hamadei was charged with assisting in the 1985 hijacking of a TWA flight to LebAnon. In spite of several complicating factors, the West German government successfully prosecuted Hamadei who was sentenced to thirteen years in prison. States must be willing to give up whatever ideological interests they wish to protect and adhere faithfully to the prosecute or extradite principle. The end of the Cold War and the change of regimes in Eastern Europe ARE facilitating this, but there are still problems beyond Europe. U.S. refusal, for instance, to extradite certain IRA personnel to Great Britain runs counter to this need.

6. *Public Policies.* States must be careful about pronouncing ironclad policies, however. Few things do more to encourage terrorism than the constant bending of unbendable rules. The much vaunted EC policy of "making no concessions to terrorists or their sponsors" has turned to ashes. This principle was affirmed at the June 1987 meeting of the leaders of the key industrial states, but within one year, it was clear that West Germany, France, and the United States had violated it. West German officials admitted that their unwillingness to extradite one of the terrorists involved in the hijacking of a TWA jet in 1985 stemmed from their fear over the possible consequences of such an action on the German hostages held in Lebanon. The very next day an additional West German citizen was kidnapped in Beirut.[48] France secured the release of three French hostages held by pro-Iranian terrorists by releasing 670 million dollars of frozen Iranian assets held in France, by agreeing to reopen diplomatic relations with Iran, and, according to some reports, by agreeing to supply weapons to Teheran in return for Khomeini forcing Shi'ite terrorist groups to release French hostages.[49] Finally, no matter how it is couched, the Reagan administration's arms-hostage exchange with Iran did little to further U.S. credibility nor America's commitment to ironclad principles. Since it is difficult to think of any counterterrorism principle to which some exception cannot be found, it might be more prudent to keep any and all policies open and available for use under the right set of circumstances.

7 . Perspective. Finally, it is essential that terrorism be kept in perspective. Terrorists want to disrupt the normal processes of government in target countries; that is, they want to create a sense of crisis. Crisis government is seldom good government and the term "crisis" ought to be reserved for actions which legitimately threaten U.S. national interests.[50] Yet in the 1980s, virtually every terrorist incident which involved Americans was portrayed as a crisis either by the government, the media, or both. The proportion of terrorist incidents involving Americans has stayed somewhere between 20 to 32 percent of all incidents for over a decade. Moreover, the number of Americans killed by terrorists has remained between 2 and 5 percent of all terrorist-related deaths for the same period of time.[51] Neither the number of incidents nor the number of Americans killed justifies this sense of crisis.[52]

It is the brutality and capriciousness of terrorism that captures the public mind and creates the sense of crisis. The sight of dead bodies of innocent people being pushed onto an airport tarmac by seemingly anonymous hands is revolting to all but the most warped fanatics. Yet even this is not the challenge to civilization and order that it is often described as being. No single terrorist act can breech the generally and widely respected wall of civilization that sets the bounds for most human conduct. Terrorism is beyond the pale of civilized behavior not because people are killed but because it challenges one of the central tenets of the modern nation-state system—the notion that only the state, acting for society, can use force to establish its will. This becomes a threat to civilization only when it is consistently and persistently ignored or even encouraged by states. It is only the accumulated effect of many ignored terrorist incidents which challenges civilization, not any single incident itself.

Clearly it is possible for a single terrorist incident to become a legitimate crisis. A terrorist group armed with nuclear or chemical weapons, and the intent to use them, would be a crisis of major proportions. Policies to prevent this, and security measures to deter it, must be a high priority for all governments.

As terrorism increases in volume and intensity, it will become more important to begin discriminating among the events. Acknowledging that terrorism is unlikely to threaten the country's core interests unless each episode is allowed to be perceived as a crisis would be the first step in developing a practical response.[53]

An appropriate perspective may be the single most important weapon to use against terrorists. By seeing terrorism in its proper perspective—as a serious problem but something short of a national crisis—the government will have greater flexibility, the public will be less fascinated with terrorism, and the media will be less drawn to making each incident a media extravaganza.

Above all else, U.S. antiterrorist and counterterrorist activities must not go beyond the bounds of what is permitted in a democratic society. In spite of frequent calls by frustrated government officials and former intelligence officers for unlimited powers to go after terrorists, the United States must resist such temptations.[54] In this case, as in all instances, the United States must not let ends justify means. Constitutional principles must not be sacrificed on the altar of antiterrorism. The fight against terrorism must observe ethical and legal standards whether or not they are observed by the terrorists.

There is nothing that can be done which will make America invincible to terrorism. Dissident individuals and groups anywhere in the world will continue to vent their anger and frustration against America through terrorism. Every new development in airport security will lead to new terrorist techniques to evade it. For every separatist problem solved in the world, new territorial claims will arise. A mature nation with global interests, after doing all that it can to eliminate terrorism and after taking all reasonable steps to protect its citizens and officials, must focus its efforts on more serious threats to the national interests.

ENDNOTES

1. This definition is both directly and indirectly drawn from Jeffrey Scheuer, "Moral Dimensions of Terrorism," *The Fletcher Forum of World Affairs,* 14 (Winter 1990): 146, with only slight modifications.
2. Nevertheless, the words "terror" and "terrorism" were first used in a political context during the so-called "Reign of Terror" associated with the First Revolution in France in 1793 and 1794.
3. See Michael Aaronson, "Terrorism or Freedom Fighting? A Minefield in International Relations," *International Relations,* 8 (November 1986): 611-34 for a discussion of this point.

4. For a more complete discussion of this and other points raised in this section, see Paul Wilkinson, *Terrorism and the Liberal State* (London: The Macmillan Press, Ltd., 1977), Part I.

5. Perhaps the best discussion of the "just war" theory is by Michael Waltzer, *Just and Unjust Wars* (London: Allen Lane, 1977).

6. The alleged complicity of former UN Secretary General Kurt Waldheim, acting as a junior officer in the German army during World War II, and the allegations made in the spring of 1988 about the actions of a British submarine commander, operating under the U.S. Command in the Pacific during World War II, attest to the commitment liberal states have made to adhere to accepted principles even during time of war.

7. The quotation is from Adam Roberts, "Terrorism and International Order," in Lawrence Freedman and others, *Terrorism and International Order* (London: Routledge & Kegan Paul, 1986), 20.

8. Tim Timmermann, "The American Bombing of Libya," *Survey,* 29 (May/June 1987): 206. Unfortunately for the American government, this "evidence" was not publicized since, it was claimed, publication would compromise the sources and methods by which it was gathered. It is commonly known, however, that these directives were sent by electronic transmission from Libya to its foreign missions and that they were intercepted by U.S. intelligence agencies.

9. Again, the evidence was not made public, however, within the next two weeks the governments of Great Britain and West Germany reviewed the evidence and accepted it as compelling. See Timmermann, "The American Bombing of Libya," 206.

10. The quotation from Arafat as well as general information about this particular hijacking may be found in *The Sunday Times* (London), 17 April 1988, A12 and 24 April 1988, A13.

11. A much more complete review of the history of terrorism may be found in Walter Laqueur, *Terrorism* (London: Weidenfeld & Nicholson, 1977).

12. Walter Laqueur's argument that tyrannicide during Greek and Roman times was terrorism is merely an example of loose definitions. It was often revolutionary in that it brought a new regime into power but it was not meant to coerce or intimidate a larger population. It was meant to create a vacancy on the throne which the assassin would usually fill. See Walter Laqueur, "The Anatomy of Terrorism," Royal United Services Institute for Defence Studies, *Ten Years of Terrorism: Collected Views* (London: RUSI, 1979), 8.

13. Philip Windsor argues that this emergence of terrorism in the Middle East was the beginning of modern *unlimited* and *indiscriminate* terrorism. In contrast, he cites the story of the Russian anarchist who, at the moment he was to throw his bomb to destroy Grand Duke Nicholas, noticed the Duchess was part of the company and was arrested holding the bomb in his hand rather than harm the Duchess. See Philip Windsor, "The Middle East and Terrorism," in Freedman and others, *Terrorism and International Order,* (New York: Routledge & Kegan, 1986), 27.

14. William Echikson, "Italian Terrorism Plummets: Tough Government Stands, Public Consensus, and Patient Police Work Have Turned the Tide," *The Christian Science Monitor,* 27 March 1987, 1.

15. Paul Wilkinson, *Terrorism and the Liberal State,* 187. On the other hand, the PLO has not agreed to relax its attacks against Israel which it considers acts of war.

16. See a similar analysis by Richard Owen in "Have the Terrorists Won?" *The Times* (London), 29 January 1988, 12.

17. It is a common mistake, however, to assume that every terrorist incident which involves a Palestinian is in support of this goal. The Palestinian refugee camps created in the West Bank, Gaza, and Jordan have bred a generation of people whose entire life is devoted to armed struggle. They may engage in violence merely out of anger or revenge. Even after a decade of efforts by PLO leader Yassir Arafat to bring greater discipline into the

Palestinian movements, it is still common to see Palestinians involved in a variety of terrorist attacks, some of which are even contrary to the will of the PLO.

18. Philip Windsor, "The Middle East and Terrorism," *Terrorism and International Order* (New York: Routledge & Kegan Paul, 1986), 34.
19. See Richard Owen, "Have the Terrorists Won?" *The Times* (London), 29 January 1988, 14.
20. Paul Wilkinson, "Trends in International Terrorism and the American Response," in Freedman and others, *Terrorism and International Order* (New York: Routledge & Kegan, 1986), 42.
21. David L. Altheide, "Format and Symbols in TV Coverage of Terrorism in the United States and Great Britain," *International Studies Quarterly,* 31 (June 1987), 162.
22. Paul Wilkinson, *Terrorism and the Liberal State,* 2d ed., (London: Macmillan, 1986), 210. Wilkinson cites Rand Corporation data as his source.
23. Brian M. Jenkins, "International Terrorism: A New Mode of Conflict," in David Carlton and Carlo Schaerf, eds., *International Terrorism and World Security* (London: Croom Helm, 1975), 39.
24. Major General Yosef Geva as quoted in *Newsweek* (International Edition), 6 June 1988, 24.
25. Public Law 99-399. Other titles of this Act addressed a wide variety of terrorism issues: nuclear terrorism, multilateral cooperation to combat terrorism, compensation for victims of terrorism, security against maritime terrorism, fellowships for American students to work in U.S. diplomatic missions in certain countries, and greater security against terrorism at American military bases abroad. Title XIII of the Act, however, reveals considerable insight into the operations of Congress. It contains miscellaneous provisions having nothing to do with terrorism other than a desire to attach themselves to legislation which was sure to pass Congress and which was seen as veto-proof. One provision in this title provided for the funding of research to eradicate Amblyomma Variegatum among bovines in the Caribbean Basin!
26. L. Paul Bremer, III, Ambassador at Large for Counter Terrorism, "Practical Measures for Dealing with Terrorism," *Current Policy,* No. 913 (U.S. Department of State, Bureau of Public Affairs, Washington, D.C.), 1.
27. See several sources of data cited by Paul Wilkinson, *Terrorism and the Liberal State,* 2d ed., 211.
28. See D. J. Paletz and others, "Terrorism on Television News: The IRA, the FALN, and the Red Brigades," in W. Adams, ed., *Television Coverage of International Affairs* (Norwood, NJ: Ablex, 1982), 143-65.
29. U.S.-Egyptian relations were particularly strained in the face of what amounted to an American hijacking of an Egyptian airliner. Moreover, as the Italian government released the leader of the group, the notorious Abu Abbas, U.S. criticism brought about a severe crisis in the Italian government of Prime Minister Bettino Craxi.
30. The UN Charter suggests that the use of force is permissible only by a collective decision of the Security Council or in the case of self-defense against an actual armed attack.
31. The official policy was that military "retribution" against state sponsors would be automatic when the evidence of their involvement was "irrefutable."
32. See *Facts on File,* 44 (20 April 1984): 280 for other details of the directive and for the full statements from Reagan and Shultz.
33. By contrast, domestic terrorist groups were fairly easily penetrated and the FBI or local police departments had their own undercover agents within many such groups in the 1970s.
34. See Edward Marks and Debra van Opstal, eds., Combatting Terrorism: A Matter of Leverage (Washington, D.C.: The Center for Strategic and International Studies, Georgetown University, 1986), 15.

35. Paul Wilkinson, "Trends in International Terrorism and the American Response" in Freedman and others, *Terrorism and International Order* (New York: Routledge & Kegan, 1986), 37-55.
36. These numbers are taken from data supplied by the U.S. Department of State, Office of the Ambassador-at-Large for Counter Terrorism to the authors in 1987. The proportion of all incidents which had a Middle East connection was extrapolated from data provided by the Congressional Research Service of the Library of Congress in Issue Brief (Order Code) IB86096 dated 16 August 1986. Numbers about terrorism are very slippery and great caution is necessary in interpreting the data that exist. No two sources of data about terrorism report the same statistics due to varying definitions and counting rules.
37. See Judith Miller, "Terrorism Around the Mediterranean," *Adelphi Papers,* No. 230 (Spring 1988): 57-70.
38. Windsor, "The Middle East and Terrorism," in Freedman and others, *Terrorism and International Order,* (New York: Routledge & Kegan, 1986), 27-8.
39. Miller, "Terrorism Around the Mediterranean," 59.
40. Quoted in William Echikson, "Euroterrorists are Acting Up—But They Aren't Acting Together," *The Christian Science Monitor,* 27 March 1987, 13.
41. Wilkinson, "Trends in International Terrorism," 51. Clair Sterling's *The Terrorist Network* (London: Weidenfeld & Nicolson, 1981) makes the most popular, but over-stated, argument for Soviet direction of international terrorism. For one critical review of Sterling, see Michael Stohl, "Review Essay: The International Network of Terrorism," in *Journal of Peace Research,* 20 (1983): 87-94.
42. See Galia Golan, "The Soviet Union and the PLO," *Adelphi Papers,* No. 131 (Winter 1976) for a discussion of this point pertaining to the PLO.
43. See Che Guevara, *Guerilla Warfare* (Harmondsworth: Penguin Books, 1969), 26.
44. Max Beloff, "Terrorism and the People," *Ten Years of Terrorism* (New York: Crane, Russak, 1979), 116.
45. Jeffrey D. Simon, "Misunderstanding Terrorism," *Foreign Policy,* No. 67 (Summer 1987): 113 and 115. See also the editorial by George Ball, "Shultz is Wrong on Terrorism" in *The New York Times,* 16 December 1984, E21.
46. Miller, "Terrorism Around the Mediterranean," 62.
47. Geoffrey Kemp and Augustus Richard Norton, "US-Soviet Teamwork of Terrorism," *The Christian Science Monitor,* 10 March 1989, 18.
48. *The Sunday Times* (London), 21 January 1988.
49. *The Times* (London), 6 May 1988, 1 and *The Sunday Times* (London), 31 January 1988.
50. Much of this analysis follows that of Simon, "Misunderstanding Terrorism."
51. These numbers are from Rand Corporation reports and are reported by Simon in "Misunderstanding Terrorism," 107.
52. For comparative purposes, cigarette smoking kills about 350,000 Americans every year, about 50,000 die annually from traffic accidents, about 5,000 have died each year since 1981 from AIDS, and about 28 Americans are killed each year by terrorists. These figures come from the Department of State and from Geoffrey Cowley, "Science and the Cigarette," *Newsweek* (International Edition), 11 April 1988, 42.
53. Simon, "Misunderstanding Terrorism," 120.
54. For one example, see James B. Motley, "International Terrorism: A Challenge for U.S. Intelligence," *Journal of Intelligence and Counterintelligence,* 1 (Spring 1986): 83-96.

PART III

U.S. FOREIGN ECONOMIC POLICY-MAKING IN AN ERA OF GLOBAL INTERDEPENDENCE

The previous section concentrated on issues which the average American would consider as the core of U.S. foreign policy: conventional and strategic defense priorities, diplomacy, alliance building, and antiterrorism planning. However, in the new post-Cold War era featuring the dismantlement of the Soviet Union and a downgrading of nuclear rivalries, economic issues may have now moved up to the top tier on the U.S. foreign policy agenda.

Arguably, the United States emerged from World War II as the greatest hegemonic power that the world had ever seen, able almost singlehandedly to determine the rules of the game for interstate relations in a large part of the world.[1] This hegemony was based both on military and economic superiority, with the United States organizing a new order for four-fifths of the global economy.[2]

This final section of the book will concentrate on the theme of vincibility from both an economic and environmental perspective. In other words, emphasis will be placed on America's performance in the world economy through most of the latter half of the twentieth century, and an assessment made of how well Americans are prepared to cope with the myriad economic and environmental challenges of the twenty-first century. A key issue to be addressed is whether the United States is on an irreversible downward slope after having attained the pinnacle of global economic power in 1945. This is an important question, because the United States began the 1990s as the world's largest debtor nation and was heavily burdened with unprecedented government and trade deficits.

A growing number of foreign observers are already convinced that the United States is a declining economic power. For several decades after the end of World War II, overseas critics chastised the United States for exhibiting an arrogance of power and a lack of awareness of the needs and aspirations of people in other nations. A new type of criticism is now emerging, illustrated quite succinctly by an editorial in *The Economist* magazine:

> Yet if, today, you stop the average European, or Japanese, or Latin American, or, for full effect, Canadian in the street and ask him what he thinks about America, you are as likely to hear contempt as praise. The Japanese will probably mention idleness and self-indulgence, the European philistinism and naivety, the Latin American insensitivity and boorishness.[3]

This editorial goes on to accuse the United States of being mired in a "decadent puritanism," or in other words, "an odd combination of ducking responsibility and telling everyone else what to do."[4] A Japanese business leader adds that the United States is doomed as a superpower because of economic self-indulgence, indiscipline, and executive greed, emphasizing that the "time will never again come when America will regain its strength in industry" and that there will be "a totally new configuration in the balance of power in the world."[5] As outside observers situated across the Atlantic and across the Pacific, are these foreigners able to ascertain changes in the U.S. society and economy which many Americans seem to overlook, or are they simply engaging in the popular overseas pursuit known as "Yankee bashing"?

Because this section will dwell on economic issues, many readers will probably approach it with the same sense of agony they feel prior to making a visit to the dentist's office. After all, economics is famous for jargonese and many people seem to agree with the statement that the job of an economist is to take what is obvious and try to make it as incomprehensible as possible. And indeed, the ensuing chapters will introduce such well-known household phrases as current account deficits, countervailing duties, and foreign direct investment.

To add to the reader's misery, economics is widely considered a dull subject, and the ebb and flow of U.S. foreign economic policy do not exactly keep Americans awake at night. In fact, if a person were to take time to read the memoirs of the past few presidents and several leading foreign policy practitioners such as Henry Kissinger, Zbigniew Brzezinski, and Cyrus Vance, they would be hard-pressed to find more than a few paragraphs that even mention foreign economic policy. Therefore, if the national leaders who once supervised U.S. foreign policy generally ignore or disdain economic matters, why should the average American take an interest in the topic?

In addition, readers may not only agonize over the economic jargon, but they may also be disturbed by the underlying message of the next few chapters. This message is that the United States is definitely losing ground in the global competitiveness race, and that the nation's economic policy process is often parochial, chaotic, and very shortsighted. As the Presidential Commission on Industrial Competitiveness has written: "Our world leadership is at stake and so is our ability to provide for our people the standard of living and opportunities to which they aspire."[6] The commission added that U.S. national security and government funding for vital domestic programs were also integrally linked to the ability of American industry to compete both at home and abroad.[7] Richard Darman, who would later become the director of the Office of Management and Budget in the Bush administration, added this stinging indictment of contemporary American society:

> We have allowed ourselves to accept very much less than the development of the full human potential in our schools, at work, in our management. . . . If you have a complacent national effort, where it's okay to be second or third, you would be on your way down.[8]

In the next chapter, we assess U.S. economic competitveness in a world which is becoming far more complex and interdependent. Chapter 11 will then focus on international problems linked to the environment, energy, and immigration. Chapter 12 will discuss how U.S. foreign economic policy is made, and Chapter 13 will then look at some of the policy options which might permit the United States to maintain economic prosperity at home while promoting economic competitiveness overseas.

ENDNOTES

1. As Bruce Russett has stated, "Virtually all analysts of the regimes school agree that the United States in about 1946 came closer to meeting the criteria of global hegemony than has any other state in world history." See Russett, "America's Continuing Strengths," *International Organization* 39 (Spring 1985): 213-14.
2. In Robert O. Keohane and Joseph S. Nye, *Power and Interdependence: World Politics in Transition* (Boston: Little, Brown, 1977), 44, the authors define hegemony as a condition in which "one state is powerful enough to maintain the essential rules governing interstate relations, and willing to do so." Russett, in "Strengths," p. 213, argues that right after World War II, the United States was able to organize a new economic order for 80 percent of the global economy, and a system of collective security to maintain political and economic control over this 80 percent.
3. *Economist,* 28 July 1990, 11.

4. *Economist,* 28 July 1990, 11.
5. These comments were made by Akio Morita, chairman of the Sony Corporation. See *The New York Times,* (National Edition), 8 November 1989, A21.
6. President's Commission on Industrial Competitiveness, *Global Competition: The New Reality,* by John Young, Chairman, Vol. 1 (Washington, D.C.: Government Printing Office, 1985), 1.
7. President's Commission, *Global Competition,* 1.
8. Peter Behr, "The U.S. Economy: Great Ambitions, Narrower Options," *Washington Post,* 17 April 1987, A18.

10

AMERICAN COMPETITIVENESS IN AN INTERDEPENDENT WORLD

INTERDEPENDENCE AND THE AVERAGE AMERICAN

Although the United States remains the world's dominant economic power, it is showing major weaknesses in the areas of global market competition, worker productivity, corporate performance, educational achievement, and overall creativity and innovation. Furthermore, Americans are more vulnerable than ever before to the repercussions of economic actions or decisions rendered outside the borders of the United States.

A few actual and hypothetical illustrations of this phenomenon known as "interdependence" would be helpful. The United States is dependent on foreign sources for almost one-half of its petroleum needs. A decision taken in the Middle East by the major producers of oil to restrict shipments and raise prices would affect each and every American who drives a car or works in an industry that uses imported petroleum or products derived from petroleum (such as plastics). After a decision by the Middle Eastern members of OPEC in October 1973 to halt oil exports to the United States, America suffered a major shortage of petroleum, leading to long lines at gas stations, occasional rationing, and huge increases in oil and gas prices.

Brazil and Mexico are the largest debtor countries in the developing world. A policy announcement made simultaneously in Brasilia and Mexico City that these nations would no longer pay their foreign debt would send shock waves through the American financial community. U.S. financial institutions have made tens of billions of dollars in loans to developing nations, particularly those in Latin America. The nine largest banks in the United States, including Chase Manhattan, Citicorp, and Bank of America, have collectively made loans to Third World nations which at one time equaled their primary capital bases. Thus, a major default among Latin American countries would lead to distress in the U.S. banking industry and many depositors would feel a keen sense of anxiety. In addition, as banks write off some of these foreign loans, American consumers are asked to pay part of the tab in the form of higher interest rates for domestic loans, higher fees for a variety of banking services, and higher taxes to permit the U.S. government to bail out some of the more vulnerable banking institutions.

Furthermore, many Third World countries have had to cut back on buying products from the United States because a good part of their earnings must go to pay the interest on their foreign debts. About 40 percent of U.S. farmland in production is used to service overseas customers. One job in six in the U.S. manufacturing sector is also directly linked to exports. Because of this U.S. dependency on international markets, a decision by Venezuelans to buy fewer American products in order to pay interest on their debts could cause financial hardships for both the farmer in Iowa and the steelworker in Pennsylvania.

Because of heavy losses in the European automobile sector, the managers of Renault in Paris might one day decide to lay off a substantial number of their work force. This decision would likely lead to job losses in Allentown, Pennsylvania; Atlanta, Georgia; Chicago, Illinois; Hagerstown, Maryland; Bridgewater, New Jersey; and Dallas, Texas. Why? The state-owned Renault company controls Mack Trucks in the United States, and Mack Trucks' facilities are located in each of these cities. Moreover, because Renault is owned by the French government, it may be more palatable politically to dismiss workers in the far-off United States than at home in France.

Renault's stake in Mack Trucks is known as a foreign direct investment. Quite recently, the United States has emerged as the number one host nation in the world for this type of investment which gives an investor in one country a controlling interest in the management of an enterprise in another country. Five million Americans now work for foreign-controlled companies in the United States which in 1993 included the likes of Toyota, Pillsbury, Baskin-Robbins, Carnation, Columbia Pictures, Holiday Inn, Standard Oil, Firestone, and Burger King. This means that decisions made in corporate headquarters in Tokyo, Paris, London, or Toronto could have a major impact on the job prospects for an increasing number of Americans.

In effect, the so-called "average American" will have to learn to cope with the special challenges to be found in a very complex and highly interdependent global economic system. Because of this growing vulnerability to international market conditions, U.S. foreign policy-makers must pay much closer attention to economic issues in the future. The average citizen will also have to keep abreast of economic matters in order to recognize how individuals will be affected by policy decisions made in Washington, D.C. and major cities around the world.

AMERICAN ECONOMIC LEADERSHIP IN THE POST-WORLD WAR II PERIOD

The Costly Legacy of the 1930s

The United States emerged from the Second World War as the world's foremost economic superpower, accounting by itself for an amazing one-half of the world's total production. In addition, there were no serious economic competitors on the horizon. Germany and Japan were in ruin and much of the European continent was devastated. The Soviet Union had suffered over 20 million casualties and some of its major cities were in rubble. In contrast, the U.S. was spared from having to fight battles on its own territory, and the war effort had required a feverish pace of industrial development.

Because of its completely dominant economic position, the United States assumed the role of chief architect of the post-World War II international economic strategy which has helped bring unprecedented prosperity to many people in Europe, Asia, North America, and the Pacific. Even before the war effort against the Axis powers (mainly Germany, Japan, and Italy) had ended, the Allied nations were making plans for new international economic arrangements. As stipulated by the leading Allied countries in the 1944 Bretton Woods accord, an agreement hammered out at a resort in the White Mountains of New Hampshire, the United States was to assume the preeminent position in rebuilding the postwar economy. The dollar was to be king and U.S. productivity was to spur economic development worldwide. The fixed exchange value of foreign currencies was to be linked directly to the dollar and the par value of the dollar itself was eventually pegged at 35 dollars per ounce of gold.

The Allies had learned from bitter experience that economic cooperation was far superior to nationalistic beggar-thy-neighbor tactics.[1] The developed countries had precipitated a very bitter trade war in the early 1930s and everyone wound up a loser. As economic conditions worsened during this period, national governments clamped restrictions on imports in a vain effort to protect jobs at home. In the case of the United States, the infamous Smoot-Hawley Act of 1930 raised the average tariff on a dutiable good to a record high 59 percent. The tariff walls did indeed limit imports, with shipments into the U.S. in 1932 falling back to the level of 1909. However, a large number of nations reacted to these new American restrictions by increasing their own import duties. This abrupt trade war was partially responsible for increasing U.S. unemployment to a staggering 25 percent, and real per capita income retreated to the level achieved back in 1907.

This economic warfare was also pivotal in fomenting World War II. The widespread economic privation during the Great Depression soon led to political instability and extremism. For example, Germany was hard hit during the Depression, with unemployment increasing from 1.3 million in September 1929 to over 6 million in January 1933. In the July 1932 elections to the Reichstag, the fanatical right-wing National Socialist party received 14 million votes and won 230 seats, whereas in 1928 the party had garnered only 12 seats. To the far left, the Communist party won 89 seats in the Reichstag, compared with only 54 in 1928. In essence, in the midst of economic turmoil, German citizens turned to extremist political solutions for relief. Adolf Hitler, the leader of the National Socialist movement, pledged to restore national pride and full employment to the German nation. Once he came to power, Hitler was able to fulfill part of his pledge, but only by resorting to very draconian measures. He first repudiated provisions in the Versailles Treaty and rearmed Germany, sending one-half million young men into military service. He then systematically eliminated Jews, Gypsies, the infirm, and other groups whom he despised, thereby decreasing the pool of people in need of work. Eventually, Hitler's militarism, racism, and thirst for expansion plunged Europe into a catastrophic war, with the roots of the conflict linked to the earlier economic deprivation which helped spawn fanatical leaders such as Hitler in Germany and Mussolini in Italy.

The U.S. as Chief Architect of the International Economic System

Once World War II ended, a war responsible for the deaths of from 35 to 60 million people, an earnest effort was made to restore economic cooperation and rebuild tattered national economies.2 The International Monetary Fund (IMF), the World Bank (formally known as the International Bank for Reconstruction and Development-IBRD), and later the General Agreement on Tariffs and Trade (GATT) would provide institutional mechanisms through which the United States could assert international leadership in trade, investment, and monetary policy. The very generous Marshall Plan (referred to in formal terms as the European Recovery Program) and other aid programs would also help prime the pump for economic recovery in Europe and elsewhere. From 1947 to 1954, the U.S. government provided through the Marshall Plan 12 billion dollars in assistance to 16 European nations. This was a vast sum of money, being equivalent to almost 70 billion 1990 dollars, and by and large the Europeans used the funding judiciously. By the early 1950s Western Europe was well on its way to economic recovery.

Beginning in 1949 and attributable in part to efforts to help struggling nations elsewhere in the world, the United States began to experience balance-of-payments deficits. In plain English, this means that more money was leaving the United States than was entering. U.S. expenditures abroad included payments for imports, the costs of maintaining military forces overseas, money invested in other countries by American businesses, and foreign aid given in the form of grants and loans. These expenditures were greater than funds flowing into the United States from payments for exports and services, profits on U.S. foreign investment, repayments of U.S. government loans, and so on.

This massive effort launched by America to help rebuild the economies in other nations was carried out in part to help alleviate the suffering of tens of millions of people. In addition, leaders in Washington recognized that the U.S. needed strong trading partners in order to expand America's own economy, so it was natural to help Europe, Japan, and other nations to recover. Washington was also extremely concerned about the spread of international communism, which at the time was perceived by most American leaders as monolithic and directed exclusively from the Kremlin. During the war, communists in France and Italy had formed the backbone of the resistance to the German occupation and fascist governments. In the early period following the war, communists actually played an active part in the governments of France and Italy. U.S. officials worried that these major European nations, along with several other countries, were vulnerable to Moscow's influence and that the communists would do everything possible to exploit the severe economic problems on the European continent.

In order to counter this perceived threat, Washington agreed to help rebuild Europe and pledged money to those nations willing to support predominantly capitalist economic systems. For those that were not interested in the capitalist road to recovery, such as the Soviet Union, Yugoslavia, Czechoslovakia, Poland, and some neighboring countries, Marshall Plan money simply would not be made available. Consequently, for both strategic and economic reasons, it was important for the United States to send financial assistance to reconstruct a good part of the European continent. On the other hand, the amount of money involved in the recovery programs was very large and illustrated American concern for the plight of people elsewhere in the industrialized world. Ironically, such tangible assistance and concern have never been manifested to the same degree for inhabitants in the developing nations.

In the postwar era, Washington also took a particular interest in remolding the political and economic systems of the defeated Axis powers. Both the German and Japanese constitutional documents bear many resemblances to the U.S. Constitution. Under the tutelage of U.S. General Lucius Clay and others, the part of Germany under Western control gradually emerged from its pariah status and was integrated into the mainstream of European society, first through the formation of a separate nation known as the Federal Republic of Germany in 1949, then through its entry into the European Coal and Steel Community (the precursor to the European Community) in 1951, and finally in 1955 through its membership in the North Atlantic Treaty Organization (NATO). General Douglas MacArthur had an even greater impact on Japan's postwar development. Whereas Germany had been divided into American, British, French, and Russian zones after the war, Japan was essentially under the exclusive control of the United States. As Supreme Commander of the Allied Powers, MacArthur was given the responsibility of making Japan safe for democracy and for capitalism. With large infusions of U.S. aid and very generous U.S. trade concessions, MacArthur could justifiably claim that his mission was successful.

At the multilateral level, both the IMF and the World Bank were created at the June 1944 Bretton Woods conference which had brought together representatives from 44 nations. The purpose of the IMF is to promote international monetary cooperation and the expansion of international trade, and to insure stability in the exchange of major currencies. The IMF also helps nations to overcome balance-of-payments difficulties through special loans. In order to procure such loans, however, the affected nations must agree to abide by certain conditions, such as cutting back on imports, devaluing their currencies, or reducing the size of their public bureaucracies. These conditions are determined by the major Western industrialized nations, by virtue of the fact that they control the majority of votes in the IMF. Unlike the United Nations General Assembly, where each nation is entitled to one vote, a weighted voting system has been instituted in the IMF, with votes calculated in accordance with a nation's contribution to the fund. Currently, the United States is entitled to about one-fifth of the total votes, with the major Western European nations and Japan sharing a hefty portion of the remaining votes. In 1991 alone, the IMF issued 10.5 billion dollars in loans.[3]

The IMF and the World Bank each have a membership of approximately 170 nations and are headquartered next to one another in Washington, D.C., with their spacious premises located only a few blocks from the White House. The weighted voting system is also used in the World Bank, with the United States controlling over 17 percent of the total votes. In addition, the president of the World Bank has always been an American. The Bank provides loans and technical assistance to developing countries to help them modernize and expand their economies. Common projects involving World Bank financing would include the development of hydroelectric facilities, roads, ports, and heavy industries.[4]

The member states pledge funds to the World Bank, which can then use this government backing to sell its own bonds in global financial markets. Money raised from the bond markets is then loaned out to nations at competitive interest rates. During the 1992 fiscal year, the World Bank made loan and credit commitments totaling 21.7 billion dollars for 222 projects in 83 countries.[5] Once again, strings are attached to these loans and the strings generally reflect the policy preferences of the leading capitalist nations. For example, in return for a sizeable loan, a developing nation may be required to sell off government-owned businesses, lower government deficits, and reduce import barriers for certain products.

It is not uncommon for Americans to perceive that the World Bank simply gives money away to the poorer nations of the world. This is an erroneous assumption. It is true that an affiliate of the World Bank, the International Development Association (IDA), does provide interest-free loans to the poorest nations, loans which may stretch over a 50 year period. But such loans are only a fraction of the total lending activity of the World Bank, and the Bank generally makes profits exceeding 1.5 billion dollars per year by investing funds in capital markets.[6]

The General Agreement on Tariffs and Trade (GATT) was established in 1947 and is headquartered in Geneva. Its major task is to facilitate trade links among the member nations and to lower both tariff and nontariff barriers in international trade. A tariff is a duty on an imported product, whereas a nontariff barrier is any device other than a duty which impedes import activity. Quotas, product content standards, and customs' regulations are a few examples of nontariff barriers. Nearly 110 nations have joined GATT and through a series of multilateral trade rounds in the post-World War II period, duties have been lowered substantially. Unfortunately, as duties have come down, many nontariff barriers have been erected to take their place. The major Western nations' voting power is distributed more widely in GATT than in the IMF and World Bank, but they remain the pivotal actors and the United States continues to play a major role in GATT proceedings.

Because of its economic might and its dominance in such international organizations, the United States has clearly set many rules of the game for the postwar international economic system. Indeed, the United States was clearly the world's only economic superpower entering the 1960s, and American businesses were gaining huge market shares around the globe. In the early part of that decade, French publisher Jean-Jacques Servan-Schreiber wrote a book entitled *The American Challenge,* warning Europeans that if they did not wake up, the third greatest industrial power in the world after the United States and the USSR would be American multinational corporations in Europe.[7]

Early Challenges to U.S. Economic Leadership

However, U.S. mastery of the world economy began to flounder noticeably in the late 1960s, with the Vietnam War accelerating this downward spiral. The conflict in Southeast Asia exacerbated America's balance-of-payments problems, prompting some countries to question not only U.S. strategic priorities, but also the soundness of the American dollar. President Charles de Gaulle of France openly challenged the role of the dollar as the world's only reserve currency and began to cash in dollars for gold. The resurgence of the Western European and Japanese economies also prompted leaders in some of these countries to demand the establishment of another means of exchange which could replace the dollar as the world's dominant currency. In response to these demands, the IMF created Special Drawing Rights (SDRs) in 1969. The SDR is an international reserve currency which is backed by the IMF member states and can be used as a means of exchange around the world. Its value is linked to a so-called basket of currencies which includes the U.S. dollar, the British pound, the Japanese yen, the German mark, and the French franc. At the time, some prognosticators insisted that the SDR would soon overtake the dollar and become the dominant currency for global transactions. Their predictions concerning the demise of the dollar proved to be highly exaggerated, and the dollar eventually solidified its position as the world's major reserve currency.

Nonetheless, the erosion of U.S. economic power continued into the 1970s, precipitating two devaluations of the dollar. The convertibility of dollars into gold was also suspended by President Richard Nixon on August 15, 1971, effectively bringing to an end the postwar fixed exchange rate system established at Bretton Woods. In its place, a rather ad hoc floating exchange system was instituted, with supply and demand forces in international exchange markets and national governmental policies largely determining the relative value of currencies. This floating exchange system is still in place today and the value of the dollar has fluctuated dramatically over the past two decades.

On the same day that he ended the dollar's convertibility into gold, President Nixon slapped a ten percent surcharge on dutiable goods entering the United States. He took this step as a means of dampening America's enthusiasm for foreign products and to combat the nation's chronic balance-of-payments deficit and worsening trade picture. Moreover, he was sending a message to the major Western nations to cooperate with the United States in efforts to overcome its economic problems. The so-called "Nixon Shock" of 1971 served its purpose, and the Smithsonian agreement concluded by the West's major trading countries in December of that year permitted the United States to devalue its currency by almost 9 percent in return for dropping the import surcharge. An additional 10 percent devaluation occurred in 1973.

What impact does a currency devaluation have on international trade? With the dollar dropping in value vis-à-vis other major currencies, American consumers would have to pay more for overseas products. Conversely, American exporters would benefit from the devalued dollar and find it easier to sell their products in foreign markets. Thus, demand for imports would eventually drop and foreign demand for American-made products would increase, thereby improving the trade performance of the United States. Washington was also signaling to other nations that the United States would be intent on improving its own economic position in the world, and should no longer be expected to make the major unilateral concessions which had helped to rebuild the shattered economies in Europe and Asia after the Second World War. Likewise, the rejuvenated members of the European Community and Japan were now to be considered as major economic competitors, prompting the United States to devote much more time to safeguarding its own special interests both at home and abroad.

THE CURRENT BALANCE SHEET: AMERICAN SUCCESSES

In spite of the growing competition from Europe, Japan, and newly industrialized countries such as South Korea, Taiwan, and Brazil, the United States still remains a very formidable international economic actor. In 1992, the United States accounted for slightly more than one-fifth of the world's total production. Japan and the Germany ranked a distant second and third. America, whose annual production of goods and services (labeled as gross domestic product or GDP) added up to almost 5.9 trillion dollars in 1992, also created 20 million net new jobs from the latter part of 1982 until the end of the decade. This is a remarkable statistic, especially when compared with the rather stagnant job growth performance of Europe during most of the same period.

Furthermore, the United States continues to be the foremost trading nation with annual imports and exports of goods and services easily surpassing 1.2 trillion dollars in 1992. Germany ranks number two with about four-fifths of the U.S. total.[8] The challenge from the SDR has also been met for the time being, with the U.S. dollar in 1990 being the currency used for 70 percent of trade transactions in the Western world, and accounting for over one half of reserves held by central banks around the globe.[9]

Americans have also invested more abroad than citizens of any other country. In the domain of foreign direct investment, Americans had made 450 billion dollars in overseas investments by the beginning of 1992. Without any doubt, a large number of multinational corporations headquartered in the United States, including corporations of the stature of Ford, IBM, General Motors, and Exxon, continue to play significant roles in many foreign markets.

The United States is also the home of the largest, best integrated, and most affluent market on earth. Using a purchasing power parity (PPP) index which controls for fluctuations in currency values, the American consumer ranks number one in terms of what goods and services can be bought with the average paycheck. Inflation in the United States dropped from the 12 percent range in 1980 to 3 percent in 1992, and unemployment declined from the 10 percent level in 1982 to the 7 percent range at the end of 1992.

Moreover, the United States remains the major breadbasket for the rest of the world and is richly endowed with many natural resources. In physical terms, it is the fourth largest nation in the world and also ranks as the third most populated country, with one-quarter billion inhabitants. The population base and the affluency of most Americans provide product diversification and economy-of-scale advantages for American firms which are often not available to their counterparts in other countries. For example, the second largest nation in the world territorially is America's northern neighbor, Canada. Canada is richly endowed in terms of natural resources, but over one-half of its land mass is subject to permafrost (permanently frozen ground). Canada also has a population of only 27.5 million people, smaller than that of California, and four-fifths of its people are clustered within 200 miles of the U.S. border. Japan, on the other hand, has a population in excess of 120 million people, but its population is squeezed into an area the size of Montana. Moreover, Japan is a very mountainous island nation possessing very few natural resources and very limited habitable space.

THE CURRENT BALANCE SHEET:
THE NEGATIVE FEATURES

The United States is certainly an economic power to be reckoned with, but on the opposite side of the coin, the U.S. is registering some "record" performances which give cause for grave concern.

1. The United States has experienced the worst trade deficits in history. In absolute dollar terms, no other nation has ever come close to matching America's recent annual trade deficits. During the 1980s, the red ink in U.S. merchandise trade exceeded one trillion dollars, and it is still not clear when U.S. exports will once again equal or surpass U.S. imports (see Figure 10-1).[10] Perennial trade deficits represent a relatively new phenomenon for the United States, because it enjoyed annual merchandise trade surpluses during the entire period spanning 1894 and 1970.

2. The United States is the largest debtor nation in history. At the beginning of 1992, the United States owed foreigners 362 billion dollars more than they owed Americans, an external debt greater than the combined debts of Brazil, Mexico, Venezuela, Russia, and Nigeria. Ironically, the United

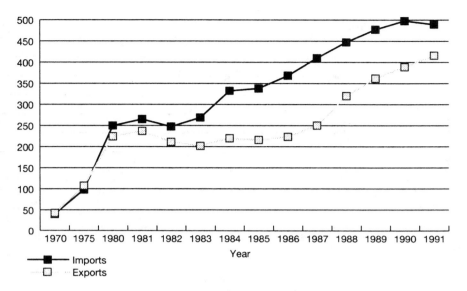

FIGURE 10-1
U.S. Merchandise Imports and Exports, 1970–1991
Billions of Dollars

TABLE 10-1 U.S Merchandise Imports and Exports,* 1970-1991, Billions of Dollars

YEAR	IMPORTS	EXPORTS
1970	$ 40.0	$ 42.5
1975	98.2	107.1
1980	249.8	224.3
1981	265.1	237.0
1982	247.6	211.2
1983	268.9	201.8
1984	332.4	219.9
1985	338.1	215.9
1986	368.4	223.3
1987	409.8	250.2
1988	447.2	320.2
1989	477.4	361.7
1990	497.6	388.7
1991	489.4	416.0

*Excludes military imports and exports
Source: Survey of Current Business, June 1992.

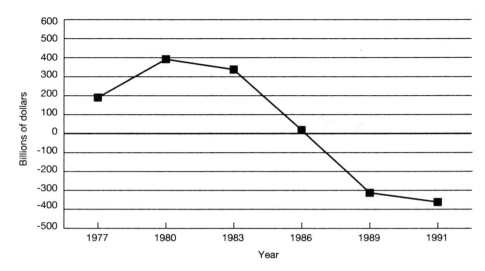

FIGURE 10-2
U.S. International Investment Position, 1970-1991, Current Cost Formula

TABLE 10-2 U.S. International Investment Position, 1970-1991, Current Cost Formula

Year	Billions of Dollars
1977	$190.5
1980	392.5
1983	337.4
1986	18.7
1989	-312.3
1991	-361.5

States had ranked as the world's largest creditor nation from 1914 until the 1980s, and enjoyed a net surplus of 18.7 billion dollars as recently as 1986 (see Figure 10-2).

This external debt is still a relatively small percentage of gross domestic product (about 7 percent at the end of 1990 compared with 31 percent in Brazil and 41 percent in Mexico), and the U.S. has the luxury of repaying its external obligations with money it can run off on its own government printing presses.[11] The statistics also reveal that foreign investors maintain a high level of confidence in the stability and dynamism of the U.S. economy, holding claims to 2.3 trillion dollars in U.S. assets at the end of 1991.[12] Nonetheless, the need to service this external debt will add to the country's already severe current account problems, with the current account defined as the broadest measure of trade in goods and services, and including transactions such as the repatriation of dividends, interest earnings, and corporate profits (see Figure 10-3). Furthermore, the U.S. economy has now become much more vulnerable to the consequences of a rapid withdrawal of foreign investment from the American marketplace.

3. The United States has the largest government debt in history. At the end of 1992, the federal government's cumulative debt had surpassed four trillion dollars ($4,000,000,000,000), up 400 percent since 1980. The costs of servicing this swelling debt are mounting steadily, in spite of the 1990 deficit-reduction law and tax reform. For example, about 14 percent of the federal government's budget was devoted to debt servicing in 1992, compared with 7 percent in 1980, and this and entitlement payments have been the fastest growing categories in the entire budget. Annual net interest payments on this debt approached 200 billion dollars in 1992, up from 53 billion dollars in 1980. These payments are greater than Washington's combined spending for education, the environment, law enforcement, agriculture, transportation, and foreign aid.

As a percentage of GDP or on a per capita basis, the U.S. federal government's debt and the funds needed to service the debt are not as large as those to be found in several other nations, including America's neighbor to the north, Canada. Nevertheless, in terms of absolute dollars, Washington's debt is the largest ever recorded and is growing much faster than government red ink in most other countries. To put this debt accumulation in perspective, at the beginning of World War I, the U.S. government's total debt was 1.2 billion dollars. At the end of World War II, it was up to 258.7 billion dollars. In 1981, it finally reached 1 trillion dollars, and only five years later it surpassed the 2 trillion dollar mark. At the 4 trillion dollar level reached in 1992, each man, woman, and child in the United States owed 16,000 dollars as his or her share of the mushrooming debt.

COMPETITIVENESS

Beyond the various debt dimensions, one must also begin to wonder about the competitiveness of the United States in the world economy. At the end of World War II, the United States produced at least one-half of the world's total production. In 1960, the U.S. produced almost 40 percent, but in the 1990s its share is down to a little more than 20 percent, about the same as the European Community's and about one-third larger than Japan's.[13]

U.S. merchandise exports are a small part of GDP, and American exports as a percentage of the world total were down significantly from about 20

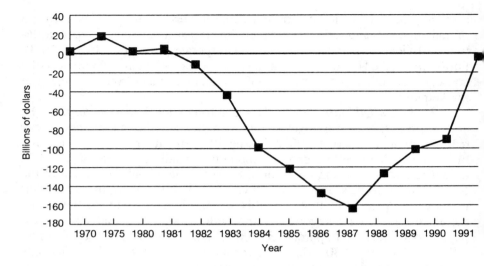

FIGURE 10-3
U.S. Current Account Balances, 1970-1991

TABLE 10-3   U.S. Current Account Balances, 1970-1991

Year	Billions of Dollars
1970	2.3
1975	18.1
1980	2.3
1981	5.0
1982	-11.4
1983	-43.6
1984	-98.8
1985	-121.7
1986	-147.5
1987	-163.5
1988	-126.7
1989	-101.1
1990	-90.4
1991	-3.7

Source: *Survey of Current Business,* June 1992.

percent in the early 1950s to only 10 percent at the end of the 1980s, before rebounding to the 13 percent range in 1992. Indeed, in the late 1980s, total annual U.S. exports were surpassed by Germany and were only somewhat higher than Japan's, the nations once "tutored" by the United States and which have less than one-third and one-half the U.S. population respectively. Both the U.S. manufacturing and agricultural sectors have also suffered from intense competition from abroad, and even in the high-technology area, long considered as America's strong suit, problems have arisen. For the first time ever in the mid-1980s, the United States actually began to run a yearly trade deficit in high-technology products.

At close inspection, the performance of the United States in creating jobs is also somewhat mixed. Although close to 20 million net new jobs were created from the end of the recession in 1982 through the remainder of the decade, the vast majority were to be found in the services sector and paid an average yearly wage between 9,000 and 15,000 dollars. To put this into perspective, the government's official poverty line for a family of four in 1990 was about 12,700 dollars. Moreover, the Federal Bureau of Labor Statistics, which is responsible for compiling these figures, counts anyone as "employed" who works more than one hour per week. Of the more than 120 million Americans counted as employed at the beginning of 1990, almost a quarter was actually working part-time. During portions of the past decade, the U.S. either lost or had negligible job gains in manufacturing, export-oriented industries, and in businesses subject to direct import competition. Many of these lost jobs have traditionally paid a much higher wage than those in retailing or in many other service sectors.

The job picture is also muddled by America's inability to control its own borders. Although annual figures are difficult to pin down, perhaps five million aliens entered the country illegally during the 1970s and 1980s.[14] Many of these illegal aliens secured employment, although some were certainly exploited by unscrupulous employers. In 1986, Congress finally passed a new immigration law providing amnesty to many illegal residents but also penalizing employers who hired any new people entering the United States clandestinely. The effectiveness of this new legislation on illegal immigration flows has apparently been quite minimal.[15]

Legal immigration, on the other hand, should be very good for the U.S. economy. As Americans get older and the ratio of active workers to retirees decreases, new job seekers will be needed. In the late 1940s, there were 13 workers per retiree, compared with 4 in 1990 and a projected 2.3 in the year 2030. During the 1980s, 8.7 million immigrants entered the United States legally or were granted amnesty after having entered illegally, the largest immigration wave since the first decade of the twentieth century. During the 1960s, immigrants accounted for about 11 percent of America's total population growth, and this increased to

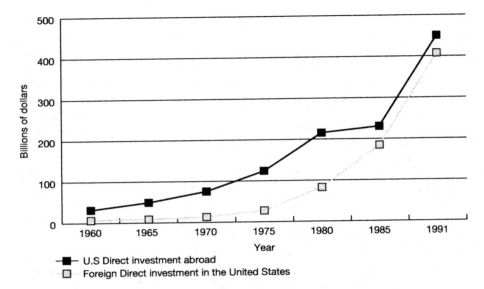

FIGURE 10-4
U.S. Direct Investment Overseas and
Foreign Direct Investment in the United States, 1960-1991
Cumulative on an Historical Cost Basis, Billions of Dollars

TABLE 10-4   U.S. Direct Investment Overseas and Foreign Direct Investment in the United States, 1960-1991, Cumulative on an Historical Cost Basis, Billions of Dollars

Year	*U.S. Direct Investment Abroad*	*Foreign Direct Investment in the United States*
1960	31.9	6.9
1965	49.5	8.8
1970	75.5	13.3
1975	124.1	27.7
1980	215.4	83.0
1985	230.3	184.6
1991	450.2	407.6

Source: *Survey of Current Business* (various) and *Statistical Abstract of the United States* (various).

33 percent during the 1970s and 39 percent during the 1980s.[16] Almost 90 percent of the legal applicants were approved for entry because of family ties in the United States, and the remaining 10 percent because they possessed skills needed in the U.S. work force. As time passes, more emphasis may have to be placed on attracting overseas residents with skills which will help America to become more competitive globally, and this has been reflected in part in the 1990 Immigration Act which will increase quotas for skilled men and women wanting to enter the United States. The overall implications of legal and illegal immigration for the United States are discussed in greater detail in Chapters 5 and 11.

In the direct investment arena, foreign firms have in recent years put more money into the United States than American corporations have invested overseas. At the end of 1970, individuals and firms from the United States had invested 75 billion dollars abroad, whereas foreigners had invested only 13 billion dollars in the U.S. At the beginning of the 1980s, these figures were 188 billion dollars and 55 billion dollars respectively. At the beginning of 1992, U.S. direct investment abroad totaled 450 billion dollars, in comparison to 408 billion dollars in foreign direct investment in the United States. Thus, during the 12-year period from 1980 through 1991, American direct investment overseas increased by 142 percent while foreign investment in the United States catapulted by 642 percent (see Figure 10-4).

These figures are somewhat skewed by the use of tax havens such as the Netherlands Antilles by U.S. corporations. Moreover, the market value of U.S. investment abroad is still larger than foreign investment in the United States, mainly because Americans have had their investments for a much longer period of time.[17] Nevertheless, the trend is still abundantly clear. The American business community has slowed its penetration of foreign markets, whereas foreign firms have now made the United States the number one host nation in the world for direct investment. As mentioned earlier, several million Americans now work for foreign-controlled enterprises in the United States such as Shell Oil, Sony, Nissan, Nestle, and Renault. Through acquisitions, foreign residents or corporations also control such "traditional" American companies and product lines as Firestone, Timex, Alka-Seltzer, Burger King, Geritol, and Pepsodent (see the partial list of foreign-controlled firms and products in Table 10-5). In the early 1990s, Japanese firms were capable of manufacturing over 1.5 million cars and trucks in the United States, and through a combination of their imports and U.S. production, they could supply almost 40 percent of the American domestic market, compared with 23 percent at the end of the 1980s. Americans accustomed to the dominance of the Big 3 (General Motors, Ford, and Chrysler) may have to think again, for their share of the U.S. market may soon fall to the 50 percent range, and there are now more Japanese automakers in the United States than U.S. automakers. Japanese banks also command about 10 percent of the market for

TABLE 10-5   Foreign-Owned Companies and Products in the United States, 1993

Company or Product	Company or Product	Company or Product
A&P	Alcan Aluminum	Alka-Seltzer
Alpo	B. Dalton	Bantam Books
Barnes & Noble	Baskin-Robbins	Bass Shoes
Benetton	Bic	Brooks Brothers
Capitol Records	Carnation	CBS Records
Celanese Corp.	Cineplex Odeon	Clorox
Dalton	Dell Publishing	Doubleday
Dr. Pepper	Dunkin' Donuts	Dunlop Tire
Elizabeth Arden	Encyclopedia Americana	Fireman's Fund
Firestone	First Boston	Foster Grant
Frigidaire	G. Heileman	General Tire
Geritol	Giant Food Stores	Good Humor
Green Giant	Grolier, Inc.	Haagen-Dazs
Hardee's	Harper & Row	Hilton International
Int'l House of Pancakes	J&B Scotch	Jacuzzi
Keebler	Kennecott Copper	KitchenAid
Knorr Foods	Lawry's Foods	Libbey-Owens-Ford Glass
Libby fruits and vegetables	Lux	Mack Trucks
Maalox	MCA	*McCalls*
Miles Laboratories	MJB	Mrs. Butterworth's
MTV	Nestle	Noranda
Norelco	Northern Telecom	Omni Hotels
Ovaltine	Peoples Drug Store	Pepsodent
Philco	Pillsbury	Polygram Records
Q-Tips	Ragu spaghetti sauce	Ramada
RCA Records	Reebok	Rockefeller Center
Ronson	Roy Rogers Restaurants	Saks Fifth Avenue
7-Eleven	Shell Oil	Singer sewing machines
Smith Corona	Smith and Wesson	Spiegel
Standard Oil of Ohio	Stouffer Hotels	Sylvania
Taster's Choice	Thomas J. Lipton, Inc.	Tiffany
Travelodge	*TV Guide*	Twentieth Century Fox
Uniroyal Goodrich Tire	Van de Kamp	Vaseline
Washington Times	Westin Hotels	Wilson Sporting Goods
Yale Locks	Zale Corp.	Zenith Computers

business loans within the United States, and have provided about 50 percent of the U.S. market for municipal letters of credit.[18]

The relative decline of the United States in competitiveness is shown in other ways as well. In 1960, there were 175 U.S.-based companies among the top 275 industrial corporations in the world in terms of overall sales, representing 64 percent of the total number.[19] Among the top 275 industrial corporations in 1991, there were only 84 U.S. firms left on the list, accounting for 34 percent of the total.[20] Among the top 500 industrial corporations in 1991, 31 percent were American, 24 percent were Japanese, and 27 percent were from the European Community.[21] In 1960, 20 U.S. banks (33 percent) were to be found among the top 60 in the world. A decade later, 17 (28 percent) U.S. banks had places on the list. At the end of 1991, only 4 U.S. banks (7 percent) ranked in the top 60 banks in terms of assets. Among the top 100, 7 were American, 28 were Japanese, and 48 were from the European Community.[22] In 1990, Japanese banks also controlled 38 percent of all international lending, versus 14 percent for U.S. banks.[23] Foreign institutions currently control roughly one-quarter of all banking assets in the United States, up from 14 percent in 1982 and 4 percent in 1973.[24] These foreign banks also hold almost 30 percent of all U.S. business loans.[25]

Furthermore, the United States may be losing the innovation race. A large number of computer and electronics firms are having difficulty keeping up with foreign competition, costing them market shares both at home and abroad. Perhaps a sign of the times is the fact that almost one-half of the patents issued by the U.S. Patent and Trademark Office at the end of the 1980s were to foreign residents and foreign corporations, compared with only 11 percent back in 1961 and 24 percent in 1972.[26]

In 1974, the United States designed about 70 percent of the advanced technology in the world. A decade later, this had fallen to 50 percent, and by the mid-1990s it may be down to 30 percent.[27] To use more concrete terms to describe this competition gap, one should remember that in 1960 the United States singlehandedly produced three-quarters of the world's cars, versus only one-quarter in 1990. In the automotive industry, U.S. plants now take 40 percent longer to achieve the same amount of production as plants in Japan, and still produce cars with twice the number of defects as their Japanese competitors.[28] Americans also invented the color television, but more than one-half of color TVs are now made in East Asia and only a minuscule number are still made in the U.S. Americans first developed the videocassette recorder, but Asian companies now provide the great bulk of VCR production.[29] In addition, the U.S. accounted for almost one-quarter of all machine-tool exports in 1964, but only 4 percent by the mid-1980s.[30]

VINCIBILITY AND THE FOREIGN ECONOMIC POLICY CHALLENGES FACING THE UNITED STATES IN THE TWENTY-FIRST CENTURY

Some critics contend that the United States is now in an inevitable state of economic decline, much as Great Britain was at the end of the nineteenth century.[31] In retrospect, Great Britain prevailed economically during most of the nineteenth century, then passed the baton on to the United States, which prevailed during most of the twentieth century. In place of the United States, perhaps an Asian or European bloc of nations will prevail in the twenty-first century. If this scenario is accurate, the halcyon days of U.S. economic hegemony have now ended and the United States will be relegated to the role of one major actor among many on the global economic landscape. Quite frankly, for some critics, the "land of opportunity" has become a "nation of reduced expectations and limited options."[32] The gravy train has ended and the United States, a "diminished giant," is now dying a death by 1,000 cuts.

Others add that Americans have never before been so vincible to international developments, insisting that many economic and environmental problems are now beyond the purview of Washington to solve unilaterally. These controversial perspectives, especially the one alleging that the American economic dynasty is over, will be the focus of attention in the next few chapters.[33]

ENDNOTES

1. Beggar-thy-neighbor tactics involve trying to take advantage of other nations while giving up very little in return. For example, Nation X would want to export as much as possible to Nation Y, while severely limiting the amount of imports from Nation Y. Thus, each country wanted to run a balance-of-trade surplus, but this goal was not achievable. As one nation erected trade barriers, others retaliated, leading to a drop in overall global trade and a horrendous loss of jobs.
2. Only a few nations have been able to provide reliable or precise statistics on the number of military and civilian deaths caused directly or indirectly by World War II. It is assumed, however, that Poland lost almost 20 percent of its prewar population, and both the Soviet Union and Yugoslavia about 10 percent each.
3. Statistics provided by the IMF's Public Affairs Office.
4. The World Bank Group consists of the International Bank for Reconstruction and Development (IBRD), established in 1945, the International Finance Corporation (IFC), established in 1956, the International Development Association (IDA), established in 1960, and the Multilateral Investment Guarantee Agency (MIGA), established in 1988. The IFC promotes development through support of the private sector in less developed countries and invested 1.8 billion dollars in 167 projects in fiscal year 1992. MIGA helps developing countries to attract foreign investment from private sources and from public sector companies.
5. World Bank, *The World Bank Annual Report 1992* (Washington, D.C.: World Bank, 1992), 18, 176-7. These were commitments made by the IBRD and the IDA.

6. In 1992, the World Bank's net income was 1.6 billion dollars. See *Annual Report, 1992,* 70.
7. Jean-Jacques Servan-Schreiber, *The American Challenge* (New York: Avon, 1968), 3. This is the English translation of his book, *Le défi américain.*
8. In 1991, the United States accounted for 14.4 percent of global merchandise exports, Germany for 12.6 percent, and Japan for 9.8 percent. See *The Wall Street Journal,* (National Edition), 28 July 1992, A1.
9. On the other hand, the U.S. dollar accounted for 80 percent of currency reserves held by central banks worldwide as recently as the mid-1970s. See *The Wall Street Journal,* (National Edition), 6 July 1992, 10.
10. These figures include trade-related transportation and insurance costs.
11. Debt statistics for Brazil and Mexico are found in the Central Intelligence Agency, *The World Factbook 1991* (Washington, D.C.: Government Printing Office, 1991), 40. 205-06.
12. U.S. Department of Commerce study reported in *The Wall Street Journal,* (National Edition), 3 July 1992, A2.
13. *IMF Survey,* 26 October 1992, 321.
14. Michael J. Mandel and Christopher Farrell, "The Immigrants: How They're Helping to Revitalize the U.S. Economy," *Business Week,* 13 July 1992, 116.
15. After leveling off for a few years, attempted illegal entries at the U.S.-Mexican border increased in the early 1990s according to statistics compiled by the U.S. Immigration and Naturalization Service.
16. Mandel and Farrell, "The Immigrants." In 1990, there were a record 18 million foreign-born residents in the United States. These residents represented 8.6 percent of the U.S. population compared with 4.7 percent in 1970.
17. A Federal Reserve study estimated that in 1989 the market value of American foreign direct investment abroad was 785 billion dollars, versus 466 billion dollars for foreign direct investment in the United States.
18. Diane Harris and Andrea Rock, "The Japanese are Here to Stay," *Money,* May 1987, 140-148.
19. Earl H. Fry, *The Politics of International Investment* (New York: McGraw-Hill, 1983), 20-21.
20. "Fortune Guide to the Global 500," *Fortune,* 27 July 1992, 178-83.
21. "The Global 500 by Country," *Fortune,* 27 July 1992, 178-83.
22. See Fry, *Politics,* 21; *The Rand McNally International Bankers Directory,* 1985 edition (Chicago: Rand McNally, 1985), 47-8, "Top 500 Banks in the World," William Glass-gall, "A Nightmare Year for Japan's Bankers," *Business Week,* 6 July 1992, 62-63; and *American Banker,* 27 July 1992, 16A. One should add, however, that in 1991, 4 of the world's 10 most profitable banks, and 19 of the top 50, were American according to the London-based rating agency, ICBA. See *U.S.A. Today,* 13 November 1992, 4B.
23. This estimate is made by the Basle-based Bank of International Settlements (BIS).
24. *The Wall Street Journal,* (National Edition), 8 June 1990, B3B.
25. At the beginning of 1990, foreign banks held 28.5 percent of American business loans. See *The New York Times,* (National Edition), 18 June 1990, A1.
26. In 1960, fewer than 8,000 of 47,000 U.S. patents were issued to foreign firms and individuals. In 1988, foreign entities received 48 percent of the 77,924 patents issued by the U.S. Patent and Trademark Office, with Japanese-owned companies receiving 16,158 of these patents. Eight of the top ten corporations which received the most U.S. patents were foreign-owned. See the *World Almanac and Book of Facts, 1990* (New York: Pharos Books, 1989), 162.
27. "Can America Compete?," *Business Week,* 20 April 1987, 57.

28. Michael L. Dertouzos, Richard K. Lester, and Robert M. Solow, *Made in America* (Cambridge: MIT Press, 1989), 20.
29. Dertouzos, Lester, and Solow, *Made in America,* 58.
30. David S. Broder, "U.S. Competitiveness: A Campaign Code Word," *Washington Post,* 16 April 1987, 1.
31. Paul Kennedy, *The Rise and Fall of the Great Powers* (New York: Random House, 1987).
32. David S. Broder, "Competitiveness a Complex Issue on 1988 Agenda," *Washington Post,* 16 April 1987, A14.
33. Not everyone agrees that America's economic future is gloomy. For much more optimistic appraisals, consult Joseph S. Nye, Jr., *Bound to Lead: The Changing Nature of American Power* (New York: Basic Books, 1990), Richard Rosecrance, *America's Economic Resurgence: A Bold New Strategy* (New York: Harper and Row, 1990), and Henry R. Nau, *The Myth of America's Decline* (Oxford: Oxford University Press, 1990).

11

EMPLOYMENT, RESOURCES, AND THE ENVIRONMENT
INTERNATIONAL CHALLENGES FACING THE UNITED STATES

As Americans prepare to move into a new century, they are increasingly aware of the challenges of global interdependence. In terms of environmental, energy, resource, and population issues, the world is rapidly being transformed into a global village with spillover occurring from one village to the next. To a certain extent, Americans are frustrated at Washington's inability to solve unilaterally the problems of ozone deterioration, global warming, resource shortages, illegal immigration, and other pressing issues. On the other hand, a growing number recognizes that many issues transcend the boundaries of individual nation-states and require regional and global cooperation in order to derive satisfactory solutions.

POPULATION GROWTH, IMMIGRATION, AND JOBS

The United States is now home to a quarter of a billion people, ranking as the third most populous nation in the world after China and India. Nonetheless, these 250,000,000 people represent less than 5 percent of the world's total population. In 1987, the global population surpassed 5 billion, and by 1998, the population should exceed 6 billion, with an average of 4 1/2 babies born every second. To put this explosive population growth into perspective, the world's population at the time of the birth of Christ was approximately 250 million. In the year 1650, the population had doubled to 500 million; in 1850 it topped 1 billion for the first time; in 1930 it surpassed 2 billion; and in 1975 the population doubled once again to 4 billion (see Table 11-1).[1]

The United Nations currently predicts that the global population will approach nine billion by the year 2030.[2] Such predictions are at times hazardous, of course, as evidenced by Malthusian projections which were much too high, or by a U.S. Census Bureau study in 1946 which estimated that the United States would have a population of a mere 165 million in 1990.[3]

What is incontestable, however, is that population growth is causing strains for many societies, both directly and indirectly.[5] Most of the growth is now confined to developing nations, which are already experiencing major difficulties in providing adequate health care and in creating new jobs. Almost 90 percent of all children born today live in developing nations, and 60 percent will be part of families whose annual income is less than the subsidy provided by the European Community in 1990 for one dairy cow (about 350 dollars). In a frantic search for job opportunities, millions of people from these countries will eventually migrate, either legally or illegally, to the advanced industrial nations of the West.

Ironically, among these so-called Western nations, population has generally leveled off, or in certain cases is actually declining. The "West" is generally defined as the 24 nations affiliated with the Paris-based Organization for Economic Cooperation and Development (OECD). This mostly affluent group includes the United States and Canada, most of Western Europe, the "Eastern" nation of Japan, and Australia and New Zealand, both located in the Southern hemisphere. To illustrate the current population trends, the West at the end of World War II accounted for about one-fourth of the world's population, only one-seventh in 1985, and perhaps only one-twenty-fifth by the year 2065.[6] Some of these nations, in an effort to encourage families to have more children, are now offering birth bounties and family allowances.

TABLE 11-1   The Doubling of Earth's Population[4]

Date	Estimated World Population	Doubling Time
1 A.D.	250,000,000	1,650 years
1650	500,000,000	200 years
1850	1,000,000,000	80 years
1930	2,000,000,000	45 years
1975	4,000,000,000	35 years
2010	8,000,000,000	

Under the authoritarian leadership of the late Nicolae Ceausescu, the government in the Central European nation of Romania even resorted to harsh measures banning abortions and establishing birth-monitoring systems to prevent the termination of pregnancies.[7]

In spite of this variety of inducements for greater fertility, most of the industrialized nations continue to experience low birthrates, with only nine of the OECD Western nations maintaining fertility rates above replacement levels since the 1970s.[8] A laundry list of reasons for this decline would include more effective contraception, delayed marriages, higher divorce rates, ready access to abortion clinics, urbanization pressures, better educational opportunities, higher income and standard of living aspirations, environmentalist concerns, and a rapid growth in the number of women entering the work force.[9]

In marked contrast, many of the developing countries are experiencing massive increases in population, with 1 million babies born every 4 1/2 days. After all, in the absence of highly developed systems of social security and insurance, families in developing countries view children as an asset, not a liability. In certain nations, such as Kenya and Syria, the population is actually doubling over a 20-year period.[10] To show the disparities in population growth between Northern and Southern nations, consider the following: in 1900, France was the fifth largest independent country in the world; in 1960 the tenth; in 1980 the fifteenth; and in the year 2000 it will likely be the twentieth.[11] In 1950, the combined population of the United States and Canada exceeded that of Latin America and the Caribbean; in 1980 the latter group of nations had 120 million more people; by the year 2000 the population gap should increase to 265 million; and by 2025 this gap should widen further to 520 million.[12] Unless current trends are altered drastically, the projected population growth through the mid-twenty-first century for all of Europe, North America, and the republics in the former Soviet Union will be less than the additions expected in either Bangladesh or Nigeria.[13] Most of the people who will be added to the global population rolls over the next half century will be in the Indian subcontinent, Africa, the Middle East, and Latin America, areas already plagued by high unemployment and low living standards.

Although the population continues to grow in most parts of the Third World, death also stalks many young people and expectant mothers. Approximately 15 million children die each year in the developing world from poor nutrition, diarrhea, malaria, pneumonia, measles, whooping cough, and tetanus. In addition, 500,000 women die annually from pregnancy or childbirth complications. Although figures remain alarmingly high, the infant mortality rate is actually beginning to fall due to improvements in nutrition and the use of vitamin supplements, better public hygiene, and medical programs involving widespread use of smallpox and childhood disease vaccines, antibiotics, malaria control procedures, and oral rehydration therapy to combat acute diarrhea. The United Nations World Health

Organization (WHO) constantly pleads with the rich nations for additional funding, claiming that a boost in spending on health care amounting to 5 dollars per child per year would save the lives of millions of young people who now die prematurely from treatable or preventable diseases.[14]

In spite of far too many children succumbing to illness in the Third World, the developing countries are relatively young when compared to the Northern tier of nations. In the year 2000, almost half of the world's population will be under age 25, with the great bulk of these people to be found in the developing countries. These young people deserve a proper education, but over 100 million children, of which two-thirds are girls, are deprived of even basic schooling.[15] They will also need jobs; but unfortunately, few will be available in their own home countries.

The population problem is also exacerbated by limited habitable land and by food production and distribution difficulties. The great bulk of the earth's inhabitants live on only 10 percent of the earth's land surface.[16] The overall population density on earth is about 83 per square mile, but Bangladesh has over 1,600 people per square mile, compared to just 61 in the United States. To put this comparison into clearer perspective, the 110 million residents of Bangladesh live in an area the size of Iowa.

Even Northern countries with very limited population growth rates, such as the Federal Republic of Germany, Japan, and the United Kingdom, have density rates in excess of 700. Urbanization also compounds the population problems in the Third World, with the lure of jobs persuading hundreds of millions of inhabitants to migrate to urban areas. The United Nations estimates that the urban share of the world's population will be 50 percent at the turn of the century, up from only 29 percent in 1950.[17] At the beginning of the past decade, the two major metropolitan areas in the world were the Northern cities of Tokyo and New York City. At the end of the current decade, the two most populated municipalities in the world will be the Southern cities of Mexico City, with over 26 million people, and Sao Paulo, with 24 million.

Although Third World population growth remains explosive, current levels of world grain output, which increased by 260 percent since 1950, provide sufficient supplies to furnish an adequate energy intake for each and every person on earth.[18] The problem is that many developing countries are still not able to grow or distribute enough food to feed all of their own citizens, and about one-fifth of the precious topsoil found on cropland has already been lost.[19] Many people also lack the purchasing power necessary to buy adequate foodstuffs. In 1980, it is estimated that 340 million people in 87 developing countries were not getting adequate calories to prevent stunted growth and serious health problems. This number of hungry people is the largest ever, although it was slightly below 1970 figures in terms of a share of total world population.[20]

Over the past decade, more than 100 nations were importing grain from the United States. Agricultural land is a very precious commodity in many parts of the world. In a long list of countries, acreage is shrinking due to expanding cities, salination, erosion of topsoil, desertification, and the loss of soil fertility. The Green Revolution, which began in earnest in the 1950s and 1960s, has dramatically helped Third World agriculture through more efficient use of hardier and higher-yielding seeds, fertilizers, pesticides, farm equipment, and watering techniques. Unfortunately, an acceleration in the loss of arable land, when combined with continued population increases and major distribution roadblocks, adds up to serious problems now and in the future.

Population growth is a difficult issue for decision-makers around the world to confront. Cynics would argue that if individual nations permit their populations to grow at unreasonable rates, they should be responsible for dealing with the repercussions and not expect the richer countries to bail them out. For example, quite a few Americans might initially sympathize with the "lifeboat ethics" scenario provided by biologist Garrett Hardin. Hardin depicts the growing world population as being comparable to a group of lifeboats afloat on the sea. Americans are portrayed as fifty people occupying a lifeboat with a capacity of sixty. One hundred swimmers have been forced overboard from other overcrowded boats. They are begging to be pulled aboard the U.S. boat. Those in the U.S. boat have three options: (1) let anyone board, although this would eventually sink the boat; (2) pull in ten people, leaving those already in the boat with the traumatic decision of determining which ten should be rescued; or (3) permit no one else to board, thereby assuring the comfort and the safety of the original fifty occupants.

Hardin proceeds to apply his "lifeboat ethics" scenario to policy options in the area of food assistance. The first option would be for the United States to provide food assistance to all of the world's hungry. The second option would be to concentrate food assistance on a selected group of countries. The final option would be to deny all food requests. Hardin concludes that the first two options would permit many Third World countries to continue to experience population growth without regard to the dire consequences. The third option, however, would make each nation responsible for the welfare of its own inhabitants. The prospect of starving, according to Hardin, would eventually put an end to population growth and force national governments to adopt sane and reasonable demographic policies. Hardin would therefore select this final option.[21]

Individual national governments must certainly take responsibility for solving some of the grievous problems facing their citizens, and some have been eminently or at least modestly successful in limiting population growth, including Singapore, Taiwan, South Korea, Thailand, Indonesia, and the People's Republic of China. Furthermore, one must keep in mind that world population has increased in part because of positive achievements in medicine and science. For example, medical breakthroughs and better education are helping many people to live longer and enjoy an improved quality of life. In the period between 1960 and 1987, life expectancy in the developing world rose from 46 years to 62 years, and the mortality rate for children under 5 was halved.[22] The percentage of the world's children fully immunized against a number of serious but preventable diseases also increased from 15 percent to 73 percent in the decade prior to 1990.[23] Because of the high birthrate in many parts of the Third World, and the fact that people are generally living longer and healthier lives, the net annual difference between births and deaths was approximately 92 million in 1992.[24]

Undoubtedly, solving the problems linked to a burgeoning population in the developing world will prove to be arduous and controversial. After all, religious beliefs certainly have a pervasive influence on birthrates in many parts of the world. Moreover, few people would favor governments taking draconian actions such as forced sterilization or mandatory abortions to bring down birthrates. In the long run, most government leaders hope that improved education, expanded family planning services, easier access to contraceptive devices, more food, and better medical treatment will help to mitigate some of the problems commonly associated with rapid increases in population. Unfortunately, passive concern for the effects of population growth, combined with apathy and a lack of cooperation at the international level, may well turn this crisis into a global catastrophe.

THE UNITED STATES AND THE DEBT AND POPULATION ISSUES

Running counter to the diffident attitude personified in the lifeboat scenario, troubles afflicting many of the 4 billion people in the Third World should be of concern to Americans in general and foreign policy decision-makers in particular. Above all, one should have sympathy for and be willing to help those people who suffer. Several years ago, the Brandt Commission made the following startling observation: "In the North, the average person can expect to live for more than 70 years; he or she will rarely be hungry, and will be educated at least up to the secondary level. In the countries of the South, the great majority of people have a life expectancy closer to 50 years; in the poorest countries one out of every four children dies before the age of five; one-fifth or more of all the people in the South suffer from hunger and malnutrition; 50 percent have no chance to become literate."[25] Some improvements in living conditions have occurred since this report was released, but the North-South gap continues to be colossal.[26]

To complicate the problem further, most residents of the Third World are not protected by the so-called "safety net" which is so commonplace in many Western countries. The safety net includes such innovations as pensions, social security benefits, and insurance covering unemployment, disability, and health care. Over one-half of the world's population lives in countries where the average annual income is less than 500 dollars, and in the 42 poorest nations, which have a combined population of nearly 500 million, the average is only 225 dollars.[27] Tragically, many people in developing countries face absolute poverty in areas characterized by massive unemployment and under-employment, overcrowded cities, inadequate food distribution, and deteriorating environmental conditions.

For humanitarian reasons, most "Northerners" would certainly like to see a major improvement in the quality of life of poor people around the world. The North, including Eastern Europe, has one-fifth of the global population, but four-fifths of the world's income. The South, in contrast, is home to four-fifths of all people on earth but survives on only one-fifth of global income. In many respects, the contemporary world is composed of "islands of plenty surrounded by seas of poverty,"[28] and living standards in many of these seas of poverty have actually been deteriorating over the past decade.[29]

Foreign aid and contributions to international organizations such as the World Bank, the International Monetary Fund, the United Nations Children's Fund (UNICEF), and the World Health Organization, all of which are affiliated with or directly attached to the UN, are the major routes used by Northern governments to transfer some of their wealth to the 160 or so developing nations. In absolute dollar terms, Japan and the United States contribute much more than any other nation in multilateral and bilateral aid to the Third World. On the other hand, many Northern countries contribute more than the United States as a percentage of gross national product. In fiscal year 1993, U.S. foreign aid, including military assistance, added up to about 14 billion dollars, or about 0.24 percent of GDP. When military assistance is excluded, this aid package dropped to well below 0.2 percent of GDP. The stated goal of the United Nations for official development assistance by the rich nations of the North is a minimum of 0.7 percent.

The intense poverty found in various parts of the Third World also calls into question societal priorities. For example, much of the foreign assistance received by governments in the South is in the form of military weapons, weapons which do little to provide food or increase productivity. Moreover, development assistance invariably returns to the age-old argument of guns versus butter. As the Brandt Commission emphasizes, the cost of a modern tank would pay for storage facilities for 100,000 tons of rice or would provide 1,000 classrooms for 30,000 children. For the price of one jet fighter, 40,000 village pharmacies could be built and stocked with a wide variety of medicines. Some experts insist that one-half of 1 percent of one year's military expenditures would pay for all the farm equipment and supplies needed to permit food-deficit countries to gain self-sufficiency within a decade.[30] Indeed, global military expenditures now hover near one trillion dollars, greater than the combined income of the poorest half of humanity.[31]

Others would argue, however, that military assistance is needed because no price can be placed on the attainment or preservation of freedom. Those Americans critical of foreign aid in general also insist that much of the assistance winds up in the hands of the rich or the corrupt, and rarely reaches those who are desperately in need of help. Others contend that it is unfortunate that so many people elsewhere in the world are suffering, but point out that the United States has its share of poverty in Appalachia, in the lower Mississippi Delta Valley, and in many large cities and other regions of the country. They emphasize that the United States must first improve the lot of its own people before embarking on assistance programs targeted at faraway countries. Indeed, it is distressing that nationwide 36 million Americans, including 20 percent of the 65 million children under the age of 18, now live below the government's official poverty line.[32] In addition, 35 million Americans, of which 12 million are children, have no health insurance coverage whatsoever, and America's infant mortality rate is higher than that of any other major Western nation and actually rivals that of some developing countries.[33] Astonishingly, the life expectancy for a male in Harlem is less than that for a male in Bangladesh.[34]

Still others would assert that the U.S. has provided over 400 billion dollars in foreign aid in the post-World War II period, only to find later on that several of the major beneficiaries have turned their backs on the United States and have openly repudiated what America stands for. These skeptics do not want to see future U.S. foreign aid "wasted" on ingrates. In addition, some believe strongly that the hard-working American taxpayer is being short-changed because once aid is shipped to a developing country, it rarely winds up in the hands of the needy. In other words, they insist that foreign aid goes from the poor in rich countries to the rich in poor countries.

There is a kernel of truth in all of these allegations, but the fact remains that the United States cannot insulate itself from the festering problems in the Third World, nor can Washington logically maintain its decade-long policy of insisting that economic development will suffice to solve the population problem. Without any doubt whatsoever, the problems linked to population growth, joblessness, poor health conditions, and burgeoning debt in other countries are now clearly having a significant impact on the U.S. economy.

Third World Debt

One of the most serious problems in the Third World is an external debt which surpassed 1.3 trillion dollars in 1991.[35] This debt continues to mount, and over the past several years, more money has been transferred from the South to the North than vice-versa. Some of this transfer is in the form of "flight capital," with many of the wealthy in the Third World, who lack confidence in the political and economic futures of their own countries, channeling their money into the United States, Europe, and other rich nations for investment purposes.[36] The reluctance of commercial banks in the industrialized countries to make any new loans to the developing world, when combined with an onerous repayment schedule for existing loans, also helps account for the net northward flow of funds. In addition, population pressures certainly contribute to the debt accumulation of Third World nations as their governments labor to provide food, jobs, education, and health care services. As Lester Brown asserts, "nations with low fertility are invariably the lenders; those with high fertility, the borrowers."[37]

In sub-Saharan Africa, foreign debt represented 115 percent of that region's gross product at the end of the 1980s, compared with 28 percent at the beginning of the decade. In 1990, debt servicing alone absorbed more than one-quarter of the value of export earnings from sub-Saharan Africa, and the net outflow of money exceeded 5 billion dollars. This outflow of money is very painful, for this is the region that has the greatest human misery on earth. Of the 44 countries listed by the United Nations in 1990 as having "low human development," 33 were in Africa (see Table 11-2).[38] Globally, the poor nations have recently been paying the rich ones 50 billion dollars each year in debt and interest payments beyond what they receive in new loans and grants, although the annual interest and debt repayments as a proportion of their exports have begun to decrease for many of these countries.[39]

Although improvement has occurred in recent years, Latin America remains heavily in debt, with Brazil at the end of 1990 owing 122 billion dollars, Mexico 96 billion dollars, Argentina 60 billion dollars, and Venezuela, Chile, Peru, Colombia, and Bolivia combined an additional 90 billion dollars.[40] The bulk of this Latin American debt is owed to U.S. banks, with smaller amounts owed to the U.S. government or international organizations heavily funded by the U.S. government. As discussed earlier, if this external debt is not repaid, or if repayments are slowed to a trickle, U.S. banks which are heavily exposed in the Third World will suffer. The customers of these banks may also be hurt because of bank losses and the need for banks to recoup lost revenue from domestic sources. The banks will also have less money to loan out, which would be a contributing factor to higher interest rates and a slowdown in economic expansion. But much more important than the fate of banks is the disturbing trend of the past decade for the rich nations to get richer and the poor nations to get poorer. Throughout much of Africa and Latin America, the 1980s brought rising debt, falling earnings, and contracting food supplies. About one-quarter of humanity, or 200 million more than in 1980, exist in absolute poverty, defined by Robert McNamara as "a condition of life so limited by malnutrition, illiteracy, disease, squalid surroundings, high infant mortality, and low life expectancy as to be beneath any reasonable definition of human decency."[41]

TABLE 11-2 Human Development Index*

Country	Life expectancy at birth (years) '87	Adult literacy rate (%), '85	Read GDP per head (ppp-adj'd) '87, $	HDI	Rank by GNP per head	Rank by HDI
Niger	45	14	452	0.116	20	1
Mali	45	17	543	0.143	15	2
Burkina Faso	48	14	500	0.150	13	3
Sierra Leone	42	30	480	0.150	27	4
Chad	46	26	400	0.157	4	5
Guinea	43	29	500	0.162	31	6
Somalia	46	12	1,000	0.200	23	7
Mauritania	47	17	840	0.208	40	8
Afganistan	42	24	1,000	0.212	17	9
Benin	47	27	665	0.224	28	10
Burundi	50	35	450	0.235	18	11
Bhutan	49	25	700	0.236	3	12
Mozambique	47	39	500	0.239	10	13
Malawi	48	42	476	0.250	7	14
Sudan	51	23	750	0.255	32	15
Central African Rep.	46	41	591	0.258	29	16
Nepal	52	26	722	0.273	8	17
Senegal	47	28	1,068	0.274	43	18
Ethiopia	42	66	454	0.282	1	19
Zaire	53	62	220	0.294	5	20
Rwanda	49	47	571	0.304	26	21
Angola	45	41	1,000	0.304	58	22
Bangladesh	52	33	883	0.318	6	23
Nigeria	51	43	668	0.322	36	24
Yemen Arab Rep.	52	25	1,250	0.328	47	25
Liberia	55	35	696	0.333	42	26
Togo	54	41	670	0.337	24	27
Uganda	52	58	511	0.354	21	28
Haiti	55	38	775	0.356	34	29
Ghana	55	54	481	0.360	37	30
Yemen, PDR	52	42	1,000	0.369	39	31
Côte d'Ivoire	53	42	1,123	0.393	52	32
Congo	49	63	756	0.395	59	33
Namibia	56	30	1,500	0.404	60	34
Tanzania	54	75	405	0.413	12	35
Pakistan	58	30	1,585	0.423	33	36
India	59	43	1,053	0.439	25	37
Madagascar	54	68	634	0.440	14	38
Papua New Guinea	55	45	1,843	0.471	50	39
Kampuchea, Dem.	49	75	1,000	0.471	2	40
Cameroon	52	61	1,381	0.474	64	41
Kenya	59	60	794	0.481	30	42
Zambia	54	76	717	0.481	19	43
Morocco	62	34	1,761	0.489	48	44
Egypt	62	45	1,357	0.501	49	45
Laos	49	84	1,000	0.506	9	46
Gabon	52	62	2,068	0.525	93	47
Oman	57	30	7,750	0.535	104	48
Bolivia	54	75	1,380	0.548	44	49
Burma	61	79	752	0.561	11	50
Honduras	65	59	1,119	0.563	53	51
Zimbabwe	59	74	1,184	0.576	45	52
Lesotho	57	73	1,585	0.580	35	53
Indonesia	57	74	1,660	0.591	41	54
Guatemala	63	55	1,957	0.592	63	55
Vietnam	62	80	1,000	0.608	16	56
Algeria	63	50	2,633	0.609	91	57
Botswana	59	71	2,496	0.646	69	58
El Salvador	64	72	1,733	0.651	56	59
Tunisia	66	55	2,741	0.657	70	60
Iran	66	51	3,330	0.660	97	61
Syria	66	60	3,250	0.691	79	62
Dominican Rep.	67	78	1,750	0.699	51	63
Saudi Arabia	64	55	8,320	0.702	107	64
Philippines	64	86	1,878	0.714	46	65

TABLE 11-2, continued

Country	Life expectancy at birth (years) '87	Adult literacy rate (%), '85	Read GDP per head (ppp-adj'd) '87, $	HDI	Rank by GNP per head	Rank by HDI
China	70	69	2,124	0.716	22	66
Libya	62	66	7,250	0.719	103	67
South Africa	61	70	4,981	0.731	82	68
Lebanon	68	78	2,250	0.735	78	69
Mongolia	64	90	2,000	0.737	57	70
Nicaragua	64	88	2,209	0.743	54	71
Turkey	65	74	3,781	0.751	71	72
Jordan	67	75	3,161	0.752	76	73
Peru	63	85	3,129	0.753	74	74
Ecuador	66	83	2,687	0.758	68	75
Iraq	65	89	2,400	0.759	96	76
United Arab Emirates	71	60	12,191	0.782	127	77
Thailand	66	91	2,576	0.783	55	78
Paraguay	67	88	2,603	0.784	65	79
Brazil	65	78	4,307	0.784	85	80
Mauritius	69	83	2,617	0.788	75	81
North Korea	70	90	2,000	0.789	67	82
Sri Lanka	71	87	2,053	0.789	38	83
Albania	72	85	2,000	0.790	61	84
Malaysia	70	74	3,849	0.800	80	85
Columbia	65	88	3,524	0.801	72	86
Jamaica	74	82	2,506	0.824	62	87
Kuwait	73	70	13,843	0.839	122	88
Venezuela	70	87	4,306	0.861	95	89
Romania	71	96	3,000	0.863	84	90
Mexico	69	90	4,624	0.876	81	91
Cuba	74	96	2,500	0.877	66	92
Panama	72	89	4,009	0.883	88	93
Trinidad and Tobago	71	96	3,664	0.885	100	94
Portugal	74	85	5,597	0.899	94	95
Singapore	73	86	12,790	0.899	110	96
South Korea	70	95	4,832	0.903	92	97
Poland	72	98	4,000	0.910	83	98
Argentina	71	96	4,647	0.910	89	99
Yugoslavia	72	92	5,000	0.913	90	100
Hungary	71	98	4,500	0.915	87	101
Uruguay	71	95	5,063	0.916	86	102
Costa Rica	75	93	3,760	0.916	77	103
Bulgaria	72	93	4,750	0.918	99	104
USSR	70	99	6,000	0.920	101	105
Czechoslovakia	72	98	7,750	0.931	102	106
Chile	72	98	4,862	0.931	73	107
Hongkong	76	88	13,906	0.936	111	108
Greece	76	93	5,500	0.949	98	109
East Germany	74	99	8,000	0.953	115	110
Israel	76	95	9,182	0.957	108	111
USA	76	96	17,615	0.961	129	112
Austria	74	99	12,386	0.961	118	113
Ireland	74	99	8,566	0.961	106	114
Spain	77	95	8,989	0.965	105	115
Belgium	75	99	13,140	0.966	116	116
Italy	76	97	10,682	0.966	112	117
New Zealand	75	99	10,541	0.966	109	118
West Germany	75	99	14,730	0.967	120	119
Finland	75	99	12,795	0.967	121	120
Britain	76	99	12,270	0.970	113	121
Denmark	76	99	15,119	0.971	123	122
France	76	99	13,961	0.974	119	123
Australia	76	99	11,782	0.978	114	124
Norway	77	99	15,940	0.983	128	125
Canada	77	99	16,375	0.983	124	126
Holland	77	99	12,661	0.984	117	127
Switzerland	77	99	15,403	0.986	130	128
Sweden	77	99	13,780	0.987	125	129
Japan	78	99	13,135	0.996	126	130

Countries with population over 1 million. GDP refers to gross domestic product, GNP to gross national product, and PPP to purchasing power parity.

The Linkage Between Debt and Trade. The need for developing nations to spend so much of their earnings on repaying this external debt has also hurt the U.S. business community. In 1986, for example, Latin American countries purchased 8 billion dollars less in U.S. products than they had purchased just 6 years earlier. Part of this deterioration in trade is explained by the need for Latin American countries to divert money to debt repayments. Part is also due to the need to encourage export activity and discourage imports in order to build up hard currency reserves required to pay off external obligations.[42] Consequently, several of these nations devalued their currencies vis-à-vis the U.S. dollar, thereby making their exports more attractive in the American market, but at the same time making U.S. imports into their countries prohibitively expensive. In Mexico, for example, the peso was worth 22 to a dollar in 1981, but then plummeted to almost 3,000 to a dollar entering the 1990s. With a peso worth so little in comparison to the U.S. dollar in the mid to late 1980s, it became very difficult for many Mexicans to purchase goods made in the United States. The U.S. Department of Commerce estimates that each billion dollars in exports creates approximately 25,000 jobs in the United States. The loss of 23 billion dollars in exports to Latin America during the first part of the 1980s could have conceivably cost the United States 575,000 jobs, many of which were in the already depressed manufacturing sector.

Jobs and Illegal Immigration

Another spillover effect impacting upon American society is in the domain of illegal immigration. We discussed the political implications of immigration in Chapter 5 and here will talk about economic implications. Some of the people in developing nations, recognizing the limited employment and income prospects in their own home countries, have decided to vote with their feet and find a new homeland, regardless of whether they are officially welcomed or not in their "adopted" country. Illegal immigration has plagued the United States for a number of years and has emerged as an important foreign policy issue. It will probably become an even more acute issue in the future because the International Labor Organization (ILO) estimates that up to 1 billion jobs will be needed worldwide for new workers between the mid-1980s and the year 2000, with 880 million of those looking for these new jobs residing in the Third World.[43]

In many respects, the United States itself is a land of immigrants, with approximately 40 million arriving between 1820 and 1950 and another 25 million between 1950 and 1992. Prior to the 1920s, few barriers were placed in the way of immigrants, with the major exception being restrictions placed on Chinese immigration beginning in 1882 and informal restrictions on Japanese immigration commencing in 1907. In 1924, country preferences were established which heavily favored immigrants from the British Isles and

Northwest Europe. However, this restrictive policy was not extended to the Western hemisphere, with open borders still being available at that time to U.S. neighbors to the north and south.[44] This immigration policy which had so heavily discriminated against people from various parts of the globe was officially changed in 1965, but strict limits were placed on the number of people entering the United States from anywhere in the world. The Immigration Law of 1990 has boosted quotas by 40 percent and has authorized 675,000 people to enter the United States annually over the next decade.[45] In addition, over 130,000 refugees will be welcomed to the United States on a yearly basis.

Lack of employment opportunities at home prompted a massive wave of illegal immigrants, mainly from Mexico and Latin America, to enter the United States during the 1970s and 1980s. Some also crossed U.S. borders to escape very unstable political and economic conditions at home. For example, it is estimated that one-fifth of the entire population of El Salvador now resides in the United States, with most entering the country illegally.[46] It is difficult to pinpoint how many illegal immigrants have actually settled in the United States, but certainly a few million had established roots by the beginning of the 1990s.[47] The motivations for such immigration are easy to understand. Before a modest improvement registered in the 1989-92 period, the average Mexican had suffered a 40 percent decline in his living standards during most of the 1980s, and unemployment and underemployment were estimated to be close to 40 percent. In 1993, an employed Mexican who worked for 240 days at the minimum wage, would earn a little more than 1,000 dollars. In contrast, the earnings on a job in the United States at the minimum wage would be almost 8,200 dollars. If an undocumented worker were caught by agents of the U.S. Immigration and Naturalization Service (INS), not carrying a weapon, the penalty would simply have been deportation back across the border. The person could then once again attempt to reenter the United States, and if caught, would face deportation one more time. In effect, the benefits to be gained from employment in the United States far outweigh the potential penalties.

Furthermore, a fair number of these illegal immigrants do not intend to remain in the United States on a permanent basis. For example, a Colegio de Mexico study estimates that undocumented workers in the United States contribute at least one-half of the income for 100 or more villages in Mexico. Many of these people work in the United States on a seasonal basis and then return to their home villages. This transfer of funds from the Mexican workers in the U.S. back to Mexico is estimated to be the third largest source of foreign revenue for Mexico.[48]

Moreover, the issue of immigration is highly complex. Most Americans are alarmed at the entry of so many illegal immigrants and wonder aloud what methods should be utilized by a sovereign nation to defend its own borders. In effect, can a nation maintain political and economic stability and prosperity if anyone can choose to take up residency? On the other hand, for the first 140 years of its existence, the United States maintained open borders and emerged at the end of that period as the dominant economic power in the world, with a highly stable and responsive republican system of government.

The vast majority of U.S. citizens do believe that immigration should continue, but at moderate and controlled levels. Nonetheless, some resent any form of immigration, believing that the country already has enough people, or fearing that new arrivals might take jobs away from Americans, particularly those in unskilled or low-skilled occupations. Others insist that taxpayers unfairly bear the brunt of higher social welfare payments associated with the arrival of impoverished illegal immigrants. Still others are simply xenophobic (an irrational fear of foreigners or strangers) or downright racist. The open hostility to the Chinese, Japanese, non-Western Europeans, and Jews manifested in earlier U.S. immigration laws also indicates that even the U.S. government has at times engaged in blatant discrimination.

On the opposite side of the coin, "brain drain" immigration must certainly be considered as a major plus for America's future. Many highly skilled people have entered the United States with aspirations of carrying forth with their professional activities. Almost one-third of all living American Nobel Prize winners are immigrants, as are one-quarter of the members of the National Academy of Sciences. These figures would be much higher if one were to add those illustrious citizens whose parents or grandparents had previously immigrated to the United States.[49]

In addition, migrant laborers, often from south of the border, have been willing to harvest a good part of America's crop production. Such jobs, which pay very little and require intense physical labor under arduous conditions, but which are critical to U.S. economic prosperity, are often not of interest to American citizens.

Moreover, Americans are living in an aging society, with young men and women representing an increasingly smaller percentage of the overall population. In stark contrast, over 50 percent of the people in the Third World are under the age of 18. Eventually, the United States may have dire need of younger people from around the world to fill manufacturing and service-related jobs.[50]

The United States may also serve its own interests in acting as a "safety valve" until Mexico and other neighboring nations can achieve economic success.[51] As long as some of the unemployed and discontented in these countries can find work in the United States, the chances of political turmoil or even revolution south of the border are diminished. Without this safety valve, the possibilities of major upheavals increase dramatically, leaving the United States with the specter of having unstable and perhaps even hostile neighbors to the south. A massive deportation of illegal immigrants back to their home countries would also exacerbate an already precarious economic climate in these nations.

Mexico is also very special in terms of the historical development of the United States. In the short period between 1845 and 1853, the U.S. government either confiscated or purchased over one-half of Mexico, with most of the land seized by conquest. The territory encompassing much of California, Nevada, Utah, Arizona, New Mexico, Colorado, and Texas, comprising almost one-third of the land area of the continental United States, was once part of Mexico. Thus, from an historical vantage point, a Mexican might have ambivalent feelings about the legality or illegality of setting up a residence in the southwestern portion of the United States.

On the other hand, even if the speculative points mentioned above are accurate, Americans do want new entrants to arrive in the country legally and in an orderly fashion. In an effort to cut back dramatically on the entry of illegal aliens, the Congress of the United States passed into law the Immigration Reform and Control Act of 1986. This act permits illegal immigrants who can prove that they arrived in the United States before January 1, 1982, to apply for temporary residency status, and later on for permanent residency. Over 2 million people have now been granted temporary residency status as a result of this new law. However, those arriving after 1982 can no longer remain in the country, and employers now face stiff sanctions for knowingly hiring an illegal alien. The rationale put forward by Congress is that if employment opportunities are no longer available, illegals will not have an incentive to enter the country. Conversely, employers feel that too much of the burden has been placed on their shoulders, and some Hispanic groups contend that Spanish-speaking Americans may now face open discrimination in the work place. It is still too early to ascertain if the new legislation will drastically curtail illegal immigration, or what negative impact it might have on Hispanic Americans.

RESOURCE DEPENDENCY

Even though the United States is one of the most richly endowed nations in the world, it remains dependent on other countries for many raw materials needed to maintain its strategic readiness and its citizens' standard of living.[52] Americans still bitterly remember the severe costs in time, money, and convenience of the U.S. dependence on OPEC oil suppliers in the 1970s. Currently, the United States depends on the volatile Persian Gulf region for 10 percent of its oil supply, and this is expected to increase by the end of the 1990s.[53]

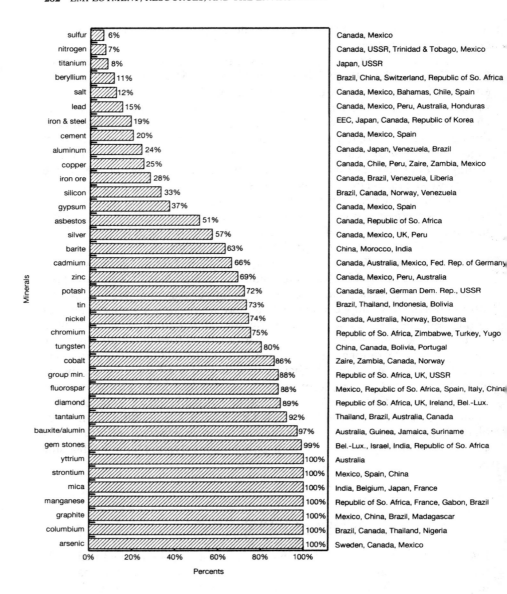

Mineral	Percent	Source countries
sulfur	6%	Canada, Mexico
nitrogen	7%	Canada, USSR, Trinidad & Tobago, Mexico
titanium	8%	Japan, USSR
beryllium	11%	Brazil, China, Switzerland, Republic of So. Africa
salt	12%	Canada, Mexico, Bahamas, Chile, Spain
lead	15%	Canada, Mexico, Peru, Australia, Honduras
iron & steel	19%	EEC, Japan, Canada, Republic of Korea
cement	20%	Canada, Mexico, Spain
aluminum	24%	Canada, Japan, Venezuela, Brazil
copper	25%	Canada, Chile, Peru, Zaire, Zambia, Mexico
iron ore	28%	Canada, Brazil, Venezuela, Liberia
silicon	33%	Brazil, Canada, Norway, Venezuela
gypsum	37%	Canada, Mexico, Spain
asbestos	51%	Canada, Republic of So. Africa
silver	57%	Canada, Mexico, UK, Peru
barite	63%	China, Morocco, India
cadmium	66%	Canada, Australia, Mexico, Fed. Rep. of Germany
zinc	69%	Canada, Mexico, Peru, Australia
potash	72%	Canada, Israel, German Dem. Rep., USSR
tin	73%	Brazil, Thailand, Indonesia, Bolivia
nickel	74%	Canada, Australia, Norway, Botswana
chromium	75%	Republic of So. Africa, Zimbabwe, Turkey, Yugo
tungsten	80%	China, Canada, Bolivia, Portugal
cobalt	86%	Zaire, Zambia, Canada, Norway
group min.	88%	Republic of So. Africa, UK, USSR
fluorospar	88%	Mexico, Republic of So. Africa, Spain, Italy, China
diamond	89%	Republic of So. Africa, UK, Ireland, Bel.-Lux.
tantaium	92%	Thailand, Brazil, Australia, Canada
bauxite/alumin	97%	Australia, Guinea, Jamaica, Suriname
gem stones	99%	Bel.-Lux., Israel, India, Republic of So. Africa
yttrium	100%	Australia
strontium	100%	Mexico, Spain, China
mica	100%	India, Belgium, Japan, France
manganese	100%	Republic of So. Africa, France, Gabon, Brazil
graphite	100%	Mexico, China, Brazil, Madagascar
columbium	100%	Brazil, Canada, Thailand, Nigeria
arsenic	100%	Sweden, Canada, Mexico

FIGURE 11-1
U.S. Dependency on Mineral Imports
Source: U.S. Department of the Interior. Bureau of Mines.
Mineral Commodity Summaries 1988, p. 2.

Figure 11-1 indicates the degree of U.S. dependence on various minerals and the main foreign suppliers of such minerals. Entering the 1990s, the United States remains dependent on overseas sources for one-half of its oil, and also imports 50 percent or more of 37 strategic minerals required to maintain the U.S. national security and industrial base. To illustrate U.S. vulnerability, one should remember that to manufacture a single jet fighter engine requires various amounts of cobalt, chromium, columbium, tungsten, and tantalum, all of which appear on the dependency list.

Eighteen countries or groups of nations supply at least 20 percent of one or more of the minerals on the strategic minerals list. Five of these are considered as major U.S. suppliers: Canada, Mexico, Australia, the Western European group, and South Africa. South Africa is particularly important as a leading supplier of chromium, fluorspar, manganese, platinum group metals, and vanadium.[54]

This resource dependency makes the United States vulnerable to supply cutoffs, dramatic mineral price fluctuations, and disruptions in shipping. Yet in spite of potential dire consequences, U.S. policy towards resource dependency has been inconsistent and erratic, prompting one critic to charge that "in many cases we have simply stuck our head in the sand in the belief that if we ignore the problem long enough, it will go away."[55]

Several options should certainly be considered by decision-makers in Washington. First of all, the United States can make a concerted effort to maintain good relations with the supplier nations, thus minimizing the risk of supply disruptions and unanticipated increases in prices. This option may be very practical in the case of Canada, Mexico, and Australia, but may be extremely difficult insofar as relations with the republics in the former Soviet Union and South Africa are concerned.

Secondly, the United States could establish buffer stocks which would provide up to a three-year supply of the strategic minerals in the event of a national emergency.[56] In case of political or economic uncertainty, this stockpile could be used until such time as international conditions improved or new supplies could be acquired elsewhere. Washington took a modest step in this direction with the establishment of a National Defense Stockpile and a Strategic Petroleum Reserve. Oil, for example, has been purchased overseas and then pumped into converted salt mines, providing the United States with a couple of month's supply in the case of an emergency.[57] Contingency planning regarding oil is also helped by the fact that the United States has domestic sources of oil and natural gas which can be drilled and refined over a period extending from several months to a few years.

By the mid-1980s, the United States had also stockpiled over 100 percent of its stated goal for manganese, 95 percent for chromium, 50 percent for cobalt, 40 percent for the platinum group metals, and smaller percentages for several other minerals.[58] Because of the U.S. government's budgetary problems, and confidence that the United States could rely on friendly suppliers in times of emergency, a National Security Council report has recommended that the current stockpile goals be drastically trimmed, a recommendation which has not been supported by the Congress.[59] Such a policy would certainly ease pressure on Washington's budget, but at the expense of growing U.S. vulnerability to supply cutoffs by other countries. When one recalls that the United States produced 310,000 aircraft during World War II, the need for strategic minerals in times of national emergency certainly becomes of paramount importance.[60]

Thirdly, Washington can encourage recycling, new processing technologies, and the use of substitute products for raw materials now obtained from potentially unreliable overseas suppliers. This latter strategy is referred to as import substitution, and would help lessen U.S. dependence on other nations. Unfortunately, suitable substitutes are only available for a small number of critical resources.

Fourthly, conservation efforts could be encouraged, similar to what occurred during the oil crisis of the 1970s and early 1980s. In 1973, for example, a car in the United States averaged 13 miles per gallon. That average has now been more than doubled. Better fuel-efficient equipment, greater reliance on mass transit, and the expanded use of insulation material have also helped to reduce reliance on overseas petroleum products. Nevertheless, as global petroleum prices fell and U.S. domestic production was curtailed, America's reliance on foreign oil increased by more than half just over the past decade.

In an overall perspective, the United States is much richer in raw materials than either the European Community or Japan. Nonetheless, policymakers must face up to the fact that America is increasingly dependent on raw materials and goods and services from abroad. Furthermore, reliance on the second option listed above can certainly be prohibitively expensive and siphon funds away from more constructive endeavors. On the other hand, a welcome benefit of the end to the Cold War has been markedly higher shipments of key minerals from nations in the former Soviet Union and in Eastern Europe. Without any doubt, a world in which tensions have eased should certainly diminish the prospects of future resource wars. Consequently, fostering international cooperation and agreement on the ground rules for buying, selling, and transporting key raw materials must be a policy priority for future U.S. administrations.[61]

ENVIRONMENTAL CONCERNS

Few issues illustrate the concept of U.S. vincibility more dramatically than environmental concerns. The human species is rather fragile, and relatively small changes in the earth's life-support systems could do irreparable damage to civilization and life as we now know it. In addition, most of the problems confronting humankind in the environmental arena are beyond the control of individual nation-states. In 1986, a chemical spill into the Rhine River from a plant located in Switzerland caused significant environmental damage in Germany and the Netherlands. That same year, the Chernobyl nuclear plant explosion in the Soviet Union resulted in an increased risk of cancer for thousands of people throughout Europe. Emissions from smokestacks in Ohio are causing the demise of forests and lakes in the Canadian provinces of Ontario and Quebec. The release into the atmosphere of chlorofluorocarbons (CFCs) from a plant in Poland can increase the risk of cancer for sunbathers on the beaches of southern California. Obviously, joint international action to combat environmental deterioration is required, and Washington will be burdened with the responsibility of helping to initiate and maintain fruitful consultations with nations around the globe. National leaders must also grapple with convincing their own rank-and-file citizens that environmental problems are a societal priority and that not only tax money must be allocated for this purpose, but that the daily lives of these citizens may have to change dramatically in order to stave off both environmental and resource deterioration. As former Prime Minister Gro Harlem Brundtland of Norway has admonished: "Unless we are able to translate our words into a language that can reach the minds and hearts of people young and old, we shall not be able to undertake the extensive social changes needed to correct the course of development."[62]

Ecology and economic development are also closely intertwined. As the UN-sponsored World Commission on Environment and Development, otherwise known as the Brundtland Commission, has noted: "Ecology and economy are becoming ever more interwoven—locally, regionally, nationally, and globally—into a seamless net of causes and effects."[63] As the Commission observes, deforestation by highland farmers is causing flooding on lowland farms, and factory pollution in urban areas is threatening the catch of people who fish hundreds of miles away.[64]

From birth to death, Americans reportedly spend 95 percent of their lives indoors. Yet the current era requires a great awareness and sensitivity for what is transpiring on, below, and above the earth's surface.[65] Some of the environmentally-related issues which will demand action by the U.S. foreign policy community include the following.

The Greenhouse Effect. The earth's atmosphere is a fragile thin blue layer encircling the crust of the planet, and is less than 1/1000th the size of the earth's diameter. This atmosphere is suffering from a buildup of carbon dioxide and five other major gases.[66] Almost 80 percent of the carbon dioxide emissions emanate from cars and factories in the industrialized countries, but there is now a rapid growth in such discharges from the developing nations as well. Over several decades, this buildup could potentially lead to the greenhouse effect which would raise the earth's temperature from three to eight degrees Fahrenheit, having a dramatic impact on which land would be suitable for crop production, which land would be too arid, and which land would likely be under water.[67] As a result of higher surface temperatures, severe flooding could occur in low-lying coastal cities and river deltas; in addition, temperature changes affect the distribution of rainfall, the intensity of storms and droughts, and the direction of prevailing winds and ocean currents. To show the potential impact of just a few degrees change in temperature, many scientists estimate that the last ice age started when temperatures dropped on average by as little as four degrees Fahrenheit.

On the positive side, some progress has definitely been made in a few countries toward controlling certain carbon dioxide emissions. For example, air over the United States now contains less sulfur and lead than 20 years ago, even though economic production rose 80 percent, the population increased by 20 percent, and the number of cars in use grew by 50 percent. Over 750 billion dollars was spent on clean air projects during that period, and 80 billion dollars is currently being expended annually, mostly private spending to comply with mandated fuel and equipment standards. The amount of energy that Americans use to produce 1 dollar's worth of output actually fell by nearly one-third during the past 2 decades.[68] The implementation of the 1990 Clean Air Act will result in further progress in coping with air quality problems in the United States.

Nonetheless, America's air is very dirty in many metropolitan areas. At the global level, continued economic expansion, population growth, and persistent reliance on burning fossil fuels for transportation and manufacturing will result in greater emissions into the atmosphere, increasing the probability of a severe greenhouse effect. Indeed, six of the seven warmest years in recorded history occurred during the period 1980-91.[69]

This environmental issue, as well as most others, indicates very clearly that possible solutions are beyond the purview of the individual nation-state. Even if Washington were to launch an even more comprehensive campaign to decrease carbon dioxide emissions, the greenhouse effect could still occur because of inaction in other countries. In addition, it will be extremely costly to make the transition globally from fossil fuels to alternate energy sources. Fossil fuels currently provide 78 percent of the world's total energy, with oil providing 33 percent, coal 27 percent, and natural gas 18 percent.[70]

Finding multilateral solutions to global warming is further complicated by the fact that some poor nations simply cannot afford to shift from the use of fossil fuels. Others also have huge coal reserves at their disposal, and coal is a major source of the troublesome carbon dioxide emissions. Thus, if the coal-rich People's Republic of China persists with plans to build 200 coal-fired generating stations, any savings in the United States might be negated. A potential solution to this dilemma may be the transfer of significant aid from the North to the South to help developing countries to use alternative energy sources, thereby improving the standard of living of their people while at the same time slowing the process of environmental degradation. Alarmingly, issues of economic growth, national sovereignty, and inadequate North-South transfers may well impede the resolution of this potentially devastating environmental problem.

Ozone Deterioration. Ozone is located in the stratosphere about 30 miles above the earth's surface and helps absorb and reflect most of the harmful ultraviolet rays from the sun. Through the introduction of commercially used inert gases such as CFCs and halons into the atmosphere, ozone molecules are being broken down and the ozone layer is decomposing, leading to a thinning atmospheric hole about the size of the continental United States. Such a deterioration will lead to greater exposure to ultraviolet radiation and could lead to higher incidents of skin cancer and blindness, reduced crop yields, and damage to marine life.[71] Over the Antarctic, about a 50 percent depletion in the ozone layer has already taken place, prompting some scientists to fear that the destruction of this critical atmospheric shield is occurring at a much more rapid rate than first suspected.

The principal commercial uses for these chlorine compounds are as propellants in aerosol sprays, as fluids in refrigeration systems, and as ingredients in plastics manufacturing. The United States, Canada, and parts of Scandinavia have already banned or restricted nonessential aerosol uses and have limited the industrial use of some chlorine compounds, such as CFCs. In 1985, the United Nations Environment Program brought together most of the industrialized nations in Vienna to discuss the issue. A document was signed pledging to give serious consideration to reducing chlorine emissions, but a timetable on specific control measures was not worked out. As was emphasized at the Vienna meeting, the ozone problem is not simply a national or regional problem, for "the ozone layer protects every square meter of our planet and therefore every person from every continent and country."[72]

At a 1987 conference in Montreal, a protocol was adopted which would slowly reduce these harmful emissions, and at a 1990 session in London and a 1992 meeting in Copenhagen, 86 nations agreed to hasten the phasing out of the production and use of chlorofluorocarbons. Because the eventual ban on CFCs will place an additional burden on developing countries, the major Western nations will be expected to contribute to an international fund earmarked for economic development in the Third World.

Acid Rain. This destructive form of precipitation is produced when sulfur dioxide and nitrogen oxides mix with rainwater and fall to earth as snow or rain. Acid rain may travel hundreds or even thousands of miles and is capable of destroying both plant and animal life. Primarily as a result of acid rain, over 15,000 lakes in North America and Europe are now biologically dead and more than 75 million acres of forests have been badly damaged, an area almost the size of Texas. Moreover, acid rain is no respecter of boundaries, with more than 50 percent of the acid rain which has fallen on Canada in recent years emanating from sulfur dioxide and nitrogen oxide emissions in the United States. The Canadian government estimates that 14,000 lakes have been acidified, more than 300,000 other lakes are threatened, and 84 percent of the most productive agricultural lands in eastern Canada suffer from dangerous levels of acid deposits. In addition, 55 percent of eastern Canada's forests, which generate more than 10 billion dollars worth of forest products, are in areas where acid rain falls. Moreover, almost 80 percent of all Canadians live in areas where acid rain deposits are high.[73]

The costs of cleaning up acid rain are immense. In the case of the United States, most of the problem is linked to power plants and manufacturing facilities in the Midwest, an area which has not prospered significantly in recent years. Tens of billions of dollars will be needed to retrofit plants, install scrubbers, and introduce limestone injection processes which would reduce the buildup of sulfur dioxide. Thousands of jobs will probably be lost and workers dislocated during the transition period to cleaner plants and to the use of low-sulfur coal. Moreover, would the high price tag be picked up by the customers of the utilities and plants causing the acid rain, or would the U.S. taxpayer be expected to foot the bill? Would Canada's problems be sufficiently important to convince Washington to proceed full speed with reforms, or must more damage occur within the United States before the issue would be moved from the foreign policy backburner to the domestic policy frontburner? What sort of international arrangement can be made to eradicate acid rain, and who will bear the costs of the cleanup? As can be readily seen, the issue is very complex and certainly illustrates quite well that in an age of growing interdependence, the line between "foreign" policy and "domestic" policy has been blurred substantially.[74] In 1990, Washington at least began the process of reducing acid rain emissions through the passage of a long overdue Clean Air Act. However, the United States and the other advanced industrial societies will have to do much more before this killer of plant and animal life is eradicated.[75]

Nuclear Power Plant Accidents. The Chernobyl nuclear power plant accident which occurred in 1986 originally caused the deaths of more than 30 people. It also spread a cloud of radiation which eventually circled the globe. This cloud has increased the chances that thousands of people, particularly in the former Soviet Union and in Europe, will eventually contract cancer.

At the beginning of 1990, 5 percent of the energy consumed worldwide was generated by 426 commercial nuclear reactors, with France receiving 75 percent of its electricity from nuclear reactors, Germany over 30 percent, Japan 28 percent, the United Kingdom 22 percent, the United States 20 percent, and the former USSR, site of the Chernobyl disaster, 12 percent.[76] In spite of this dependency on nuclear power as a source of electricity, can these nuclear reactors be operated safely without a repeat of the Chernobyl disaster or the near catastrophe at the Three-Mile Island facility in Pennsylvania? This issue will vex policy-makers for years to come.

Nuclear Waste Disposal. Once fuel has been used up by nuclear power plants, the waste material which remains is highly radioactive and extremely dangerous to all forms of life. Few areas want to be repositories for the spent fuel and governments have had extreme difficulty in agreeing either nationally or internationally to acceptable methods for disposing of progressively larger amounts of nuclear waste.[77] Disposal is further complicated by the fact that some of the spent nuclear fuel can actually be used in the production of nuclear weapons.

Chemical Accidents and Chemical Waste Disposal. Approximately 70,000 chemicals are now used on a daily basis, with about 1,000 new ones being invented every year. Unfortunately, some manufacturers and users have been negligent if not criminal in their fabrication and disposal of these chemicals. For example, a major part of a town in northern New York was found in 1983 to have been built on a site contaminated by highly dangerous chemicals. Similar sites have been found in various nations around the world, increasing the risk of serious illness for unsuspecting residents. Some of this waste is also carried on waterways or in underground streams to other nations, making the problem international in scope. Although domestic penalties for such careless disposal practices have increased substantially, many dangerous waste deposits remain and only marginal action has been taken to deal with this problem at the international level.

Chemical plant accidents may also be just as dangerous as nuclear plant catastrophes. For example, the 1984 leak at a pesticides factory owned by a U.S. firm in Bhopal, India killed more than 2,000 people and injured another 150,000. International standards for the maintenance and inspection of chemical plants are needed in order to avoid the repetition of Bhopal-like disasters, and nations must also work together to formulate and implement policies which will protect people from the improper use of toxic chemicals.

Loss of Fresh Water. Many nations, including the United States, are now suffering from decreasing stream flows, falling water tables, and aquifer depletion. In the U.S., for example, one-fifth of the irrigated cropland is supported by the Ogallala aquifer (an underground water reserve), and perhaps one-half of this aquifer has already been depleted in certain parts of Texas, New Mexico, and Kansas.[78]

Because fresh water is an absolute necessity for human and animal life, as well as crop production, the issue is becoming increasingly important on the international agenda. Dirty water may be responsible for killing 25 million people a year in the developing world, and in these countries water is believed to be the principal transmission agent for 80 percent of the diseases that afflict their citizens. With the exception of the People's Republic of China, 2 out of 4 people in the developing countries do not have access to clean water, and 3 of 4 suffer from an unacceptable level of sanitation. In contrast, 9 of 10 people in the developed countries have access to clean, piped water and to an acceptable level of sanitation.[79]

Technology already exists to provide clean water and proper sanitation facilities to earth's inhabitants, but the costs are generally beyond the capacity of many developing nations to pay. As for the problem of diminishing fresh water, one solution is to convert salt water into fresh water, but the costs are ten times greater than using conventional freshwater sources. Better conservation methods, the recycling of agricultural water, the use of drip irrigation, water diversion projects, improved watersheds, the cleaning of lakes, rivers, and streams, and other innovations must be adopted in order to confront this problem head on.

Depletion of Fisheries. Almost 70 million tons of fish are being removed from the earth's oceans and waterways every year. Many believe that overfishing is occurring in various parts of the world, prompting a 15 percent decrease in the fish catch since 1970.[80] Cod stocks are dwindling off North America's Atlantic coast, driftnet fishing in the north Pacific is taking a toll on salmon, steelhead, porpoises, and seabirds, and up to 100,000 dolphins have perished each year in the nets used by commercial fishing vessels to catch tuna in the eastern Pacific.[81] Because oceans are generally considered as international waterways, a multilateral agreement on the rules for fishing and replenishing fish stocks is the best alternative available for coping with this growing problem, but thus far negligible progress has been made.

Desertification, Deforestation, and Soil Erosion. The total surface area of the earth is almost 200 million square miles, but 70 percent of the surface is covered by water and only 30 percent by land. Eleven percent of the land is permanently under ice, 10 percent is tundra (a treeless plain with a permanently frozen subsoil), and another one-third is arid or semiarid. About one-tenth of the total ice-free land area, or about 1.5 billion hectares (3.7 billion acres), can be readily cultivated, with another 13 percent cultivable at great effort and expense.[82] Currently, this relatively small proportion of productive land on earth is being destroyed at alarming rates. Approximately 6 percent of 'forest land has been lost over the past decade and perhaps one-third of the world's rain forests has been decimated, mainly due to population pressures, inappropriate farming techniques, and the demand by Western consumers for tropical hardwoods, exotic fruits, and beef.[83] About one-half of the world's population also relies primarily on biomass for its energy needs, mainly in the form of firewood. Most of these people are cutting down trees faster than new ones are being planted, creating a major deforestation problem.[84] Thousands of species of plant and animal life are also becoming extinct as forests disappear.

In addition, topsoil vital to growing crops is being eroded at a much more rapid rate than new soil is being formed, with approximately 240 billion tons lost globally during the 1980s, an amount equal to about one-half of the total topsoil on U.S. cropland.[85] A related phenomenon, known as desertification, refers to rangeland deterioration. The United Nations Environment Program estimates that 35 percent of the earth's land surface, on which over 1 billion people depend on their livelihood, is threatened by desertification.[86] Improper grazing patterns contribute to this phenomenon, and desertification is to be found in very productive countries such as the United States, and in very marginal agricultural areas such as parts of Africa. In Africa alone, more than 10 million people have become nomadic "refugees" because of the loss of once productive land to desertification.

Energy Depletion. Much of the world's energy comes from nonrenewable fossil fuel sources (gas, oil, coal) or from nuclear plants which pose substantial risks in case of accidents. As discussed earlier, the burning of some of these fossil fuels may also cause pollution and structural damage to the atmosphere. For the moment, the major renewable sources of energy include hydropower, solar thermal power, solar water heating, wind power, and alcohol fuels. Falling water (hydropower) currently provides about one-quarter of the world's electricity, but the other sources have hardly been tapped. For example, renewable energy sources supply only 10 percent of the electricity used in the United States. Eventually, the United States and the world community of nations will have to resort to conservation measures and to cleaner, less dangerous, and renewable sources of energy, with planning, implementation, and coordination needed at the national, regional, and international levels.

CONCLUSION

Foreign policy-makers in the United States will have their hands full in tackling such diverse issues as global warming, ozone depletion, population growth, water and air pollution, destruction of forests and rangelands, waste disposal, and the proliferation of harmful weapons, issues which were not even on the foreign policy agenda a decade or two ago. In view of these serious international problems, Robert Heilbroner has been prompted to make the following observation: "We are entering a period in which rapid population growth, the presence of obliterative weapons, and dwindling resources will bring international tensions to dangerous levels for an extended period."[87]

The obliterative weapons which exist today have 18,000 megatons of explosive power, or the equivalent of over 3 tons of TNT for every man, woman, and child on the earth.[88] However, with the end of the Cold War and new accords which are designed to reduce strategic weapons held by the United States and the former Soviet republics, many now believe that the threat from obliterative weapons has actually diminished. If this is true, then are human beings finally willing to devote greater attention to making peace with the planet which they inhabit? Are Americans and their counterparts in the North willing to share their bounty and expertise with the far less prosperous people of the South, and will people everywhere embrace the concept of a "sustainable society," a society which satisfies its needs without jeopardizing the prospects of future generations?[89]

Will the world of the twenty-first century be able to find acceptable substitutes for fossil fuels such as oil, natural gas, and coal, as well as for nuclear power? Will conservation measures and innovations in the use of solar, wind, geothermal, and hydropower lead to a far cleaner atmosphere while at the same time not jeopardizing the standard of living of the Northern nations and not hindering economic development in the Third World?[90] Will hunger and starvation finally be conquered?

As for the United States, the big question is whether it is prepared, both in terms of its domestic and foreign policy capacities, to embrace global solutions and to work hand in hand with other nations to develop common responses to these unprecedented environmental, humanitarian, and resource challenges. Certainly, there are some encouraging signs. The United States has participated in several major international conferences dealing with global warming, ozone deterioration, the transportation and disposal of hazardous waste, and other pressing environmental issues. For example, at the UN-sponsored World Environmental Summit held in Rio de Janeiro in June 1992 with representatives of 178 nations in attendance, Washington joined with other governments in signing a global warming convention which will require countries to return to the 1990 level of potentially harmful emissions within a reasonable period of time.[91] The 1990 Clean Air Act, when fully implemented, will contribute significantly to easing the acid rain problem between the United States and Canada, and international protocols are already helping to reduce CFC emissions which will hopefully slow the destruction of the ozone layer. Voters in the major democracies are also better informed about environmental issues, and so-called "Green" parties have actually won seats in several national legislatures and in the European Parliament. In the United States, an increasing number of environmental causes has been championed by representatives of both major political parties.

On the other hand, only marginal substantive progress has been made at the national, regional, or international levels in actually solving many of the environmental problems discussed in this chapter. Even though a plethora of lofty proclamations has been issued, governments around the world have been very hesitant to take the often costly and painful steps to improve environmental quality. Tragically, in the absence of decisive government action, the environment is destined to suffer further degradation, and Americans risk seeing their own quality of life deteriorate.

ENDNOTES

1. Richard Clinton, "Population Dynamics and Future Prospects for Development," in *Ecological Perspectives on World Order,* ed. David W. Orr and Marvin S. Sorous (Chapel Hill: University of North Carolina Press, 1979), 62.
2. Others estimate a population of eight billion by the second or third decade of the next century. See, for example, Just Faaland, "Introduction," in *Population and the World Economy in the 21st Century* (Oxford: Basil Blackwell, 1982), 4, and Lester R. Brown, Christopher Flavin, and Sandra Postel, "Earth Day 2030," *World-Watch* March 1990, 13.
3. In his treatise, "An Essay on the Principle of Population," Thomas Malthus, a nineteenth-century British economist, asserted that global poverty was unavoidable because population was increasing geometrically while food supplies were increasing arithmetically. His projections of population growth proved to be highly inaccurate. The U.S. Census Bureau projections are discussed in Allen Kelley, "The Birth Dearth: The Economic Consequences," *Public Opinion* , 8 (December/January 1986): 57.
4. Clinton, "Population Dynamics," 62.
5. In Paul R. Ehrlich and Ann H. Ehrlich, *The Population Explosion* (New York: Simon & Schuster, 1990), the authors argue that overpopulation is the number one environmental problem, causing hunger, acid rain, smog, global warming, deforestation, and the destruction of other species.
6. Ben J. Wattenberg and Karl Zinsmeister, "The Birth Dearth: Geopolitical Consequences," *Public Opinion* , 8 (December/January 1986): 12.
7. Some commentators believe that the lack of births in the developed countries is actually a major problem for the future. See, for example, Ben J. Wattenberg, *The Birth Dearth* (New York: Pharos Books, 1987).
8. Faaland, *Population and the World Economy,* 3. The replacement level is generally considered to be 2.1 children per woman.
9. Faaland, *Population and the World Economy,* 3.
10. Lester R. Brown, "Stopping Population Growth," in *State of the World, 1985,* ed. Lester Brown et al. (New York: W.W. Norton, 1985), 200.
11. Paul Demeny, "Population Policies," in Faaland, *Population and the World Economy,* 211.
12. Demeny, "Population Policies," 211.
13. Demeny, "Population Policies," 205. The United Nations estimates that 94 percent of the global population growth between 1992 and 2025 will be in developing countries.

14. World Health Organization Report released in April 1990, and Alan Durning, "Life on the Brink," *World-Watch,* March 1990, 2. As Durning emphasized, the world spent 1 trillion dollars for military purposes in 1988, but could not come up with the five dollars per child to eradicate the diseases that killed 14 million that year.

15. See the proceedings of the UN-sponsored World's Summit for Children held in September 1990, and *The New York Times,* 1 October 1990, A10.

16. George A. Schnell and Mark Stephen Monmonier, *The Study of Population* (Columbus, Ohio: Charles E. Merrill, 1983), 41.

17. This issue is discussed in Brown, *World 1985,* 25.

18. T. Kelly White, director of the U.S. Department of Agriculture's Economic Research Service, contends that the world's food system is capable of feeding every inhabitant for at least the next two or three decades, although localized food crises are likely to occur. See Bruce Stokes, "Crowds, Food and Gloom," *National Journal,* 16 September 1989, 2263-66.

19. Lester R. Brown, "The Illusion of Progress," in *State of the World, 1990,* Lester Brown et al., eds. (New York: W.W. Norton, 1990), 3.

20. The World Commission on Environment and Development, *Our Common Future* (Oxford: Oxford University Press, 1987), 29.

21. Hardin's proposal is discussed in Marvin S. Sorous, "Lifeboat Ethics Versus One-Worldism in International Food and Resource Policy," in Orr and Sorous, 131-49. U.N. Development Program, *Human Development Report 1990* (New York: Oxford University Press, 1990), 19-20.

22. In sub-Saharan Africa, life expectancy was only 51 years, compared with 62 for all developing nations and 74 for industrialized countries. The infant mortality rate (under age 1) was nearly 200 deaths per 1,000 births in 1960 compared with 79 in 1987, and the child mortality rate (under age 5) dropped from 243 deaths per 1,000 births to 121. See the UN Development Program, *Human Development Report 1990* (New York: Oxford University Press, 1990), 19-20.

23. This statistic was compiled by UNICEF. See *The New York Times,* 30 June 1990, I, 8.

24. Lester R. Brown et al., *State of the World, 1992* (New York: W.W. Norton, 1992), 3.

25. The Brandt Commission, *North-South: A Program for Survival* (Cambridge, Mass.: MIT Press, 1980), 32.

26. The Washington, D.C.-based Population Crisis Committee released a report in May 1992 detailing the "misery scale" in 141 countries. This group used 10 indicators of well-being: life expectancy, daily calorie intake, access to clean water, infant immunization, secondary school enrollment, per capita income, inflation rate, number of telephones per 1,000 people, political freedom, and civil rights. Approximately 3.5 billion people on earth were considered to endure high suffering, of which 430 million were subject to extreme suffering. Three-quarters of the world's population "live in countries where human suffering is the rule rather than the exception." See *Facts on File,* 9 July 1992, 495.

27. Of these 42 poorest countries, 28 are in Africa, 9 in Asia, 1 in the Americas, and 4 are island nations. See *The New York Times,* 13 February 1990, A3, and the World Bank report on average incomes released in September 1990. In 1989, the average income was 30,270 dollars in Switzerland, 21,100 dollars in the United States, and only 120 dollars in Ethiopia and Tanzania.

28. Faaland, *Population and the World Economy,* 18.

29. The World Commission, *Our Common Future,* 6.

30. The World Commission, *Our Common Future,* 6.

31. Brown, "Stopping Population Growth," 197, and World Commission, *Our Common Future,* 7. According to calculations made by the Stockholm International Peace Research Institute, global spending on defense was 950 billion dollars in 1989, a 2 percent decrease from 1988's spending levels. See "No Peace Dividend Just Yet," *Washington*

Post, 23 May 1990, A38. This annual spending is generally considered to have remained below one trillion dollars during the first part of the 1990s.

32. Louis S. Richman, "Struggling to Save Our Kids," *Fortune,* 10 August 1992, 34, and the U.S. Census, *Reports on Income and Poverty,* 3 September 1992. The official poverty level for a family of four in 1991 was 13,924 dollars.

33. In her book, *Drawing the Line* (Washington, D.C.: Urban Institute, 1990), Patricia Ruggles argues that the U.S. government's formula for determining poverty has not been revised since the early 1960s and is now outdated. If poverty were determined by the U.S. government's current criteria for low-income housing subsidies, the poverty rate for 1987 would have increased from 13.5 percent to 23.4 percent. In 1992, according to a report by the American Public Health Association, the United States ranked nineteenth in the world in terms of infant mortality and twenty-eighth in low birth-weight babies.

34. "Smoking: the Intolerance Spreads," *Economist,* 28 April 1990, 31. Statistics from a *New England Journal of Medicine* study are quoted.

35. The World Bank estimates that at the end of 1991 sub-Saharan Africa's external debt burden was 176 billion dollars, East Asia and the Pacific region's 245 billion dollars, the Mediterranean region's 173 billion dollars, Latin America's 429 billion dollars, the North Africa and Middle East region's 136 billion dollars, and South Asia's 122 billion dollars. See the *Globe and Mail,* 17 August 1992, B1, and the World Bank, *World Debt Tables, 1991-92,* Vol. I (Washington, D.C.: World Bank, 1991), 13.

36. The International Monetary Fund estimates that 184 billion dollars of "flight capital" has left the world's 13 most heavily indebted countries, representing almost one-half of their outstanding foreign debts. See "Looking Beyond Europe's Crisis: The IMF Claims that the World Economy is Poised to Recover," *Economist,* 19 September 1992, 81-82.

37. Brown, "Stopping Population Growth," 200.

38. Report of the UN Development Program. This report ranked 130 developing nations according to a "human development index" which took into account life expectancy, adult literacy rates, and per capita income. Mauritius ranked forty-ninth, the highest of any sub-Saharan African nation (the Republic of South Africa was not included in the survey).

39. Durning, "Life on the Brink," 25. The debt-service ratio was down to 14 percent in 1991 from 32 percent in 1986, and from 45 percent in 1986 to 31 percent in 1991 for the 15 most indebted countries. See "Economic and Financial Indicators," *Economist,* 29 August 1992, 92.

40. *World Factbook, 1991,* 15, 36, 40, 62, 68, 205-6, 249, and 331.

41. *World Factbook,* 24. Another definition for absolute poverty is the "lack of sufficient income in cash or kind to meet the most basic biological needs for food, clothing, and shelter."

42. A hard currency is one which can be used for international commercial transactions. These currencies would primarily include the U.S. dollar, Japanese yen, German mark, British pound, and French franc.

43. Olivia Ward, "Life Without Work?" *World Press Report,* October 1984, 41. Approximately 55 million jobs must be filled each year in the Third World to keep pace with population growth. See "The Year of the Refugee: Voting with their Feet, their Trabants and their Oars," *Economist,* 23 December 1989, 27.

44. These provisions were outlined in the 1924 Immigration and Nationality Act. See Milton D. Morris, *Immigration—The Beleaguered Bureaucracy* (Washington, D.C.: Brookings Institution, 1985), 58.

45. The 1990 Immigration Law permits 465,000 new immigrants annually on the basis of family preferences, 130,000 skilled workers, 10,000 investor-immigrants (mainly millionaires), and 70,000 who fulfill other criteria.

46. *The Wall Street Journal,* 14 May 1987, 54.

47. The immigration phenomenon is discussed in detail in Nathan Glazer, ed., *Clamor at the Gates: The New American Immigration* (San Francisco: Institute for Contemporary Studies Press, 1985). From 1971 through 1980, the Immigration and Naturalization Service seized 8.3 million illegal immigrants, up from 1.6 million in the previous decade. See Morris, *Immigration,* 51.

48. *The Wall Street Journal,* 14 May 1987, 54.

49. Glazer, *Clamor at the Gates,* 18.

50. In his book, *Friends or Strangers: The Impact of Immigrants on the U.S. Economy* (New York: Basic Books, 1990), at 223-25, George J. Borjas argues that the United States should screen legal immigrants more carefully because unskilled immigrants impose an economic cost on U.S. society. He suggests consideration of options such as selling visas to potential immigrants or ranking visa applications on the basis of observable skills.

51. A discussion of Mexican immigration patterns is provided in Silvia Pedraza-Bailey, *Political and Economic Migrants in America: Cubans and Mexicans* (Austin: University of Texas Press, 1985).

52. The Strategic and Critical Materials Stock-Piling Act of 1979 defines strategic and critical materials as "those that (a) would be needed to supply the military, industrial, and essential needs of the United States during a national emergency, and (b) are not found or produced in the United States in sufficient quantities to meet such need." See Kenneth A. Kessel, *Strategic Minerals: U.S. Alternatives* (Washington, D.C.: National Defense University Press, 1990), 14.

53. This forecast was made by CIA Director William Webster in 1989.

54. See Ewan W. Anderson, "Ensuring America's Mineral Supply," *Enterprise,* November/December 1985, 13-15.

55. See Kessel, *Strategic Minerals,* 201. A case study of the battles between the White House and Congress over strategic resource policy in the 1980s is found in Ewan W. Anderson, *The Structure and Dynamics of U.S. Government Policymaking: The Case of Strategic Minerals* (New York: Praeger, 1988).

56. The three-year supply was recommended by the Reagan administration in 1982. See Executive Office of the President, *National Materials and Minerals Program Plan and Report to Congress,* 15 April 1982, 27.

57. The U.S. Strategic Petroleum Reserve is stored in salt caverns along the Louisiana and Texas coasts at a cost of more than 20 billion dollars over the past decade. It now contains about 600 million barrels, enough to replace imports for 50 to 60 days.

58. "The Defense Stockpile: A Measure of Security," *Enterprise,* November/December 1985, 16-18.

59. "The Defense Stockpile," 17.

60. "The Defense Stockpile," 18.

61. A good discussion of the resource dependency issue is found in Ewan W. Anderson, *Strategic Minerals: The Geopolitical Problems for the United States* (New York: Praeger, 1988).

62. *Southam Environmental Project,* 7 October 1989, 3.

63. The World Commission, *Our Common Future,* 5.

64. The World Commission, *Our Common Future,* 5.

65. This statistic is derived from a U.S. Atomic Energy Commission study and is quoted in Michael J. Cohen, *How Nature Works* (Walpole, NH: Stillpoint Publishing, 1988), 17.

66. In the United States, 33 percent of carbon dioxide emissions come from electric plants, 31 percent from vehicles, 24 percent from industries, and 12 percent from residences.

67. There are still many skeptics concerning the greenhouse effect. Although almost everyone is in agreement that the earth's temperature has increased by 1.1 degrees Fahrenheit over the past century, some scientists believe that increased cloud formations and water

vapor which result from warmer temperatures will counterbalance the trend toward even higher temperatures. See *The New York Times*, 16 April 1990, A11.

68. *International Herald Tribune*, 23 April 1990, 4.

69. Brown, *World, 1992*, 3. Record-keeping dates from the mid-nineteenth century.

70. Christopher Flavin, "Slowing Global Warming," in *World, 1990*, ed. Brown, 22.

71. Ozone deterioration and other environmental issues are discussed in detail in Mostafa K. Tolba's *Saving Our Planet* (London: Chapman & Hall, 1992).

72. This statement was made by Mr. Tolba, executive director of the United Nations Environment Program. See the *International Herald Tribune*, 23 April 1990, 20.

73. Canada, Ministry of Environment, *Stopping Acid Rain* (Ottawa: Minister of Supply and Services Canada, 1987).

74. Even if the issue gains domestic notoriety, there is some doubt about the "will" of Washington to solve the problem of clean air. In 1970, Congress passed what many considered a revolutionary Clean Air Act. Although much good has resulted from this legislation, almost 80 million Americans were living in areas with unhealthy air in 1990. The Clean Air Act of 1990 is a hopeful step in the right direction, but much more remains to be accomplished. See *The Wall Street Journal*, 6 April 1987, 52.

75. An excellent jargon-free description of acid rain and other environmental problems is found in *Southam Environmental Project*.

76. Irene Franck and David Brownstone, *The Green Encyclopedia* (Englewood Cliffs, NJ: Prentice Hall, 1992), 211-12.

77. The classification of nuclear waste actually goes beyond the power plant dimension. Spent fuel, high-level waste, and transuranic waste are general by-products of nuclear fuel reprocessing. In addition, low-level waste is generally composed of items such as paper, filters, tools, and gloves utilized by commercial, medical, and industrial enterprises using radioactive material. Mill tailings are another category of nuclear waste and are the by-product of uranium mining and processing. Unless closely supervised and controlled, these types of waste are extremely dangerous to plant and animal life.

78. Brown, *World, 1985*, 51-52.

79. *Southam Environmental Project*, 12-13.

80. Lester R. Brown, *State of the World, 1986* (New York: W.W. Norton, 1986), 10. In 1992, the United States, Mexico, Venezuela, and Vanuatu reached an agreement to ban the setting of nets around schools of tuna that include dolphins. See *The New York Times*, 16 June 1992, D9.

81. *Southam Environmental Project*, 13.

82. Geoffrey Lean, Don Hinrichsen, and Adam Markham, *Atlas of the Environment* (New York: Prentice Hall, 1990), 11. Also consult World Resources Institute, *World Resources 1988-89* (New York: Basic Books, 1988).

83. The Western demand for beef leads to forest land being cleared in order to provide grazing areas.

84. Timothy E. Wirth, "Introduction," in *The Challenge of Global Warming*, Dean Edwin Abrahamson, ed., (Washington, D.C.: Island Press, 1989), xvii.

85. Lester R. Brown and John E. Young, "Feeding the World in the Nineties," in Brown, ed., *World, 1990*, 60.

86. *Southam Environmental Project*, 13.

87. Robert Heilbroner, *An Inquiry into the Human Prospect* (New York: Norton, 1980), 127.

88. Ruth Leger Sivard, *World Military and Social Expenditures, 1989* (Washington, D.C.: World Priorities, 1989), 7.

89. In 1989, Congress enacted a law requiring the federal government to calculate both GNP and "gross sustainable productivity" statistics. The latter would take into account the environmental consequences of expanded economic activity, including resource depletion and damage to the environment. See Brown, *World, 1990*, 9. An informative book

which discusses both the dangers of antienvironmentalism and radical environmentalism is Martin W. Lewis' *Green Delusions* (Durham, NC: Duke University Press, 1992).

90. See Brown and others, "Earth Day 2030," 12-21.
91. However, at the Rio Summit, Washington refused to sign a pact to protect biodiversity (the protection of species and ecosystems), claiming that provisions in the treaty were ill-defined and threatened patents and copyrights issued to U.S.-based companies.

12

U.S. FOREIGN ECONOMIC POLICY

As the previous two chapters have emphasized, the United States remains the foremost economic power in the world, but its lead over other nations has narrowed dramatically. Policy-makers in Washington are facing severe problems in coping with the special challenges now confronting the United States, especially the vulnerability which is a natural by-product of global economic interdependence.

This chapter will indicate how complicated the foreign economic policy process is in the United States, and will illustrate some of the major problems currently facing Washington in trying to keep the economic ship of state on course. Washington's problems may be linked directly to:

1. the relative insularity and parochialism of the United States in an era of economic globalization, which is defined as "the increasing interdependence and interconnectiveness of national economies, including consumers, suppliers, competitors, and markets in general;"[1]

2. complacency and malaise in American society in general and in the U.S. educational system in particular;

3. the insufficient attention accorded to international economic issues in top foreign policy-making circles;

4. institutional weaknesses at the national level which accentuate insularity and hinder policy coordination and long-term planning in the economic sphere;

5. basic infrastructure and business management weaknesses;

6. a significant proliferation in actors at the national and subnational governmental levels and in the private sector who have a direct stake in international economic issues, thereby making it more difficult for the United States to speak with "one voice" on economic matters; and

7. inadequate interactive and decision-making structures bridging together the United States and the other major global economic actors.

These problems, which are linked both to policy-making institutions and processes, are having a dramatic impact on how the U.S. government is reacting to current crises in trade, investment, exchange rates, debt, and overall competitiveness. Whether these problems can be solved satisfactorily will determine to a great degree the future role of the United States in the world economy, and the future openness and stability of the international economic system.

AMERICANS AND THE INTERNATIONAL ECONOMY

After punching fourteen numbers on a push-button phone, the average American in Peoria or Poughkeepsie can be in instantaneous contact with a friend or relative residing in Perth, Australia. Through the satellite-beamed Worldnet system, leaders in Washington can be in visual touch with U.S. representatives and local officials in Beijing, China. Computers linked via satellite can relay financial information within seconds from Wall Street to Tokyo's financial district. And a business executive can enjoy lunch at the Charles de Gaulle Airport in Paris, hop on the Concorde, and be in downtown Manhattan within six hours.

Yet, in spite of these amazing advances in information and transportation which have literally brought the world closer together, the United States remains in many ways a very parochial nation. Just as many people in Galileo's day believed that the universe revolved around the planet earth, so do many Americans persist in believing that the rest of the world revolves around and is dependent upon the United States of America. Moreover, for a good portion of the American people, what occurs outside the United States is relatively unimportant. Even for those people who do view international activities as having a bearing on America's future, many are caught up with the notion that the American "way of life" (in other words, basic values linked to business, government, law, morality, and so on) is exportable and can bring great benefits and blessings to societies around the globe. In this respect, Woodrow Wilson's messianic quest is still alive and well, with exchanges at the international level still viewed by far too many Americans as unidirectional, starting in the United States and then spreading abroad.

American parochialism is especially pronounced in the economic arena. Public opinion surveys consistently find that a majority of Americans, regardless of age, family income, or area of residence, opposes foreign direct investment in the United States, especially the acquisition of existing U.S. firms by foreign enterprises. Up to one-half of Americans believe that foreign trade is either irrelevant or harmful to U.S. interests.[2]

American disinterest or ignorance concerning international phenomena is manifested in other areas as well. The *Dallas Times Herald* commissioned tests in geography, science, and math to twelve-year-olds in eight industrialized countries in 1983. In one group of American students, 20 percent could not find the United States on the world map. On another question, 20 percent of the American students identified Brazil as the United States. The lack of knowledge about specific places, dates, or events should not be construed as meaning that Americans are totally unconcerned or do not possess commonsense perspectives towards such major international problems as nuclear proliferation, strategic and conventional security, or poverty and hunger. Nonetheless, and as will be discussed in greater detail in the next chapter, Americans tend to perform abysmally on these types of tests and the dearth of awareness about what exists both within and outside the boundaries of the United States is very disturbing. The overall foreign policy implications of this lack of awareness have already been discussed in an earlier section of the book.

THE AMERICAN POLITICAL SYSTEM AND ECONOMIC INTERDEPENDENCE

The general lack of interest and awareness among the American public concerning international activities does not necessarily mean that Americans are inherently in favor of parochial or even xenophobic solutions to the serious problems facing the United States in the international economy. On the other hand, it may mean that there will not be a groundswell of resistance among the public to protectionist policies advocated by the executive, legislative, or even at times the judicial branches of government. In addition, the risk of protectionism increases because American consumers are so poorly organized as a pressure group. Recent studies indicate that the average American family may be paying up to 2,000 dollars more per year for goods, services, and taxes because of protectionist rules currently in force in the United States, ranging from quotas on steel to "Buy American" provisions at the state and local government levels.[3] Quotas on Japanese automobiles during the early 1980s may have cost consumers 2,000 to 3,000 dollars extra per car.[4] In terms of consumer costs versus job losses in industries heavily impacted by imports, the U.S. Federal Trade Commission estimated in the mid-1980s that consumers would save almost 13 billion dollars per year if import quotas on automobiles, textiles, sugar, and steel were terminated. According to this report, for every U.S. auto industry job protected during the period of "voluntary" quotas on Japanese cars, consumers paid 240,000 dollars in higher costs. For each dollar in lost wages in the textile, steel, and sugar sectors, consumers would save respectively 19 dollars, 35 dollars, and 24 dollars.[5] With Americans now paying far above the world price for sugar, some academics have concluded that if the price differential were accumulated for just two years, it would exceed the total capital value of all the sugar producers in the United States.[6] The main message to be learned is that American consumers bear the brunt of the costs for tariff and nontariff barriers, but because they are such a disparate group, short-term job preservation strategies usually take precedence over more innovative and long-term trade adjustment policies.

As a consequence, consumers are a numerically strong but organizationally weak pressure group in a political and governmental system which habitually caters to powerful interest groups. Other features of the American system also contribute to the difficulties faced in responding rationally to the special challenges of economic interdependence. For example, in many respects the United States is a highly decentralized society.[7] Stephen Krasner suggests that the United States has been able to maintain a weak political structure because (1) the U.S. was "born strong" and did not need a strong state to destroy a traditional society, (2) until recently, the United States has not confronted a serious external threat to its territorial and political integrity, and (3) the U.S. system has generally been characterized by material abundance and relatively high levels of social equality, conditions which do not foster widespread demands for centralized government.[8]

Fragmentation is certainly a prevailing feature of the contemporary American political and governmental system, especially insofar as foreign economic policy-making is concerned. For one thing, the United States has a federal system of government which constitutionally divides authority to govern among national and regional units. As will be explained in detail later on, these regional or subnational governmental units are now integrally involved in international economic activities and must be considered as very significant actors in certain arenas impacting upon U.S. foreign economic policy. The United States also has a highly fragmented quasi-presidential system which bears little resemblance to the parliamentary systems found in most Western advanced industrial societies.

To the north, Canada has a federal system of government which is much more decentralized than its U.S. counterpart, but its parliamentary system generally permits the opportunity for much more coherent and consistent economic policy-making at the national level. As long as a majority government is seated on Parliament Hill in Ottawa, and party discipline remains a hallmark of the Canadian parliamentary system, the incumbent government will be able to formulate and enact into law most of its economic priorities in a relatively short period of time. In contrast, the United States has a system of separation of powers and checks and balances, which gives each of the three branches of government (executive, legislative, and judicial) some voice in the determination of policies. Except for impeachable offenses, the president is not answerable to Congress for his actions, but neither is Congress required to support the policy positions of the White House. A strong committee and subcommittee system in Congress, and the absence of both highly disciplined and integrated political parties and powerful legislative leaders, make the policy process even more disjointed.

Elections every two years for all members of the House of Representatives and one-third of the members of the Senate, and a campaign contribution system which continues to make private donations the lifeblood of a politician's existence in Washington, insure that locally and nationally based interest groups will have significant clout in the economic policy-making process. The electoral college system for the selection of the American chief executive also works in favor of special or regional interests. As an illustration, the 9 largest steel-producing states in the United States account for 225 of the 270 electoral votes needed to win the presidency. It is therefore politically expedient for a presidential candidate to cater to the steel lobby on certain very sensitive trade-related issues. Far too often these myriad institutional arrangements lead to support for the status quo or for protectionist measures, rather than the promulgation of creative policies to confront the new challenge of economic interdependence.

THE MAKING OF FOREIGN ECONOMIC POLICY IN THE UNITED STATES

A Disjointed Policy Process Favoring Protectionism

U.S. foreign economic policy is formulated and implemented by a variety of departments, agencies, and committees in Washington, D.C. Indeed, far too many people have their fingers in the foreign economic policy pie. Over sixty executive agencies have some role, as do two-thirds of the standing committees in the U.S. Senate and over one-half in the House of Representatives. This plethora of players makes it extremely "difficult to locate the 'center of gravity' for the formulation and execution of foreign economic policy."[9]

Key institutional actors include the Office of the U.S. Trade Representative (USTR), the Department of Commerce, the Department of the Treasury, the State Department, the Department of Agriculture, the Council of Economic Advisers, the National Security Council, the International Trade Commission (ITC), and various cabinet councils and special committees. Depending on the issue involved, the Defense Department (technology transfer, foreign investment, and national security concerns), the Department of Justice (extraterritorial and special legal concerns), the Labor Department (equal opportunity and worker-related concerns), the Interior Department (resource-related concerns), and a bevy of other agencies might be included in the policy-making process. Lawyers representing these institutions seem to be omnipresent and highly technical legal ruminations are an inevitable part of any discussion.

Each agency also has its own constituency and is closely identified with various interest groups. For example, USTR, which is part of the Executive Office of the President, has a staff of approximately 140, but averages seven private-sector advisers for every employee. Its constituency generally consists of those large U.S. companies which are actively involved in international commerce. There is, consequently, a built-in bias favoring an open international trade and investment regime and the enhancement of U.S. business interests overseas. The State Department also generally favors an open regime, but has been criticized from time to time for rendering American commercial interests subservient to diplomatic concerns. Indeed, because of this perceived bias, the State Department's lead role in international trade talks was stripped away by Congress in 1962. With few exceptions, the constituency groups closely aligned with the other departments and agencies in Washington, D.C. have a checkered record concerning advocacy for international economic, business, and labor issues.

In international trade negotiations, American officials fondly refer to the United States as the world's foremost free-trade nation. Yet in spite of this self-laudatory perception, protectionism is alive and well in the nation's capital, with more than 8,000 tariffs and 3,000 nontariff restrictions currently on the government's ledgers.[10] In 1992, for example, quotas and other barriers resulted in Americans paying twice the world price for sugar, and being limited per capita to 7 imported peanuts, 1 pound of imported dairy cheese, and 1 spoonful of imported ice cream. The importation of fresh milk and cream was banned altogether.[11] There are also a plethora of options available to restrict international commerce in the future. Some of these options would include:

Section 201 of the Trade Act of 1974. This escape clause and safeguards statute sets a procedure for granting domestic producers relief from injury caused by rising imports of competitive products. A 201 case may be initiated by an industry group, labor union, or a specific firm, or at the request of the president, USTR, the ITC, the Finance Committee of the U.S. Senate, or the Ways and Means Committee in the U.S. House of Representatives. The president makes the final determination on whether import relief should be granted after having received a recommendation from the ITC. Relief may include tariff increases, quotas, tariff rate quotas (tariff rates which increase once a specified amount of imports have entered the country), orderly marketing agreements (accords which are reached between governments to restrain trade in specified products), or other measures. Compensation may also be provided to trading partners in an attempt to avoid retaliation.

Countervailing Duties. Various tariff acts dating from 1930 stipulate that a countervailing duty may be imposed on products which receive subsidies from foreign governments. In most cases, it must also be substantiated that the subsidized import has injured an American industry. Various groups and the Department of Commerce can initiate a complaint. The Department of Commerce is then authorized to determine whether or not a product is being subsidized, and the ITC determines if a U.S. industry has been injured by the subsidized import. Countervailing duties equal to the amount of the net subsidy can then be imposed on the imports.

Dumping. The Tariff Act of 1930, and subsequent amendments, permit antidumping duties to be imposed on imports which are sold at less than fair value and are injuring competing U.S. products. The criteria for determining an antidumping case include whether or not a product is being sold in the American market for less than it is being sold in the market of the exporting nation or third country markets, and whether a U.S. company producing the same product is being materially injured or "threatened" with being injured by the import. A variety of parties, or the Department of Commerce, can initiate a case, and the Department of Commerce determines whether dumping is occurring and the ITC ascertains whether a U.S. firm has been injured or is threatened with injury. Duties equivalent to the dumping margin can then be assessed.

Section 301. The president is empowered in Section 301 of the Trade Act of 1974 to enforce U.S. rights under bilateral and multilateral trade agreements and to seek the elimination of practices in other countries which discriminate against or restrict U.S. commerce. This authority was expanded substantially in the Omnibus Trade and Competitiveness Act of 1988. A petition may be filed by various parties, or even the president can initiate an investigation. USTR is assigned responsibility for investigating the case and making recommendations to the president. A GATT dispute settlement mechanism may also be pursued in relevant cases. The president may impose duties, quotas, or other trade restrictions, suspend or withdraw trade concessions from the offending nations, or take other "appropriate" actions. The executive branch's review powers cover not only goods, but also services, high technology products, and foreign investment activity. In addition, USTR can initiate its own investigations without waiting for formal complaints to be filed by U.S. industry groups.

The Omnibus Trade and Competitiveness Act of 1988 also created "Super 301," which requires the executive branch to investigate alleged unfair trading practices of other nations and to compile an annual list of major offenders. In 1989, Japan, Brazil, and India were placed on the first annual list. Super 301 instructs the president to negotiate satisfactory solutions to these unfair trade practices with each of these nations. If solutions were not agreed upon, then the United States could proceed to place onerous tariffs on products coming from these countries.

As a result of negotiations, Japan and Brazil were removed from the annual offender's list released in 1990, with India alone cited for a continuation of unfair trading practices harming the interests of American companies. Super 301 has now lapsed, but various members of Congress have threatened to renew it in order to punish nations allegedly engaging in discriminatory trading practices.

Unfair Import Practices. Authority for this action comes from Section 337 of the Tariff Act of 1930 and is an umbrella approach for investigating such unfair practices as infringements on patent, trademark, copyright, or property rights, false advertising, monopolistic practices, theft of trade secrets, etc. A complaint is filed by an interested party or initiated by the ITC. The ITC then determines whether an unfair trade practice has occurred, but the president is left the final say concerning actions to be taken. Products may be excluded from entry into the U.S. and companies and individuals may be issued cease and desist orders. The affected party does retain the right to appeal the decision to the federal court of appeals.

Voluntary restraint agreements (VRAs), orderly marketing agreements (OMAs), trigger price mechanisms (TPMs), tariffs, quotas, tariff rate quotas, rules of origin restrictions, export and technology transfer controls, special Customs Service provisions, subsidies, government procurement and investment codes, antitrust regulations, taxation policies, and the suspension of trading, licensing, and access to credit privileges, are just some of the weapons available to the U.S. federal government to influence import and export activity. This abundant arsenal of protectionist weapons, when combined with the pervasive influence of special interest groups and the disjointed economic policy-making process in Washington, have made it increasingly difficult for the United States to maintain its adherence to an open international trading regime. Indeed, during the 1980s, nontariff restrictions were applied to about 12 percent of U.S. manufactured imports at the beginning of the decade, and nearly 23 percent by the end of the decade. Because of these nontariff barriers, it is now more difficult and more expensive for Americans to buy automobiles, trucks, machine tools, clothing, shoes, semiconductors, steel, sugar, and numerous other products, adding about 50 billion dollars in annual costs for consumer purchases.[12] Moreover, as result of America's huge and lingering trade deficit, there is little reason to believe that protectionist actions will decrease significantly in the foreseeable future.

Steel provides a good case study showing the problems faced by policy-makers in Washington today. The U.S. steel industry was once the dominant global actor, accounting for over 40 percent of world crude steel production in 1955.[13] It was able to maintain its position as the globe's largest and most efficient steel industry into the 1960s, but over the past 2 decades, it has suffered through a spate of major financial upheavals.[14] Between 1979 and 1985, 46 percent of the work force was dismissed and the industry as a whole recorded multi-billion dollar losses. The industry has consistently blamed unfair international competition for its woes and pushed vigorously for governmental assistance. Yet in spite of government support through the imposition of tariff and nontariff barriers, the U.S. steel manufacturers' share of the American market dropped from 98 percent in 1956 to 75 percent in 1990, and it would have been much lower without these stiff barriers.

Steelmakers filed their first case against foreign subsidies as far back as 1923, and have kept up the pressure off and on ever since. During the 1980s, the steel industry used 3 major approaches in its effort to persuade Washington to restrict steel imports even further. First, it filed literally dozens of antidumping and subsidy suits. Secondly, it convinced certain members of Congress to introduce bills which would limit steel imports to a maximum of 15 percent of the U.S. domestic market, down from the 25 percent share at the time. And thirdly, it initiated a Section 201 case at the U.S. International Trade Commission. The ITC eventually ruled that imports were harming the U.S. steel industry, and President Reagan was given 60 days to decide what type of relief, if any, would be given to the industry. In its final report, the ITC recommended 5 years of quotas and additional tariffs, but stressed that this should be coupled with specific pledges from the steel industry to cut management and labor costs and to modernize. The lobbyists for the steel industry understood, of course, the workings of the American political system. President Reagan's decision in this case had to be rendered only a few weeks prior to the national elections of November 1984. Moreover, as was mentioned earlier, the nine largest steel-producing states in the United States account for over 80 percent of the electoral votes needed to select a new chief executive.

Once the ITC had rendered its decision, an interagency group was established to provide options to President Reagan and his small cadre of key White House officials. This group met for a few weeks and prepared several position papers for presidential consideration. A large number of quite disparate preferences was expressed at this interagency gathering, a phenomenon which is not too surprising when one considers the missions and constituency interests of the various departments and agencies. In the end, a prioritized list of options was forwarded to the chief executive. The White House eventually decided on the imposition of 21 VRAs with other nations which would limit their total steel imports to 18 to 20 percent of the U.S. domestic market for a five-year period.

This presidential decision was much more protectionist than had been recommended by the interagency group, but indicates clearly the powerful influence which domestic lobbying can have on the foreign economic policy process in the United States. In effect, President Reagan and his closest political advisors had added up the electoral benefits of steel protection, and decided to placate both the steel industry and the states where the industry is a dominant economic actor.

The restrictions placed on steel imports, with some minor modifications, were extended for an additional 2 1/2 years by the Bush administration in 1989. During the 1988 presidential campaign, George Bush had pledged to the steel-producing states that he would extend the quotas if he were to become the new occupant of the White House. This followed a period when the U.S. steel industry had taken advantage of the lower-valued dollar to amass 2 billion dollars in profits in 1988 alone. In addition, the presidential edict in favor of extended protection was issued in spite of data showing that this protectionism was costing American companies which used steel an extra 7 billion dollars a year and was hindering their ability to be internationally competitive.[15]

Moreover, as is commonplace when protectionist measures are implemented, only modest progress was made in dealing with the structural problems of the U.S. steel industry. First of all, only a token effort was made to modernize plants and to move away from the outmoded techniques used in integrated steel facilities. For example, the United States still makes only about one-half of its steel with efficient continuous casters, versus 95 percent in Japan. Secondly, when relief was offered by Washington, it was not linked to ironclad pledges of improved performance standards by the domestic steel industry and its affiliated unions. Far too frequently, management practices at steel plants were archaic and rigid labor rules thwarted creativity. Companies also tended to take profits, largely derived from protectionism, and to funnel them into nonsteel-related industries such as oil and gas.

In addition, only a few years ago, the wages of unionized steelworkers were 80 percent higher than U.S. manufacturing workers in general, a differential which is incomprehensible.[16] This gap has now been narrowed, but steelworkers continue to be paid much more than their counterparts in most other industrial sectors. However, the price for maintaining this differential has been steep, with 250,000 steelworkers having lost their jobs over the past 15 years.[17] Thirdly, multilateral discussions on the rationalization of steel policy were a rare occurrence and generally unproductive. Hard questions should have been posed at these international forums. For example, why should the United States be expected to be a fair trader in steel when over 45 ercent of the world's steel production, and more than 50 percent in Europe, was fabricated by nationalized (government-controlled) plants? Moreover, even if nationalization were to be phased out internationally, how would a U.S. steelworker earning 5 times more than his South Korean counterpart ever be productive enough to compensate for the huge wage differential? Furthermore, should countries be expected to maintain steel industries for national security reasons even if the industries remain uncompetitive and unprofitable? These are troublesome issues which have yet to be resolved satisfactorily at either the national or multilateral levels.

The Executive Branch

In the U.S. domestic setting, foreign economic policy does not enjoy a lofty position on the overall policy-making agenda of the executive branch of government. Within the Executive Office of the President, only USTR deals primarily with international economic issues, and this office is not even located in the White House-Old Executive Office Building compound. The U.S. Trade Representative does hold a seat in the cabinet, but rarely has this person been a close confidant of the president. The permanent staff of the National Security Council, which has lately numbered about fifty, has had only four or five people at a time who deal extensively with economic matters. The Council of Economic Advisers is generally preoccupied with domestic issues and its chairperson has rarely been close to the chief executive. Moreover, an average of only one or two mid-range members of the White House staff have had assignments within the Executive Office which zero in on important international economic issues.

Not only is foreign economic policy grossly underemphasized in the executive branch, but the policy process itself leaves much to be desired. The process is often very disjointed, complicating efforts to formulate a consistent and coherent economic policy. For example, during the early 1980s, the Cabinet Council on Commerce and Trade was chaired by the Secretary of Commerce. The Trade Policy Committee, which is expected to iron out policy differences between departments and agencies, was headed by the U.S. Trade Representative. The Senior Interagency Group on International Economic Policy was directed by the secretary of the treasury. The National Security Council, headed by the national security adviser, was given responsibility for monitoring and evaluating specific events which might impact upon the international economy. And an Economic Policy Council was created to concentrate on trade and investment issues and to solicit expertise from both within and outside the executive branch.

Assignments for fulfilling specific tasks are also spread among various agencies, and often lack consistency. As an illustration, investment talks with Japan were headed at one time by the State Department, at another time by the

Treasury Department, and yet another time by USTR. The State Department was placed in charge of certain trade negotiations with Japan, while at the same time the Commerce Department was assigned the responsibility for reviewing Japan's "voluntary" quotas on automobiles. USTR attempts to provide some semblance of order by chairing interagency meetings and coordinating the preparation of position papers for the White House. However, at times "coordinators" become "advocates" and this may complicate efforts to reach an interagency consensus on critical trade issues.[18]

Congress

The situation in Congress is even more muddled than in the executive branch, for as one foreign observer quipped, "by tradition, Congress works out its trade policy in a panic."[19]

Some members of Congress have developed a great expertise on international economic issues and work closely with the relevant agencies in Washington. In particular, very important work is done in the trade subcommittees of the Ways and Means Committee in the House of Representatives and of the Finance Committee in the Senate. On the whole, however, the senators and representatives on Capitol Hill are much more concerned with domestic political and economic issues and receive a great deal of pressure from organized interest groups that want to be protected from mounting international competition. For example, many members of the House of Representatives and Senate receive the bulk of their campaign funds from special-interest groups, and well-organized groups that benefit from protectionism have a membership which both vote and make political contributions, whereas the representatives of foreign firms hurt by a high duty might make contributions, but they cannot vote. Very few members of Congress admit publicly that unilateral protectionist actions on the part of the United States may be highly injurious to the international trading system, and may invite retaliation overseas against U.S. industries which have become internationally competitive. Moreover, American consumers are victims of such protectionism, but as pointed out earlier, they do not constitute a powerful organized pressure group and their influence on Congress has been inordinately weak.

Fortunately, much of what occurs in Congress is simply talk aimed at placating domestic constituency groups, and many of the protectionist-oriented bills introduced in Congress are never passed. The president can also veto the more onerous protectionist bills passed by Congress, such as periodic textile legislation, and it is often difficult for Capitol Hill to come up with the two-thirds majority needed in each chamber to override a presidential veto. However, logrolling and pork barrel politics are alive and well and continue to complicate efforts to formulate coherent legislation governing U.S. foreign economic policy. In an infamous episode of panic and parochialism, Congress managed to add almost 1,000 amendments to the legendary Smoot-Hawley

Tariff Act of 1930, and this amending process continues to be a hallmark of the American legislative system. Far too often, Congress represents an obstruction to the formulation of a comprehensive U.S. foreign economic policy, rather than a creative force helping to adapt such a policy to the imperatives of complex global interdependence. The absence of a presidential line-item veto, which is available to 43 governors at the state level, also impedes efforts by the chief executive to fine tune trade legislation passed by the Congress.

The Judicial Branch

The judicial branch is only sporadically involved in the foreign economic policy process, but once again its role has generally been more negative than positive. On a comparative basis, the U.S. judicial system has a greater influence on the development of governmental, economic, business, and social policy than any other judicial system in the world. Not too surprisingly, U.S. society is far more litigious than other societies. For example, there are twenty times as many lawyers in the United States on a per capita basis as in Japan. Far too often, judges apparently consider that the "world" of business is destined to be governed by U.S. laws, and as a result, their decisions may have significant extraterritorial consequences. This is illustrated by the numerous cases where judges have ordered the overseas affiliates of U.S. multinational corporations to obey American law instead of the laws of the countries where their subsidiaries are located. These judgments have naturally precipitated heated exchanges between these nations and the United States, with the overseas countries accusing the U.S. of violating their national sovereignty.

The U.S. government is also inundated with lawyers, whose overriding concern with legal technicalities and precedents makes it very difficult at times to conclude economic accords with other nations. Furthermore, a common practice in Washington is for lawyers to work for government agencies for a few years and then join law firms which represent companies having a stake in the passage of laws or regulations affecting U.S. foreign economic policy. Through extensive lobbying and the use of the judicial system, these people can be highly effective at times in representing firms which support protectionism.

In addition, as economic interdependence has become more pronounced in the United States, many more cases currently before the courts are linked to international trade and investment activity. Typically, these cases may deal with antitrust considerations, takeover and acquisition provisions, employment codes, compensation practices, product liability and warranty standards, plant closures, trade secret violations, export controls, visa restrictions, and a broad range of other issues.

Many leaders in government and industry profess to believe in free trade, but the U.S. political system is clearly skewed in the direction of parochialism and insularity. In response to perennial trade deficits, Capitol Hill, and to a lesser extent, the White House, have been more than willing to protect industries impacted negatively by foreign competition, rather than to help these industries make short-term adjustments in order to become more competitive in the long run. In an era of interdependence when at least 70 percent of American-made products face direct competition from foreign products in the U.S. domestic marketplace, the siren song of protectionism seemingly becomes even more seductive.

The Subnational Governmental Dimension

The foreign economic policy-making labyrinth in the United States is made even more perplexing because of the nature of the American federal system. At the grassroots level, U.S. state and local officials are keenly aware of the impact which both national and global competition is having on the people they represent. In the spirit of "thinking globally and acting locally," more than four-fifths of the states have now opened 160 offices abroad in 24 different countries to promote trade, investment, and tourism, almost 3 times the number of offices opened in 1986. To put this subnational governmental activity in perspective, the federal government currently operates about 130 special foreign commercial posts in 68 countries, less than the combined total of state overseas offices but with facilities in almost 3 times as many countries.[20] In addition, more states now maintain offices in Tokyo than in Washington, D.C.[21] Moreover, over the past several years California's Export Finance Office alone has issued almost as many loan guarantees as the Export-Import Bank of the United States has made nationwide.[22] Even major cities are now sponsoring annual international trade and investment missions, and about 1,000 of America's 36,000 municipal and township governments are actively involved in international programs.[23] All of this subnational activity has occurred during a period when the U.S. Foreign and Commercial Service, the federal agency assigned to help American companies to export, has seen its budget cut by 20 percent in real terms over the past few years and its staffing reduced by 10 percent.[24]

Especially in the last decade, state and local governments in the United States have been actively engaged in developing subnational economic development strategies, with the goal of protecting and enhancing the interests of the constituencies who live within their fixed jurisdictions.[25] Without any doubt, a major motivation for this new emphasis is the shrinking transfer payments from Washington, D.C. In constant dollars, federal aid to the states and cities peaked in 1978, and fell by almost 40 percent in real terms during the 1980s.[26] Washington's deficit-reduction measures are expected to exacerbate even further the transfer problems in the 1990s, and the federal government already spends much more on interest payments on the national debt than on state and local government programs.

In an effort to achieve some semblance of self-sufficiency and economic diversity at the subnational level, state economic development agencies are devoting over one-half of their time to in-state business development, almost one-third to attracting firms elsewhere in the United States, and about 15 percent to attracting foreign companies.[27] At the county and municipal levels, an additional 11,000 economic development groups have been formed across the United States, excluding the 9,000 local chambers of commerce.[28] Some observers now refer to the state governments as the "dynamos" of the U.S. federal system, and there is no doubt that their policies will have a growing impact during the 1990s upon U.S. commercial relations at home and abroad.[29]

The ability of U.S. state and local governments to influence domestic and international commerce positively or negatively should not be underestimated. Nearly two-thirds of the countries in the world have fewer than 10 million people, and nearly one-third fewer than 1 million. If one were to rank the top 25 nations in the world by gross national product, it would be possible to add 10 states to the list. Moreover, America's smallest state, as measured by gross state product, would still rank ahead of more than 100 nation-states around the globe. California, with its 30 million people, now accounts for more than 700 billion dollars in annual gross state product, and would rank as the seventh largest country globally. New York is not far behind with its top 10 ranking, and Texas alone produces almost twice as much as neighboring Mexico. These states are also important trading clients for many countries, with California ranking as Japan's second leading partner after the rest of the United States.

Furthermore, the annual budgets of states such as California and New York, which now each top 50 billion dollars, are surpassed by only a handful of national governments.[30] To put this purchasing power in perspective, California's budget is several times larger than the budget of Russia, a nation with 150 million people. At the municipal level, New York City's annual budget is also twice as large as that of the Philippines with its 56 million people, and the four-county Los Angeles metropolitan area, with an annual production of goods and services exceeding 250 billion dollars, ranks as the eleventh largest economic power in the world ahead of Australia, Switzerland, and India.

State and local governments are now allocating hundreds of millions of dollars each year in an effort to attract foreign direct investment to their areas of jurisdiction. For example, 35 states entered the bidding for the Volkswagen plant in the late 1970s. Pennsylvania won the bidding war by offering an incentive package of grants, subsidized loans, and other special favors worth almost 70 million dollars.[31] Nissan was courted by 39 American states as potential sites for a truck-assembly plant. Tennessee won the contest and agreed to provide Nissan with about 66 million dollars in incentives. Honda also received 70 million dollars from Ohio, Mazda 120 million dollars from

Michigan, and Toyota an estimated 325 million dollars from Kentucky spread over a 20-year period.[32]

Municipal governments have also been actively engaged in international economic activities. Atlanta's municipal leadership has pledged to make its city the gateway for U.S. trade with Africa. The leaders of Dallas promised to transform that Texas metropolis into an "international city," and proceeded to establish a local task force on international trade and to create a Dallas-based free-trade zone.[33] In an effort to provide more jobs for local residents and to diversify its textile-oriented economic base, the South Carolina city of Spartanburg initiated an active campaign almost two decades ago to attract foreign investors. More than 50 foreign firms have now located in that city and have invested in excess of 1.2 billion dollars.[34] The U.S. Conference of Mayors has sponsored periodic investment conferences in Europe and Asia since 1980, and the leaders of many major cities travel abroad on a regular basis seeking out new commercial contacts.

State governments continue to exercise broad powers in the areas of land use, insurance and banking, environmental controls, hazardous waste disposal, labor relations, civil rights, and corporate taxation and chartering, all of which may impact upon international commercial activities. In general, state governments are much more involved than ever before in regulating businesses, whether foreign or domestic. Forty-three state legislatures met annually in 1992, compared with only 18 in 1960. State legislative staffs have increased dramatically and state legislators have shown a growing interest in business activities. In the early 1980s, seven times as many business-related laws and regulations were passed by state legislatures as by the U.S. Congress. Sixteen times as many bills of all categories are currently being passed at the state level as at the federal level.[35] Moreover, the chances of a particular piece of legislation actually being enacted by a state legislature are much higher than legislation introduced in the U.S. Congress. Because of the impact which subnational government laws and statutes can have on the business community, three-quarters of the largest U.S. corporations are currently engaging in lobbying activity at the state level. Moreover, nearly one-half of the companies which employ state-government relations officers have hired them just since 1975.[36]

In certain respects, state governments are developing industrial policies. More than two dozen states are now directly involved in the venture capital game, and over twenty offer export assistance to local firms. Several states have also signed special economic accords with subnational governments in other nations, and groups of states are cooperating in regional banking projects. In addition, over forty states invoke Buy American provisions and maintain discriminatory government procurement standards which give a preference in bidding to local firms. About the same number of states has also enacted anti-takeover measures which are aimed at thwarting domestic and foreign corporations from making hostile takeovers of local companies. Over the past decade, several state governments have also placed special restrictions on commercial activity with the former Soviet Union, South Africa, and Arab states in the Middle East.

Strong views concerning moral issues have also prompted significant and at times controversial state and local government decisions which impact upon international commercial transactions. Following the downing of the Korean Airlines passenger jet in September 1983 by Soviet aircraft, 15 states placed a temporary embargo on the sale of spirits from the USSR. Currently, over 160 municipal, county, and state governments sponsor total or partial disinvestment policies prohibiting public employee pension funds from holding shares in companies which do business with South Africa, and some prohibit these companies from bidding on public contracts.[37] The impact of these policies may be quite substantial, for California's Public Employees Retirement System alone controls more than 65 billion dollars in assets.[38] A half-dozen states, including Massachusetts, also officially endorse the MacBride principles which are aimed at eliminating anti-Catholic discrimination in Northern Ireland. These states instruct businesses within their areas of jurisdiction which maintain subsidiaries in Northern Ireland to comply fully with these principles.

State governments are also actively engaged in entering into formal arrangements with their counterparts in other nations. Eleven New England governors and Eastern Canadian premiers have met annually since 1973 and have agreed on a broad range of institutional accords. Governors from eight states and premiers from two Canadian provinces have signed a charter to protect water rights in the Great Lakes. Representatives of Alaska, British Columbia, and the Yukon also meet on a regular basis, and periodic conferences are held between the governors of the U.S. and Mexican border states. In a meeting held in December 1987, the governors of New Mexico, California, Arizona, and Texas discussed economic development strategies, particularly maquiladora operations (in-bond assembly plants), with governors from Baja California, Sonora, Chihuahua, Coahuila, Nuevo Leon, and Tamaulipas. On the other hand, geographic proximity is not a prerequisite for close international working relationships, as illustrated by the success of the Southeast U.S.-Japan Association which has annually brought together public and private officials from the two nations for over a dozen years.

State governments also insist that much better coordination is needed between state and federal officials in tackling international economic issues. The National Governors' Association has requested that the Office of the U.S. Trade Representative consult with state representatives on any foreign policy initiative which might adversely affect state interests, especially federal policies linked to foreign investment. Many states also cooperate with federal agencies such as the U.S. and Foreign Commercial Service, the International

Trade Administration, and the U.S. Export-Import Bank in promoting export activity.

The expansion of state and local government activities abroad does, however, raise some interesting constitutional issues. The U.S. Congress is vigilant in upholding constitutional provisions which prohibit the states from entering into foreign treaties, but it has had few qualms about state governments signing hundreds of international pacts, agreements, and understandings. For example, the state of Illinois has entered into special economic cooperation agreements with the Chinese province of Liaoning and with the Russian Republic before the demise of the Soviet Union. Constitutionally, should the supremacy clause require prior congressional approval before Illinois or any other subnational government enters into such international arrangements? A few states, including California, also maintain a modified system of unitary taxation which taxes subsidiaries of multinational corporations based on the global earnings of the parent firm, and not just on the activities of the subsidiary within the state. Many foreign governments have complained that the unitary system is a form of double taxation and violates U.S. bilateral tax treaties. In view of the commerce clause, should state governments have the right to implement a system of taxation which might have extraterritorial consequences and exacerbate U.S. relations with other countries? Some state governments also provide direct financial subsidies for exporters, while a few place significant restrictions on certain types of foreign direct investment. At GATT meetings, Washington's official position is that export subsidies should be eliminated and most barriers to foreign direct investment dismantled. Constitutionally, should Washington implement one set of standards on issues critical to international trade and commerce, and still permit state governments to maintain a conflicting set of standards?

Without any doubt, a much richer literature is needed to explain the theoretical and constitutional dimensions of intergovernmental relations in an age of complex interdependence, an interdependence which spawns a vulnerability which is beyond Washington's capacity to control, and which penetrates deep into the heartland of the nation.

TOWARD THE TWENTY-FIRST CENTURY

Undoubtedly, the international activities of state and local governments will continue to expand as the U.S. economy becomes progressively intertwined with the global economy, resulting in the well-being of local constituencies being linked not only to domestic prosperity, but to the vitality of the international economic system as well. This proliferation of subnational government ties beyond America's borders will greatly complicate intergovernmental relations as questions of jurisdiction, propriety, and efficiency arise time and time again. On the other hand, such grassroots' initiatives emphasizing globalization are a direct response to growing vincibility and may be imperative if America hopes to compete effectively in a very complex international arena.

This concluding section will offer recommendations on what should be done to improve the economic policy-making process in Washington, D.C., whereas the next chapter will address what America as a nation must do to enhance its international economic competitiveness. Without any doubt, current institutional and procedural mechanisms for coping with foreign economic policy in the United States must undergo a major transformation. Much greater priority must be given to economic issues at the highest policy-making levels, and government leaders must have a thorough knowledge of both the opportunities and the vicissitudes of an interdependent economy. As William Diebold, Jr. has pointed out, "[t]he internationalization of the American economy has outrun people's understanding of its implications. More than ever before, we cannot put our own house in order except by relating the American economy to the rest of the world." He adds that in trying to adapt to the challenges of interdependence, the United States has "trouble because our pluralistic methods greatly complicate our dealings with other countries."[39]

Institutionally, an important foreign economic policy unit should be established in the White House itself. Perhaps this could be done by beefing up the National Security Council or the Council of Economic Advisers. The resurrection of the Council on International Economic Policy might be an even better option. Moreover, USTR should be trimmed to about thirty professionals and given much greater access to the chief policy-makers. USTR would then assume a coordinating function for all foreign economic policy in the executive branch. Currently, USTR is too big to carry out this important function and has become just one of the players among the myriad departments and agencies which have a say in international economic matters. A trimmed-down USTR could, in certain respects, be "above" administrative politics and carry out the function of presenting viable policy alternatives to the president. None of this revamping will work, however, unless the chief executive and his small cadre of key advisers begin to recognize the growing importance of economic issues on the policy agenda, and to comprehend the new challenges, vulnerabilities, and opportunities facing the nation in an era of complex interdependence.

The creation of a Department of International Trade also has some merit, but not as outlined by recent congressional proponents. Bills introduced in Congress over the past several years would piece together a department which is far too large and which lacks focus. A truly "lean and mean" agency should be created which would be responsive to the concerns of domestic industries, but not serve as a doormat for protectionist whims. Such a department should also work closely with state and local governments and assume an informal coordinating role in making sure that policies at all governmental levels promote U.S. interests at home and abroad.

Most of the burden for increasing the U.S. trade presence abroad must fall to private industry, but Washington should be expected to help open foreign markets through special foreign economic policy programs and through the GATT process. For the moment, companies that desire to export can receive some limited assistance by establishing Foreign Sales Corporations (FSCs). These FSCs provide special tax benefits for companies which are export oriented.

The Export-Import Bank (Eximbank) of the United States also provides a variety of assistance, especially loans at competitive interest rates to overseas buyers willing to purchase U.S. goods. Major problems have plagued the Eximbank, including insufficient funding, noncompetitive interest rates, and an overemphasis on big-ticket items such as aircraft, which crowd out the small exporters that are seeking assistance. The Foreign Credit Insurance Association (FCIA), composed of a group of U.S. property, casualty, and marine insurance companies, works with the Eximbank, private firms, and a variety of government agencies to provide export credit insurance for American companies. The Overseas Private Investment Corporation (OPIC), a quasigovernmental entity, also provides insurance to Americans for overseas investment activity. This insurance covers the companies against losses due to revolution, expropriation, or foreign government prohibitions on the repatriation of profits. The U.S. Foreign and Commercial Service, which is part of the Department of Commerce, also furnishes market information to U.S. companies. Commercial officers have been placed in major U.S. embassies and consulates around the world and have been given the responsibility of keeping abreast of possible trade opportunities for American firms. These programs are generally helpful, but currently lack the financial and infrastructure support which many European and Asian governments offer to their own national firms.[40]

Washington must also grapple with the increasingly important issues of technology transfer and countertrade. The U.S. government has attempted to limit the transfer to unfriendly nations of technology which might have a military, atomic energy, or a dual (military-civilian) application. The Export Administration Act (EAA) provides the mechanism and ground rules for determining whether or not technology may be transferred. Almost everyone in the private and public sector agrees that certain sensitive technology should not fall inadvertently into hostile hands. On the other hand, some American firms have registered vociferous complaints against the EAA. First of all, they complain that the agencies which administer the guidelines are far too bureaucratic and take too much time to make decisions. Secondly, they insist that Washington has lost touch with the fact that other nations also possess sensitive technology, and if their firms are able to supply potentially hostile countries, why should U.S. companies be eliminated from the competition, especially in the new post-Cold War era? In other words, why place another administrative roadblock in the way of U.S. firms which are already struggling in a rapidly evolving international trade arena? And finally, these critics argue that the list of sensitive goods is far too long and should be pared substantially.

The major Western nations do work together in an effort to limit the transfer of sensitive technology from the West to hostile countries, which through most of the post-World War II era were Soviet-bloc nations. The main steering group is the Coordinating Committee for Export Controls (COCOM), an organization established at about the same time as the formation of NATO in 1949. The United States, Canada, Japan, and twelve European countries are members of COCOM, with the organization maintaining a permanent secretariat and national delegations in Paris. It is widely perceived that the U.S. government is much more sensitive to the technology transfer issue than its Western allies, but COCOM has begun to lift many restrictions as a result of the dynamic changes in the former Soviet Union and Eastern Europe.

Countertrade, which means international trade by barter or the exchange of goods rather than an exchange of money, has been officially frowned upon by Washington. Both Capitol Hill and the White House worry that such trade could complicate efforts by governments to collect revenues on trade transactions. On the other hand, nations which depend on trade in raw materials and semifinished goods may find that countertrade will be more productive for them than using currency as an intermediary. Classic examples of countertrade would be the exchange of oil for aircraft, or natural gas for grain. Very little progress has been made at the multilateral level to formulate acceptable rules of the game for this growing phenomenon known as countertrade, and other Western nations have generally been more adept than the United States in taking advantage of this bartering system.

Washington must also reconsider the wisdom of clinging to trade protectionist policies. Although many U.S. industrial sectors have been hurt by intense foreign competition, including high technology and electronics' firms, most of the structural problems related to international competitiveness have historically been concentrated in four industrial groups: (a) automobiles, (b) steel, (c) textiles and apparel, and (d) shoes. Many other sectors remain highly competitive, and even though the services' arena is becoming increasingly important as a percentage of overall GNP and as a provider of jobs, the United States is not in the process of deindustrializing.[41] Consequently, creative solutions devoid of knee-jerk protectionist measures are needed to deal with the problems plaguing America's industrial core.

Without any doubt, protectionist measures have rarely benefitted the U.S. economy as a whole, and have almost always placed additional burdens on the American consumer. The voluntary restraints placed on Japanese cars in the early 1980s may have helped Detroit recover temporarily, but they also resulted in a shift of imports to European sources, a significant increase in Japanese automobile export prices, accessory upgrading by the Japanese car industry which has led to even higher prices for their products in the American market, and for a time, record profits for the U.S. auto industry. In spite of intense foreign competition, some companies in the auto, steel, textile, and shoe industries are showing that they can compete effectively. Washington should insure that foreign competitors of these industries do not engage in unfair trading practices, and that adjustment assistance is provided to displaced workers, the area where the greatest human tragedy has occurred as a result of a decline in U.S. industrial competitiveness. However, quotas and import surcharges are usually not the avenue to follow, for they cause great problems for competitive industries and for consumers while doing little to insure that protected industries will improve their level of performance.[42]

Finally, the United States is certainly not the only nation which has a less than stellar record in the formulation and implementation of foreign economic policy. Moreover, on a comparative basis, the United States may be less protectionistic than most of the members of the OECD group of industrial societies. On the other hand, the United States remains the largest industrial power and trading nation in the world, so the impact of its economic policies on other countries can be substantial and it can still play a prominent role in pushing for liberalized trade relations worldwide.

In conclusion, policy-makers in Washington, D.C. have three major options available in steering U.S. trade policy in the 1990s. The first is the *unilateral option* best represented by the 1988 Omnibus Trade and Competitiveness Act. This law made the U.S. government judge, jury, and executioner in regard to the trade policies pursued by other nations. With both the blessing and prodding of Congress, the executive branch decides which nations are engaging in "unfair trade practices," what must be done by these nations to rectify their harmful policies, and what penalties will be exacted if they fail to comply with U.S. directives. The strength of this approach is that it is fairly simple and straightforward. Most Americans believe that the United States is being treated unfairly on an unlevel playing field and therefore has the right to change the rules in order to balance competitive advantages and disadvantages. Moreover, because so many nations are dependent on shipping their products to the United States, Washington anticipates that they will probably make major concessions in order to retain access to the largest national market in the world. Furthermore, many Americans are suspicious of GATT's multilateral process, perceiving it to be too slow and cumbersome and too preoccupied with helping other countries to develop strong export markets at America's expense.

Conversely, the potential costs of the unilateral approach can be very prohibitive. Most other nations would deeply resent U.S. unilateralism, perceiving it as a Rambo-style gunboat economic strategy designed to force compliance by America's major trading partners. Because American companies are still the largest traders and investors in the world, their business activity would undoubtedly be put in jeopardy if other nations were to retaliate and implement reciprocal policies towards the United States. The 1930s stand as a grim testament to the consequences of rampant trade protectionism and unilateral "beggar-thy-neighbor" policies.

The second approach is *bilateral.* In this case, the United States would conclude a series of bilateral trade and investment agreements with nations whose views on international economic issues generally coincide with those of Washington. In 1989, the U.S.-Canada Free Trade Agreement was implemented, thereby creating the largest bilateral market in the world with annual two-way trade surpassing 200 billion dollars. The United States, Canada, and Mexico have also negotiated the North American Free Trade Agreement (NAFTA) which may be implemented in 1994 and may establishe a free trade zone from the Yukon to the Yucatan with 360 million people and annual production surpassing 6 trillion dollars. In addition, a significant number of officials from other nations has also approached American leaders formally and informally to express interest in negotiating similar trade pacts with the United States. This approach would definitely permit the United States to pick and choose its partners and form both regional and transoceanic economic alliances with nations sympathetic with the American vision of the international trade arena.

On the other hand, a proliferation of bilateral agreements would undoubtedly weaken the GATT multilateral approach and perhaps give rise to regional trading blocs in Europe, East Asia, and the Americas. In effect, nations within each trading bloc would enjoy fairly open trading ties, but relations between the blocs could be very protectionist. Moreover, developing countries which were not invited to join any of the rich trading blocs of the North could once again find their economic prospects in jeopardy.

The final approach is *multilateral* and would require full U.S. cooperation in the GATT, World Bank, the International Monetary Fund, and other international economic organizations. In the ideal sense, this is the best approach to deal with the problems associated with economic, resource, and environmental interdependence because so many of these problems are beyond the capacity of Washington or any other national capital to solve. It would also require Americans to view themselves increasingly as residents of a fragile planet earth who must be interested in what transpires not only in their own home country, but in other regions of the world as well.

Yet even with the multilateral approach there are some inherent problems. First of all, national sentiments are firmly entrenched in the United States and elsewhere, meaning that many people still prefer taking care of their own national problems and own citizens before venturing forth to help others in distant and unfamiliar places. The sense of globalization and interdependence is still very weak in the psyches of many people, and a disturbingly large number of Americans continues to know very little about what transpires outside their national borders. Crises in global warming and ozone deterioration may eventually help to build a sense of a common global destiny, but that time may still be decades away. Secondly, both U.S. policy-makers and the American public must be convinced that the multilateral approach will benefit their nation while at the same time helping other countries. Frequently, Americans perceive that Uncle Sam is played for Uncle Sucker internationally, particularly in the domain of foreign aid and foreign trade. These innate suspicions will have to be overcome before Washington can give wholehearted support to the multilateral process. In particular, substantial progress within GATT on issues of prime concern to the United States, namely liberalized trade in agriculture and services, and the creation of an effective dispute settlement mechanism, would go a long way toward building public confidence in multilateralism as a workable solution to America's growing sense of vincibility.

With this in mind, multilateral negotiations covering trade, investment, monetary, and debt concerns must be pursued vigorously and persistently. In particular, ongoing GATT discussions must reach substantive agreements in the areas of services, investment, agriculture, government procurement policies, the protection of trademarks, copyrights, and patents, and other related issues which will liberalize trade around the world. Although the tangible benefits from such discussions might initially be quite modest, they would nonetheless represent a step away from protectionism and would help focus the attention of U.S. policy-makers on the substantial role which America should be playing in the interdependent global economy of the twenty-first century.

ENDNOTES

1. This definition is provided by Catherine Johnston of the Conference Board of Canada.
2. See the *Journal of Commerce*, 3 August 1984, for a look at some of the Roper Poll data.
3. *Journal of Commerce*, 25 April 1984. These figures were calculated by the Consumers for World Trade coalition.
4. Hobart Rowen, "Detroit's Quota Crutch," *Washington Post*, 10 May 1984, A19.
5. See "The High Cost of Import Quotas," *Deseret News*, 25 February 1985, 8A. Robert Crandall estimates that the U.S. auto restraints agreed to by the Japanese in 1981 cost U.S. consumers 160,000 dollars for every U.S. job which was saved in the auto industry. See Rahul Jacob, "Export Barriers the U.S. Hates Most," *Fortune*, 27 February 1989, 89.
6. J.R. Kearl, "Cutting Off One's Nose to Spite One's Face: Protectionism and Declining Economic Well-Being," Brigham Young University Forum address, 21 May 1985.
7. Peter J. Katzenstein suggests that the United States is highly fragmented and organizationally decentralized both in the government and the business spheres. See his article, "Conclusion: Domestic Structures and Strategies of Foreign Economic Policy," in

Between Power and Plenty: Foreign Economic Policies of Advanced Industrial States (Madison: University of Wisconsin Press, 1978), 311 and 325.

8. Stephen D. Krasner, "United States Commercial and Monetary Policy: Unravelling the Paradox of External Strength and Internal Weakness," in Katzenstein, *Between Power and Plenty*, 62-63.

9. James A. Caporaso and Michael D. Ward, "The United States in an Interdependent World: The Emergence of Economic Power," in *Challenges to America*, ed. Charles W. Kegley, Jr., and Patrick I. McGowan (Beverly Hills, CA: Sage, 1979), 165.

10. James Bovard, *The Fair Trade Fraud* (New York: St. Martin's Press, 1991), 306.

11. *The New York Times,* 7 February 1992, A1.

12. Mordechai E. Kreinin, *International Economics: A Policy Approach,* 5th ed. (San Diego: Harcourt Brace Jovanovich, 1987), 331, and Doug Bandow, "Fair Trade with Japan," Copley News Service, 29 May 1990.

13. See Michael Borrus, "The Politics of Competitive Erosion in the U.S. Steel Industry," in *American Industry in International Competition,* ed. John Zysman and Laura Tyson (Ithaca, NY: Cornell University Press, 1983), 68.

14. See Robert W. Crandall, *The U.S. Steel Industry in Recurrent Crisis* (Washington, D.C.: Brookings Institution, 1981), vii.

15. Gary Hufbauer, "Wean the Steel Barons from Protection," *The Wall Street Journal,* 27 December 1988, A10.

16. Gene Bylinsky, "Can Smokestack America Rise Again?" *Fortune,* 6 February 1984, 82.

17. U.S. employment in the steel industry hit an all-time high of 650,000 in 1953. During the 1970s, the average was 335,000 jobs, compared with 170,000 jobs in 1988.

18. One of the authors served as special assistant in the Office of the U.S. Trade Representative in 1983 and 1984 and had the privilege of participating in several of these interagency sessions.

19. "Look Out, Japan, the Americans are Coming," *Economist,* 30 March 1985, 37.

20. *Business America,* World Trade Week 1992 edition, 22.

21. These figures are for the year 1990. See the *Governors' Weekly Bulletin,* 30 March 1990, 1, and *Nation's Cities Weekly,* 1 July 1991, 6. Thirty-three states maintained offices in Washington, D.C. at the beginning of 1990 compared with 39 in the Tokyo-Osaka corridor. In 1989, governors from 41 of the 55 U.S. states and territories made 82 trips to 35 countries. Forty-eight trips were primarily to encourage exports and 32 to increase investment. Japan was the leading country visited, with 19 trips, followed by 13 trips to Belgium.

22. Elliot King, "Bridging the Finance Gap for Mid-Sized Exporters," *Global Trade,* July 1989, 18. This statement was made by L. Fargo Wells, executive director of the California Export Finance Office.

23. The international involvement of municipalities in the United States and Canada is detailed in Earl H. Fry, Lee H. Radebaugh, and Panayotis Soldatos, eds., *The New International Cities Era: The Global Activities of North American Municipal Governments* (Provo, UT: David M. Kennedy Center for International Studies, Brigham Young University, 1989).

24. *San Francisco Chronicle,* 6 November 1989, C3. The export promotion staff of the U.S. & Foreign Commercial Service, which is part of the U.S. Department of Commerce, was cut from 142 in 1985 to 115 in 1989, with trade specialists in U.S. field offices cut from 365 to 291, and trade staff in overseas offices, including foreign nationals, cut from 690 to 679.

25. The notion of subnational "fixed jurisdictions" deserves further explanation. Obviously, U.S. state and local governments have limited territorial boundaries, whereas businesses can be much more mobile. For example, in 1987 the sales of affiliates of U.S.-based

multinational corporations (MNCs) surpassed 1 trillion dollars, whereas U.S. exports were in the range of 250 billion dollars. The affiliates of U.S.-based MNCs also produce about 500 billion dollars' worth of products in the European Community each year, while U.S. exports to all of Europe amount to only 70 billion dollars annually. With this in mind, Gary Hufbauer has been prompted to conclude that the changes to be implemented in the European Community at the end of 1992 may be a "bonanza for U.S. multinationals, but a question mark for U.S. exporters." (Hufbauer quoted in Bruce Stokes, "Multiple Allegiances," *National Journal*, 11 November 1989, 2757). For state and local governments, the "bonanza" is clearly in the form of exports from their areas of jurisdiction, whereas the U.S.-based MNCs may have a far different agenda for maximizing profits.

26. As a fraction of total federal spending, aid to state and local governments fell from one-sixth in 1979 to one-ninth in 1990.

27. These figures are based on a 1988 NASDA survey and are found in *The NASDA Newsletter*, 15 November 1988.

28. Donald Haider, "Marketing Places," *Economic Development Commentary*, Spring 1989, 15. In his address to the 1989 Congress of Cities, National League of Cities' President Terry Goddard emphasized the theme of "self-sufficiency," stressing that municipal governments could no longer count on assistance from Washington, D.C. (*Nation's Cities Weekly*, 4 December 1989, 1). Some state government leaders have used even more brutal terms to refer to the dwindling assistance from Washington, D.C., utilizing such expressions as "fend-for-yourself federalism." The governor of Michigan bluntly stated that "Washington has gone from revenue sharing to revenue bleeding." A National Governors' Association official added the following: "The 'feds' have been living on the credit card for years. Now, by mandating us to do the things they can't afford, they're trying to use ours. The idea is they get the credit, we get the bills. But we don't have their ace in the hole: deficit financing" (*Nation's Cities Weekly*, 28 August 1989, 8).

29. In Neal R. Peirce, "States: Dynamos of the Federal System," *State Government News*, December 1989, 23, the author asserts that the "1980s indisputably have been the decade of state governments. Those in doubt need only take a look at virtually any major domestic policy-making arena—welfare reform, early childhood care, education, environmental protection, homelessness, infrastructure, foreign trade promotion and health-care cost containment."

30. These state budgets include funds transferred to the states by the federal government.

31. For a case study of the VW investment, see Earl H. Fry, *Financial Invasion of the U.S.A.* (New York: McGraw-Hill, 1980), 128-31.

32. See Earl H. Fry, "State and Local Governments in the International Arena," *The Annals of the American Academy of Political and Social Science*, 509 (May 1990): 118-27.

33. Craig Savoye, "States, Cities Look for Ways to Help Small Businesses to Sell Goods Abroad," *Christian Science Monitor*, 21 June 1983, 4.

34. See Fry, *Financial Invasion*, 131-34, and David A. Ricks, "The Impact of Foreign Direct Investment in Spartanburg," *Business and Economic Review* 2 (December 1982): 29-33.

35. The Conference Board, *Managing Business-State Government Relations* (New York: Conference Board, 1983).

36. Conference Board, *Managing Business-State*.

37. For example, San Francisco bars these businesses from bidding on municipal contracts which are over 5,000 dollars. See Michael H. Shuman, *Building Municipal Foreign Policies* (Irvine, CA: Center for Innovative Diplomacy, 1987), 4, and *The Wall Street Journal*, 23 November 1992, A10.

38. This was the pension plan's asset base in January 1992. See *The New York Times*, 30 January 1992, D18.

39. William Diebold, Jr., "The United States in the World Economy: A Fifty Year Perspective," *Foreign Affairs* 62 (Fall 1983): 97.

40. A Cornell University report comparing the U.S. export-promotion program with those of Canada, the United Kingdom, France, West Germany, Japan, Singapore, Taiwan, South Korea, and Brazil was completed in March 1989. The U.S. effort in export promotion was ranked last in overall efficacy. See the *Journal of Commerce,* 3 April 1989, 1A and 5A.

41. See Robert Z. Lawrence, *Can America Compete?* (Washington, D.C.: Brookings Institution, 1984), and William C. Freund, "America Still a Tough Competitor," *The New York Times,* 5 August 1984, F2.

42. The problems faced by internationally competitive sectors of the American economy resulting directly from U.S. protectionism are illustrated in a recent specialty steel case. In response to U.S. quotas on specialty steel imports from Western Europe, the European Community imposed higher tariffs on U.S. soybeans, corn, and fine chemicals. Thus, these sectors lost market shares as a direct result of economic sanctions imposed in an entirely different business sector. As I.M. Destler recommends in his book, *American Trade Politics,* 2nd edition (Washington, D.C.: Institute for International Economics, 1992), 256, the way to compete internationally is to maintain "a dynamic, flexible economy that rewards our industrial winners, not our losers."

13

COPING WITH THE ECONOMIC CHALLENGES OF THE TWENTY-FIRST CENTURY

AMERICA AT THE CROSSROADS

As highlighted in the first chapter of this book, many foreign observers now harbor serious doubts about America's future role in the global economy, and even a solid majority of the American people now believe that Japan has emerged as the world's leading economic power. Do these perceptions coincide with reality, is the United States a "hegemon in decay," and is it destined to become a second-rate economic power?[1]

This chapter will reflect on America's economic future and will outline what steps would have to be taken if the United States hopes to maintain a strong leadership role in the increasingly interdependent global economy of the twenty-first century.

FACTORS FAVORING THE CONTINUATION OF AN AMERICAN LEADERSHIP ROLE

Except for the very bleak scenario of a major world or regional war, it is totally unrealistic to expect that the United States will ever again regain the 40 percent or even 50 percent share of global economic production which it enjoyed during the late 1940s and early 1950s. This huge proportion of world production was based on the unprecedented human and physical devastation which racked Europe and Asia during the 1940s, and must be considered as a strictly aberrant condition. Indeed, the U.S. share of global production today is comparable to what it was before World War II, and its share of manufacturing production is also about the same as it was in 1913 and 1938.[2]

There are many factors which should work to America's benefit as it attempts to maintain a significant leadership position in the global economy.

First of all, it is still far and away the world's largest economy and its citizens enjoy more purchasing power than anyone else on earth.

Secondly, no single nation anywhere else on the planet has a richer and more diverse natural resource base than the United States. In comparison, Japan and the European Community are very resource poor and are heavily dependent on imports of raw materials from other parts of the world.

Thirdly, the United States has been spending close to 300 billion dollars per year on its defense sector and has contributed more than half of the spending for the maintenance of the 16-member NATO alliance. In view of the revolutionary changes that have recently occurred in the former Soviet Union and Eastern Europe and which have decreased East-West tensions, the United States should be the greatest beneficiary of the so-called "peace dividend." This was manifested in fiscal year 1992 when 178,000 members of the armed forces were removed from the active-duty payroll, the largest cutback in 20 years.[3] Literally tens of billions of dollars in decreased defense spending should now be available annually to pare the government's debt and to improve America's capacity to compete in the global economy.

And lastly, America's chief economic competitors also face their share of challenges as the new century approaches. Japan is a small, resource-poor island nation of 123 million people. It has an aging population and because of cultural biases, the Japanese have found it difficult to open their doors to immigrants who would be able to provide the work force needed for the twenty-first century. The Japanese hope that their investments abroad will provide them with an overseas work force and a production and resource base which will permit them to remain highly competitive in the decades ahead. This increasing reliance on foreign direct investment to offset demographic problems may prove to be a very tenuous strategy in an era when nationalism still remains a powerful political force.

The European Community is one of the great success stories of recent history and stretching from the mountains of Mourne to the Peloponnese, it is creating a unified and integrated common market of 340 million people with a combined gross national product rivaling that of the United States. Moreover, with the changes in Eastern Europe, the European Community may well expand in the future to include most of the continent. Conversely, the community is still comprised of individual nation-states which have their own national interests to safeguard. Even the newly unified Germany is much smaller than the United States, with a population one-third the size, a gross national product one-fourth the size, and an area equivalent to half the size of the state of Texas.

The former Soviet Union was once the world's largest nation geographically and ranked third in terms of population. It was also rich in natural resources and was world class in the military and space sectors. But in many other ways, it was an economic disaster which had more in common with developing countries than with the industrialized nations. It had been unable to feed its own people and was widely known for producing shoddy goods. Its ruble was not convertible internationally, which hampered the USSR's ability to participate fully in the global economy. A popular maxim among Soviet workers was "they pretend to pay me and I pretend to work," reflecting both the perils of a weak currency and a weak economy in general. Moreover, the Kremlin has now lost its Eastern European satellites and the fifteen constituent republics of the former USSR have declared their own independence. All of these factors portend difficult economic challenges for Russia and the other former constitutent units of the Soviet Union over the next couple of decades.

Thus the very large, highly affluent, well-diversified, and resource-rich American economy enjoys many advantages not to be found in other major industrialized societies, advantages which should serve it well in the decades ahead. The strong sense of political unity in the United States also stands in sharp contrast to the erosive forces of extreme nationalism and ethnicity in Europe and elsewhere in the world.

CHARTING A PAINFUL COURSE
TO RETAIN U.S. COMPETITIVENESS

American Complacency

The United States is now back at pre-World War I and World War II levels in terms of its share of global production, and a smaller U.S. portion of total world production is not necessarily a negative phenomenon. For example, if economies continue to expand globally, especially in the Third World, Americans should welcome a smaller percentage of what has become a much larger economic pie. In other words, Americans should continue to prosper while others around the world also taste prosperity, many for the first time ever.

On the other hand, America may now be coasting along, resting on past laurels, and expecting that former achievements will provide the momentum for a strong and vibrant economy for the next century. Unless tough decisions are made and implemented, America *will* be a declining economic power, both in absolute and relative terms.

The Debt Constraint

Little of a substantive and positive nature has been done to tackle the serious economic and societal problems now facing the United States, problems which impact directly on America's global competitiveness. Above all, the nation cannot continue to pile up a huge government debt, placing the burden for repayment on future generations and funneling funds to interest obligations instead of for more productive economic development purposes. The federal government's debt surpassed 4 trillion dollars in 1992 and almost 3 trillion dollars in additional debt is expected to be added just during the 1990s, placing the United States at a distinct disadvantage as it enters the twenty-first century. For the sake of future competitiveness, the yearly deficit must be steadily reduced without the use of accounting gimmicks or other "smoke and mirror" deceptions.

This task will not be easy, even if tens of billions of dollars are freed up by the "peace dividend." The crisis in the savings and loan and banking sectors represents America's largest financial fiasco since the Great Depression and will add hundreds of billions of dollars in extra tax burdens over the next three decades. It is quite possible that the savings-and-loan catastrophe alone will cost taxpayers 500 billion dollars over the next two decades. To put this costly episode in perspective, the entire financial cost of the United States fighting in World War II was 460 billion dollars (measured in 1990 dollars), including service-related veterans' benefits.[4]

Adding insult to injury, the U.S. federal government is not the only entity in America which in up to its neck in debt. In 1990, the total U.S. debt outstanding was 12.5 trillion dollars, compared with only 2 trillion dollars in 1975.[5] Over three-quarters of this debt is private, with both businesses and households having incurred unprecedented financial liabilities. This burden of indebtedness will definitely hamper the United States as it competes in the international economic system.

Infrastructure Improvements

In addition, America's infrastructure of highways, bridges, harbors, airports, and mass transit and water systems is aging. One of every four bridges in the country is considered as unsafe, and 65 percent of the interstate highway system is no longer in good shape.[6] A congressionally mandated group, the National Council on Public Works Improvement, has recommended that annual spending on infrastructure be doubled to 90 billion dollars by the end of the 1990s, concluding that "the quality of America's infrastructure is barely adequate to fulfill current requirements and insufficient to meet the demands of future growth and development."[7] Without a modern, first-class infrastructure, the United States will certainly fall behind in the global marketplace, but the costs of modernization will add to the ominous budgetary dilemma facing the nation as a whole. Consequently, if real progress is to be made in lowering annual government deficits, many budget items will have to be trimmed and some taxes raised. Except for the poor, all segments of U.S. society should be expected to bear some of the brunt of reduced government services and higher tax bills.

Business Myopia

Dramatic changes are also needed in America's business community. Most U.S. firms have no interest in exporting, even though international trade in goods and services now surpasses 4 trillion dollars annually. Even more importantly, if America's small and medium-sized enterprises do not produce globally competitive goods, they may find their market share at home threatened by both large U.S. and foreign companies. In the early 1960s, only 20 percent of the goods produced in the United States faced direct competition domestically from foreign products. In the 1990s, this figure is 70 percent and growing. Unless these small and medium-sized U.S. businesses view the world as their marketplace and begin to produce world-class goods, they may be the dinosaurs of the twenty-first century.

Industrial productivity is another issue which must be faced head on. In its study of eight U.S. industrial groups, an MIT commission pinpointed six recurring patterns of weakness in America's productivity performance:

1. outdated strategies;
2. short time horizons;
3. technological weaknesses in development and production;
4. neglect of human resources;
5. failure to cooperate within companies and industrial groups and between management and labor; and
6. lack of coordination between government and industry.[8]

Unless dramatic changes are made in both the corporate boardroom and the shop floor, U.S. productivity growth will continue to lag behind that of the major competitors across the Pacific and the Atlantic.

America's stock market system is also geared to short-term profits and may prove to be disastrous for long-term U.S. international competitiveness. Wall Street has been transformed into a type of casino, with stocks being turned over on a rapid basis. In the early 1960s, only 15 percent of the shares of New York Stock Exchange companies traded annually. In 1987, 95 percent of the shares were turned over, and commissions and fees linked to this turnover equalled one-sixth of total U.S. corporate profits that year.[9] A majority of trading is now done by pension and mutual funds, and not individual investors. These institutional investors are prone to trade often, make a quick profit, and generally ignore the long-term fundamentals of American industry. This fixation on quarterly profits encourages myopia at corporate headquarters, as business leaders are prone to sacrifice long-term planning and research-and-development funding in order to concentrate on short-term financial gains. In contrast, Japanese companies, and to a lesser extent their European counterparts, can implement strategies for the long term. For example, Japanese companies lost billions of dollars initially as they built up market share against the dominant U.S. companies in the semiconductor industry. Today, the Japanese firms are the world leaders in semiconductors and are reaping unprecedented profits. In the meantime, several of their U.S. competitors who were not able to spend as much on research and new product development are no longer major players in this highly lucrative international market.

The Education Deficit

America may have a vast natural resource base, but it has sorely neglected the needs of its most important resource, human beings. We spoke in Chapter 5 about the potential impact of education on foreign policy. In this chapter we stress the relationship between education and economic growth and productivity. The first high school graduating class of the twenty-first century is already making its way through the school system. On a positive note, more Americans than ever before are persevering and graduating from high school, with a record 76 percent of those aged 25 and over having received high school diplomas and 20 percent having finished at least four years of college.

Tragically, however, almost three-quarters of a million American teenagers are now dropping out of school each year, with 5 million young people between the ages of 16 and 24 not having completed high school. On an annual basis, another 700,000 are receiving degrees but leaving school as functional illiterates, unable to read their high school diplomas.[10] Almost 20 percent of the entire U.S. work force may be functionally illiterate, compared with 1 percent in Japan. To illustrate the implications of functional illiteracy, 25 million American adults cannot read with adequate comprehension the poison warning on a can of pesticide, and one-quarter of all adults, when given their paycheck and the stub showing deductions, cannot figure out if the paycheck is correct.[11]

This problem is especially acute within minority groups. Among urban blacks and Hispanics, the high school dropout rate is sometimes as high as 40 to 50 percent, and in Texas nearly one-half of Hispanics statewide are not finishing their secondary education.[12] This is an ominous trend, for over the next decade, more than 80 percent of the new job entrants in the United States will be minorities, women, or recent immigrants. If America's educational system cannot adequately train these traditionally disadvantaged groups and prepare them for skilled positions, a high price will be paid both in terms of societal cohesion and international competitiveness.

Even those who remain in school face competitive disadvantages. The average school day is longer in Europe and Japan, and the academic year is only 180 days in the United States, compared with 235 days in Germany and 240 days in Japan. Consequently, both the quality and quantity of educational training available to young people in the United States must be substantially improved. Already, two-thirds of the businesses contacted by the National Alliance of Business are reporting that they are not getting the kind of applicants they need, and the U.S. Chamber of Commerce estimates that American businesses are spending 40 billion dollars a year on remedial training and developing basic reading, writing, and mathematical skills among new employees.[13]

At the university level, fewer American citizens received science and engineering Ph.D.s in 1985 than in 1970.[14] Currently, almost 50 percent of all postgraduate science students enrolled in U.S. institutions of higher learning are foreigners, with 45 percent of science and engineering doctorates awarded in 1991 going to citizens of other nations.[15] Only 8.5 percent of first-year college students decided to pursue an engineering curriculum in 1987, compared with 12 percent in 1982. This waning interest now permits Japan, with one-half the U.S. population, to graduate more engineers each year than the United States.

Education and Global Awareness

The world is becoming more interdependent economically, but few Americans seem to care. A far higher percentage of U.S. high school students studied a foreign language in 1915 than in 1980. In 1915, 85 percent of America's colleges and universities required a prospective student to pass a competency test in a foreign language before being admitted; in 1980, only 8 percent of institutions had a similar requirement.[16] Fortunately, both high school and especially college enrollment is much higher today than several decades ago; nevertheless, only 5 percent of America's college students now possess any significant fluency in a foreign language. Far too many Americans believe that English is the lingua franca of the world, and thus there is no need to study a foreign language. Even in corporate boardrooms, many American executives share this perception, forgetting that the most important language in the world of business is the language spoken by their customers.

As for knowledge about the world in general, 78 percent of college students surveyed in the United States in 1950 could identify the principal country through which the Amazon river runs; in 1984 the number was down to 27 percent.[17] In a 1988 survey, 75 percent of Americans could not find the Persian Gulf on a map, 45 percent could not identify Central America, and 45 percent did not associate apartheid with South Africa.[18] One in 7 adults cannot locate the United States on a world map, nearly 40 percent of Boston high school seniors who were surveyed could not identify the 6 New England states, and 25 percent of students surveyed in Dallas failed to name Mexico as the nation which shares a southern border with the United States.[19]

The consequences of insularity, complacency, and ignorance of what is going on in the world can be traumatic. In the early 1960s, just before the massive buildup of American troops in Vietnam, no member of the U.S. Embassy staff in Saigon could speak the language of the native people. In Tokyo today, only a few members of the U.S. Embassy staff speak Japanese with any proficiency, and less than a half dozen are truly fluent.[20] In addition, only a small percentage of the U.S. business community in Japan can read and speak Japanese. Without the ability of their representatives to communicate, both the U.S. government and the corporate community face serious difficulties in gaining an accurate assessment of the political, economic, business, and social climates in Japan and in other overseas nations.

Quite frankly, America is ill-equipped to enter into the new age of information and brainpower. It is estimated that 85 percent of the scientists who have ever lived are alive today.[21] New knowledge is being added at unprecedented rates and technological change is proceeding at a record pace. America's children have been tested in a variety of disciplines against their counterparts around the world and generally rank in the bottom 25 percent.[22] Continued failures in the primary and secondary schools will make it a Sisyphean task for America to compete effectively against nations which consider education as the lifeblood of future prosperity.

The Policy-Making Quagmire and Citizen Responsibility

Both the political and decision-making environment in the nation's capital is resistant to the changes needed to preserve and promote U.S. economic competitiveness in the twenty-first century. Pundits are fond of referring to Washington, D.C. as "Disneyland East" or "69 square miles surrounded by reality." Occupants of the White House and Capitol Hill are often accused of living by the motto, "there is no problem too big that you can't run away from it."

These quips underline some of the serious challenges facing national leadership. For example, very little has been done in Washington, D.C. to tackle the problems outlined in the last few chapters. Debt continues to mount, protectionism continues to expand, and ubiquitous pork barrel and logrolling practices continue to subordinate the national interest to those of local and special interest groups.

The link between elected officials and special interest groups is fortified by outmoded campaign financing laws. Over 4,500 Political Action Committees (PACs) representing special interest groups are making record levels of campaign donations, with almost 90 percent of those donations earmarked for congressional races going to incumbents.[23] Large staffs, generous office and travel allowances, free mailings, in-house media operations, and other perks estimated to be worth 3.5 million dollars per year per senator and 1 million dollars per year per representative also provide incumbents with tremendous advantages during election campaigns. In 1988, for example, the odds against a challenger defeating an incumbent in the House of Representatives were 58 to 1, with almost 99 percent of incumbents who sought reelection retaining their seats.[24] In 1990, 96 percent of the incumbents seeking reelection in the House and 97 percent in the Senate emerged victorious. In 1992, 93 percent of the House and Senate incumbents who ran in November retained their seats. This is about the same rate of retention as for the British House of Lords, where members lose their seats only in the event of death.

Citizens of the United States must also make their representatives on Capitol Hill, in the White House, and in statehouses around the country more accountable for their economic decisions. In most cases, logrolling and the pork barrel add to the severe budgetary woes facing the nation. Americans must also be better informed on issues and expect more than a photogenic face and a glib personality from their political leaders. As one critic has charged, many Americans are seemingly chained to their televisions, and TV has turned political reporting into "melodramas and cliches, expressing the superficial and the controversial, making the politician a prisoner of promises he cannot keep in exchange for popularity he cannot sustain."[25] Quality policy-making will return when the electorate demands more of substance from candidates, better understands the ramifications of executive and legislative decisions, and holds those making these policies directly responsible for their actions.

International Cooperation versus Parochialism

The world trading system in particular and the global economic system in general have been described as "more and more like one single interacting organism."[26] This organism can still suffer from major cramps and indigestion, but it nonetheless has the potential of bringing the global community of nations closer together in an effort to achieve shared prosperity. Coordination must certainly be a hallmark of this system, with greater attention paid to the contributions which can be made by the General Agreement on Tariffs and Trade (GATT) and other international organizations. In effect, nation-states such as the United States and Japan must be willing to work out their differences and plan for a more efficient system through multilateral consultations and agreements.

Moreover, if economic reforms continue to be made within the former Soviet Union and Eastern Europe, these countries should be permitted to join the GATT, helping to bring standardized rules of the trading game for the great bulk of humanity. Because of the dominant Western influence in GATT and the weighted voting formula used in the IMF and the World Bank, these new entrants would be unable to block proposals supported by the major OECD nations. On the other hand, the nations of the former Soviet bloc which are interested in improving the standard of living of their citizens through enhanced trade opportunities and cooperative economic development projects would be valuable players in the multilateral process.

International cooperation is also desperately needed in the area of exchange rates. The rollercoaster ride taken by the U.S. dollar during the 1980s and early 1990s has had a profound impact upon U.S. economic fortunes. In the period when the dollar reached lofty levels, American firms were unable to sell their products abroad, leading to bankruptcies, corporate restructurings, and massive worker layoffs in export-related industries. When the dollar dipped in value beginning in the mid-1980s, new export opportunities eventually opened up for American firms, but they initially found it very difficult to recapture lost markets. The value of currencies has a dramatic impact on the trading fortunes of modern nations, and the problem of floating exchange rates can only be tackled at the multilateral level. For several years, the leading trading nations have relied on annual economic summits and periodic meetings of the G-5 (the United States, Japan, West Germany, Great Britain, and France) and later the G-7 (the G-5 members plus Canada and Italy) in an effort to resolve major problems in international monetary, trade, and investment transactions. In September 1985, the G-5 members met in New York City and orchestrated the Plaza Agreement which resulted in a coordinated and generally successful effort to bring down the value of the U.S. dollar. The problem which was not resolved, however, was how far the dollar should fall vis-à-vis the Japanese yen, German mark, and other currencies of major Western nations and selected newly industrialized countries such as Taiwan and South Korea. In addition, what should have been expected of the U.S. government in implementing fiscal and monetary policies which would help stabilize the value of the dollar over a period of months and years? Such questions remained unanswered.

In the twenty-first century, a more permanent consultative structure will be needed, and rules of the game for exchange rates will have to be spelled out clearly and concisely. Without such rules, currencies will continue to fluctuate erratically and the trading fortunes of nations will fluctuate with them.

Ultimately, Americans must realize that they are an integral part of an interdependent world and that many decisions will have to be made at the multilateral level instead of exclusively in Washington, D.C. This will be a difficult transition for most U.S. citizens, because for well over 100 years Americans were content to be isolated and insulated from much of the rest of the world, perfectly satisfied to be buffered and protected by the massive Atlantic and Pacific oceans. Ironically, Commodore Perry of the United States was instrumental in 1854 in forcing Japan to open up and trade with America after three centuries of Japanese isolation. In spite of this intrusion, Japan remained in many ways a very insular nation and is even today only slowly emerging from its island cocoon. Nonetheless, global trends are beginning to affect lifestyle preferences in Japan and elsewhere, slowly helping to break down nationalistic barriers. As Kenichi Omhae has observed, two decades ago the "Japanese slept on mats in cotton quilts, shopped daily, grabbed a quick meal at a noodle shop and drank green tea at breaks. Now they sleep in beds under sheets, shop once a week to fill their freezers, hit McDonald's for fast food, and have coffee and doughnuts at teatime."[27] One could argue incessantly as to whether this predominantly Americanization process is actually good for Japan, but it is certainly helping to erode parochial attitudes and prejudices which have persisted for centuries.

Interestingly enough, traditional Japanese insularity shares certain common characteristics with its American counterpart across the Pacific. It is true that the United States emerged briefly to fight in the last two years of World War I, the last four years of World War II, and to play the role of Western protector in the post-1945 period. In many respects, however, the U.S. remained a parochial nation with many of its residents longing for a Fortress America which would permit their country to be self-sufficient, prosperous, and isolated. There was also a strong inclination to believe in the superiority of American cultural and religious values, leaving people with the impression that very little could be learned from foreign countries. This Fortress America image, which is completely anathema to global interdependence, still permeates the psyche of many U.S. citizens.[28] Until such time as Americans consider themselves as "global players" who must both compete and cooperate incessantly in a world economic arena, America's relative decline is unlikely to be arrested.

Above all, the American people must recognize the prohibitive costs of protectionism. Many fingers are pointed toward the Japanese for their restricted markets which help keep beef and rice prices many times higher than those in the United States. Other fingers are pointed at some of the members of the European Community who have placed restraints on the importation of automobiles, textiles, steel, sewing machines, and a broad range of other goods.[29] On the other hand, U.S. protectionist barriers have been estimated to cost American consumers over 50 billion dollars each year and these barriers have been increasing.[30] Protectionism for an industry which is not internationally competitive also invites retaliation from overseas. Ironically, this retaliation would generally be aimed at U.S. firms which are already internationally competitive, such as aircraft, telecommunications, and computers. Thus, even though some workers in the textile sector may retain their jobs because of U.S. import barriers, workers with Boeing, McDonnell-Douglas, ITT, and IBM might face layoffs because of retaliatory steps taken by foreign governments.

TOWARD THE TWENTY-FIRST CENTURY

Without any doubt whatsoever, the major task now facing the United States is to put its own economic house in order, but many of the problems discussed in this book are beyond the control of America alone. This points out one of the great paradoxes of international society at the dawning of the twenty-first century. The world has grown increasingly interdependent economically, but in political terms it is still fragmented into 190 separate nation-states, each very jealous and highly protective of its political and economic sovereignty. As one observer has commented, "the problem is determining how to adapt the political interests of individual nations to the collective priorities of an integrated world economy."[31]

As for the United States, it currently faces a degree of economic vulnerability unknown since the Great Depression. Moreover, even though the United States may have been history's greatest hegemonic power during the late 1940s and early 1950s, it can no longer be considered as a "superpower" in the international economic system. The United States is now a vincible nation, but so are all the other countries around the globe. It still ranks as the single most important national economic actor in the world, but its well-being is linked increasingly to constant cooperation with other national, regional, and international actors in building a global system based on economic stability and sustainable development. In economic and resource terms, the twenty-first century will be a major success or colossal failure based on the willingness of nation-states to relinquish some national sovereignty in order to find global solutions to problems which now transcend the capacity of individual governments to solve unilaterally. The first major step toward such a cooperative framework should be taken in Washington, D.C.

ENDNOTES

1. As cited in Chapters 1 and 9, the first characterization was made by David Calleo and the second by Richard Darman.
2. Peter Petre, "Lifting American Competitiveness," *Fortune,* 23 April 1990, 56-66.
3. *The New York Times,* 12 November 1992, A12.
4. *The Wall Street Journal,* 9 August 1990, A9.
5. *The New York Times,* 11 November 1990, IV, 4.
6. W. John Moore, "The Bridge is Out," *National Journal,* 2 April 1988, 868.
7. *The Wall Street Journal,* 29 March 1988, 29. The Council gave the following grades: highways, C+; mass transit, C; aviation, B-; water resources, B; water supply, B-; waste water, C; solid waste, C-; hazardous waste, D.
8. Michael L. Dertouzos, Richard K. Lester, and Robert M. Solow, *Made in America* (Cambridge: MIT Press, 1989), 44.
9. Louis Lowenstein, "Regulate the Wall Street Casino," Fortune, 27 February 1989, 125-26.
10. Nancy J. Perry, "Saving the Schools: How Business Can Help," *Fortune,* 7 November 1988, 42.

11. Jonathan Kozol, *Illiterate America* (Garden City, NY: Anchor Press, 1985), 4, 5, 9, 16.
12. William H. Kolberg, "Our Education System Needs to Get an MBA," *Los Angeles Times,* 15 January 1989, IV, 3, and John Paul Newport, Jr., "Texas Faces Up to a Tougher Future," *Fortune,* 13 March 1989, 112.
13. William H. Kolberg, "Our Education System Needs to Get an MBA," *Los Angeles Times,* 15 January 1989, IV, 3.
14. The Cuomo Commission on Trade and Competitiveness, *The Cuomo Commission Report* (New York: Touchstone, 1988), 73.
15. Michael J. Mandel and Christopher Farrell, "The Immigrants: How They're Helping to Revitalize the U.S. Economy," *Business Week,* 13 July 1992, 114, 116.
16. Paul Simon, "The U.S. Crisis in Foreign Language," *Annals of the American Academy of Political and Social Science* 449 (May 1980): 32.
17. Congress, Senate, Committee on Labor and Human Resources, *Hearings on Geography Education,* 100th Cong., 1st sess., 29 October 1987, 34 and 47.
18. This survey was commissioned by the National Geographic Society and completed by the Gallup organization.
19. See the Stephen Green column, Copley News Service, 28 February 1989, and Richard Wood, "For Americans, the World Is Terra Incognita," *Christian Science Monitor,* 28 February 1989, 19.
20. Clyde V. Prestowitz, *Trading Places* (New York: Basic Books, 1988), 263.
21. Walter B. Wriston, "Technology and Sovereignty," *Foreign Affairs* 67 (Winter 1988/89): 63.
22. See, for example, the Princeton-based Educational Testing Service results of 1986 which tested the math and science skills of 13 year olds in the United States, South Korea, Ireland, Spain, the United Kingdom, and four Canadian provinces. Other relevant cross-national tests include the International Mathematics Study examination and the geography survey sponsored by the National Geographic Society.
23. According to the Federal Election Commission, PACs made 63.5 million dollars in donations to congressional candidates in the 15-month period from January 1989 to March 1990. Congressional incumbents received 89 percent of these donations, compared with 87 percent for the same 15-month period in the 1987-88 cycle.
24. See the article by John Dutton on Congress, "Perks Help Keep Incumbents in Office," *Deseret News,* 28 May 1990, 10A.
25. Felix G. Rohatyn, *The Twenty-Year Century* (New York: Random House, 1983), 20.
26. This statement was made by Akio Morita, Sony's chairperson. See Richard I. Kirkland, Jr., "We're All in this Together," *Fortune,* 2 February 1987, 26.
27. Richard I. Kirkland, Jr., "We're All in this Together," *Fortune,* 2 February 1987, 26.
28. It should be noted that some observers believe that the United States could go it alone in the international economy. Dominick Salvatore, for example, contends that the United States is the only nation which could withdraw from the world trading system and still survive without a drastic decline in its standard of living. See his book, *International Economics* (New York: Macmillan, 1983), 3.
29. For example, several EEC members have placed "voluntary" restraints on the importation of Japanese automobiles. In 1987, Great Britain limited Japanese imports to 11 percent of its market, France to 3 percent, and Italy to only a few thousand cars. In comparison, Japan's "voluntary" agreement with the United States allowed it to capture about 20 percent of the American automobile market through export activity.
30. The Institute for International Economics in Washington estimated that these protectionist barriers cost U.S. consumers 55 billion dollars in 1984 alone. See the *Economist,* 25 April 1987, 18.
31. Sidney L. Jones, "Cooperation and Competition in an Integrated World Economy," (photocopy), May 1985, 2.

14
THE FUTURE

In a prefatory note to his final volume on the history of World War II, Winston Churchill sardonically described the "lesson" of the conclusion of that great struggle: "How the Great Democracies triumphed, and so were able to resume the follies which had so nearly cost them their life."[1] One of the permanent tragedies of history is that, at the moment of triumph over a compelling threat or pressing problem, the opportunities opened by that resolution are dissipated by forgetting the lessons of the recent challenges and by the sudden depression of the spirit engendered by the realization that mundane issues remain.

The period from the Great Depression to the end of the Cold War has been one of the most dramatic in history. It has witnessed a clash of titans swept up in the vortex of power struggles and ideological contests. Great armies have clashed, petty chieftains have contended, and millions of people have suffered and died. Perhaps only the strains of a Wagnerian opera could do artistic justice to this heroic age. As we survey this past and assess the present, we face another heroic challenge, a conceptual one: What kind of world is emerging from the struggles of the twentieth century and how will or should the American people respond?

With the conclusion of the drama of the immediate past, one can well understand Francis Fukuyama's pronouncement that history itself is at an end, by which he means the end of the historical clash of great organizing ideas. The victory of liberal democracy, free markets, and open societies now definitively provides, in his view, the global center of gravity.[2] Yet, the difficult demands of these social orders and the persistence even of bad ideas, sometimes in changed garb, make this judgment problematical at best. In effect, as we contemplate the "new" world, however orderly or disorderly it may be, we are saddled with the task of distinguishing that which is constant from that which is novel in today's headlines, and determining what in fact are the relevant lessons of the recent past. Perhaps most importantly from the vantage point of this study, we must consider what may be permanent and what may be transitory in the status of the United States in world affairs.

OF CHANGE AND CONTINUITY

As we compare the present to the period after World War II, we can clearly discern certain political, economic, and social patterns that have been transformed and have provided the presuppositions of this book. Central to these changes are the passing both of the Soviet empire and the unified Soviet state and the rise to global prominence once again of Japan and the states of Central and Western Europe.

The circumstances of this geopolitical transfiguration are, however, in many respects quite different from such transitions in the past. Global economic interdependence and an intertwined global society may be the defining reality of the new world and a dominant shaper of political and social power. Although the jargon of interdependence has suffused the talk of academics and policy-makers for years, economic interdependence may now be so quantitatively extensive and institutionalized as to constitute a qualitatively different phenomenon. Moreover, cultural mores and social norms are clearly cutting across territorial boundaries and defining a global social order. This order is not that of a homogeneous village, however, but of a heterogeneous "greater" Los Angeles or New York. Economic, social, religious, and cultural ties have always transcended state borders, but the richness and extent of these ties have now reached historic proportions, driven by the forces of modern technology in information systems, communications, and transportation.

In all of this, there are still many things that would be quite comprehensible to the chroniclers of the past—a Thucydides, a Gibbon, or a Toynbee. Despite the interdependency of peoples, tribal sentiments are flourishing under many guises—ethnicity, nationalism, mercantilism, protectionism, and religious exclusiveness. Moreover, there not only persists but there are newly energized struggles in many parts of the world to develop modes of political organization that will at the same time provide public safety and order, maximize material benefits, establish a sense of unique community, and protect the boundaries of that community from external interference. If there are forces of integration abroad, there are surely forces of disintegration. And, indeed, the fact that different areas of the globe exhibit differential rates of economic growth need not push the various human communities into which the globe is still divided into ever greater forms of political cooperation. At least as likely is that the habits of the past and the tribal preferences of the present may rupture even those institutions of international integration that have been developed.

In the face of such divergent possibilities, it is by no means easy to discern what lessons of the past can shape most advantageously the contours of the future. The geostrategist Colin Gray recently reminded many of us of Arnold J. Toynbee's reflections on the onset of World War I:

> The general war of 1914 overtook me expounding Thucydides to Balliol undergraduates . . . and then suddenly my understanding was illuminated. The experience that we were having in our world now had been experienced by Thucydides in his world already. I was re-reading him with a new perception . . . to which I had been insensible until I, in my turn, had run into that historical crisis that had inspired him to write his work. Thucydides, it now appeared, had been over this ground before. He and his generation had been ahead of me and mine in the stage of historical experience that we had respectively reached [in 431 B.C. and A.D. 1914]; in fact, his present had been my future. But this made nonsense of the chronological notation which registered my world as "modern" and Thucydides' world as "ancient." Whatever chronology might say, Thucydides' world and my world had now proved to be philosophically contemporary.[3]

With this perspective in mind, Gray noted how unhelpful a recent editorial in *The New York Times* might be when it suggested that in plotting the U.S. national security posture in the post-cold War world, Americans must clearly distinguish between "clear and present dangers" and "overblown and distant threats."[4] Unless one clearly understands the nature of one's historical epoch and the real nature of the choices available, it is not always easy to make that distinction. The diversity of the "lessons of history" and the contradictions of the present render judgments on the future at best an exercise in the sophisticated reading of entrails.

Sensitive to such difficulties, however, nations, especially the United States, cannot escape making these judgments. Over the past chapters we have assessed both the nature of the American political culture and the character of the global political, economic, and strategic environment. Our central theme has been that the United States is "vincible." It should be clear by now that this is a provocative way of pointing to the contingent nature of American power. The United States has always seen itself as both exemplary and detached—a political and moral model for the world and a community spared many of the fundamental dangers and moral ambiguities found elsewhere around the globe. The cataclysmic collapse of nations and empires in our century and the leadership thrust upon the American Republic by the clashes of our time reinforced this sense of destiny. If the past pages have demonstrated anything, however, it is that America has become intertwined in a host of transnational political, economic, and social ties and that its internal strengths are neither absolutely preeminent nor even necessarily relevant compared to outside states. Moreover, the passing of the galvanizing international struggles of this century has rendered the American people peculiarly sensitive both to the vulnerabilities of their situation and to the demands of the domestic agenda. American global leadership may still be central of the emergent international system, but the conditions of that leadership have been transformed.

THE UNITED STATES IN THE
TWENTY-FIRST CENTURY

Charles Schulz in his comic strip *Peanuts* depicts Lucy leaving her house one day while Linus is standing in the front yard making a snowball. She suddenly whirls on her heels and says to Linus: "Life is full of choices. You may choose, if you so wish, to throw that snowball at me. You may also choose if you so wish not to throw that snowball at me. Now, if you choose to throw the snowball at me, I will pound you right into the ground! If you choose not to, your head will be spared!" At which point Linus throws the snowball away and says, "Life is full of choices, but you never get any!"

Influence is to a substantial degree delimiting the choices of others and expanding the range of one's own. When we speak of positions of strength, balances of power, deterrence, market dominance, cash reserves, and so forth, we are at one and the same time pointing to the limits that we are placing on others and the possibilities that are open to us. The most certain and stable foundation of such influence is one's internal strengths and the patterns of relationships established with others. Economic growth and competitiveness, stable public finances, social harmony, political unity—all these elements define the internal strength of the United States. International commercial and financial arrangements, political and military alignments and institutions, and social and cultural ties—these factors constitute the pattern of international power. These internal and external elements of influence are intertwined. The United States cannot, for instance, resolve imbalances in its international trade apart from its internal fiscal and monetary policies nor can it exercise political-military influence in the Middle East without taking into account domestic political considerations.

American influence in the twenty-first century will be determined by the reciprocal relationship between the constitution of new or renewed forms of economic strength and social harmony within the nation, and of new or renewed forms of cooperation and competition outside its borders. Over the past chapters we have signalled a number of key choices in institutional processes, defense structures, education, energy and the environment, immigration, and taxation and spending that will determine the foundations of American power and influence in the years ahead. None of the choices can be made in isolation from the outside world, for the very character of interdependence is that the boundaries between "inside" and "outside" are eroded. Politicians often speak of resolving America's problems apart from the outside world or of responding unilaterally to an external exigency, but the reality, as we have seen, is far more complex.

It is possible to act as if U.S. choices are unconstrained by international forces or the costs of unilateral initiatives, whether they be in the economic or political-miliary realm, but this would be foolhardy. The constraints are real and the costs can be excruciatingly high. The United States possesses enormous power and a considerable range of choice, but the evolution of international power in this century has enmeshed it in a global security, economic, social, and political nexus. Moreover, that web of power has generally served the American people well—undergirding both their security and their economic welfare. Whatever must be done to strengthen the domestic foundations of American power, it has been the thesis of this study that such actions should be undertaken within the framework of an international economic and security order that reflects both fundamental American values and the interests of the broader international community. In many respects, this may very well be the lesson of the Cold War to which Americans should hold fast.

The Cold War is typically seen in terms of Soviet-American competition. At least as important, however, is the cooperation of those states who joined together to pursue the policy of containment. The understandings and links forged among the states of North America, Western Europe, and Japan, as well as lesser connections with associated states, gave rise to an international political, economic, and social order that is unprecedented in its geographical scope and depth of connections. Perhaps more important to the Cold War struggles than the periodic clashes of arms and strategic confrontation was this remarkable association.

It is true that this alignment was closely related to the utterly preeminent position of the United States after World War II and the willingness of that state to engineer diplomatic bargains wherein strategic and economic interests were linked and balanced. For instance, in order to forge a strategic position of strength in the western end of Eurasia, the Americans were prepared not only to accept but to encourage the rise of a common market in Western Europe that clearly established a preferential economic zone potentially at odds with an international liberal economic regime. Similarly in Asia, the United States was remarkably benign in its reaction to the rise of a Japanese economic power that would erode America's international competitive position. It is probably the case that the Americans were for too long complacent about the international shift in the economic balance. But is equally certain that successive American administrations were prepared to accept certain trade-offs in the interest of a unified position via-à-vis the Soviet Union.

With the collapse of the Soviet threat, and the accumulating evidence of a U.S. economic position in relative decline in relationship to the other major industrial states, many Americans are far more prepared to seek protectionist measures against erstwhile friends even at the risk of major ruptures in these traditional linkages. So intertwined has American welfare become with those states, however, that the United States would do well to resist some of the more extreme measures of mercantilism and trade protectionism. Indeed, as discussed throughout the pages of this book, the major task facing the United States is to reforge and renew the political, economic, and social ties that underpinned its Cold War strategies and to extend those same ties to include even states that were once the object of U.S. competitive strategies. Nevertheless, the ability of the United States to revive and extend this association depends on the willingness of the American people and their government to undertake fundamental reforms in the institutions and practices that undergird national power: education; fiscal, monetary, and social policies; and relations between the public and private sectors and between the different levels of the public sector. In other words, national priorities and international responsibilities go hand in hand as the United States prepares to venture forth into the twenty-first century.

ENDNOTES

1. Winston S. Churchill, *Triumph and Tragedy,* volume 6 of *The Second World War* (Boston: Houghton Mifflin Company, 1935), 1st Preface.
2. Francis Fukuyama, *The End of History and the Last Man* (New York: The Free Press, 1992).
3. Arnold Toynbee, *Civilization on Trial* (London: Oxford University Press, 1953), 7-8, as cited in Colin Gray, "Strategic Sense, Strategic Nonsense," *The National Interest,* Number 20 (Fall 1992): 12.
4. *The New York Times,* 19 February 1992, as cited in Colin Gray, "Strategic Sense, Strategic Nonsense," *The National Interest,* Number 20 (Fall 1992): 14.

INDEX

framework for, 9, 17, 25, 34-35, 42, 49-
51, 55, 64, 67, 71, 73, 85, 98-99,
104, 124, 141, 143, 183
geographic conditions for, 105-107, 125
and interest groups, 120
leaders in, 15, 18, 41, 52-54, 57-59, 61,
66-67, 72, 74-75, 80-83, 86-88,
91-92, 94, 96, 104, 118, 125, 142,
145, 199
and national values, 114, 116, 125
political challenges to, 13-14, 34, 39-40,
42, 65, 74, 78, 110, 125, 142,
146, 154
and powers of Congress, 18-19, 27, 32,
37-38, 63
and powers of the president, 18-21, 24,
26, 28-29, 33, 37, 42-43, 50, 63
Foreign Relations Committee, 31, 35, 94
Foreign Service, 75-78
Foreign Service Officers (FSOs), 72-74, 77-
78, 80
Forrestal, James, 68
France, 136, 195
banks, 5
and economic power, 5
French Direct Action, 218
and international relations, 161, 170
Paris, 62
and political power, 171
Franklin, Benjamin, 72
Frederick the Great, 3
Fukuyama, Francis, 339

–G–

General Agreement on Tariffs and Trade
(GATT), 178, 248, 251, 305, 316-17,
320-21, 334
Geography, 136
and foreign policy, 105-107, 125
Georgia, Atlanta, 314
Germany
decentralization of, 160
and economic power, 142
Federal Republic of, 204, 270
and global power, 135-36, 146, 195
and international relations, 20, 130, 139,
200

people of, 22
unification of, 162-63, 167, 192
Gettysburg, Battle of, 146
Global system, 8, 51-52, 123
Goldwater, Barry, 32-33
Goodpaster, Andrew, 58
Gorbachev, Mikhail, 141-42, 181-86, 191,
196
Government Accounting Office, 23
Gray, Colin, 341
Great Britain, 130, 136-37
British empire, 140
and economic power, 5
and education, 122
and foreign policy, 106, 116
and international relations, 158, 161, 170
and Parliament, 42
pax britannica, 6
people of, 6, 116
and population density, 270
the U.S. Embassy in, 73
Great Depression, The, 248
Great Lakes, 22
Great Powers, 6, 189-90, 198, 206
Green Revolution, The, 271
Grenada, 20, 85, 198
Gritz, Bo, 67
Guevara, Che, 232
Gulf of Tonkin Resolution, 30
Gulf War, 20-21, 31, 136, 141, 148, 187
"Operation Desert Storm," 21

–H–

Haig, Alexander, 57, 60, 82, 107
Hamilton, Alexander, 20, 26, 29, 129
Hanoi, 22
Hardin, Garrett, 271
Harmel, Pierre, 179
Hegemony, 3, 7, 79, 146, 196
Helms, Jesse, 24
Heurta, Victoriano, 25
Hezbollah, 213, 218
Hitler, Adolf, 106
Hoffmann, Stanley, 51
House and Senate Armed Services Commit-
tees, 152